STUDY GUIDE

PARKIN

MACROECONOMICS

SECOND EDITION

STUDY GUIDE

PARKIN

MACROECONOMICS

SECOND EDITION

DAVID E. SPENCER
Brigham Young University

ADDISON-WESLEY PUBLISHING COMPANY
Reading, Massachusetts • Menlo Park, California • New York
Don Mills, Ontario • Wokingham, England • Amsterdam • Bonn
Sydney • Singapore • Tokyo • Madrid • San Juan • Milan • Paris

Reprinted with corrections, May 1993.

Reproduced by Addison-Wesley from camera-ready copy supplied by the author.

ISBN 0-201-58637-1
3 4 5 6 7 8 9 10-BA-96959493

CONTENTS

PREFACE: TO THE STUDENT ix

PART 1 INTRODUCTION

Chapter 1 What is Economics? 1
Chapter 2 Making and Using Graphs 9
Chapter 3 Production, Specialization, and Exchange 23
Chapter 4 Demand and Supply 39

PART 2 INTRODUCTION TO MACROECONOMICS

Chapter 5 Inflation, Unemployment, Cycles and Deficits 55
Chapter 6 Measuring Output and the Price Level 67
Chapter 7 Aggregate Demand and Aggregate Supply 81

PART 3 AGGREGATE DEMAND FLUCTUATIONS

Chapter 8 Expenditure Decisions and GDP 97
Chapter 9 Expenditure Fluctuations and Fiscal Policy 111
Chapter 10 Money, Banking, and Prices 125
Chapter 11 The Federal Reserve, Money, and Interest Rates 137
Chapter 12 Fiscal and Monetary Influences on Aggregate Demand 153

PART 4 AGGREGATE SUPPLY, INFLATION AND RECESSION

Chapter 13 Productivity, Wages, and Unemployment 173
Chapter 14 Inflation 191
Chapter 15 Recessions and Depressions 209

PART 5 MACROECONOMIC POLICY

Chapter 16 Stabilizing the Economy 223
Chapter 17 The Deficit 239

PART 6 INTERNATIONAL ECONOMICS

Chapter 18 Trading with the World 251
Chapter 19 The Balance of Payments and the Dollar 267

PART 7 GROWTH, DEVELOPMENT, AND REFORM

Chapter 20 Growth and Development 281
Chapter 21 Economic Systems in Transition 293

GUIDE TO SECOND EDITION CONTENTS: ECONOMICS, MICROECONOMICS, MACROECONOMICS

ECONOMICS Hardcover Parent Text Part / Title	Chapter / Title	MICRO Paperback Split Part	MICRO Paperback Split Chapter	MACRO Paperback Split Part	MACRO Paperback Split Chapter
Part 1: Introduction	Chapter 1: What Is Economics?	Part 1	Ch. 1	Part 1	Ch. 1
	Chapter 2: Making and Using Graphs		Ch. 2		Ch. 2
	Chapter 3: Production, Specialization, and Exchange		Ch. 3		Ch. 3
	Chapter 4: Demand and Supply		Ch. 4		Ch. 4
Part 2: How Markets Work	Chapter 5: Elasticity	Part 2	Ch. 5		
	Chapter 6: Markets in Action		Ch. 6		
Part 3: Households' Choices	Chapter 7: Utility and Demand	Part 3	Ch. 7		
	Chapter 8: Possibilities, Preferences, and Choices		Ch. 8		
Part 4: Firms' Choices	Chapter 9: Organizing Production	Part 4	Ch. 9		
	Chapter 10: Output and Costs		Ch. 10		
Part 5: Markets for Goods and Services	Chapter 11: Competition	Part 5	Ch. 11		
	Chapter 12: Monopoly		Ch. 12		
	Chapter 13: Monopolistic Competition and Oligopoly		Ch. 13		
Part 6: Markets for Factors of Production	Chapter 14: Pricing and Allocating Factors of Production	Part 6	Ch. 14		
	Chapter 15: Labor Markets		Ch. 15		
	Chapter 16: Capital and Natural Resource Markets		Ch. 16		
Part 7: Markets, Uncertainty, and Distribution	Chapter 17: Uncertainty and Information	Part 7	Ch. 17		
	Chapter 18: The Distribution of Income and Wealth		Ch. 18		
Part 8: Markets and Government	Chapter 19: Market Failure	Part 8	Ch. 19		
	Chapter 20: Public Choice		Ch. 20		
	Chapter 21: Regulation and Antitrust Law		Ch. 21		
Part 9: Introduction to Macroeconomics	Chapter 22: Inflation, Unemployment, Cycles, and Deficits			Part 2	Ch. 5
	Chapter 23: Measuring Output and the Price Level				Ch. 6
	Chapter 24: Aggregate Demand and Aggregate Supply				Ch. 7
Part 10: Aggregate Demand Fluctuations	Chapter 25: Expenditure Decisions and GDP			Part 3	Ch. 8
	Chapter 26: Expenditure Fluctuations and Fiscal Policy				Ch. 9
	Chapter 27: Money, Banking, and Prices				Ch. 10
	Chapter 28: The Federal Reserve, Money, and Interest Rates				Ch. 11
	Chapter 29: Fiscal and Monetary Influences on Aggregate Demand				Ch. 12
Part 11: Aggregate Supply, Inflation, and Recession	Chapter 30: Productivity, Wages, and Unemployment			Part 4	Ch. 13
	Chapter 31: Inflation				Ch. 14
	Chapter 32: Recessions and Depressions				Ch. 15
Part 12: Macroeconomic Policy	Chapter 33: Stabilizing the Economy			Part 5	Ch. 16
	Chapter 34: The Deficit				Ch. 17
Part 13: International Economics	Chapter 35: Trading with the World	*Part 9	*Ch. 22	Part 6	Ch. 18
	Chapter 36: The Balance of Payments and the Dollar				Ch. 19
Part 14: Growth, Development, and Reform	Chapter 37: Growth and Development			Part 7	Ch. 20
	Chapter 38: Economic Systems in Transition	*Part 9	*Ch. 23		Ch. 21

PREFACE:
TO THE STUDENT

My objective in preparing this *Study Guide* to accompany *Macroeconomics, Second Edition,* by Michael Parkin is to help you master course material in order to do well on examinations. If that objective is realized, you will not only achieve a higher grade in the course but you will develop a deeper understanding of economics and the many economic issues that play such an important role in all our lives.

A study guide, however, is not a substitute for the text. Before you approach a chapter in the *Study Guide,* you should carefully read the corresponding chapter in the text. The major purpose of this *Study Guide,* then, is to *reinforce* and *deepen* your understanding of economics, not to initiate that understanding. I have tried to keep that purpose sharply in focus as I have prepared each chapter. Each chapter of the *Study Guide* contains two parts. The first part contains four sections intended to enhance your individual study effectiveness while the second part consists of several self-test sections followed by answers to all the self-test questions. Let's take a look at the basic content of each chapter by discussing each of these sections.

CHAPTER CONTENTS

Chapter in Perspective: As students proceed from chapter to chapter through the text, they frequently get bogged down in the detail and lose sight of the broader picture. The purpose of this first section of each *Study Guide* chapter is to put each chapter of the text into perspective by indicating how it relates to preceding and following chapters and by highlighting some of the central issues that are examined.

Learning Objectives: This section simply repeats the learning objectives from the text. As you work through each chapter of the *Study Guide,* it would be a good idea to ask yourself if you have achieved each of these objectives.

Helpful Hints: When you encounter difficulty in mastering concepts or techniques, you will not be alone. Many students find certain concepts difficult and often make the same kinds of mistakes. A major purpose of this section is to help students avoid these common errors. An additional purpose is to highlight or supplement the text's discussion of key concepts.

Key Figures and Tables: Each chapter of the text contains numerous figures and tables but not all are equally important. Some are designated as "key" figures or tables and identified in the textbook by a diamond-shaped icon. In this section each of these is discussed to help you focus your study on the most important diagrams.

Self-Test: Along with the Helpful Hints, this will be the most useful section of the *Study Guide.* The questions are designed to give you practice and to test the skills and techniques you must master to do well on exams. The Self-Test section contains five parts (listed below) and is followed by an Answer section.

Concept Review: This section contains simple "recall" questions designed to check your knowledge of the basic terminology and fundamental concepts of each chapter. These questions should build your confidence. This part is not a test of deep understanding, or mastery of analytical skills.

True or False: These questions test your basic knowledge of chapter concepts as well as your ability to apply these concepts. These are the first questions to challenge your understanding to see if you can identify mistakes in statements using basic concepts.

Multiple Choice: These more difficult questions test your analytical ability by asking you to apply concepts to new situations, to manipulate information, and to solve numerical and graphical problems. Since most examinations will consist mainly—if not exclusively—of multiple choice questions, these questions will provide useful practice.

Short Answer: Each chapter contains several short answer questions that ask about basic concepts and can generally be answered in a few sentences or a paragraph. Avoid the tendency simply to read the questions and think you know the answer. Writing down brief responses or answering the questions out loud in a study group will prove to be very beneficial.

Problems: The best way to learn economics is to do problems. Thus each self-test concludes with a collection of several numerical or graphical problems. In most chapters, this section will be the most challenging part of the Self-Test. It is also likely to be the most helpful in deepening your understanding of the chapter material. The problems are designed to teach as much as to test. They are purposely arranged so as to lead you through the problem-solving analysis in a gradual and sequential fashion, from easier to more difficult parts.

Answers: The Self-Test is followed by a section that contains the answers to all Self-Test items. I recommend that you complete the entire Self-Test before looking at the answers. Then, when you find a difference between your answer and the correct answer, return to the text chapter to correct or extend your understanding.

SOME FRIENDLY ADVICE

The best way to ensure a good grade in your economics course is to develop a thorough understanding of economics, and that will require effort. There is no effective method short of that. With that in mind, let me offer some advice on how to develop such an understanding and how this study guide can help.

1. *Read the chapter in the text first.* Make a commitment to yourself at the beginning of the course that you will read the relevant chapter *before* your instructor lectures on it. You may be amazed at how your instructor's ability to teach improves if you come to class prepared. In this initial reading, note the concepts and issues that seem more difficult but don't concentrate on these yet. Your purpose at this point is to get a general understanding of the concepts and issues.

2. *Read the first four sections of the study guide chapter.* Study both the Helpful Hints and Key Figures and Tables sections especially carefully. They are intended first to help you identify which ideas and concepts are relatively more important and then to help you extend and deepen your understanding of them. Hopefully, some of the difficulties you noted in your first reading of the textbook chapter will be overcome by this process.

3. *Keep a good set of lecture notes.* Good lecture notes are vital for focusing your study. Your instructor will only lecture on a subset of topics from the textbook and those topics should usually be given priority when studying for exams.

4. *Return to the text.* After your instructor's lecture, read the chapter again, but this time for mastery of the detail. Use a pencil and paper to make notes and to work through the analysis of the text, especially when graphs are involved. By the end of this experience

you should have a thorough understanding of the material and be ready to test yourself.

5. *Complete the Self-Test sections of the study guide.* To test your understanding and to identify areas of weakness, complete the Concept Review, True or False, Multiple Choice, Short Answer, and Problem sections of the Self-Test. I recommend using a pencil to write your answers in the *Study Guide.* This will allow you to erase your mistakes and have neat, completed pages from which to study. I also recommend writing the answers to the Multiple Choice questions on a separate sheet of paper so that these questions can be freshly reviewed later.

Avoid the mistake of thinking that because your test will only contain multiple choice questions, you will not benefit greatly from completing the Short Answer and Problem sections. Indeed, these may be the most instructive exercises.

As you respond to the Short Answer questions, you will learn more if you will take the time *actually to write* brief responses rather than simply saying to yourself: "I know the answer to that one." The act of physically writing answers will reveal weaknesses of which you are yet unaware. This is at least as true for working through the Problems section. The problems are generally sequential and intended to guide you step-by-step through some important aspect of economic analysis. In many cases, your deepest learning will take place as you work these problems.

Once you have tested your understanding and identified areas where that understanding might be weak, you should review the relevant parts of the textbook chapter.

6. *Use your instructor and/or teaching assistants.* When you have questions about any concept, ask someone who can give you appropriate help. Depending on the arrangements at your university, your instructor or the teaching assistants assigned to your class are anxious to respond to your questions and, indeed, expect you to ask them.

7. *Carefully prepare for each exam.* If you have followed the previous six suggestions, you are an unusually wise student and your preparation for exams will be much less frustrating than for many of your colleagues. In preparation for an exam, review your lecture notes as well as each chapter in the text paying special attention to the Review sections and to each Chapter Summary. For each chapter, take another look at the Helpful Hints and Key Figures and Tables sections of the *Study Guide.* Also, quickly review the sections of the Self-Test, *except* the Multiple Choice section. If you used paper and pencil as you previously worked through the Short Answer and Problems sections, your review will likely proceed more quickly. Then, as a final preparation, complete the Multiple Choice section of the study guide again. This time, however, be sure not only to know why the correct choice is correct, but also to see if you *know why each incorrect choice is incorrect.* If you can do this, you will be very well prepared.

If available, working old exams your instructor has given in previous years is an excellent additional preparation. In addition to providing useful practice, old exams give you a feel for the style of question your instructor may ask. Remember, though, that old exams are a useful study aid only if you use them to *understand* the reasoning behind each question. Do not try to memorize answers in the hope that your instructor will ask the same question again.

8. *Form a study group.* A very useful way to motivate your study and to learn economics is to discuss the things you are learning with other students. As you discuss concepts and issues *aloud*, your understanding will deepen and your areas of weakness will become apparent. When you answer a question in your head only, you often skip steps in the chain of reasoning without realizing it. When you are forced to explain your reasoning out loud,

gaps and mistakes quickly appear, and you (and your fellow group members) can readily correct your reasoning.

As you effectively use the textbook and study guide together, you will not only be well prepared for tests, but, more important in the long run, you will have developed analytical skills and powers of reasoning that will benefit you throughout your life.

DO YOUR HAVE ANY FRIENDLY ADVICE FOR ME?

I have attempted to make this *Study Guide* as clear and as useful as possible, and to avoid errors. No doubt, I have not been entirely successful. This study guide has been carefully checked for errors but, most likely some were not detected. If you discover errors or have other suggestions for improving the *Study Guide*, please let me know. Send your correspondence to

Professor David E. Spencer
Department of Economics
Brigham Young University
Provo, UT 84602

ACKNOWLEDGMENTS

One cannot teach bright and motivated economics students without learning much from them about how to do a better job. Thus, I am grateful to the many students I have had the privilege of knowing. I would also like to express appreciation to Barbara Rifkind, Marjorie Williams, Cindy Johnson, Kari Heen, Amy Willcutt, and Sarah Hallet Corey at Addison-Wesley Publishing Co. Above all, I am grateful to my wife, Jan, whose love and support, both direct and indirect, continue to be invaluable.

Provo, Utah D.E.S.

1 WHAT IS ECONOMICS?

CHAPTER IN PERSPECTIVE

This first chapter introduces the *subject* of economics by briefly discussing what kinds of questions economics tries to answer and why these questions are interesting and important. The fundamental economic problem is scarcity. Because wants exceed the resources available to satisfy them, we cannot have everything we want and must make choices. This problem leads to economizing behavior – choosing the best or optimal use of the resources available. Economics, as a subject, is the study of how we use limited resources to try to satisfy unlimited wants.

This chapter also introduces the *method* of economics: how economists use economic theory and models to answer economic questions and to analyze and understand how people and economic systems cope with the fundamental problem of scarcity.

LEARNING OBJECTIVES

After studying this chapter, you will be able to:

- **State the kinds of questions that economics tries to answer**
- **Explain why all economic questions and economic activity arise from scarcity**
- **Explain why scarcity forces people to make choices**
- **Define opportunity cost**
- **Describe the function and the working parts of an economy**
- **Distinguish between positive and normative statements**
- **Explain what is meant by an economic theory and how economic theories are developed by building and testing economic models**

HELPFUL HINTS

1. The definition of economics (the study of how people use limited resources to satisfy unlimited wants) leads us directly to three important economic concepts—choice, opportunity cost, and competition. Since wants exceed resources, we cannot have everything we want and therefore must make *choices* among alternatives. In making a choice we forgo alternatives that we might have chosen and the *opportunity cost* of any choice is the value of the best forgone alternative. The fact that wants exceed resources also means that wants and individuals must *compete* against each other for the scarce resources.

2. Another fundamental point of this chapter is that economics is a science. It is important to understand that, like other sciences, economics seeks to enlarge our understanding of the world by constructing, examining, and testing *economic models*. Such models are highly simplified representations of the real world. Rather than making models less useful, this simplicity actually enhances their usefulness. By selectively abstracting from the less relevant complexity of the real world, economic models allow us to focus more clearly on those factors that are most important for the question under investigation.

Models are frequently compared to maps, which are useful because they "abstract from" real world detail. A map does not indicate every feature of the landscape (e.g., trees, streetlamps, etc.) but rather offers a simplified view, which is carefully selected according to the purpose of the map.

3. The most important purpose for studying economics is not to learn *what* to think about economics but *how* to think about economics. The "what" — the facts and descriptions of the economy — can always be found in books. The principal value of a course in economics is the ability to think critically about economic problems and to understand how the economy works. This comes through the mastery of economic theory and model-building.

KEY FIGURE

Figure 1.1 A Picture of the Economy

This figure illustrates the flow of goods and services as well as flows of money in the economy. There are three decision-making sectors (households, firms, and governments) and two groups of markets (goods markets and factor markets). Households supply factors of production to firms through factor markets for which they receive payment of wages, interest, rent, and profits. Firms supply goods and services to households through goods markets for which they receive money payments. Governments collect taxes from both households and firms and supply goods and services to both in addition to other benefits (transfer payments) to households and subsidies to firms.

SELF-TEST

CONCEPT REVIEW

1. The fundamental and pervasive fact that gives rise to economic problems is ______________. This simply means that human wants ______________ the resources available to satisfy them. The inescapable consequence is that people must make______________.
2. When we choose an action, the value of the best forgone alternative is the ______________ cost of that action.
3. The process of evaluating the costs and benefits of our choices in order to do the

best we can with limited resources is called __________.

4. An economy is a mechanism that determines __________ is produced, __________ it is produced, and __________ __________ it is produced.
5. The three groups of decision makers in the economy are __________, __________, and __________.
6. Factors of production are classified under three general headings. The physical and mental resources of human beings are called __________, natural resources are called __________, and manufactured goods used in production (e.g., machines and factories) are called __________.
7. While all economies must have some way of coordinating choices, there are two fundamental mechanisms. The __________ mechanism relies on the authority of some kind of central planning, while the __________ mechanism relies on the adjustment of __________ in economic markets. A(n) __________ economy has elements of both of these fundamental mechanisms.
8. An economy that is economically linked with other economies in the world is called __________.
9. Statements about what *is* are called __________ statements, while those about what *ought* to be are called __________ statements.
10. The branch of economics that studies the choices of individual households and firms is called __________, while the branch which studies behavior of the economy as a whole is called __________.

TRUE OR FALSE

____ 1. Scarcity is a problem only for capitalist (market) economies.

____ 2. Economics is the study of how to use unlimited resources to satisfy limited wants.

____ 3. Scarcity can be eliminated through cooperation.

____ 4. The notion of opportunity cost is illustrated by the fact that because Fred studied for his economics exam last night he was unable to see a movie with his friends.

____ 5. Competition is a contest for command over scarce resources.

____ 6. The opportunity cost of any action is the cost of all forgone alternatives.

____ 7. To economists, capital is the money used by businesses to buy assets.

____ 8. The pair of scissors a barber uses to cut hair is an example of capital as a factor of production.

____ 9. In an economy in which economic activity is coordinated by a command mechanism, the decisions of *what, how,* and *for whom* are the result of price adjustment.

____10. A mixed economy is one in which there is both internal and international trade.

____11. The U.S. is a pure market economy.

____12. In economics, a closed economy is one in which there is very limited economic freedom.

____13. The U.S. is an open economy.

____14. Careful and systematic observation and measurement are basic components of any science.

____15. Economics is not a science since it deals with the study of willful human beings and not inanimate objects in nature.

____16. "An increase in the income tax rate will cause total tax revenue to fall." This is an example of a positive statement.

____17. Science is silent on positive questions.

____18. A positive statement is about what *is,* while a normative statement is about what *will be.*

____19. One of the key assumptions of an economic model is that people make choices which they expect to make them as well-off as possible.

____20. Economic models are of very limited value in helping us understand the real world because they abstract from the complexity of the real world.

____21. Models are complete descriptions of reality.

____22. Microeconomics is concerned with the economy as a whole.

____23. Macroeconomics includes the study of the causes of inflation.

____24. Testing an economic model requires comparing its predictions against real world events.

____25. When the predictions of a model conflict with the relevant facts, a theory must be discarded or modified.

Multiple Choice

1. The fact that human wants cannot be fully satisfied with available resources is called the problem of
   a. opportunity costs.
   b. scarcity.
   c. normative economics.
   d. what to produce.

2. The problem of scarcity
   a. exists only in economies which rely on the market mechanism.
   b. exists only in economies which rely on the command mechanism.
   c. exists in all economies.
   d. means that at least some prices are too high.

3. When the government chooses to use resources to build a dam, those resources are no longer available to build a highway. This illustrates the concept of
   a. microeconomics.
   b. macroeconomics.
   c. opportunity cost.
   d. optimizing.

4. Sally has the chance to either attend an economics lecture or play tennis. If she chooses to attend the lecture, the value of playing tennis is
   a. equal to the value of the lecture.
   b. greater than the value of the lecture.
   c. not comparable to the value of the lecture.
   d. the opportunity cost of attending the lecture.

5. The opportunity cost of getting a $10 haircut is
   a. the customer's best alternative use of the $10.
   b. the customer's best alternative use of the time it takes to get a haircut.
   c. the customer's best alternative use of both the $10 and the time it takes to get a haircut.
   d. the value of $10 to the barber.

6. *All* decision makers in an economy
   a. coordinate choices between groups.
   b. supply factors of production.
   c. make choices.
   d. produce goods or services.

7. Which of the following is an example of capital as a factor of production?
   a. Money held by General Motors
   b. A General Motors bond
   c. An automobile factory owned by General Motors
   d. All of the above

8. All of the following are factors of production *except*
   a. government.
   b. natural resources.
   c. land.
   d. labor.

9. A closed economy is one that
   a. has strict government control of production.
   b. has no economic links with other economies
   c. maintains strict control of its borders.
   d. is characterized by a dominant agricultural sector.

10. The U.S. economy is best described as a
    a. closed economy.
    b. market economy.
    c. command economy.
    d. mixed economy.

11. A normative statement is one about
    a. what is usually the case.
    b. the assumptions of an economic model.
    c. what ought to be.
    d. what is.

12. "The rich face higher income tax rates than the poor" is an example of
    a. a normative statement.
    b. a positive statement.
    c. a negative statement.
    d. a theoretical statement.

13. An economic model is tested by
    a. examining the realism of its assumptions.
    b. comparing its predictions with the facts.
    c. the Testing Committee of the American Economic Association.
    d. the detail of its descriptions.

14. Which of the following is <u>NOT</u> a key assumption of an economic model?
    a. People have preferences.
    b. People economize.
    c. People are constrained by a given technology and a fixed amount of resources.
    d. People's choices are not coordinated.

15. When economists say that people are rational, it means they
    a. do not make errors of judgment.
    b. make the best decision from their perspective.
    c. act on complete information.
    d. will not later regret any decision made now.

16. The branch of economics that studies the decisions of individual households and firms is called
    a. microeconomics.
    b. macroeconomics.
    c. positive economics.
    d. normative economics.

17. All of the following are microeconomic issues EXCEPT
    a. wages and earnings.
    b. distribution of wealth.
    c. production.
    d. unemployment.

18. Which of the following would NOT be considered a macroeconomic topic?
    a. The reasons for a decline in the price of orange juice
    b. The cause of recessions
    c. The effect of the government budget deficit on inflation
    d. The determination of aggregate income

SHORT ANSWER

1. What is meant by scarcity?

2. Why does the existence of scarcity mean that we must make choices?

3. Why will cooperation not eliminate scarcity?

4. What is meant by opportunity cost? What is the opportunity cost of spending two hours studying for an economics exam?

5. Sarah takes five courses each school term. She is considering taking economics as her fifth course this term. If she decides to do so, what is the opportunity cost of taking the economics course?

6. What are the three broad classifications of factors of production? Give two examples of each.

7. Why is the U.S. economy considered to be mixed?

8. Is the following statement normative or positive? *Why?* "All college students should take an economics course."

9. How are economic models tested?

PROBLEMS

1. It takes one hour to travel from Boston to New York by airplane and five hours by train. Further, suppose that air fare is $100 and train fare is $60. Which mode of transportation has the lower opportunity cost for the following people?
    a) A person who can earn $5 an hour
    b) A person who can earn $10 an hour
    c) A person who can earn $12 an hour

2. Suppose the government builds and staffs a hospital in order to provide "free" medical care.
    a) What is the opportunity cost of the free medical care?
    b) Is it free from the perspective of society as a whole?

3. Indicate whether each of the following statements is positive or normative. If it is normative (positive), rewrite it so that it becomes positive (normative).
    a) "The government ought to reduce the size of the deficit in order to lower interest rates."

b) "Government imposition of a tax on tobacco products will reduce their consumption."

4. Suppose we examine a model of plant growth which predicts that, given the amount of water and sunlight, the application of fertilizer stimulates plant growth. How might you test the model?

ANSWERS

CONCEPT REVIEW

1. scarcity; exceed; choices
2. opportunity
3. optimizing
4. what; how; for whom
5. households; firms; governments
6. labor; land; capital
7. command; market; prices; mixed
8. open
9. positive; normative
10. microeconomics; macroeconomics

TRUE OR FALSE

1. F	6. F	11. F	16. T	21. F
2. F	7. F	12. F	17. F	22. F
3. F	8. T	13. T	18. F	23. T
4. T	9. F	14. T	19. T	24. T
5. T	10. F	15. F	20. F	25. T

MULTIPLE CHOICE

1. b	5. c	9. b	13. b	17. d
2. c	6. c	10. d	14. d	18. a
3. c	7. c	11. c	15. b	
4. d	8. a	12. b	16. a	

SHORT ANSWER

1. Scarcity is the universal condition that human wants always exceed the resources available to satisfy them.

2. The fact that goods and services are scarce means that individuals cannot have all of everything they want. It is therefore necessary to choose among alternatives.

3. Scarcity is a problem of essentially infinite wants and limited resources. While cooperation is one way to organize our activity as we confront the problem of scarcity, it cannot eliminate it and therefore cannot eliminate economic problems.

4. Opportunity cost is the best forgone alternative (opportunity). The opportunity cost of spending two hours studying for an economics exam is the best alternative activity you would have chosen. This, obviously, will be different for different individuals. It might be attending the opera, watching TV, or sleeping.

5. The opportunity cost of choosing the economics course is the course Sarah would have chosen otherwise. If her *next* best choice is a sociology course, then that would be the opportunity cost.

6. *Labor*: the effort and skill of a carpenter, the ability of an actor.
Land: trees, water.
Capital: a tractor, a factory building.

7. The U. S. economy is a mixed economy because it relies on both the market and command mechanisms. Most coordination is carried out through the market mechanism, but there are many economic decisions which are either made by or regulated by the government.

8. The given statement, however wise, is normative because it is about what ought to (should) be rather than what is.

9. Economic models are tested by comparing the model's predictions with the facts of the real world. If the predictions of the model are in conflict with those facts, the model is rejected, otherwise we do not reject the model.

PROBLEMS

1. The point here is to recognize that the opportunity cost of travel includes the best alternative value of travel time as well as the train or air fare.
   a) Thus, if the opportunity cost of the time spent traveling is the $5 an hour that could have been earned (but wasn't), the opportunity cost of train travel (in dollars) is the $60 train fare plus the $25 ($5 an hour times five hours) in forgone income for a total of $85. In this case the opportunity cost of air travel is the $100 air fare plus $5 in forgone income, for a total of $105. Therefore, for a person whose best alternative use of time is to earn $5 an hour, the opportunity cost of traveling by train is less than the opportunity cost of traveling by air.
   b) For a person who can earn $10 an hour, the opportunity cost of train travel will be $110 ($60 fare plus $50 in forgone earnings) and the opportunity cost of air travel is $110 ($100 fare plus $10 in foregone earnings). In this case the opportunity costs are the same.
   c) For a person who could have earned $12 an hour the opportunity cost of train travel ($120) exceeds the opportunity cost of air travel ($112).

2. a) Even though medical care may be offered without charge ("free"), there are still opportunity costs. The opportunity cost of providing such health care is the best alternative use of the resources used in the construction of the hospital and the best alternative use of the resources (including human resources) used in the operation of the hospital.
   b) These resources are no longer available for other activities and therefore represent a cost to society.

3. a) The given statement is normative. The following is positive:
   "If the government reduces the size of the deficit, interest rates will fall."
   b) The given statement is positive. The following is normative:
   "The government ought to impose a tax on tobacco products."

4. The prediction of the model can be tested by conducting the following experiment and carefully observing the outcome. Select a number of plots of ground of the same size which have similar characteristics and will be subject to the same amount of water and sunlight. Plant equal quantities of seeds in all the plots. In some of the plots apply no fertilizer and in some of the plots apply (perhaps varying amounts of) fertilizer. When the plants have grown, measure the growth of the plants and compare the growth measures of the fertilized plots and the unfertilized plots. If plant growth is *not* greater in fertilized plots, we discard the theory (model).

2 MAKING AND USING GRAPHS

CHAPTER IN PERSPECTIVE

As a science, economics is characterized by systematic observation and measurement as well as the development of economic theory. In both of these components of economic science the use of graphs plays an important role.

Economic theory describes relationships among economic variables and graphs offer a very convenient way to represent such relationships. Indeed, the use of graphs allows us to economize in the sense that we are able to obtain much information with little effort. Graphs give a "picture" of the behavior of measured economic variables. Representing data graphically can be extremely useful for quickly conveying information about general characteristics of economic behavior.

As we will see in the next few chapters, graphical analysis of economic relationships is especially helpful when we are interested in discovering the theoretical consequences of a change in economic circumstances. Given the pervasive use of graphs in economics, this chapter reviews all the concepts and techniques you will need to construct and use graphs in this course.

LEARNING OBJECTIVES

After studying this chapter, you will be able to:

- **Make and interpret a time-series graph and a scatter diagram**
- **Distinguish among linear and nonlinear relationships and relationships that have a maximum and a minimum**
- **Define and calculate the slope of a line**
- **Graph relationships among more than two variables**

HELPFUL HINTS

1. The chapters of the text discuss numerous relationships among economic variables. Almost invariably these relationships will be represented and analyzed graphically. Thus an early, complete understanding of graphs will greatly facilitate mastery of the economic analysis of later chapters. Avoid the common mistake of assuming that a superficial understanding of graphs will be sufficient.

2. If your experience with graphical analysis is limited, this chapter will be crucial to your ability to readily understand later economic analysis. You will likely find significant rewards in occasionally returning to this chapter for review. If you are experienced in the construction and use of graphs, the chapter may be "old hat." Even in this case, the chapter should be skimmed and the Self-Test in this *Study Guide* completed. The main point is that you should be thoroughly familiar with the basic concepts and techniques of this chapter.

3. Slope is a *linear* concept since it is a property of a straight line. For this reason, the slope is constant along a straight line but is different at different points on a curved (nonlinear) line. When we are interested in the slope of a curved line, we actually calculate the slope of a straight line. The text presents two ways of choosing such a straight line and thus two alternative ways of calculating the slope of a curved line: (1) slope across an arc, and (2) slope at a point. The first of these calculates the slope of the *straight line* formed by the arc between two points on the curved line. The second calculates the slope of the *straight line* that just touches (is tangent to) the curve at a point.

4. Pay particular attention to graphing relationships among more than two variables.

KEY FIGURES

Figure 2.8 Positive Relationships
Variables that move up and down together are positively related. Three different positive relationships are illustrated in this figure. In each case, as the variable measured on the horizontal axis increases, the variable measured on the vertical axis also increases. Part (a) illustrates a positive linear relationship while parts (b) and (c) illustrate positive relationships that are not linear.

Figure 2.9 Negative Relationships
This figure is a companion to Fig. 2.8 and illustrates negative relationships. Variables that move in opposite directions are negatively related. Three different negative relationships are illustrated in this figure. In each case, as the variable measured on the horizontal axis increases, the variable measured on the vertical axis decreases. Part (a) illustrates a negative linear relationship, while parts (b) and (c) illustrate negative relationships that are not linear.

Figure 2.10 Maximum and Minimum Points
The relationship in part (a) reaches a maximum. As the variable measured on the horizontal axis increases, the value of the variable measured on the vertical axis increases, reaches a maximum at point *a* and then decreases. Similarly, the relationship in part (b) reaches a minimum at point *b*.

Figure 2.11 Variables with No Relationship
If there is no relationship between two variables, changes in one will have no effect on the other. The two parts of this figure illustrate how we can represent such a lack of relationship. Part (a) illustrates the fact that changes in the variable measured on the horizontal axis leave the variable measured on the vertical axis unchanged. Part (b) illustrates that changes in the variable measured on the vertical axis leave the variable measured on the horizontal axis unchanged.

Figure 2.12 The Slope of a Straight Line

The slope of a straight line tells us how much and in what direction the variable on the vertical axis changes when the variable on the horizontal axis changes. The slope is computed by dividing the change in y (the *rise*) by the change in x (the *run*). When both x and y move in the same direction, as in part (a), the slope is positive and when x and y move in opposite directions, as in part (b), the slope is negative.

Figure 2.13 The Slope of a Curve

Slope is a linear concept, so even when we measure the slope of a curve we do so by calculating the slope of a straight line. This figure illustrates the two ways of choosing a straight line to do this. Part (a) calculates the slope of the straight line that just touches (is tangent to) the curve at a point. Part (b) calculates the slope of the straight line formed by the arc between two points on the curved line.

Figure 2.14 Graphing a Relationship Among Three Variables

When graphing a relationship among three variables, we can reduce the problem to grap hing the relationship between two variables by holding one of the variables constant and graphing the relationship between the other two. This is illustrated in this figure using as an example the relationship among ice cream consumption, the price of a scoop of ice cream, and air temperature. Part (a) shows the negative relationship between ice cream consumption and the price of a scoop of ice cream if the air temperature is held constant (at 70^0 F and also at 90^0 F). Part (b) shows the positive relationship between ice cream consumption and air temperature if the price of a scoop of ice cream is held constant. Finally, part (c) shows the positive relationship between the air temperature and the price of a scoop of ice cream if the consumption of ice cream is held constant.

SELF-TEST

CONCEPT REVIEW

1. A graph that measures an economic variable on the vertical axis and time on the horizontal axis is called a(n) ____________-____________ graph.
2. The tendency for a variable to rise or fall over time is called the ____________ of the variable.
3. Suppose the value of one economic variable is measured on the x-axis and the value of a second is measured on the y-axis. A diagram that plots the value of one variable corresponding to the value of the other is called a(n) ____________ diagram.
4. If two variables tend to move up or down together they exhibit a(n) ____________ relationship. Such a relationship is represented graphically by a line that slopes ____________ (to the right).
5. Two variables that move in opposite directions exhibit a(n) ____________ relationship. Such a relationship is represented graphically by a line that slopes ____________(to the right).
6. Suppose variables A and B are unrelated. If we measure A on the y-axis and B on the x-axis, the graph of A as we increase B will be a(n) ____________ line.

7. The slope of a line is calculated as the change in the value of the variable measured on the ____________ axis divided by the change in the value of the variable measured on the ____________ axis.
8. A straight line exhibits ____________ slope at all points.
9. To graph a relationship among more than two variables we simply graph the relationship between ____________ variables, holding all others constant.

TRUE OR FALSE

____ 1. A time-series graph measures time on the horizontal axis.

____ 2. A time-series graph gives information about the level of the relevant economic variable, as well as information about changes and the speed of those changes.

____ 3. A graph that omits the origin will always be misleading.

____ 4. A two-variable time-series graph can help us see if the two variables tend to move together over time.

____ 5. A one-dimensional graph that represents measured rainfall along a horizontal line is an example of a scatter diagram.

____ 6. If the graph of the relationship between two variables slopes upward (to the right) the variables move up and down together.

____ 7. If variable *a* rises when variable *b* falls and falls when *b* rises, then the relationship between *a* and *b* is negative.

____ 8. If the relationship between *y* (measured along the vertical axis) and *x* (measured along the horizontal axis) is such that *y* reaches a maximum as *x* increases, then the relationship must be negative before and positive after the maximum.

____ 9. If the value of *y* (measured along the vertical axis) doesn't change as we increase *x* (measured along the horizontal axis), the graph of the relationship between *x* and *y* is horizontal.

____ 10. The graph of the "relationship" between two variables that are in fact unrelated will be either horizontal or vertical.

____ 11. The slope of a straight line is calculated by dividing the change in the value of the variable measured on the horizontal axis by the change in the value of the variable measured on the vertical axis.

____ 12. The slope of a curved line is not constant.

____ 13. If we want to graph the relationship among three variables, we must hold two of them constant as we represent the third.

____ 14. Refer to Fig. 2.1. The value of *y* increased between 1970 and 1971.

Figure 2.1

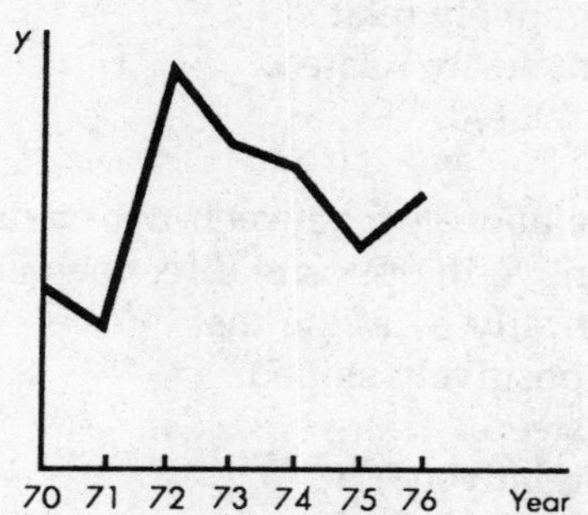

____15. Refer to Fig. 2.1. The value of y increased much more rapidly between 1971 and 1972 than between 1975 and 1976.

____16. Figure 2.1 is a scatter diagram.

____17. In Fig. 2.2, the relationship between y and x is first negative, reaches a minimum, and then becomes positive as x increases.

Figure 2.2

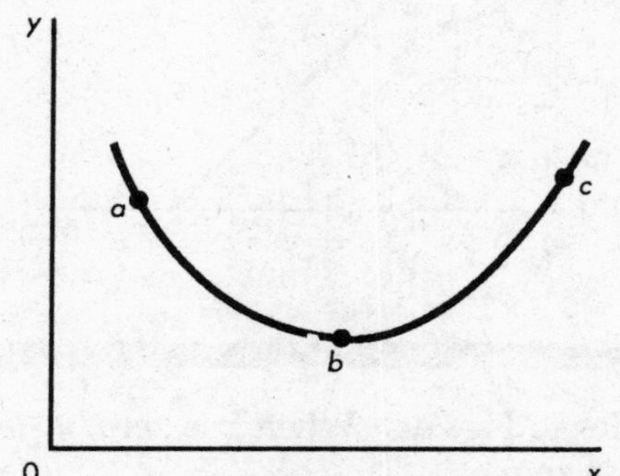

____18. In Fig. 2.2, the slope of the curve is increasing as we move from point b to point c.

____19. In Fig. 2.2, the slope of the curve is approaching zero as we move from point a to point b.

____20. In Fig. 2.2, the value of x is a minimum at point b.

____21. For a point on a two-variable graph, the length of the line running from the point to the vertical axis is the y-coordinate.

____22. The slope of a line can be described as "rise over run."

____23. For a straight line, if a small change in y is associated with a large change in x, the slope is large.

MULTIPLE CHOICE

1. The behavior of a single economic variable over time is best illustrated by a
   a. one-variable graph.
   b. two-variable graph.
   c. time-series graph.
   d. scatter diagram.

2. Figure 2.3 is a
   a. one-variable time-series graph.
   b. two-variable time-series graph.
   c. scatter diagram.
   d. both b and c.

3. The dotted line in Fig. 2.3 represents variable y. Which of the following statements best describes the relationship between x and y in Fig. 2.3?
   a. x and y tend to move in opposite directions over time.
   b. x and y tend to move together over time.
   c. x tends to move in the same direction as y, but one year later.
   d. y tends to move in the same direction as x, but one year later.

Figure 2.3

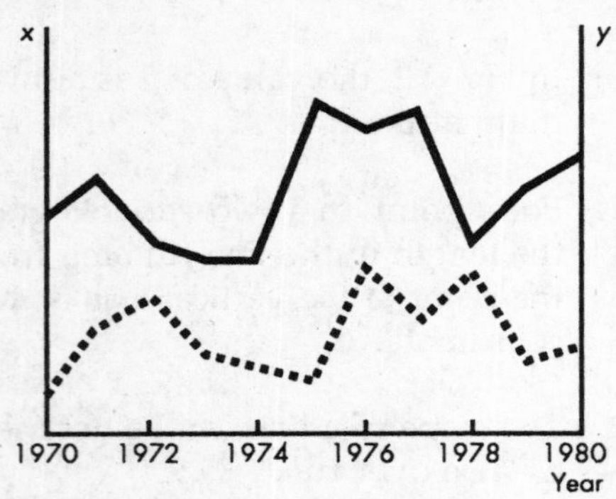

4. The data in Table 2.1 could NOT be represented by
   a. two one-variable time-series graphs.
   b. one two-variable time-series graph.
   c. a three-variable time-series graph.
   d. a scatter diagram.

Table 2.1

Year	x	y
1980	6.2	143
1981	5.7	156
1982	5.3	162

5. From the information in Table 2.1, it appears that
   a. x and y tend to exhibit a negative relationship.
   b. x and y tend to exhibit a positive relationship.
   c. there is no relationship between x and y.
   d. there is first a negative and then a positive relationship between x and y.

6. If variables x and y move up and down together, they are said to be
   a. positively related.
   b. negatively related.
   c. conversely related.
   d. unrelated.

7. The relationship between two variables that move in opposite directions is shown graphically by a line that
   a. is positively sloped.
   b. is steep.
   c. is relatively flat.
   d. is negatively sloped.

8. What is the slope of the line in Fig. 2.4?
   a. 1
   b. -1
   c. -5
   d. -1/5

Figure 2.4

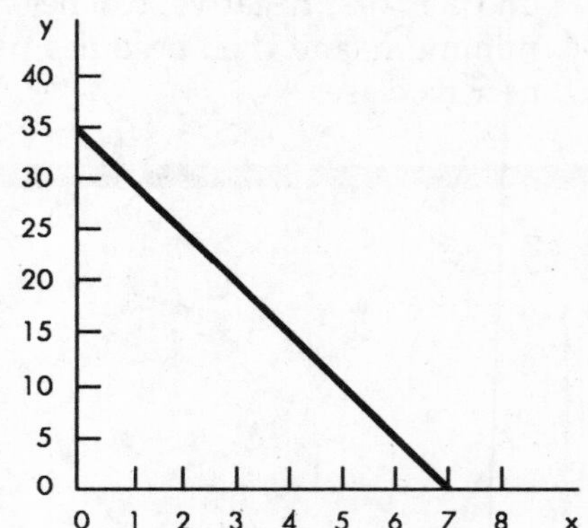

9. Refer to Fig. 2.4. When x is zero, y
   a. is zero.
   b. is 35.
   c. is 7.
   d. cannot be determined from the graph.

10. In Fig. 2.5 the relationship between x and y is
   a. positive with slope decreasing as x increases.
   b. negative with slope decreasing as x increases.
   c. negative with slope increasing as x increases.
   d. positive with slope increasing as x increases.

Figure 2.5

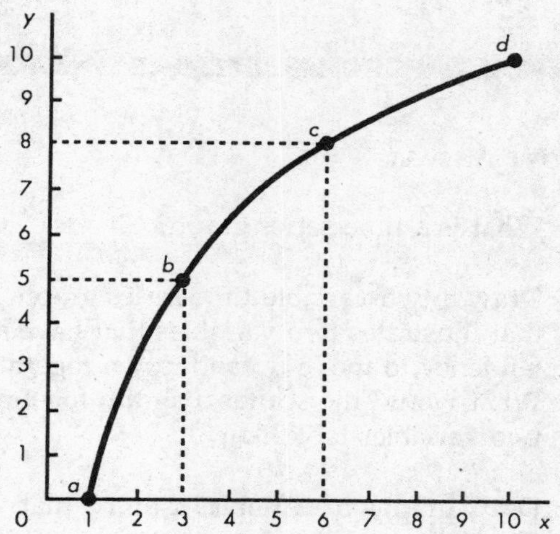

11. In Fig. 2.5, the slope across the arc between b and c is
   a. 1/2.
   b. 2/3.
   c. 1.
   d. 2.

12. In Fig. 2.5, consider the slopes of the arc between a and b and the arc between b and c. The slope at point b is difficult to determine exactly, but it must be
   a. greater than 5/2.
   b. about 5/2.
   c. between 5/2 and 1.
   d. less than 1.

13. If the price of an umbrella is low and the number of rainy days per month is large, more umbrellas will be sold each month. On the other hand, if the price of an umbrella is high and there are few rainy days per month, fewer umbrellas will be sold each month. On the basis of this information, which of the following statements is true?
   a. The number of umbrellas sold and the price of an umbrella are positively related, holding the number of rainy days constant.
   b. The number of umbrellas sold and the price of an umbrella are negatively related, holding the number of rainy days constant.
   c. The number of rainy days and the number of umbrellas sold are negatively related, holding the price of an umbrella constant.
   d. The number of rainy days and the price of an umbrella are negatively related, holding the number of umbrellas sold constant.

14. Given the data in Table 2.2, holding income constant, the graph relating the price of strawberries (vertical axis) to the purchase of strawberries (horizontal axis)
   a. is a vertical line.
   b. is a horizontal line.
   c. is a positively-sloped line.
   d. is a negatively-sloped line.

15. Consider the data in Table 2.2. Suppose family income decreases from \$400 to \$300 per week. Then the graph relating the price of strawberries (vertical axis) to the number of boxes of strawberries purchased (horizontal axis) will
   a. no longer exist.
   b. become positively sloped.
   c. shift to the right.
   d. shift to the left.

Table 2.2

Weekly family income (dollars)	Price per box strrawberries (dollars)	Number of boxes purchased per week
300	1.00	5
300	1.25	3
300	1.50	2
400	1.00	7
400	1.25	5
400	1.50	4

16. Given the data in Table 2.2, holding price constant, the graph relating family income (vertical axis) to the purchase of strawberries
    a. will be a positively sloped line.
    b. will be a negatively sloped line.
    c. reaches a maximum.
    d. cannot be drawn if we hold price constant.

17. In Fig. 2.6, x is
    a. positively related to y and negatively related to z.
    b. positively related to both y and z.
    c. negatively related to y and positively related to z.
    d. negatively related to both y and z.

Figure 2.6

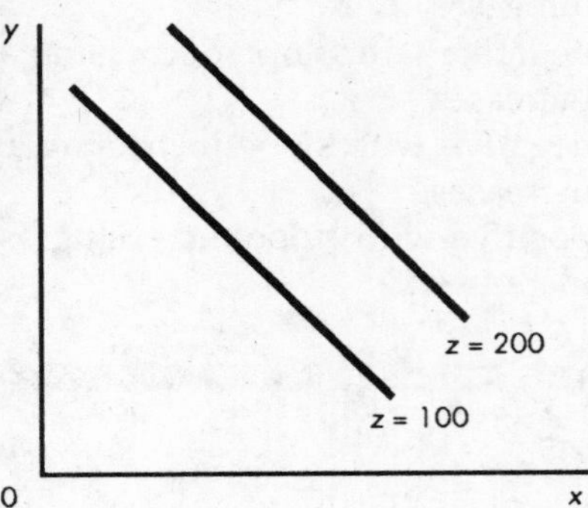

SHORT ANSWER

1. What is a time-series graph?

2. Draw a two-variable time-series graph that illustrates two variables that have a tendency to move up and down together. What would the scatter diagram for these two variables look like?

3. Draw graphs of variables x and y that illustrate the following relationships.
   a) x and y move up and down together
   b) x and y move in opposite directions
   c) as x increases y reaches a maximum
   d) as x increases y reaches a minimum
   e) x and y move in opposite directions, but as x increases y decreases by larger and larger increments for each unit increase in x
   f) y is independent of the value of x
   g) x is independent of the value of y

4. What does it mean to say that the slope of a line is -2/3?

5. Explain how we measure the slope of a curved line
   a) at a point.

b) across an arc.

6. How do we graph a relationship among more than two variables (using a two-dimensional graph)?

7. Draw a curve that is positively sloped but starts out relatively flat, becomes steeper, and then gets flatter again as the variable measured on the horizontal axis increases.

PROBLEMS

1. Consider the data given in Table 2.3.
   a) Draw a time-series graph for the interest rate.
   b) Draw a two-variable time-series graph for both the inflation rate and the interest rate.
   c) Draw a scatter diagram for the inflation rate (horizontal axis) and the interest rate.
   d) Would you describe the general relationship between the inflation rate and the interest rate as positive, negative, or none?

2. Compute the slope of the lines in Fig. 2.7 (a) and (b).

3. Draw a straight line
   a) with slope = -10 and passing through the point given by x-coordinate = 2 and y-coordinate = 80.
   b) with slope = 2 along which y = 10 when x = 6.

4. Using the graph in Fig. 2.8, compute the slope
   a) across the arc between points a and b.
   b) at point b.
   c) at point c, and explain your answer.

Table 2.3

Year	Inflation rate (percent)	Interest rate (percent)
1970	5.4	6.4
1971	3.2	4.3
1972	3.4	4.1
1973	8.3	7.0
1974	11.8	7.9
1975	6.7	5.8
1976	4.9	5.0
1977	6.5	5.3
1978	8.6	7.2
1979	12.3	10.0

Figure 2.7 (a)

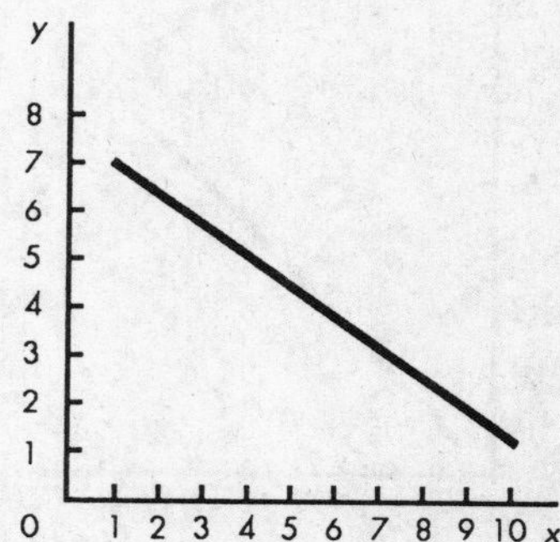

5 In Table 2.4, x represents the number of umbrellas sold per month, y represents the price of an umbrella, and z represents the average number of rainy days per month.
   a) On the same diagram, graph the relationship between x (horizontal axis) and y (vertical axis) when z = 4, when z = 5, and when z = 6. Suppose that, on average, it rains six days per month. This implies a certain average relationship between monthly umbrella sales

and umbrella price. Suppose that the "greenhouse effect" reduces the average monthly rainfall to four days per month. What happens to the graph of the relationship between umbrella sales and umbrella prices?

b) On a diagram, graph the relationship between x (horizontal axis) and z (vertical axis) when y = \$10 and when y = \$12. Is the relationship between x (horizontal axis) and z (vertical axis) positive or negative?

c) On a diagram, graph the relationship between y (horizontal axis) and z (vertical axis) when x = 120 and when x = 140. Is the relationship between y and z positive or negative?

Figure 2.7 (b)

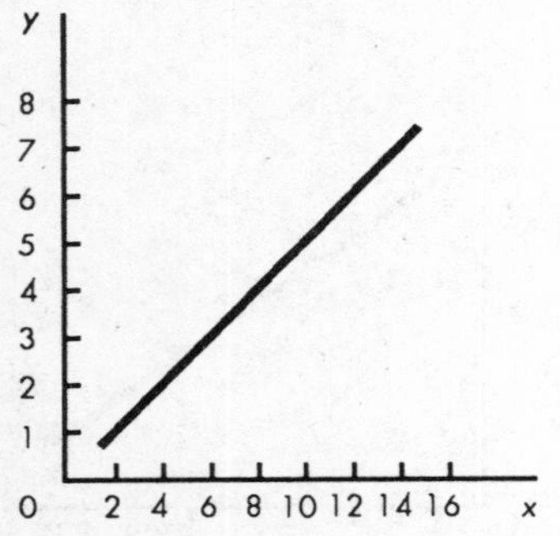

Figure 2.8

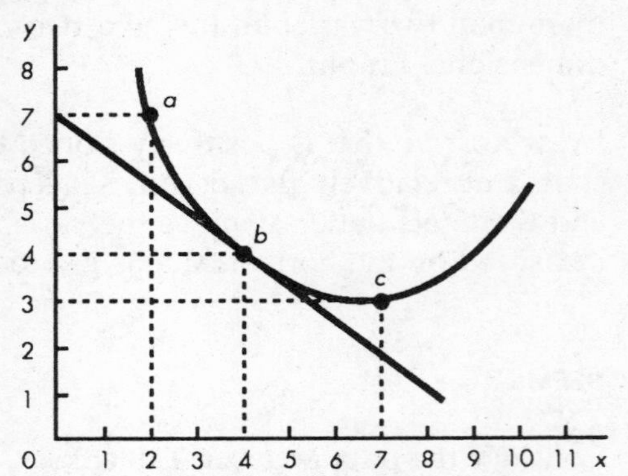

Table 2.4

Umbrellas sold per month (x)	Price per umbrella (y)	Average number of rainy days per month (z)
120	\$10	4
140	\$10	5
160	\$10	6
100	\$12	4
120	\$12	5
140	\$12	6
80	\$14	4
100	\$14	5
120	\$14	6

ANSWERS

CONCEPT REVIEW

1. time-series
2. trend
3. scatter
4. positive; upward
5. negative; downward
6. horizontal
7. vertical (y); horizontal (x)
8. constant
9. two

TRUE OR FALSE

1. T	6. T	11. F	16. F	21. F
2. T	7. T	12. T	17. T	22. T
3. F	8. F	13. F	18. T	23. F
4. T	9. T	14. F	19. T	
5. F	10. T	15. T	20. F	

MULTIPLE CHOICE

1. c	5. a	9. b	13. b	17. c
2. b	6. a	10. a	14. d	
3. d	7. d	11. c	15. d	
4. c	8. c	12. c	16. a	

SHORT ANSWER

1. A time-series graph is a graph that plots the value of the variable of interest on the vertical axis against time on the horizontal axis.

2. Figure 2.9 (a) illustrates a two-variable time-series graph of two variables with a tendency to move up and down together, while Fig. 2.9 (b) illustrates a scatter diagram for such variables.

3. Figures 2.10 (a)–(g) illustrate the desired graphs.

Figure 2.9

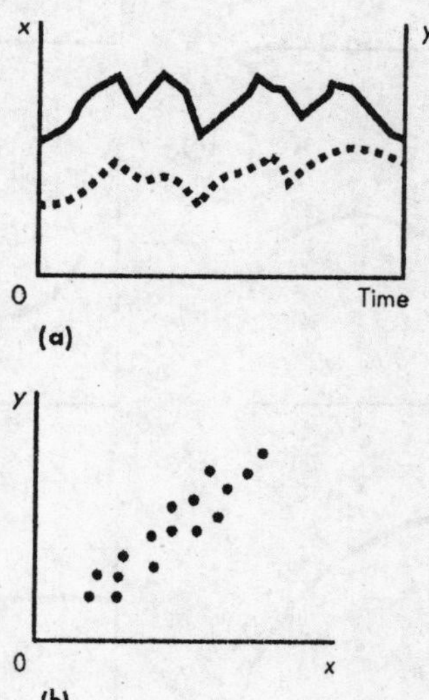

4. The negative sign in the slope of -2/3 means that there is a negative relationship between the two variables. The value of 2/3 means that when the variable measured on the vertical axis decreases by 2 units (the *rise* or Δy), the variable measured on the horizontal axis increases by 3 units (the *run* or Δx).

5. In both cases we actually measure the slope of a straight line.
a) The slope at a point is measured by calculating the slope of the straight line that is tangent to (just touches) the curved line at the point.
b) The slope across an arc is measure by calculating the slope of the straight line that forms the arc.

Figure 2.10

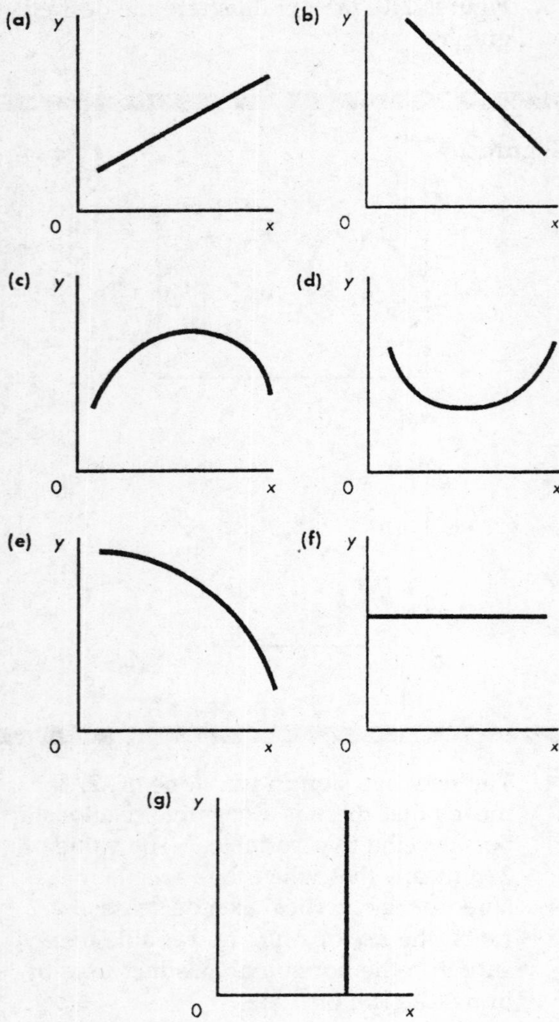

6. To graph a relationship among more than two variables we hold all the variables but two constant and graph the relationship between the remaining two. Thus we can graph the relationship between any pair of variables of interest, given the constant values of the other variables.

7. Figure 2.11 illustrates such a curve.

PROBLEMS

1. a) A time-series graph for the interest rate is given in Fig. 2.12 (a).
   b) Figure 2.12 (b) is a two-variable time-series graph for both the inflation rate and the interest rate.
   c) The scatter diagram for the inflation rate and the interest rate is given in Fig. 2.12 (c).

Figure 2.11

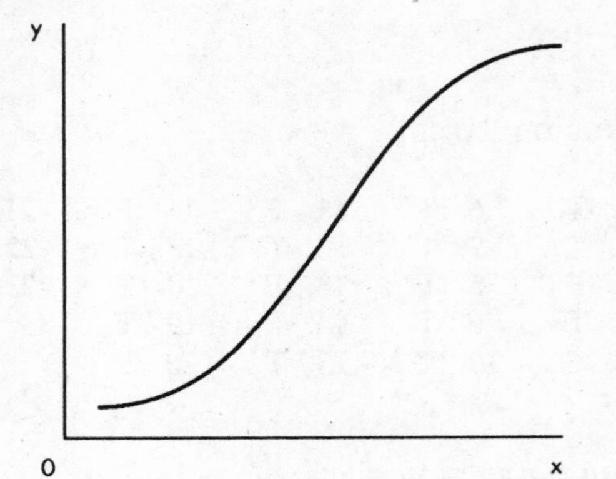

   d) From the graphs in Fig. 2.12 (b) and (c), we see that the relationship between the inflation rate and the interest rate is generally positive.

Figure 2.12 (a)

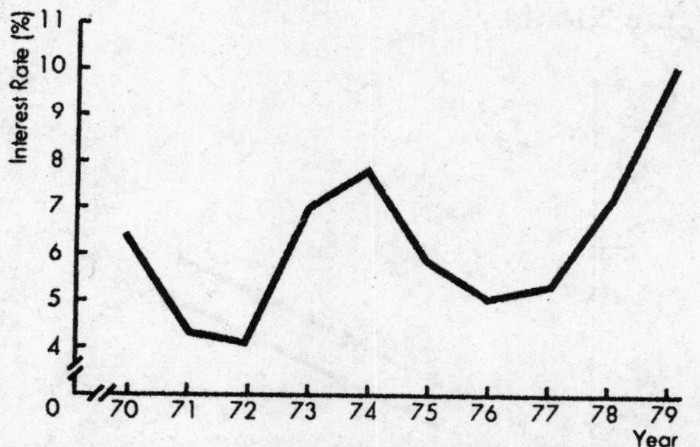

Figure 2.12 (c)

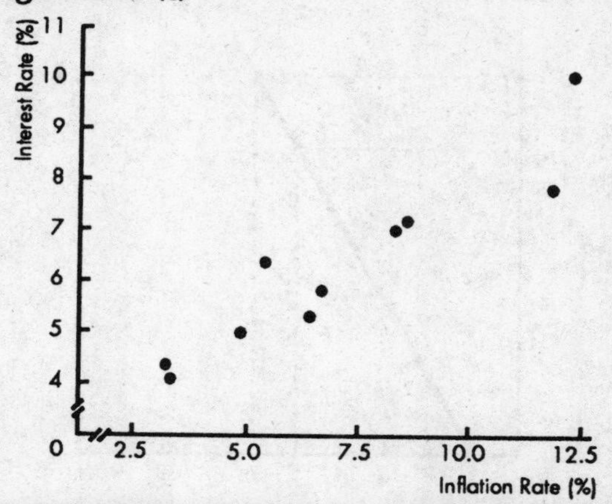

Figure 2.12 (b)

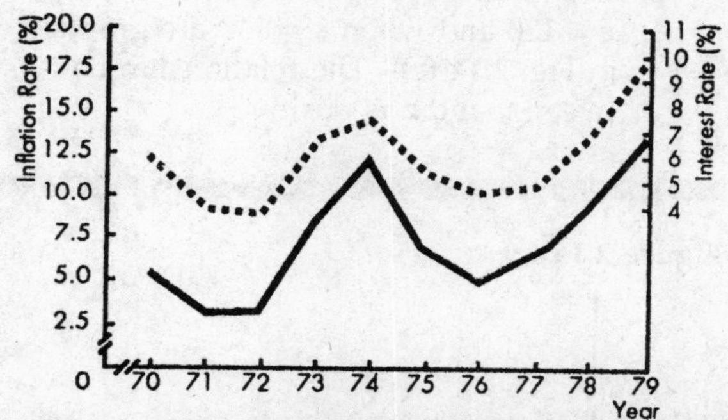

Figure 2.13 (a)

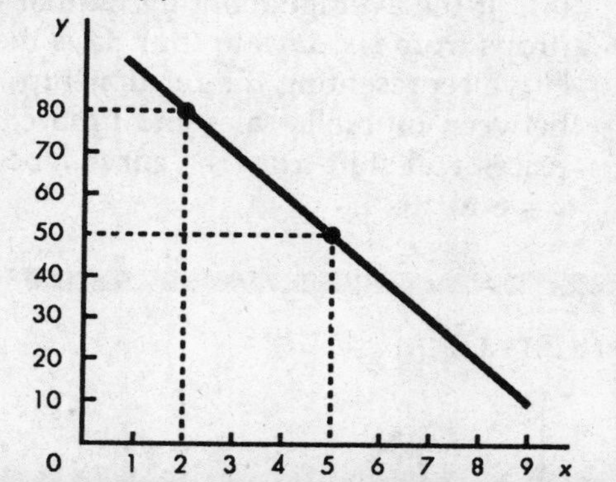

2. The slope of the line in Fig. 2.7 (a) is -2/3 and the slope of the line in Fig. 2.7 (b) is 0.5.

3. a) The requested straight line is graphed in Fig. 2.13 (a).
   b) The requested straight line is graphed in Fig. 2.13 (b).

4. a) The slope across the arc between points *a* and *b* is -3/2.
   b) The slope at point *b* is -3/4.
   c) The slope at point *c* is 0 since it is a minimum point. At a minimum point the slope changes from negative to positive; that is, it is 0.

Figure 2.13 (b)

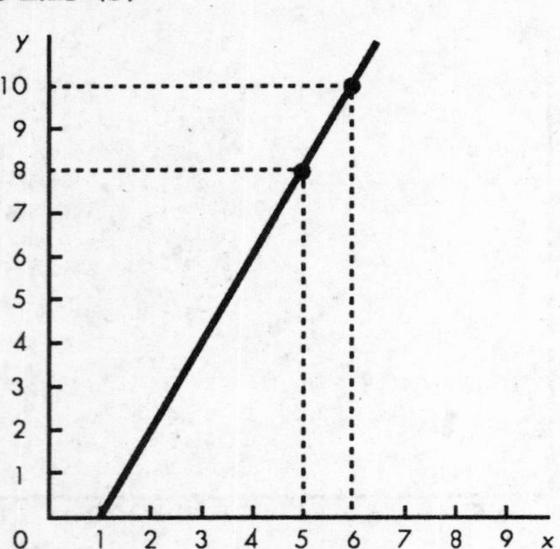

5. a) The relationships between x and y for $z = 4, 5$, and 6 are graphed in Fig. 2.14 (a). If the average monthly rainfall drops from six days to four days the curve representing the relationship between umbrella sales and umbrella prices will shift from the curve labeled $z = 6$ to $z = 4$.

Figure 2.14 (a)

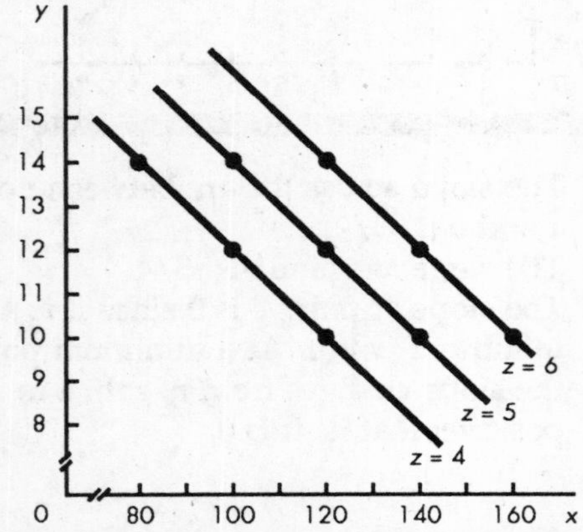

(b) The relationships between x and z when y is \$10 and when y is \$12 are graphed in Fig. 2.14 (b). The relationship between x and z is positive.

Figure 2.14 (b)

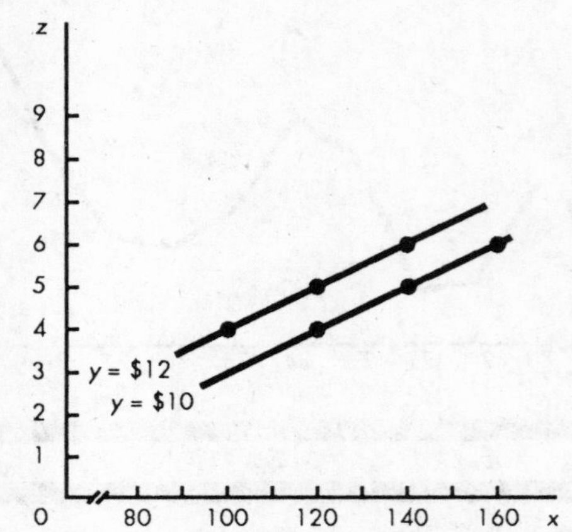

c) The relationship between y and z when $x = 120$ and when $x = 140$ are graphed in Fig. 2.14 (c). The relationship between y and z is positive.

Figure 2.14 (c)

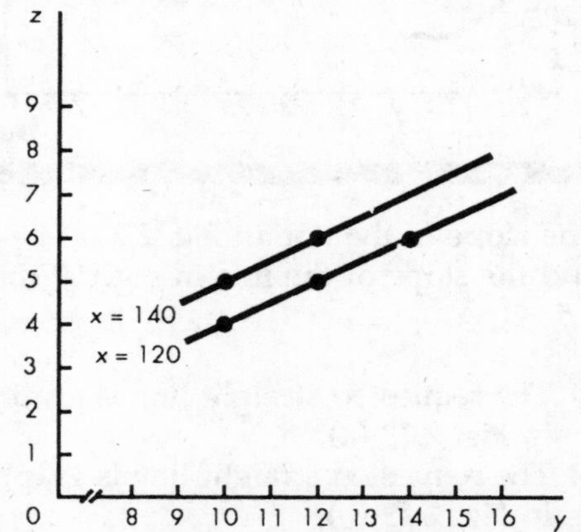

3 PRODUCTION, SPECIALIZATION, AND EXCHANGE

CHAPTER IN PERSPECTIVE

In the first chapter we learned that the existence of scarcity is the fundamental and pervasive social problem giving rise to economic activity. Because all individuals and all economies are faced with scarce resources, choices must be made, each of which has an opportunity cost. Economies that are generally considered to be successful in coping with the problem of scarcity are characterized by a broad array of goods and services produced by a highly specialized labor force. Since workers specialize as producers but consume a variety of goods and services, exchange is a necessary complement to specialization.

This chapter explains why specialization and exchange are the natural consequences of attempts to get the most from scarce resources (i.e., to optimize). It also discusses the critical role of opportunity cost in explaining why individuals and countries specialize in the production of goods and services and why tremendous gains occur from specialization and exchange.

LEARNING OBJECTIVES

After studying this chapter, you will be able to:

- **Define the production possibility frontier**
- **Calculate opportunity cost**
- **Explain why economic growth and technical change do not provide free gifts**
- **Explain comparative advantage**
- **Explain why people specialize and how they gain from trade**
- **Explain why property rights and money have evolved**

HELPFUL HINTS

1. This chapter reviews the absolutely critical concept of *opportunity cost*, which was introduced in the first chapter. It is important to recognize that the opportunity cost of an activity is *not* the *time* the activity requires but the *best alternative activity* which could have been pursued in that period of time. What matters for economic decisions is the opportunity cost of an activity, not how long it takes. Thus, when we are given information about the time involved in an activity, it is very useful to immediately make a simple opportunity cost table by asking what else could have been done.

2. A very helpful formula for opportunity cost, which works well in solving problems, especially problems that involve moving up or down a production possibility frontier is:

$$\textit{Opportunity cost} = \frac{\textit{Give up}}{\textit{Get}}$$

Opportunity cost equals the quantity of goods you must give up divided by the quantity of goods you will get. To illustrate, look again at three possibilities on Jane's production possibility frontier in Fig. 3.1 in the text.

Possibility	Corn (pounds per month)	Cloth (yards per month)
a	20	o
b	18	1
c	15	2

First consider an example of moving down the production possibility frontier. In moving from *a* to *b*, what is the opportunity cost of an additional yard of cloth? Jane must *give up* 2 pounds of corn (20 - 18) to *get* 1 yard of cloth (1 - 0). Substituting into the formula, the opportunity cost is:

$$\frac{\textit{2 pounds corn}}{\textit{1 yard cloth}} = \begin{matrix}\textit{2 pounds corn}\\ \textit{per yard of cloth}\end{matrix}$$

Next, consider an example of moving up the production possibility frontier. In moving from *b* to *a*, what is the opportunity cost of an additional pound of corn? Jane must *give up* 1 yard of cloth (1 - 0) to *get* 2 pounds of corn (20 - 18). Substituting into the formula, the opportunity cost is:

$$\frac{\textit{1 yard cloth}}{\textit{2 pounds corn}} = \begin{matrix}\textit{1/2 yard cloth}\\ \textit{per pound of corn}\end{matrix}$$

Opportunity cost is always measured in the units of the *forgone good.*

3. A production possibility frontier represents the boundary between attainable and unattainable levels of production for a fixed quantity of resources and a given state of technology. It indicates the best that can be done with existing resources and technology. Thus, the production possibility frontier will shift out if the quantity of resources increases (e.g., an increase in the stock of capital goods) even if the ability to use those resources does not change. The production possibility curve will also shift out if there is an increase in the ability to produce (i.e., a technological improvement) with no change in resources.

4. The text defines absolute advantage as a situation where one person has greater productivity than another in the production of all goods. We can also define *absolute advantage in the production of one good*. In comparing the productivity of two persons, this narrower concept of absolute advantage can be defined either in terms of greater output of the good per unit of inputs, or fewer inputs per unit of output.

It is useful to understand these definitions of absolute advantage only to demonstrate that absolute advantage has *no role* in explaining specialization and trade. The gains from trade depend only on differing comparative advantages. An individual has a comparative advantage in producing a good if he can produce it at lower opportunity cost than others.

5. One of the principle goals of this chapter is to develop a deeper appreciation of the gains (in terms of standard of living) that result from trade and institutional arrangements which enhance trade. The following thought experiments may be useful in this context. Each of them asks you to imagine how things would be different without some of the attributes of our current economic system.

a) How would your standard of living be different if there were no specialization and trade (i.e., if everyone were required to be self-sufficient)? Think of all the goods and services you now use on a regular basis (e.g., television, stereo equipment, automobiles, toothpaste, nail polish, etc.). How many of these would you not have or find it necessary to consume in lesser quantity and quality?

b) Suppose we allow specialization and exchange but have no clearly defined property rights. How would your life be different from the situation above and from what it is now?

c) Now suppose we have property rights as at present in the U. S. but that there is no money. Exchange must be conducted by barter. How would your life be different?

6. This chapter gives us our first opportunity to develop and use an economic model. It is valuable to think about the nature of that model in the context of the general discussion about such models in Chapter 1. The model developed in the chapter is a representation of the production possibilities in the two-person and two-good world of Jane and Joe. We note that the model abstracts greatly from the complexity of the real world in which there are billions of people and innumerable different kinds of goods and services. The model allows us to explain a number of phenomena that we observe in the world (e.g., specialization and exchange). The model also has some implications or predictions (e.g., countries that devote a larger proportion of their resources to capital accumulation will have more rapidly expanding production possibilities). The model can be subjected to "test" by comparing these predictions to the facts we observe in the real world.

KEY FIGURES

Figure 3.1 Jane's Production Possibility Frontier

A production possibility frontier gives the boundary between attainable and unattainable level of production for a fixed quantity of resources and a given state of technology. This figure illustrates the concept by constructing the production possibility frontier for Jane, who produces corn and cloth. Each point on the frontier shows the most cloth she is able to produce given that she is producing a particular quantity of corn. Points beyond the frontier are unattainable. Points inside the production possibility frontier are attainable but inferior to points on the production possibility frontier.

Figure 3.2 Jane's Opportunity Costs of Corn and Cloth

This figure uses information from Fig. 3.1 to calculate opportunity costs as we move along the production possibility frontier. Part (a) simply displays the increasing opportunity cost of cloth. Part (b) relates that increasing opportunity cost to movement down the frontier from points *a* to *f* as we increase the production of cloth. In moving from *a* to *b*, we give up 2 pounds of corn to get 1 yard of cloth; the opportunity cost of the first yard of cloth is 2 pounds of corn. Similar calculations show increasing opportunity cost as we increase cloth production.

Figure 3.3 Economic Growth on Jane's Island

If resources are used to produce capital goods (e.g., tools), productive capacity will increase. This is represented by an outward shift of the production possibility frontier. The greater the proportion of resources used to produce capital goods, the faster the production possibility frontier will shift out. This figure illustrates this concept using the example of Jane's production of corn and cloth. Jane can choose to use all resources to produce corn and cloth (point *e*). In this case, her production possibility frontier remains in its initial position, since Jane's ability to produce will not change. If, however, Jane decides to reduce her current production of corn and cloth in order to produce tools (e.g., point *d*) her future productive ability will increase, and so her production possibility frontier will shift out. This figure clearly illustrates the opportunity cost of increasing future production possibilities by producing tools: forgone current production (consumption) of corn and cloth.

SELF-TEST

CONCEPT REVIEW

1. The process of converting resources into goods and services is called ____________.
2. We divide production resources into three classes. Resources such as iron ore and running rivers are examples of __________, the skill of a computer programmer and the physical strength of a bricklayer are examples of ____________, and a shoe factory and an olive pitting machine are examples of ____________ resources.
3. The graphical representation of the boundary between attainable and unattainable production levels is called the ____________ ____________ ____________.
4. The ____________ ____________ of a choice is the value of the best forgone alternative choice.
5. Two key activities that can shift the production possibility frontier out are ____________ progress and ____________ accumulation.
6. The opportunity cost of producing capital goods now in order to expand future production is forgone current ____________ goods.
7. If Martha can produce salad forks at a lower opportunity cost than Jill, we say that Martha has a(n) ____________ advantage in the production of salad forks.
8. The economic system that permits private individuals to own the capital resources used in production is called ____________.
9. A system in which goods are traded directly for goods is known as ____________.
10. In order for exchange to take place in such a system there must be a double ____________ of wants.
11. ____________ is defined as a medium of exchange.

TRUE OR FALSE

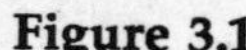

Figure 3.1

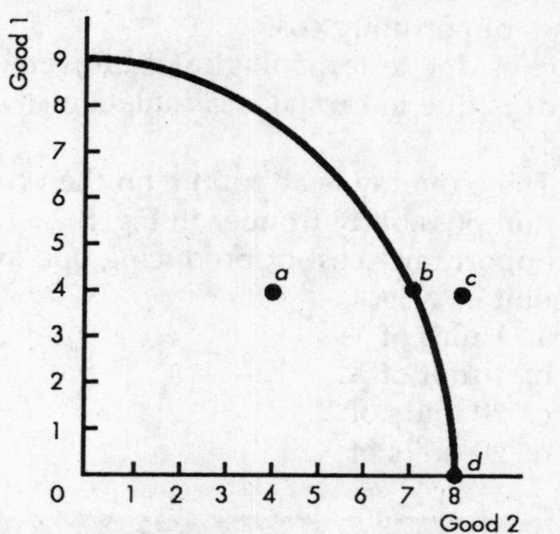

Refer to the production possibility frontier in Fig. 3.1 for questions 1-4.

____ 1. At point *b*, 7 units of good 1 and 4 units of good 2 are produced.

____ 2. Point *a* is not attainable.

____ 3. The opportunity cost of increasing the production of good 2 from 7 to 8 units is 4 units of good 1.

____ 4. Point *c* is not attainable.

____ 5. The bowedout shape of a production possibility frontier reflects decreasing opportunity cost as we increase the production of either good.

____ 6. The production possibility frontier will shift out if there is a technological improvement.

____ 7. Reducing the current production of consumption goods in order to produce more capital goods will shift the production possibility frontier out in the future.

____ 8. Bill has a comparative advantage in producing good *a* if he can do it faster than Joe.

____ 9. Consider an economy with two goods, X and Y, and two producers, Bill and Joe. If Bill has a comparative advantage in the production of X, then Joe must have a comparative advantage in the production of Y.

____10. Any time two individuals have different opportunity costs they can both gain from specialization and trade.

____11. The incentives for specialization and exchange do not depend on property rights but only on differing opportunity costs.

____12. Any system that uses capital in production is a capitalist system.

____13. With specialization and trade, a country can consume at a point outside its production possibility frontier.

____14. With specialization and trade, a country can produce at a point outside its production possibility frontier.

____15. The principle of comparative advantage helps us understand why the existence of cheap foreign labor means that sooner or later no one in other countries will buy U.S.-produced goods.

____16. A monetary exchange system requires a double coincidence of wants.

Use the following information to answer questions 17-20. In one hour, Jack can produce either four pails of water *or* eight candlesticks, while Jill can produce either 10 pails of water or 10 candlesticks.

____17. The opportunity cost of one pail of water for Jill is one candlestick.

____18. Jack has a comparative advantage in the production of candlesticks.

____19. Jill has an absolute advantage in the production of both pails of water and candlesticks.

____20. Both Jack and Jill could be made better off if Jack specialized in candlesticks and Jill specialized in pails of water and they engaged in exchange.

MULTIPLE CHOICE

1. Which of the following is NOT an example of a capital resource?
   a. A hydroelectric dam
   b. A dentist's drill
   c. A shovel
   d. A lawyer's knowledge of the law

2. If Harold can increase production of good *x* without decreasing the production of any other good, then Harold
   a. is producing on his production possibility frontier.
   b. is producing outside his production possibility frontier.
   c. is producing inside his production possibility frontier.
   d. must prefer good *x* to any other good.

3. The bowedout shape of a production possibility frontier
   a. reflects the existence of increasing opportunity cost.
   b. reflects the existence of decreasing opportunity cost.
   c. is due to technological improvement.
   d. is due to capital accumulation.

4. The economy is at point *b* on the production possibility frontier in Fig. 3.2. The opportunity cost of producing one more unit of X is
   a. 1 unit of Y.
   b. 1 unit of X.
   c. 20 units of Y.
   d. 20 units of X .

Figure 3.2

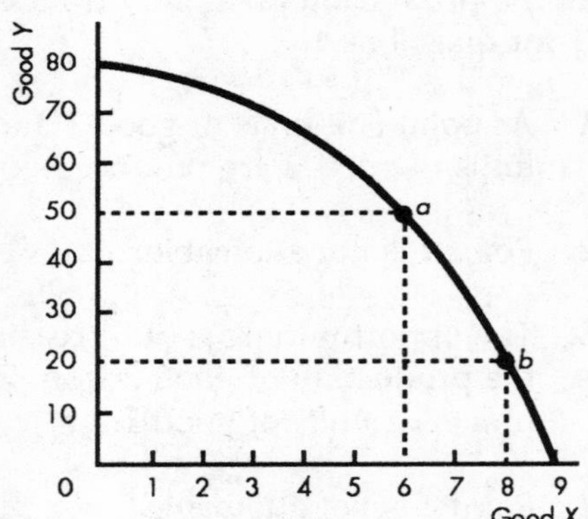

5. The economy is at point *b* on the production possibility frontier in Fig. 3.2. The opportunity cost of increasing the production of *Y* to 50 units is
   a. 6 units of X
   b. 2 units of X
   c. 8 units of Y
   d. 30 units of Y

6. Because productive resources are scarce, we must give up some of one good in order to acquire more of another. This is the essence of the concept of
   a. specialization.
   b. monetary exchange.
   c. comparative advantage.
   d. opportunity cost.

7. A production possibility frontier will shift *outward* if
   a. there is a technological improvement.
   b. there is an increase in the stock of capital.
   c. there is an increase in the labor force.
   d. all of the above.

8. The opportunity cost of pushing the production possibility frontier outward is
   a. the value of the increase in new capital resources required.
   b. the value of the increase in technological improvement required.
   c. the value of the reduction in current consumption required.
   d. the amount by which the production possibility frontier shifts.

9. In general, the higher the proportion of resources devoted to technological research in an economy,
   a. the greater will be current consumption.
   b. the faster the production possibility frontier will shift outward.
   c. the faster the production possibility frontier will shift inward.
   d. the closer it will come to having a comparative advantage in the production of all goods.

10. Refer to Table 3.1. The opportunity cost of increasing the production of X from 4 to 8 units is
   a. 4 units of X.
   b. 4 units of Y.
   c. 8 units of Y.
   d. 28 units of Y.

Table 3.1 Points on the Production Possibility Frontier for Goods X and Y

Point	Production of X	Production of Y
a	0	40
b	4	36
c	8	28
d	12	16
e	16	0

11. The diagram of the PPF corresponding to the data in Table 3.1 would be
   a. negatively sloped and linear.
   b. negatively sloped and bowed in.
   c. negatively sloped and bowed out.
   d. positively sloped for X and negatively sloped for Y.

12. From the data in Table 3.1, the production of 10 units of X and 28 units of Y is
   a. impossible given the available resources.
   b. possible but leaves some resources less than fully utilized.
   c. on the PPF between points *c* and *d*.
   d. We cannot infer whether it is possible or not from the table.

13. Mexico and Canada each produce both oil and apples using only labor. A barrel of oil can be produced with four hours of labor in Mexico and eight hours of labor in Canada. A bushel of apples can be produced with eight hours of labor in Mexico and 12 hours of labor in Canada. Canada has
    a. an absolute advantage in oil production.
    b. an absolute advantage in apple production.
    c. a comparative advantage in oil production.
    d. a comparative advantage in apple production.

14. There are two goods: *X* and *Y*. If the opportunity cost of producing good *X* is lower for Pam than for Gino, then we know that
    a. Pam has an absolute advantage in the production of *X*.
    b. Gino has an absolute advantage in the production of *Y*.
    c. Pam has a comparative advantage in the production of *X*.
    d. Gino has a comparative advantage in the production of *X*.

Fact 3.1

In an eight-hour day, Andy can produce either 24 loaves of bread or eight pounds of butter. In an eight-hour day, Bob can produce either eight loaves of bread or eight pounds of butter.

15. Refer to Fact 3.1. Which of the following statements is true?
    a. Andy has an absolute advantage in butter production.
    b. Bob has an absolute advantage in butter production.
    c. Andy has a comparative advantage in butter production.
    d. Bob has a comparative advantage in butter production.

16. Refer to Fact 3.1. Andy and Bob
    a. can gain from exchange if Andy specializes in butter production and Bob specializes in bread production.
    b. can gain from exchange if Andy specializes in bread production and Bob specializes in butter production.
    c. cannot gain from exchange because Bob does not have any comparative advantage.
    d. can exchange, but only Bob will be able to gain.

17. If individuals *a* and *b* can both produce only goods *x* and *y* and *a* does <u>NOT</u> have a comparative advantage in the production of either *x* or *y*, then we know that
    a. *b* has an absolute advantage in the production of *x* and *y*.
    b. *a* and *b* have the same opportunity cost for *x* and for *y*.
    c. *b* has a comparative advantage in the production of both *x* and *y*.
    d. the gains from trade will be large but only in one direction.

18. Which of the following would <u>NOT</u> limit private property rights?
    a. High market prices
    b. Export restrictions
    c. Laws prohibiting slavery
    d. Income taxes

19. Anything that is generally acceptable in exchange for goods and services is
    a. a medium of exchange.
    b. private property.
    c. a barter good.
    d. called an exchange resource.

20. Which of the following is an advantage of a monetary exchange system over barter?
    a. A monetary exchange system eliminates the basis for comparative advantage.
    b. Only in a monetary exchange system can gains from trade be realized.
    c. In a monetary system exchange does not require a double coincidence of wants.
    d. A monetary exchange system does not require a medium of exchange.

Short Answer

1. Explain why points *on* the production possibility frontier are best. What do points inside or outside this frontier mean?

2. Why is a production possibility frontier negatively sloped? Why is it bowedout?

3. What factors can shift the production possibility frontier outward? Inward?

4. Lawyers earn $100/hour while secretaries earn $10/hour. Use the concepts of absolute and comparative advantage to explain why a lawyer, who is a better typist than her secretary, will still *specialize* in doing only legal work and will *trade* with the secretary for typing services.

5. What would be the cost to the U.S. of increasing the production of capital goods? What would the benefits be?

6. What is meant by comparative advantage?

7. Consider an economy with two individuals (*A* and *B*) producing two goods (*X* and *Y*). If we determine that *A* has a comparative advantage in the production of *X*, explain why we know that *B* must have a comparative advantage in the production of *Y*. [Hint: If the opportunity cost of producing one unit of *X* is two units of *Y*, then the opportunity cost of producing one unit of *Y* must be 1/2 units of *X*; that is, since there are only two goods, the opportunity cost of producing one is the reciprocal of the opportunity cost of producing the other. Do you understand why?]

8. Explain why individuals can gain from specialization and trade.

9. Explain how taxes *modify* property rights. If a society must pay for its judicial system and police protection, explain how taxes *enhance* property rights.

10. Explain, using a specific example of exchange, why a monetary exchange system is more efficient than barter.

Problems

1. Suppose that an economy with unchanged capital goods (no toolmaking) has the production possibility frontier shown in Table 3.2.

Table 3.2 Production Possibilities

Possibility	Units of butter	Units of guns
a	200	0
b	180	60
c	160	100
d	100	160
e	40	200
f	0	220

a) On graph paper, plot these possibilities, label the points, and draw the production possibility frontier. (Put guns on the horizontal axis.)
b) If the economy moves from possibility *c* to possibility *d*, the opportunity cost *per unit of guns* will be how many units of butter?
c) If the economy moves from possibility *d* to possibility *e*, the opportunity cost *per unit of guns* will be how many units of butter?
d) In general terms, what happens to the opportunity cost of guns as the output of guns increases?
e) In general terms, what happens to the opportunity cost of butter as the output of butter increases?
f) Given the production possibility frontier you have plotted, is a combination of 140 units of butter and 130 units of guns per week attainable? Would you regard this combination as an efficient one? Explain.
g) Repeat the question asked in part f) for a combination of 70 units of butter and 170 units of guns.
h) If the following events occur (consider each a separate event, unaccompanied by any other), what would happen to the production possibility frontier?
   i) A new, easily exploited, energy source is discovered.
   ii) A large number of skilled workers immigrate into the country.
   iii) The output of butter is increased.
   iv) A new invention increases output per person in the butter industry but not in the guns industry.
   v) A new law is passed compelling workers, who could previously work as long as they wanted, to retire at age 60.

2. Draw a linear (straight-line) production possibility frontier and a bowedout production possibility frontier. Demonstrate that the linear frontier reflects constant opportunity cost while the bowedout frontier reflects increasing opportunity cost.

3. Suppose that the country of Quark has historically devoted 10 percent of its resources to the production of new capital goods. Use production possibility frontier diagrams to compare the consequences (i.e., costs and benefits) of each of the following.
   a) Quark continues to devote 10 percent of its resources to the production of capital goods.
   b) Quark begins now to permanently devote 20 percent of its resources to the production of capital goods.

4. Tove and Ron are the only two remaining inhabitants of the planet Melmac. They spend their 30-hour days producing widgets and woggles, the only two goods needed for happiness on Melmac. It takes Tove one hour to produce a widget and two hours to produce a woggle while Ron takes three hours to produce a widget and three hours to produce a woggle.
   a. For a 30-hour day, draw an individual production possibility frontier for Tove and for Ron.
   b. What does the shape of the production possibility frontiers tell us about opportunity costs?
   c. Assume initially that Tove and Ron are each self-sufficient. Explain what the

individual consumption possibilities are for Tove and for Ron.

d. Who has an absolute advantage in the production of widgets? Of woggles?
e. Who has a comparative advantage in the production of widgets? Of woggles?
f. Suppose Tove and Ron each specialize in producing only the good in which she/he has a comparative advantage (one spends 30 hours producing widgets, the other spends 30 hours producing woggles). What will be the total production of widgets and woggles?
g. Now, suppose Tove and Ron exchange seven widgets for five woggles. On your production possibility frontier diagrams, plot the new point of Tove's consumption; of Ron's consumption. Explain how these points illustrate the gains from trade.

ANSWERS

CONCEPT REVIEW

1. production
2. land; labor; capital
3. production possibility frontier
4. opportunity cost
5. technological; capital
6. consumption
7. comparative
8. capitalism
9. barter
10. coincidence
11. money

TRUE OR FALSE

1. F	5. F	9. T	13. T	17. T
2. F	6. T	10. T	14. F	18. T
3. T	7. T	11. F	15. F	19. T
4. T	8. F	12. F	16. F	20. T

MULTIPLE CHOICE

1. d	5. b	9. b	13. d	17. b
2. c	6. d	10. c	14. c	18. a
3. a	7. d	11. c	15. d	19. a
4. c	8. c	12. a	16. b	20. c

SHORT ANSWER

1. Points outside the production possibility frontier are unattainable and thus irrelevant. Points inside the frontier mean that some resources are not fully utilized. Points on the frontier are best because they represent more of both goods than points inside the frontier.

2. The negative slope of the production possibility frontier reflects opportunity cost: in order to have more of one good some of the other must be forgone. It is bowed out because of increasing opportunity cost.

3. The production possibility frontier will shift outward if the quantity of resources available (e.g., the stock of capital goods) increases or if there is a technological improvement. A loss of resources (e.g., during a war) or any other event that reduces ability to produce (e.g., bad weather) will shift the frontier inward.

4. The lawyer has an absolute advantage in producing both legal and typing services relative to the secretary. Nevertheless, she has a comparative advantage in legal services, and the secretary has a comparative advantage in typing. To demonstrate

these comparative advantages we can construct a table of opportunity costs. (See Table 3.3.)

Consider first the lawyer's opportunity costs. The lawyer's best forgone alternative to providing one hour of legal services is the $100 she could earn by providing another hour of legal services. If she provides one hour of typing, she is also forgoing $100 (one hour) of legal services. What would the secretary have to forgo to provide one hour of legal services? He would have to spend three years in law school, forgoing three years of income in addition to the tuition he must pay. His opportunity cost is a very large number, certainly greater than $100. If he provides one hour of typing, his best forgone alternative is the $10 he could have earned at another secretarial job. Thus Table 3.3 shows that the lawyer has a lower opportunity cost (comparative advantage of providing legal services, and the secretary has a lower opportunity cost (comparative advantage) of providing typing services. It is on the basis of comparative advantage (not absolute advantage) that the trade will take place from which both parties gain.

Table 3.3 Opportunity Cost of One Additional Hour ($)

	Legal Services	Typing
Lawyer	100	100
Secretary	100	10

5. The cost to the U.S. of increasing the production of capital goods would be the consumption goods that must be forgone when resources are switched from the production of consumer goods to capital goods. The benefit is faster growth of the production possibility frontier and therefore greater *future* consumption.

6. A person has a comparative advantage in the production of a good if his or her opportunity cost of producing the good is lower than the opportunity cost of anyone else.

7. In the simple two-person two-good model used in this chapter, the opportunity cost of producing one good is the amount of the other good that must be forgone if the first is produced. If individual a's opportunity cost of producing good x is less than individual b's opportunity cost, then we know that the reciprocals of these costs have the opposite relationship; that is, the reciprocal of a's opportunity cost of producing good x is greater than the reciprocal of b's opportunity cost of producing x. By the hint, this means that a's opportunity cost of producing y is greater than b's opportunity cost of producing y.

8. If each individual specializes in the good for which he or she has the lowest opportunity cost (i.e., a comparative advantage), then more of each good can be produced and this increase in output will be divided by exchange.

9. Taxes limit property rights directly by eliminating individual control over property which passes to the government in the form of tax payments. Without income taxes, for example, each individual would have property rights over their entire income. With income taxes, however, the individual retains property rights only over the part that remains after taxes are paid. Taxes enhance property rights by paying for the institutional enforcement necessary for an effective system of property rights. In this sense, taxes are a prerequisite for property rights.

10. The principle reason for the efficiency of a monetary exchange system relative to barter is that the monetary system does not require a double coincidence of wants to complete a successful exchange. For example, suppose you specialize in the production of apples but like to eat bananas. In a barter economy, you would likely not be able to complete an exchange with the first person you found who had bananas to trade. It would be necessary for that person to also want to trade the bananas for apples and not for carrots or some other good. In a monetary economy, you would always be able to make a successful exchange with the first person you found with bananas to trade since he or she would be willing to accept money in exchange. Similarly, in a money exchange system, you would be able to sell your apples for money to the first person you found who wanted apples (even if that person did not have bananas to sell).

PROBLEMS

1. a) The graph of the production possibility frontier is given in Fig. 3.3.
   b) In moving from *c* to *d*, in order to gain 60 units of guns, we must give up 160 - 100 = 60 units of butter. The opportunity cost per unit of guns is:

$$\frac{60 \textit{ units butter}}{60 \textit{ units guns}} = \textit{1 unit of butter per unit of guns}$$

Figure 3.3

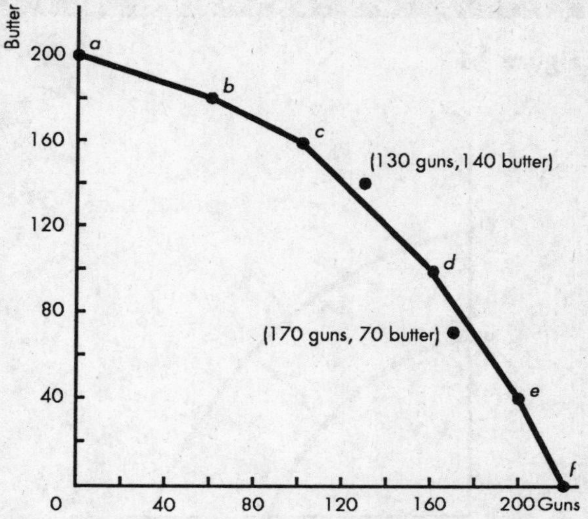

   c) In moving from *d* to *e*, in order to gain 40 units of guns, we must give up 100 - 40 = 60 units of butter. The opportunity cost per unit of guns is:

$$\frac{60 \textit{ units butter}}{40 \textit{ units guns}} = \textit{1.5 units of butter per unit of guns}$$

   d) The opportunity cost of producing more guns increases as the output of guns increases.
   e) Likewise, the opportunity cost of producing more butter increases as the output of butter increases.
   f) This combination is outside the frontier and, therefore, is not attainable. Since the economy cannot produce this combination, the question of efficiency is irrelevant.
   g) This combination is inside the frontier and is attainable. It is inefficient because the economy could produce more of either or both goods.
   h) i.) Assuming that both goods require energy for their production, the

entire frontier shifts out to the northeast as shown in Fig. 3.4.

Figure 3.4

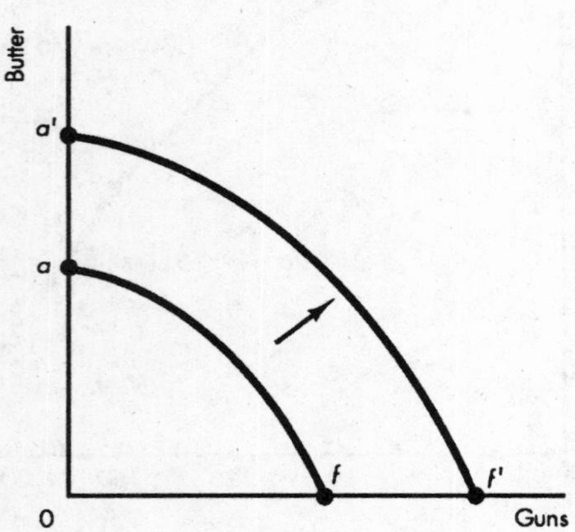

ii.) Assuming that both goods use skilled labor in their production, the entire frontier shifts out to the northeast. See Fig. 3.4.

iii.) The frontier does not shift. An increase in the output of butter implies a movement *along* the frontier to the left, not a shift of the frontier itself.

iv.) The new invention implies that for every level of output of guns, the economy can now produce more butter. The frontier swings to the right, but remains anchored at point f as shown in Fig. 3.5.

v.) The entire frontier shifts in toward the origin.

Figure 3.5

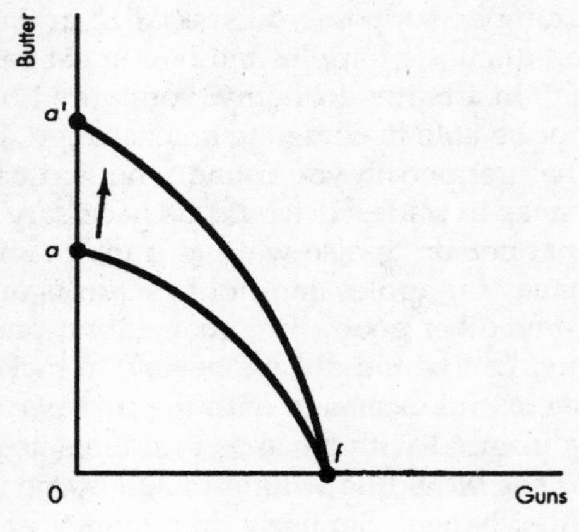

2. Parts (a) and (b) of Fig. 3.6 straight-line and bowedout production possibility frontiers respectively.

Figure 3.6

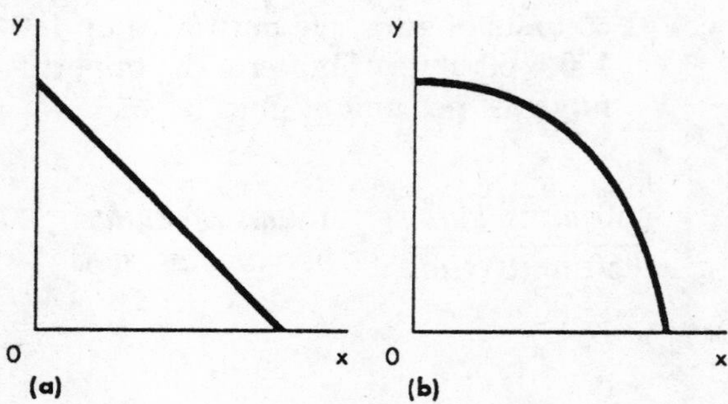

The fact that the slope of a straight line is constant implies that the amount of one good that must be given up in order to obtain one more unit of the other is constant. In the case of a bowedout curve, however, we see that the slope is becoming steeper as x increases which indicates that more of good y must be given up for each additional unit of x. Thus the bowed out production possibility frontier reflects increasing opportunity cost.

3. a) The situation for Quark is depicted by Fig. 3.7. Suppose Quark starts on production possibility frontier 1. If it continues to devote only 10 percent of its resources to the production of new capital goods, then it is choosing to produce at a point like *a*. This will shift the frontier out in the next period but only to the curve labeled 2 where, presumably, Quark will choose to produce at point *b*.

Figure 3.7

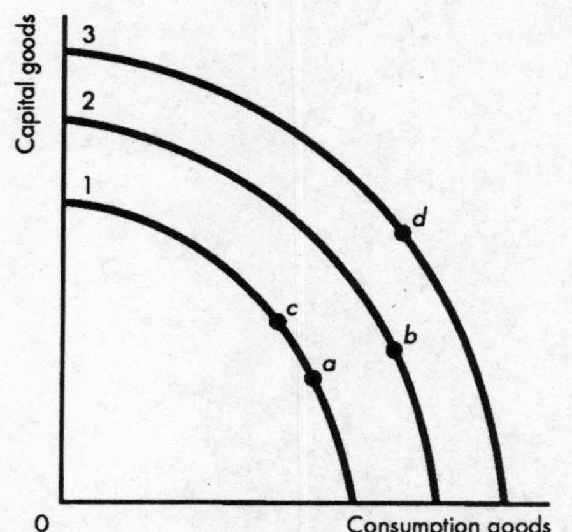

b) Starting from the same initial production possibility frontier, if Quark now decides to increase the resources devoted to the production of new capital to 20 percent, it will be choosing to produce at a point like *c*. In this case, next period's frontier will shift further – to curve 3 and a point like *d*, for example.

Thus, in comparing points *a* and *c*, we find the following costs and benefits: point *a* has the benefit of greater present consumption but at a cost of lower future consumption; point *c* has the cost of lower present consumption, but with the benefit of greater future consumption.

4. a) The individual production possibility frontiers for Tove and Ron are given by Fig. 3.8 (a) and (b) respectively.

Figure 3.8 (a)

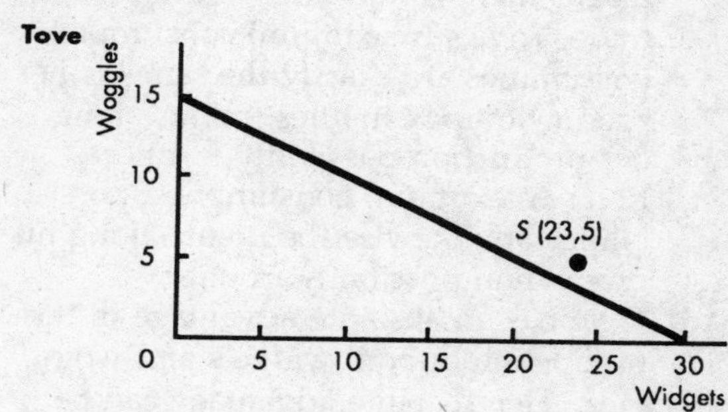

Figure 3.8 (b)

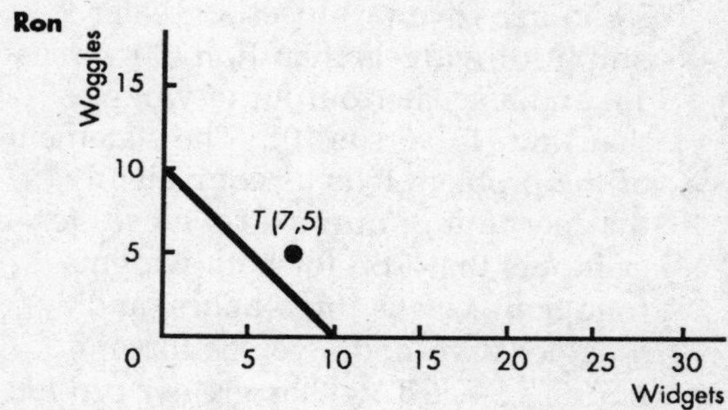

b) The linear shape of the production possibility frontiers tells us that opportunity costs are constant along each frontier.

These linear production possibility frontiers with constant opportunity costs abstract from the complexity of the real world. The world generally has increasing opportunity costs, but that fact is not essential for understanding the gains from trade, which is the objective of this problem. Making the model more complex by including increasing opportunity costs would not change our results, but it would make it more difficult to see them.

c) Individuals are self-sufficient if they consume only what they produce. This means there is no trade. Without trade, Tove's (maximum) consumption possibilities are exactly the same as her production possibilities—points along her production possibility frontier. Ron's (maximum) consumption possibilities are likewise the points along his production possibility frontier.

d) Tove has an absolute advantage in the production of both widgets and woggles. Her absolute advantage can be defined either in terms of greater output per unit of inputs or fewer inputs per unit of output. A comparison of the production possibility frontiers in Fig. 3.8 shows that, for given inputs of 30 hours, Tove produces a greater output of widgets than Ron (30 versus 10) and a greater output of woggles that Ron (15 versus 10). The statement of the problem tells us equivalently that per unit of output, Tove uses fewer inputs that Ron for both widgets (one hour versus three hours) and woggles (two hours versus three hours). Since Tove has greater productivity than Ron in the production of all goods (widgets and woggles), we say that, overall, she has an absolute advantage.

e) Tove has a comparative advantage in the production of widgets, since she can produce them at lower opportunity cost that Ron (1/2 woggle versus 1 woggle). On the other hand, Ron has a comparative advantage in the production of woggles since he can produce them at a lower opportunity cost than Tove (1 widget versus 2 widgets).

f) Tove will produce widgets and Ron will produce woggles, yielding a total production between them of 30 widgets and 10 woggles.

g) After the exchange, Tove will have 23 widgets and 5 woggles (point *S*). Ron will have 7 widgets and 5 woggles (point *T*). These new post-trade consumption possibility points lie outside Tove's and Ron's respective pre-trade consumption (and production) possibilities. Hence, trade has yielded gains that allow the traders to improve their consumption possibilities beyond those available with self-sufficiency.

4 DEMAND AND SUPPLY

CHAPTER IN PERSPECTIVE

George Bernard Shaw, the renowned Irish playwright, is reported to have said that one could make a parrot into an economist by teaching it to say "demand and supply." While no parrot has (yet) won the Nobel Prize in economics, Shaw's quip does point out the central role of the concepts of demand and supply in economic thinking. This chapter introduces these basic ideas, which will show up again and again in future chapters.

The previous chapter emphasized the tremendous economic benefits that result from specialization and exchange. Most formal exchange takes place in "markets" at prices determined by the interaction of buyers (demanders) and sellers (suppliers) in those markets. There are markets for goods (like wheat or textbooks), for services (like haircuts or tattoos), for financial assets (like IBM stock, or U.S. dollars, or government bonds). Demand and supply are very powerful tools that economists use to explain how much will be traded and at what price. Careful use of these tools will allow us to explain a wide array of economic phenomena and even predict changes in prices and quantities traded.

Given that demand and supply are so fundamental to economic analysis, extra time and effort spent to truly master the concepts discussed in this chapter will pay large dividends during the rest of the course.

LEARNING OBJECTIVES

After studying this chapter, you will be able to:

- **Construct a demand schedule and a demand curve**
- **Construct a supply schedule and a supply curve**
- **Explain how prices are determined**
- **Explain how quantities bought and sold are determined**
- **Explain why some prices rise, some fall, and some fluctuate**
- **Make predictions about price changes using the demand and supply model**

HELPFUL HINTS

1. It is important that you have a complete understanding of everything in this chapter. *Avoid the tendency to memorize*; learn for understanding. The more you can rely on logical analysis, the deeper your understanding will be. Once again, the tools discussed in this chapter will be used again and again in many different forms throughout the text. Demand and supply are two of the most important economic tools you will learn about in the course.

2. When you are first learning about demand and supply it is useful to *think in terms of examples* to help build an intuitive understanding. Have some favorite examples in the back of your mind. For example, if the situation calls for the analysis of complementary goods, you may want to think about hamburgers and french fries; if the situation calls for analysis of substitute goods, you may want to think of hamburgers and hot dogs. This will help reduce the "abstractness" of the economic theory.

3. The statement that "price is determined by demand and supply" is a shorthand way of saying that price is determined by all of the factors affecting demand (prices of related goods, income, population, expected future prices, preferences) and all of the factors affecting supply (prices of factors of production, prices of related goods, expected future prices, the number of suppliers, technology). The benefit of using demand and supply *curves* is that they allow us to systematically sort out the influences on price of each of these separate factors. Changes in the factors affecting demand will shift the demand curve and move us up or down the supply curve. Changes in the factors affecting supply will shift the supply curve and move us up and down the given demand curve.

Any demand and supply problem requires you to sort out these influences carefully. In so doing, *always draw a graph*, even if it is just a small graph in the margin. Graphical representation is a very efficient way to "see" what happens. You can avoid many mistakes by using graphs effectively. As you become comfortable with graphs, you will find that they are effective and powerful tools for systematically organizing your thinking.

Also, when you do draw a graph, be sure to *label the axes*. As the course progresses, you will encounter many graphs with different variables on the axes. It is very easy to become confused if you do not develop the habit of labelling the axes.

4. A very common mistake among students is a failure to *correctly distinguish between a shift in a curve and a movement along a curve*. This distinction applies both to demand and supply curves. Many questions in the Self-Test are designed to test your understanding of this distinction, and you can be sure that you instructor will test you carefully on this. The distinction between *shift in* versus *movements along* a curve is crucial for systematic thinking about the factors influencing demand and supply and for understanding the determination of equilibrium price and quantity traded.

Consider the example of the demand curve. The quantity of a good demanded depends on its own price, the prices of related goods, income, expected future price, population, and preferences. The term *demand* refers to the relationship between the price of a good and the quantity demanded, holding constant all of the other factors on which the quantity demanded depends. This demand relationship is represented graphically by the demand curve. Thus, the effect of a change in price on quantity demanded is already reflected in the slope of the demand curve; that is, the effect of a change in the price of the good itself is given by a movement along the demand curve. This is referred to as a *change in quantity demanded*.

On the other hand, if one of the other factors affecting the quantity demanded changes, the demand curve itself will shift; that is, the quantity demanded at each price will change. This shift of the demand curve is referred to as a *change in demand*. The critical thing to remember is that a change in the price of a good will not shift the demand curve, it will only cause a movement along the demand curve. Similarly, it is just as important to distinguish between shifts in the supply curve and movements along the supply curve.

To confirm your understanding, consider the effect of an increase in household income on the market for compact discs (CDs). (Draw a graph!) First note that an increase in income affects the demand for CDs and not supply. Next we want to determine whether the increase in income causes a shift in the demand curve or a movement along the demand curve. We ask: Will the increase in income increase the quantity of CDs demanded *even if the price of CDs does not change*? Since the answer to this question is yes, we know that the demand curve will shift to the right. Note further that the increase in the demand for CDs will cause the equilibrium price to rise. This price increase will be indicated by a movement along the supply curve (an increase in the quantity supplied) and will *not* shift the supply curve itself.

Remember: It is shifts in demand and supply curves that cause the market price to change, not changes in the price that cause demand and supply curves to shift.

5. Once we understand supply and demand analysis, we can *predict* how certain events, such as an increase in income or a technological change, will affect market price. More frequently, however, we observe changes in prices that have already taken place. Then our objective is to use supply and demand analysis to *explain* these observed price changes.

For example, suppose we observe an increase in the price of grapes. We know that this could be the result of either an increase in the demand for grapes or a decrease in supply. If, however, we know that vineyards in California suffered an infestation of grape-consuming insects, we conclude that the price increase is due to a decrease in supply. Suppose that we do not know about the insects, but we do observe a decrease in the quantity of grapes traded. This information also leads us to conclude that the price increase is not the result of an increase in demand but due to a decrease in supply.

KEY FIGURES AND TABLES

Figure 4.1 The Demand Schedule and the Demand Curve

While the content of this figure corresponds specifically to the tapes example developed by Parkin in Chapter 4, it is important to recognize that the principles illustrated are general. There are two ways to represent the relationship between the price of a good or service and the quantity demanded: the demand schedule and the demand curve. A demand schedule is a table that lists the quantities consumers demand at each price, if everything else remains constant. For example, if the price of a tape is $4, consumers would be willing to buy 3 million tapes per week, assuming that other things (like income and the price of a Walkman) remain unchanged. The law of demand is reflected by the fact that as the price of a tape increases, *ceteris paribus*, the quantity of tapes that consumers would be willing to buy decreases.

A demand curve is the graphical representation of the relationship between the quantity demanded of a good and its price, holding constant all other influences on consumers' planned purchases. Price appears on the vertical axis and quantity demanded on the horizontal axis. The demand curve in this figure tells us how many tapes consumers will be willing to buy in a week at each price, other things held constant. An equivalent interpretation of the demand curve is that it gives the highest price that consumers are willing to pay for the last unit purchased. For example, the highest price that consumers will pay for the 3 millionth tape is $4. The law of demand is reflected in the negative slope of the demand curve.

Figure 4.3 A Change in Demand Versus a Change in the Quantity Demanded

The principal purpose of this figure is to help us learn to distinguish between a change in demand (represented by a shift in the demand curve) and a change in the quantity demanded (represented by a movement along a given demand curve). As indicated above in Helpful Hint 4, failure to make the correct distinction will lead to incorrect conclusions. Remember that a change in the price of a good or service implies that the quantity demanded changes. Since this is exactly the relationship captured in the demand curve, the change in quantity demanded is represented by a movement along the curve. If there is a change in any of the other factors affecting the willingness of consumers to buy at a given price, then we say there is a change in demand which is represented by a shift in the demand curve itself.

Figure 4.4 The Supply Schedule and the Supply Curve

The purpose of this figure parallels that of Fig. 4.1. Just as there are two useful ways to represent the demand relationship, there are two ways to represent the relationship between the price of a good or service and the quantity supplied. A supply schedule is a table that lists the quantities that producers will plan to sell at each price, if everything else remains constant. For example, if the price of a tape is $4, producers will plan to sell 5 million tapes per week, assuming that other things (like the technology used to produce tapes) remain unchanged. The law of supply is reflected by the fact that the quantity supplied increases as the price increases (*ceteris paribus*).

A supply curve is the graphical representation of the relationship between the quantity of a good supplied and its price, holding constant all other influences on producers' planned sales. The supply curve in this figure tells us how many tapes producers will be willing to sell per week at each price, other things held constant. Another interpretation of the supply curve is that it tells us the lowest price that will induce producers to offer a given quantity for sale. For example, the lowest price that will induce producers to offer 5 million tapes for sale per week is $4. The law of supply is reflected in the positive slope of the supply curve.

Figure 4.6 A Change in Supply Versus a Change in the Quantity Supplied

This figure helps us learn to distinguish between a change in supply (represented by a shift in the supply curve) and a change in the quantity supplied (represented by a movement along a given supply curve). Remember that a change in the price of a good or service implies that the quantity supplied changes. Since this is the relationship represented by the supply curve, the change in quantity supplied is represented by a movement along the supply curve. If there is a change in any other factor affecting the willingness of producers to offer a given quantity for sale at a given price, then we say there is a change in supply which is represented by a shift in the supply curve itself.

Figure 4.7 Equilibrium

In this figure, the demand and supply curves are combined in the same graph in order to examine the price and quantity traded that leaves both buyers and sellers satisfied. Equilibrium price is defined as that price at which the quantity demanded is equal to the quantity supplied. The equilibrium price ($3 in the example) can be identified using either the table or the diagram. The idea of equilibrium as a point of rest is also illustrated. Note that when the price is below the equilibrium price there is a shortage which will cause the price to rise toward equilibrium. When the price is above the equilibrium price, there is a surplus which will cause the price to fall toward equilibrium. Only at the equilibrium price will there be no tendency for the price to change.

Table 4.1 The Demand for Tapes
This table specifies the law of demand: the quantity demanded increases when the price of the good or service falls and decreases when the price rises. These changes are represented by movements along the demand curve. The factors that cause changes in demand are also listed. Changes in these factors will cause the demand curve to shift. Note that the table assumes that tapes are a normal good since a rise in income will cause the demand for tapes to increase. If the good in question is inferior, a rise in income will cause demand to decrease whereas a fall in income will cause demand to increase. As implied by the name, most goods and services are normal.

Table 4.2 The Supply of Tapes
In parallel to Table 4.1, this table specifies the law of supply: The quantity supplied increases as the price rises and decreases as the price falls. These changes are represented by movements along the supply curve. The table also lists the factors that cause changes in supply. Changes in these factors will cause the supply curve to shift.

SELF-TEST

CONCEPT REVIEW

1. The __________ __________ of a good or service is the amount that consumers are willing and able to purchase at a particular price.
2. The law of demand states that, other things being equal, the higher the __________ of a good, the __________ is the quantity demanded.
3. A demand __________ is a list of the quantities of a good demanded at different __________.
4. A demand curve illustrates the __________ price that consumers are willing to pay for the last unit of a good purchased.
5. The entire relationship between the quantity of a good demanded and its __________ is referred to as demand.
6. The demand curve for most goods will shift to the right if income __________, or if the price of a substitute __________, or if the price of a complement __________, or if the size of the population __________.
7. A good is said to be __________ if the demand for it increases as income increases and __________ if demand decreases as income increases.
8. A decrease in the price of a good will cause an increase in the __________

__________; that is represented by a downward __________ __________ the demand curve.

9. The amount of a good or service that producers plan to sell at a particular price is called the __________ __________.
10. The law of supply states that the higher the __________ of a good, the __________ is the quantity supplied.
11. A supply curve shows the quantity supplied at each given __________.
12. A decrease in supply is represented by a shift to the __________ in the supply curve.
13. The supply curve will shift to the right if the price of a complement in production __________, or if the price of a substitute in production __________, or if there is a technological __________, or if the price of a productive resource __________.
14. An increase in the price of a good will cause an increase in the __________ __________; that is represented by a (an) __________ movement along the supply curve.
15. The price at which the quantity demanded equals the quantity supplied is called the __________ price.
16. If the price is above equilibrium, a (an) __________ will exist, causing the price to__________.
17. When demand increases, the equilibrium price will __________ and the quantity traded will __________.
18. When supply increases, the equilibrium price will __________ and the quantity traded will __________.
19. If demand increases and supply increases, then we know that the quantity traded must __________; but equilibrium price may increase, decrease, or remain unchanged.

TRUE OR FALSE

___ 1. If the quantity of a good demanded exceeds the quantity available, then the quantity traded will be less than the quantity demanded.

___ 2. The law of demand tells us that as the price of a good rises the demand decreases.

___ 3. The law of demand tells us that as the price of a good rises the quantity demanded decreases.

___ 4. The negative slope of a demand curve is a result of the law of demand.

___ 5. An increase in the price of apples will shift the demand curve for apples to the left.

___ 6. Hamburgers and french fries are complements. If Burger Doodle reduces the price of french fries, the demand for hamburgers will increase.

___ 7. If an increase in income causes a decrease in the demand for turnips, then turnips are inferior goods.

___ 8. A demand curve shows the least that consumers are willing to pay for the last unit.

___ 9. A demand curve is a graphical representation of the relationship between the price of a good and quantity demanded given the level of income, prices of other goods, population, and tastes.

___ 10. The law of supply implies that a supply curve will have a negative slope.

___ 11. A cost-reducing technological improvement will shift a supply curve to the right.

___ 12. If we observe a doubling of the price of mozzarella cheese (an ingredient in any pizza), we will expect the supply curve for pizza to shift to the left.

___ 13. When a cow is slaughtered for beef, its hide becomes available to make leather. Thus, beef and leather are substitutes in production.

___ 14. If the price of beef rises, we would expect to see an increase in the supply of leather and in the quantity of beef supplied.

___ 15. If the current price is such that the quantity demanded exceeds the quantity supplied, the price will tend to rise.

___ 16. If demand increases, we would predict an increase in equilibrium price and a decrease in quantity traded.

___ 17. If potatoes are inferior goods, we would expect a rise in income to result in a fall in the price of potatoes.

___ 18. A change in demand will cause equilibrium price and quantity traded to move in opposite directions.

___ 19. A decrease in the supply of a good will result in a decrease in both the equilibrium price and the quantity traded.

___ 20. Suppose there is a significant decline in the price of iron ore (used in making steel). We would predict that the equilibrium price of steel will fall and the quantity traded will increase.

___ 21. Suppose the demand for personal computers increased while the cost of producing them decreased. With this information, we can predict that the quantity of personal computers traded will increase but the price could rise or fall.

___ 22. An increase in the price of avocados and a decrease in the quantity traded is consistent with a decrease in the supply of avocados.

___ 23. When the actual price is above the equilibrium price, a shortage occurs.

Multiple Choice

1. If an increase in the price of good *a* causes the demand curve for good *b* to shift to the left, then
   a. *a* and *b* are substitutes in consumption.
   b. *a* and *b* are complements in consumption.
   c. *b* must be an inferior good.
   d. *a* must be a normal good.

2. The law of demand implies that, other things being equal,
   a. as the price of lobsters rises, the quantity of lobsters demanded will increase.
   b. as the price of lobsters rises, the quantity of lobsters demanded will decrease.
   c. as income increases, the quantity of lobsters demanded will increase.
   d. as the demand for lobsters increases, the price will rise.

3. Which of the following would lead to an increase in the demand for hamburgers?
   a. A new fad hamburger diet.
   b. A decrease in population size.
   c. An increase in the price of french fries, a complement.
   d. A decrease in consumer income.

4. Which of the following is <u>NOT</u> one of the "other things" held constant along a demand curve?
   a. Income
   b. Prices of other goods
   c. The price of the good itself
   d. Tastes

5. Good *a* is a normal good if
   a. an increase in the price of a complement causes the demand for *a* to decrease.
   b. an increase in income causes the demand for *a* to increase.
   c. an increase in the price of a substitute causes the demand for *a* to increase.
   d. it satisfies the law of demand.

6. If turnips are an inferior good, then, *ceteris paribus*, an increase in income will cause
   a. a decrease in the demand for turnips.
   b. an increase in the demand for turnips.
   c. a decrease in the supply of turnips.
   d. an increase in the supply of turnips.

7. A decrease in quantity demanded is represented by
   a. a rightward shift of the demand curve.
   b. a leftward shift of the demand curve.
   c. a movement upward and to the left along the demand curve.
   d. a movement downward and to the right along the demand curve.

8. The price of a good will tend to rise if
   a. there is a surplus at the current price.
   b. the current price is above equilibrium.
   c. the quantity demanded exceeds the quantity supplied at the current price.
   d. income decreases.

9. The fact that a decline in the price of a good causes producers to reduce the quantity of the good they plan to produce illustrates
   a. the law of supply.
   b. the law of demand.
   c. a change in supply.
   d. the nature of an inferior good.

10. Which of the following would <u>NOT</u> shift the supply curve of good x to the right?
    a. A reduction in the price of resources used in producing x
    b. An improvement in technology affecting the production of x
    c. An increase in the price of y, a complement in the production of x
    d. An increase in the price of x

11. A decrease in quantity supplied is represented by
    a. a movement down the supply curve.
    b. a movement up the supply curve.
    c. a rightward shift in the supply curve.
    d. a leftward shift in the supply curve.

12. Which of the following will shift the supply curve for good x to the left?
   a. A decrease in the wages of workers employed to produce x
   b. An increase in the cost of machinery used to produce x
   c. A technological improvement in the production of x
   d. A situation where quantity demanded exceeds quantity supplied

13. If a producer can use its resources to produce either good a or good b, then a and b are
   a. substitutes in production.
   b. complements in production.
   c. substitutes in consumption.
   d. complements in consumption.

14. If the market for good a is in equilibrium, then
   a. the scarcity of good a is eliminated.
   b. producers would like to sell more at the current price.
   c. consumers would like to buy more at the current price.
   d. there will be no surplus.

15. A shortage
   a. will exist if the price is above equilibrium.
   b. is the amount by which quantity demanded exceeds quantity supplied.
   c. is the amount by which quantity traded exceeds quantity supplied.
   d. is the amount by which quantity demanded exceeds the equilibrium quantity.

16. Which of the following correctly describes how price adjustment eliminates a shortage?
   a. As the price rises, the quantity demanded decreases while the quantity supplied increases.
   b. As the price rises, the quantity demanded increases while the quantity supplied decreases.
   c. As the price falls, the quantity demanded decreases while the quantity supplied increases.
   d. As the price falls, the quantity demanded increases while the quantity supplied decreases.

17. A surplus can be eliminated by
   a. increasing supply.
   b. government raising the price.
   c. decreasing the quantity demanded.
   d. allowing the price to fall.

18. Suppose we observe an increase in the price of oranges. Which of the following is <u>NOT</u> a possible cause?
   a. A decrease in the price of apples, a substitute
   b. A scientific discovery that oranges will cure the common cold
   c. An increase in income
   d. A freeze in Florida

19. If a is a normal good and consumer income rises, the demand for a will
   a. increase, and thus the price and quantity traded will increase.
   b. increase, and thus the price will rise but quantity will decrease.
   c. decrease, and thus the price and quantity traded will decrease.
   d. decrease, and thus the price will fall but the quantity traded will increase.

20. If *a* and *b* are complementary goods (in consumption) and the cost of a resource used in the production of *a* decreases, then
    a. the price of *b* will fall but the price of *a* will rise.
    b. the price of *b* will rise but the price of *a* will fall.
    c. the price of both *a* and *b* will rise.
    d. the price of both *a* and *b* will fall.

21. If both demand and supply increase, what will be the effect on the equilibrium price and quantity traded?
    a. Both the price and quantity traded will increase.
    b. Price will fall but the quantity traded will increase.
    c. Quantity traded will increase but the equilibrium price could either rise or fall.
    d. Price will increase but the quantity traded could either increase or decrease.

22. Which of the following will definitely cause an increase in the equilibrium price?
    a. An increase in both demand and supply
    b. A decrease in both demand and supply
    c. An increase in demand combined with a decrease in supply
    d. A decrease in demand combined with an increase in supply

23. Farm land can be used to produce either cattle or corn. If the demand for cattle increases, then
    a. demand for corn will increase.
    b. supply of corn will increase.
    c. demand for corn will decrease.
    d. supply of corn will decrease.

SHORT ANSWER

1. Explain the difference between wants and demands.

2. List three events that would likely cause an increase in the demand for peanut butter. What effect would such an increase in demand have on the price of peanut butter and the quantity traded?

3. Suppose we observe that the consumption of peanut butter increases at the same time as its price rises. What must have happened in the market for peanut butter? Is the observation consistent with the law of demand?

4. Explain how a fall in price eliminates a surplus.

5. The price of personal computers has continued to fall even in the face of increasing demand. Explain.

6. A tax on crude oil would raise the cost of the primary resource used in the production of gasoline. A proponent of such a tax has claimed that it will not raise the price of gasoline using the following argument: While the price of gasoline may rise initially, that price increase will cause the demand for gasoline to decrease which will push the price back down. What is wrong with this argument?

PROBLEMS

1. Table 4.1 gives the demand and supply schedules for cases of grape jelly.
   a) In the graph provided by Fig. 4.1 (or a similar graph you construct yourself), graphically represent the demand and supply curves for grape jelly. Be sure to properly label the axes. Label the demand and supply curves D_0 and S_0 respectively.
   b) What are the equilibrium price and quantity traded in the grape jelly market? In your diagram, label the equilibrium point *a*.
   c) Is there a surplus or shortage at a price of $40? How much?

Table 4.1

Price per case of grape jelly (dollars)	Quantity of jelly demanded (cases per week)	Quantity of jelly supplied (cases per week)
70	20	140
60	60	120
50	100	100
40	140	80
30	180	60

Figure 4.1

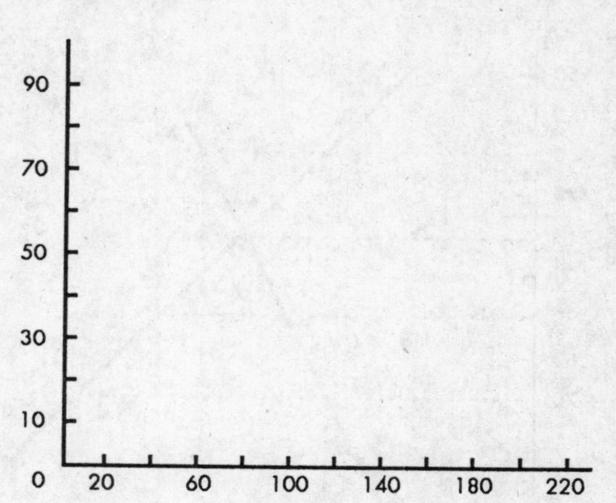

2. Suppose income increases sufficiently that the demand for grape jelly increases by 60 cases per week at every price.
   a) Construct a table (price, quantity demanded) giving the new demand schedule.
   b) Draw the new demand curve and label it D_1.
   c) Label the new equilibrium point *b*. What are the new equilibrium price and quantity traded?

3. Figure 4.2 is a graphical representation of the market for potatoes.
   a) What is the quantity of potatoes demanded at a price of $130 per ton? What is the quantity supplied at that price?
   b) What is the quantity of potatoes demanded at a price of $70 per ton? What is the quantity supplied at that price?
   c) What are equilibrium price and quantity traded?

Figure 4.2

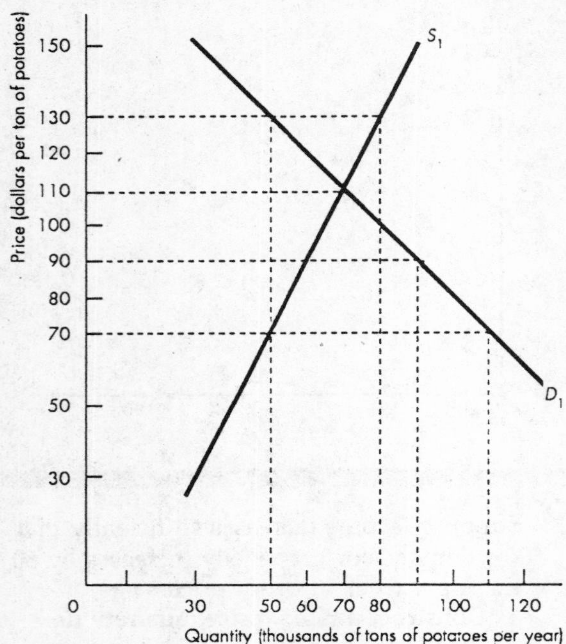

4. Now suppose that a new genetically improved strain of potatoes is developed which reduces the cost of producing any given quantity of potatoes. As a result, the supply of potatoes increases: at every price, the quantity supplied increases by 30,000 tons per year.
   a) Draw this new supply curve in Fig. 4.2. What are quantity demanded and quantity supplied at $110 per ton?
   b) What are the new equilibrium price and quantity traded?

5. Suppose further that new scientific studies demonstrate that french fries cure the common cold. As a result, the demand for potatoes increases at every price, the quantity demanded increases by 30,000 tons per year. Draw the new demand curve in Fig. 4.2. What are the resulting equilibrium price and quantity traded?

6. Soft drink makers use large quantities of sweeteners in the production of soft drinks. Both sugar and corn syrup make excellent sweeteners for this purpose. Historically, soft drink makers have used sugar, but several years ago the price of sugar rose significantly. As a consequence, soft drink manufacturers switched to the use of corn syrup. Think about the effects in the market for corn syrup as well as the market for soft drinks.
   a) Graphically show the effects in the market for corn syrup resulting from an increase in the price of sugar. What curve will shift? Why? What will happen to equilibrium price and quantity traded?
   b) Graphically show the effects in the market for soft drinks resulting from an increase in the price of sweeteners. What curve will shift? Why? What will happen to equilibrium price and quantity traded?

ANSWERS

Concept Review

1. quantity demanded
2. price; lower
3. schedule; prices
4. highest
5. price
6. increases; increases; decreases; increases
7. normal; inferior
8. quantity demanded; movement along
9. quantity supplied
10. price; higher

11. price
12. left
13. increases; decreases; improvement; decreases
14. quantity supplied; upward
15. equilibrium
16. surplus; fall
17. increase; increase
18. decrease; increase
19. increase

TRUE OR FALSE

1. T	6. T	11. T	16. F	21. T
2. F	7. T	12. T	17. T	22. T
3. T	8. F	13. F	18. F	23. F
4. T	9. T	14. T	19. F	
5. F	10. F	15. T	20. T	

MULTIPLE CHOICE

1. b	6. a	11. a	16. a	21. c
2. b	7. c	12. b	17. d	22. c
3. a	8. c	13. a	18. a	23. d
4. c	9. a	14. d	19. a	
5. b	10. d	15. b	20. b	

SHORT ANSWER

1. Wants reflect our unlimited desires for goods and services without regard to our ability or willingness to make the sacrifices necessary to obtain them. The existence of scarcity means that many of those wants will not be satisfied. On the other hand, demands refer to plans to buy and therefore reflect decisions about which wants to satisfy.

2. Any three events that are consistent with the following will increase the demand for peanut butter.
   a) An increase in the price of a substitute for peanut butter (perhaps sliced ham)
   b) A decrease in the price of a complement (perhaps bread)
   c) An increase in consumer income (assuming that peanut butter is a normal good)
   d) An increase in population size
   e) The price of peanut butter is expected to rise in the future (perhaps due to bad weather in Georgia).
   f) A change in tastes that now makes peanut butter more desirable

   Any of these will increase the demand for peanut butter and will thus cause the price of peanut butter to rise and the quantity of peanut butter traded to increase.

3. The observation that the consumption of peanut butter increases at the same time as the price of peanut butter rises is entirely consistent with the law of demand (i.e., a negatively sloped demand curve). It simply reflects that the demand for peanut butter has increased (the demand has shifted to the right).

4. The existence of a surplus means that, at the current price, the quantity supplied is greater than the quantity demanded. Thus, to eliminate the surplus, either the quantity demanded must increase or the quantity supplied must decrease (or both). As the price falls, we get exactly the necessary results (due to the laws of demand and supply): the quantity demanded increases and the quantity supplied decreases.

5. Due to the tremendous pace of technological advance, not only has the demand for personal computers been increasing, but the supply has been increasing as well.

Indeed, supply has been increasing much more rapidly than demand, which has resulted in falling prices. Thus, *much* (but not all) of the increase in sales of personal computers reflects a movement along a demand curve rather that a shift in demand.

6. This argument confuses a movement along an unchanging demand curve with a shift in the demand curve. The proper analysis is the following. The increase in the tax on crude oil will increase the cost of the primary resource used in production of gasoline and thus shift the supply curve for gasoline to the left. This will cause the equilibrium price of gasoline to increase and thus the *quantity of gasoline demanded* will decrease -- demand itself will not decrease (i.e., the demand curve will not shift). The decrease in supply causes a movement along an unchanged demand curve.

PROBLEMS

1. a) Figure 4.1 Solution graphically illustrates the demand and supply curves for the grape jelly market. They are labeled D_0 and S_0 respectively. Note the labeling of the axes.
   b) The equilibrium is given at the intersection of the demand and supply curves (labeled point *a*). The equilibrium price is $50 per case and the equilibrium quantity traded is 100 cases per week.
   c) At a price of $40 there is a shortage of 60 cases per week.

Figure 4.1 Solution

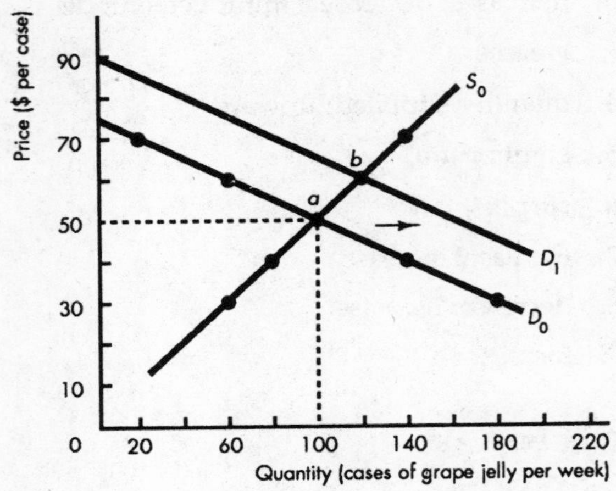

2. a) The new demand schedule is given in Table 4.3. The (unchanged) supply schedule is also included.

Table 4.3 Demand and Supply Schedules for Grape Jelly per Week

Price (per case)	Quantity Demanded (cases)	Quantity Supplied (cases)
$30	240	60
$40	200	80
$50	160	100
$60	120	120
$70	80	140

   b) The new demand curve is labeled D_1 in Fig. 4.1 Solution above.
   c) The new equilibrium is labeled point *b*. The new equilibrium price is $60 per case and the quantity traded is 120 cases of grape jelly per week.

3. See Fig. 4.2 Solution.

Figure 4.2 Solution

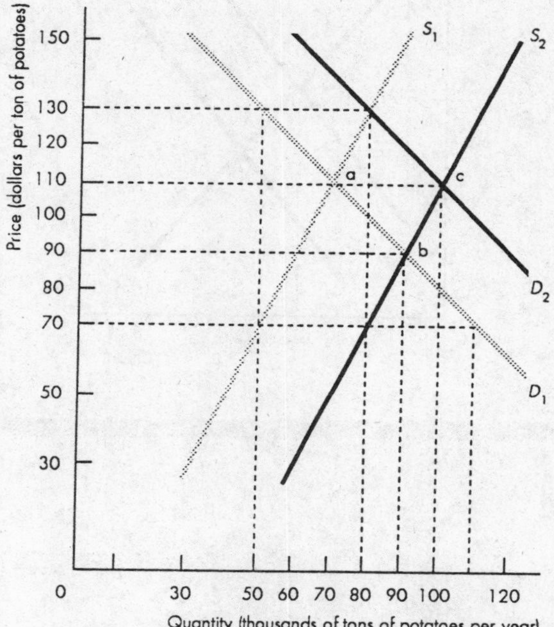

a) At a price of $130 per ton, 50,000 tons of potatoes are demanded and 80,000 tons of potatoes are supplied. Thus, at this price we observe a surplus of 30,000 tons.

b) At a price of $70 per ton, 110,000 tons of potatoes are demanded and 50,000 tons of potatoes are supplied. Thus, at this price there is a shortage of 60,000 tons.

c) The equilibrium price is $110 and the equilibrium quantity traded is 70,000 tons of potatoes per year. The equilibrium is indicated as point *a* in Fig. 4.2 Solution.

4. a) The technological advance shifts the supply curve to the right. The new supply curve is given by S_2 in the figure. After the shift, $110 is no longer the equilibrium price, since at that price, the quantity demanded remains at 70,000 tons while the quantity supplied has increased to 100,000 tons. A surplus of 30,000 tons is the result.

   b) The new equilibrium price is $90 and the new equilibrium quantity traded is 90,000 tons per year. This new equilibrium is labeled point *b* in the figure.

5. The change in tastes shifts the demand curve to the right, to D_2. The new equilibrium is labeled point *c* in the figure and corresponds to a price of $110 and quantity traded of 100,000 tons of potatoes per year.

6. a) The effect on the market for corn syrup is illustrated in Fig. 4.3. The demand curve for corn syrup will shift from D_1 to D_2 due to an increase in the price of a substitute, sugar. This will cause both price and quantity traded to increase as the market achieves a new equilibrium.

Figure 4.3

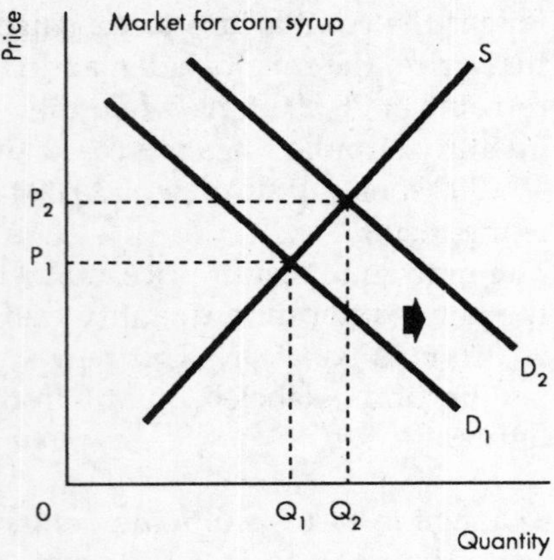

Figure 4.4

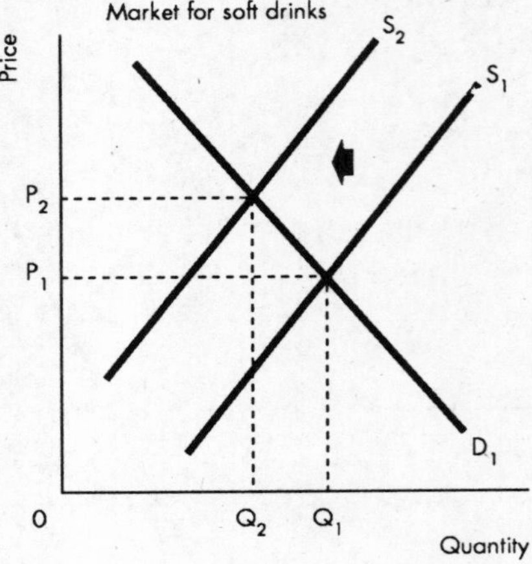

b) Figure 4.4 illustrates the effect on the market for soft drinks. The supply curve for soft drinks will shift to the left, from S_1 to S_2, because of the increase in the cost of resources (sugar or corn syrup) used in the production of soft drinks. In this market, the price of soft drinks will rise and the quantity traded will decline.

5 INFLATION, UNEMPLOYMENT, CYCLES, AND DEFICITS

CHAPTER IN PERSPECTIVE

With this chapter, we begin our study of *macroeconomics*, and so our attention will turn to the economy as a whole. In this and following chapters, we will be interested in understanding the nature of many of the economic issues that dominate the daily headlines: unemployment, inflation, recession, deficits. In this chapter, some of these basic concepts are introduced. Their causes and consequences are explored in the next several chapters.

LEARNING OBJECTIVES

After studying this chapter, you will be able to:

- **Define inflation and explain its effects**
- **Define unemployment and explain its costs**
- **Distinguish between the various types of unemployment**
- **Define gross domestic product (GDP)**
- **Distinguish between nominal GDP and real GDP**
- **Explain the importance of increases and fluctuations in real GDP**
- **Define the business cycle**
- **Describe how unemployment, stock prices, and inflation fluctuate over the business cycle**
- **Define the government budget deficit the country's international deficit**

HELPFUL HINTS

1. When the problem of inflation is evaluated for an economy, it is very crucial to know whether the inflation is *unanticipated* or *anticipated.*

Unanticipated inflation creates problems by making it difficult to determine the value of money and therefore to make certain decisions such as decisions about borrowing and saving.

Anticipated inflation does not share this problem, but it is still a problem because it continually reduces the value of money over time. This causes people to economize on the use of money and results in too many transactions.

2. Note that to be unemployed, as officially measured by the Bureau of Labor Statistics, it is not enough to be without a job. One must also be "actively" seeking a job. Most university students are without jobs but they are not counted as unemployed since they are not looking for jobs while they are attending school.

3. When economists use the term "full employment," it does not mean that everyone has a job. Rather, it means that the only unemployment is frictional and structural unemployment. When the economy is at full employment, the rate of unemployment is called the natural rate of unemployment.

It is possible for the actual rate of unemployment to be less than the natural rate of unemployment. This is the same as saying that it is possible for the level of employment to exceed full employment.

4. It is very important to understand the difference between real and nominal GDP. Nominal GDP is the value, *in terms of current prices,* of the output of final goods and services in the economy in a year. Real GDP evaluates those final goods and services *in terms of the prices prevailing in a base year.*

Nominal GDP can rise from one year to the next either because prices rise or because the output of goods and services rises. A rise in real GDP, however, means that the output of goods and services has risen.

Consider, for example, a simple economy which produces only apples. Nominal GDP tells us the value of apples produced in terms of current prices. Real GDP tells us how many apples are produced. In most cases, we are more interested in real GDP.

KEY FIGURES AND TABLES

Figure 5.1 The Price Level: 1820—1991

This figure indicates the behavior of the price level in the U. S. from 1820 to 1991. There are several features of the behavior of prices to note. Over the entire period, there has been a general tendency for the price level to rise, although the rate of growth has not been steady. The average rate of growth of the price level has historically been higher during periods of war. It has also been higher since World War II, in spite of a period of relative peace. It is also interesting to note that there was a long period of declining prices after the Civil War up to about 1900. Prices also fell during the Great Depression.

Figure 22.3 Unemployment: 1900—1991

The record of the unemployment rate in the U. S. during this century is given in this figure. We see that the rate of unemployment has fluctuated considerably although the fluctuations seem to be generally smaller since the end of World War II (1946). The worst period of unemployment was during the Great Depression when the unemployment rate reached 25 percent of the labor force. The unemployment rate has also risen during recent recessions. It also appears that the average rate of unemployment has been increasing in the period since World War II.

Figure 5.5 Real GDP: 1869—1991

Real GDP performance for the U. S. over the period from 1869 to 1991 is illustrated in this figure. The dominant feature of this performance is the general tendency of real GDP to steadily increase. The growth rate has not been constant, however, and, in fact, real GDP has actually decreased in some periods. In this regard, the Great Depression of the 1930s once again stands out.

Figure 5.6 Real GDP Fluctuations: 1869—1991

This figure clearly illustrates the uneven rate of growth of real GDP over time by plotting deviations of actual real GDP from trend real GDP. If real GDP grew faster than trend, the line is above the zero line and if real GDP grew more slowly than trend, the line is below the zero line. This figure illustrates the ups and downs of the business cycle.

Figure 5.7 The Business Cycle

The four phases of the business cycle are illustrated here by examining the behavior of real GDP deviations from trend over the 1973 to 1990 period. Note the business cycle troughs that occurred in 1975 and 1982 were followed by periods of expansion. The expansion beginning in 1975 ended with a peak in 1978, which was followed by a period of contraction.

Figure 5.8 Unemployment and the Business Cycle

The behavior of real GDP relative to trend over the business cycle is mirrored by the behavior of the unemployment rate. This is illustrated in this figure for the period between 1900 and 1990. Note that the scale of the unemployment rate measured on the right side has been inverted so that an upward movement in the unemployment rate line indicates a decline in the unemployment rate. The important feature to notice is the fact that the two curves exhibit a strong tendency to move up and down together. This indicates the close association between the two measures of economic activity over business cycles.

Figure 5.9 Stock Prices: 1871—1991

The dominant feature of the behavior of *real* (inflation adjusted) stock prices from 1871 to 1991 is fluctuation. Stock prices have been very volatile over most of this period. Two stock market crashes are indicated in the figure: the 1929 crash and the 1987 crash. The 1929 crash was followed by two successive years of steep drops in real stock prices whereas real stock prices have generally risen since the 1987 crash. There have also been periods during which stock market prices have risen rapidly. Among the most notable are the periods just before these two stock market crashes.

Figure 5.10 Inflation and the Business Cycle

While the inflation rate has generally moved systematically with the business cycle, there are some episodes where the rate of inflation seems to be unrelated to the phase of the business cycle. These facts are illustrated in this figure, which compares the behavior of inflation and deviations of real GDP from trend over the Great Depression, part (a), as well as the more recent OPEC and Volcker recessions, part (b).

During the Great Depression, the rate of inflation rose and fell with real GDP although the inflation rate was much higher than the rate of growth of real GDP relative to trend during the expansion phase. During the more recent recessions, the rate of inflation moved up and down with the business cycle except during the expansion following the Volcker recession. During this period, real GDP rose rapidly while the rate of inflation remained low.

SELF-TEST

CONCEPT REVIEW

1. An upward movement in the average level of prices is called ________. The average level of prices is called the price ________ and is measured by a price________.
2. The percentage change in the price level is called the ________ ________. When the price level is rising the value of money is ________.
3. The rate at which the currency of one country exchanges for the currency of another is the ________ ________ rate.
4. An unanticipated ________ in the inflation rate benefits borrowers and hurts lenders, while an unanticipated ________ in the inflation rate hurts borrowers and benefits lenders.
5. ________ is a mechanism which automatically links payments made under a contract to the price level.
6. ________ is measured as the number of adult workers who have jobs. The unemployment rate is ________ expressed as a percentage of the ________ ________.
7. People who do not have jobs and would like work but have stopped looking for a job are called ________ workers.
8. Unemployment that arises from normal market turnover is called ________ unemployment. Unemployment that arises when there is a decline in the number of jobs available in a particular industry is called ________ unemployment. If the number of people looking for a job equals the number of job vacancies, the economy is said to be at ________ employment and the unemployment rate is called the ________ rate of unemployment.
9. The value of all final goods and services produced in the economy is called ________ ________ ________. This does not include ________ goods which are used as inputs in the production of other goods.
10. The value of final goods and services using current prices is called ________ GDP while the value of final goods and services using the prices that prevailed in some base period is called ________ GDP.
11. The periodic but irregular up and down movement in real GDP and other macroeconomic variables over time is called the ________ ________. The part of this movement in which the pace of economic activity is slowing down is called a(n) ________, while the peri-

od during which the pace of economic activity is speeding up is called a(n) ____________.

12. A downturn in economic activity in which real GDP falls for at least two successive quarters is called a(n) ____________.

13. The total expenditure of the government sector minus the total revenue it receives is called the government ____________.

14. The difference between the value of goods and services we sell to other countries and the value of goods and services foreigners sell to us is called the ____________ ____________ ____________.

TRUE OR FALSE

____ 1. If the price of gasoline rises, we must be experiencing inflation.

____ 2. If the price of a computer falls, we must be experiencing deflation.

____ 3. If the average level of prices doubles, the value of money is half of what it was.

____ 4. If the rate of inflation is higher in the U.S. than in Japan, we would expect to see the value of the U.S. dollar fall in terms of the Japanese yen.

____ 5. If there is an unanticipated decrease in the rate of inflation, borrowers will be helped while lenders will be hurt.

____ 6. If there is an unanticipated decrease in the rate of inflation, wage earning workers will gain at the expense of employers.

____ 7. If the rate of inflation is expected to rise, people will want to hold less money on average.

____ 8. Only unanticipated inflation has a negative impact on an economy.

____ 9. The labor force is the sum of the employed and the unemployed.

____ 10. Discouraged workers are counted as unemployed but probably should not be.

____ 11. Part-time workers are counted as employed.

____ 12. Bill has just graduated from high school and is looking for his first job. Bill is frictionally unemployed.

____ 13. In order to be at full employment, it must be that there is no unemployment.

____ 14. Human capital tends to deteriorate when a worker is unemployed for a long period of time.

____ 15. When we measure GDP we do not include the value of intermediate goods and services produced.

____ 16. If nominal GDP is higher in year 2 than it was in year 1, we know that more goods and services were produced in year 2.

____ 17. Some economists believe that most of the fluctuations in real GDP are the best possible response to the uneven pace of technological change.

____18. In the contraction phase of a business cycle, the unemployment rate is rising.

____19. The behavior of stock market prices is a very reliable leading indicator of business cycle turning points.

____20. If the U.S. sells more to the rest of the world than we buy from the rest of the world, the U.S. will have a current account deficit.

MULTIPLE CHOICE

1. Price stability occurs when
   a. all prices in the economy are constant.
   b. the rate of inflation is zero.
   c. the rate of inflation is constant.
   d. the base period remains unchanged.

2. A price index
   a. is a technique used to link payments made under contract to the price level.
   b. measures the rate of inflation in a base year.
   c. measures the value of GDP in current dollars.
   d. measures the average level of prices in one period as a percentage of their level in a base period.

3. If a price index was 128 at the end of 1987 and 136 at the end of 1988, what was the rate of inflation for 1988?
   a. 4.2 percent
   b. 5.9 percent
   c. 6.25 percent
   d. 8 percent

4. If the rate of inflation is higher than anticipated
   a. lenders will gain at the expense of borrowers and workers will gain at the expense of employers.
   b. borrowers will gain at the expense of lenders and workers will gain at the expense of employers.
   c. lenders will gain at the expense of borrowers and employers will gain at the expense of workers.
   d. borrowers will gain at the expense of lenders and employers will gain at the expense of workers.

5. A fully anticipated increase in the rate of inflation
   a. is not costly since contracts can be adjusted.
   b. benefits both workers and employers.
   c. is costly because it reduces the opportunity cost of holding money.
   d. is costly because it increases the opportunity cost of holding money.

6. Which of the following is an example of an indexed loan contract? If the rate of inflation increases by 5 percent, the
   a. interest rate on an outstanding loan increases by 5 percent.
   b. interest rate on a new loan increases by 5 percent.
   c. interest rate on a new loan decreases by 5 percent.
   d. interest rate will be 5 percent.

7. Suppose that in a country with a population of 200 million, there are 90 million employed and 10 million unemployed. What is the labor force?
   a. 200 million
   b. 100 million
   c. 90 million
   d. 80 million

8. Suppose that in a country with a population of 200 million, there are 90 million employed and 10 million unemployed. What is the unemployment rate?
   a. 11 percent
   b. 10 percent
   c. 8 percent
   d. 5 percent

9. In which of the following years was the unemployment rate in the U.S. 25 percent?
   a. 1982
   b. 1959
   c. 1933
   d. 1926

10. Which of the following would be counted as unemployed in the United States?
    a. Doris only works five hours a week but is looking for a full-time job.
    b. Kathy has stopped looking for work since she was unable to find a suitable job during a two-month search.
    c. Sharon is a college student with no job.
    d. Mike has been laid off from his job but expects to be called back soon.

11. Which of the following would be considered structurally unemployed? A steelworker
    a. loses her job because of technological change.
    b. decides to look for a job as a salesperson.
    c. gives up her job because she retires.
    d. decides to leave the labor force and become a full-time student.

12. If the economy is at full employment , then the
    a. entire population is employed.
    b. entire labor force is employed.
    c. only unemployment is frictional or structural unemployment.
    d. unemployment rate is less than three percent.

13. Gross domestic product is defined as the value of all
    a. goods produced in an economy in a year.
    b. goods and services produced in an economy in a year.
    c. final goods produced in an economy in a year.
    d. final goods and services produced in an economy in a year.

14. If you want to investigate the claim that more final goods and services were produced in the economy during 1992 than 1991, you should look at
    a. intermediate GDP.
    b. nominal GDP.
    c. real GDP.
    d. current dollar GDP.

15. Nominal GDP will increase
    a. only if the average level of prices rises.
    b. only if the quantity of goods and services produced increases.
    c. only if the unemployment rate rises.
    d. if either the average level of prices rises or the quantity of goods and services produced increases.

16. Which of the following is <u>NOT</u> a reason for rising trend real GDP?
    a. advances in technology
    b. rising stock market prices
    c. growing stock of capital equipment
    d. growing population

17. Which of the following gives the correct order of the sequence of business cycle phases?
    a. expansion, peak, contraction, trough
    b. expansion, peak, trough, contraction
    c. expansion, trough, contraction, peak
    d. expansion, contraction, trough, peak

18. Which of the following has consistently fluctuated closely with real GDP fluctuations?
   a. inflation rate
   b. unemployment rate
   c. government deficit
   d. real stock prices

19. Which of the following will increase the U.S. current account deficit?
   a. Japan buys wheat from farmers in the U.S.
   b. Japan buys wheat from farmers in Australia.
   c. Japan buys U.S. Treasury bonds.
   d. The U.S. buys Toyotas from Japan.

20. Which of the following best describes the behavior of the U.S. government deficit and the U.S. current account deficit since 1982 relative to their historical behavior?
   a. The government deficit has been consistently large, while the current account deficit has been small by historical standards.
   b. The current account deficit has been consistently large, while the government deficit has been rather small by historical standards.
   c. Both of these deficits have been consistently large by historical standards.
   d. Both of these deficits have been rather small by historical standards.

Short Answer

1. What is meant by the value of money? Why does the value of money fall when there is inflation?

2. Consider borrowers and lenders. Who benefits and who is hurt when the rate of inflation is less than anticipated? Explain.

3. What are the three types of unemployment?

4. What is the natural rate of employment?

5. What are the costs of unemployment?

6. What is happening to the deviation from trend in real GDP and the unemployment rate during each of the four phases of the business cycle?

7. What is the current account balance? When is it in deficit?

Problems

1. When the rate of inflation is expected to be zero, Jennifer wants to lend money if the interest rate is at least 5 percent and Yolanda wants to borrow money if the interest rate is 5 percent or less. Thus they make a loan agreement at a 5 percent rate of interest if they expect zero inflation.
   a) If they both expect a rate of inflation of 4 percent over the period of the loan, what interest rate will they agree to?
   b) If they both expect a 2 percent rate of *deflation* over the period of the loan, what interest rate will they agree to?
   c) Suppose Jennifer expects the rate of inflation to be 4 percent but Yolanda expects it to be 6 percent. Will they be able to work out a loan agreement? If so, at what rate of interest?

2. Workers and managers in the ABC Company have worked out a wage agreement under the expectation that the rate of inflation will be zero over the period of the contract. In order to protect the workers against unanticipated inflation, however, the contract is indexed; that is, it states that at the end of each year, the wage rate will increase by the same percentage as the consumer price index (CPI). At the beginning of the contract the CPI is 214 and the wage rate is set at $10 an

hour. At the end of the first year, the CPI is 225 and at the end of the second year, the CPI is 234. What will the new wage rate become at the end of the first year? The second year?

3. Suppose nominal GDP rises by 75 percent between year 1 and year 2.
   a) If the average level of prices has also risen by 75 percent between year 1 and year 2, what has happened to real GDP?
   b) If the average level of prices has risen by less than 75 percent between year 1 and year 2, has real GDP increased or decreased?

4. Consider the following information about an economy:
   Population: 250 million
   Employment: 100 million
   Unemployment: 10 million
   a) What is the labor force in this economy?
   b) What is the unemployment rate?
   c) If 4 million of those unemployed are cyclically unemployed, what is the natural rate of unemployment?

ANSWERS

CONCEPT REVIEW

1. inflation; level; index
2. inflation rate; falling
3. foreign exchange
4. increase; decrease
5. Indexing
6. Employment; unemployment; labor force
7. discouraged
8. frictional; stuctural; full; natural
9. gross national product; intermediate
10. nominal; real
11. business cycle; contraction; expansion
12. recession
13. deficit
14. current account balance

TRUE OR FALSE

1. F	6. T	11. T	16. F
2. F	7. T	12. T	17. T
3. T	8. F	13. F	18. T
4. T	9. T	14. T	19. F
5. F	10. F	15. T	20. F

MULTIPLE CHOICE

1. b	6. a	11. a	16. b
2. d	7. b	12. c	17. a
3. c	8. b	13. d	18. b
4. d	9. c	14. c	19. d
5. d	10. d	15. d	20. c

SHORT ANSWER

1. The value of money is the quantity of goods and services that can be purchased with one unit of money. Since inflation means that prices are rising on average, it means that one unit of money will buy less. Thus the value of money falls when there is inflation.

2. Because both borrowers and lenders realize that inflation reduces the value of money, loan agreements will specify a rate of interest that reflects the anticipated rate of inflation. In particular, if they expect a high rate of inflation, they will agree to a higher interest rate. If the rate of inflation turns out to be less than anticipated, borrowers are hurt and lenders benefit since

the agreed upon interest rate, after adjusting for inflation, will be higher than expected.

3. The three types of unemployment are frictional unemployment which arises from normal labor market turnover, structural unemployment which arises when there is a permanent structural change in a region or industry, and cyclical unemployment which arises from the slowdown in the pace of economic expansion.

4. The natural rate of unemployment is the rate of unemployment that exists when the economy is at full employment; that is, the number of people looking for a job equals the number of job vacancies. When the economy is at the natural rate of unemployment cyclical unemployment is zero.

5. The clearest cost of unemployment is the loss of output and income when workers are unemployed. Furthermore, when workers are unemployed for long periods of time, their skills and abilities deteriorate; that is, human capital erodes. In addition, there are the social costs of higher crime and a loss of human dignity.

6. During the *contraction* phase of the business cycle, the rate of growth of real GDP slows down and real GDP falls below its trend. During this phase the unemployment rate is rising.

   During the *trough* phase, real GDP reaches its lowest point below trend and the unemployment rate is at its highest point over the cycle.

   The trough is a turning point between the contraction phase and the *expansion* phase during which the rate of growth of real GDP increases and the unemployment rate falls.

   At the end of an expansion, the economy reaches the *peak* phase of the business cycle. The peak is characterized by real GDP at its highest point above its trend and the rate of unemployment at its lowest point over the business cycle.

7. The current account balance is the difference between the value of all goods and services that we sell to other countries (exports) and the value of all the goods and services that we buy from foreigners (imports). The current account is in deficit if we buy more from the rest of the world than we sell to the rest of the world; that is, if imports are greater than exports.

PROBLEMS

1. a) Since both Jennifer and Yolanda expect the rate of inflation, to be 4 percent, they expect the value of money to decrease by 4 percent. Thus, they will agree to a 9 percent rate of interest to offset this, leaving a 5 percent rate of interest *really* paid after accounting for inflation.
   b) If both Jennifer and Yolanda expect a rate of *deflation* of 2 percent, they expect the value of money to *increase* by 2 percent. By the same logic as above, they will agree to a 3 percent rate of interest.
   c) If Jennifer expects a 4 percent rate of inflation she will want to loan only if the interest rate is at least 9 percent. If Yolanda expects a 6 percent rate of inflation, she will want to borrow if the rate of interest is 11 percent or less. Thus Jennifer and Yolanda could agree on any interest rate between 9 and 11 percent.

2. In order to determine the new wage rate at the end of the first year we must determine the percentage increase in the CPI and apply that percentage change to the

initial wage rate of $10 an hour. The percentage change in the CPI is ((225-214)/214) x 100, or 5.1 percent. Therefore the new wage rate at the end of the first year will be $10. x 1.051 = $10.51. During the second year, the increase in the CPI is 4 percent. Thus the new wage rate at the end of the second year will be $10.51 x 1.04 = 10.93.

3. a) Real GDP is unchanged. The increased value of goods and services is due only to increased prices.
   b) The fact that prices have risen less in proportion to the increase in nominal GDP means that real GDP has increased.

4. a) The labor force is 110 million, the sum of employment and unemployment.
   b) The unemployment rate is 9.1 percent, the number unemployed as a percentage of the labor force.
   c) The natural rate of unemployment is the rate of unemployment that would exist when all unemployment is frictional and structural and cyclical unemployment is zero. Since cyclical unemployment is 4 million, the natural rate of employment is the rate of unemployment if unemployment is only 6 million. Thus the natural rate of unemployment is 5.45 percent.

6 MEASURING OUTPUT AND THE PRICE LEVEL

CHAPTER IN PERSPECTIVE

In the introduction to macroeconomics in Chapter 5, we discussed business cycle fluctuations as the expansion and contraction of aggregate economic activity over time. We also discussed inflation, an upward movement in the price level. But how do we measure aggregate economic activity or the price level? In this chapter we address these questions in some detail.

The most widely used measure of economic activity is gross domestic product, or GDP. The behavior of GDP is frequently reported in the news. Here we discuss what it is and how it is measured. We will also examine the Consumer Price Index and the GDP deflator, two measures of the price level. As indicated in Chapter 1, one of the components of any science is careful and systematic measurement. In this chapter, we will see how measurements of the behavior of the aggregate economy are made. The concepts measured here will lay a foundation for our analysis of macroeconomic theory.

LEARNING OBJECTIVES

After studying this chapter, you will be able to:

- **Describe the flows of expenditure and income**
- **Explain why aggregate expenditure and income are equal to each other**
- **Explain how gross domestic product (GDP) and gross national product (GNP) are measured**
- **Describe two common measures of the price level: the Consumer Price Index (CPI) and the GDP deflator**
- **Explain how real GDP is measured**
- **Distinguish between inflation and changes in relative prices**
- **Explain why real GDP is not a good measure of economic well-being**

HELPFUL HINTS

1. Be sure to carefully distinguish between intermediate goods and investment goods. Both are typically goods sold by one firm to another, but they differ in terms of their use. Intermediate goods are goods that are processed and then resold, while investment goods are final goods themselves. Also note that the national income accounts include purchases of residential housing as investment because housing, like business capital stock, provides a continuous stream of value over time.

2. Note the difference between government spending on goods and services (G) and government transfer payments (TR). Both involve payments by the government, but transfer payments are not payments for currently produced goods and services. Indeed it is often useful to think of transfer payments as negative taxes, thus we define net taxes (T) as taxes (TX) minus transfer payments (TR): $T = TX - TR$.

3. There are several key equations introduced in this chapter that are important for you to understand. The first four of these key equations can be understood by careful examination of the circular flow in Figure 6.2 in the text. This figure shows a stylized view of the economy. The equations attempt to exactly measure the flows shown. As illustrated, gross domestic product can be measured in several different ways, all of which are equivalent:

(1) Income = Expenditure = Value of output (GDP)

This equation indicates that expenditures on final goods (in the goods market) are received as income (in the factor market) and that the value of the output (produced by firms) is reflected by the amount that is spent on goods and services. This equation gives rise to the two equivalent ways of computing GDP studied in this chapter.

(2) $Y = C + I + G + EX - IM$

Equation (2) reflects the expenditure approach to measuring GDP. It tells us that GDP is equal to the total amount of spending on domestic output in the economy by households, firms, government, and foreigners. Spending on imports is subtracted to account for the fact that imports are not domestically produced.

(3) $Y = C + S + T$

All income accrues to households who own the factors of production. Equation (3) indicates that income must be spent on goods and services (C) or spent as net taxes (T) or saved (S). Indeed, saving is *defined* as disposable income ($Y - T$) minus consumption expenditure (C).

(4) $I + G + EX = S + T + IM$

This equation follows from combining equations (2) and (3). It indicates that injections into the circular flow ($I + G + EX$) equal leakages from the circular flow ($S + T + IM$).

(5) GDP deflator = (Nominal GDP/Real GDP) x 100

This is the definition of the GDP deflator.

4. A price index for the current year is computed as the ratio of the value of a basket of goods in the current year to the value of the *same* basket of goods in a base year, multiplied by 100. It therefore attempts to calculate the cost of purchasing the same choice of goods in two different years. There are two major conceptual differences between the price indexes presented in this chapter.

a) The first of these differences has to do with the kinds of goods that are included in the basket of goods that is common to both the current and base years. The basket of goods used to calculate the Consumer Price Index contains goods that are purchased by a typical urban American family. The basket of goods used to calculate the GDP deflator, on the other hand, contains all goods and services included in GDP. It would, therefore, include capital goods.

b) The second difference is how the common basket is chosen. In the case of the CPI, the basket is a collection of commodities purchased in the base year. The basket used by the GDP deflator is the collection of goods purchased in the current year. Thus, the CPI uses a *fixed* basket of goods (as long as the base year is fixed), while the basket of goods used to compute the GDP deflator changes each year.

5. One should be careful not to confuse relative price changes and inflation. As demonstrated in the text, they are entirely independent phenomena; any inflation rate can occur with any behavior of relative prices. Changes in relative prices are explained by microeconomic theory and changes in the price level (e.g., inflation) are explained by macroeconomic theory.

KEY FIGURES AND TABLES

Figure 6.1 The Circular Flow of Expenditure and Income Between Households and Firms

The circular flow diagram in this figure illustrates the relationships between households and firms which give rise to alternative measures of aggregate expenditures and output. Three types of money flows are illustrated by the colored arrows. Not shown on the graphs are corresponding flows in the opposite directions.

The blue arrows show payments (income) for the use of factors of production, which flow in the opposite direction.

The red arrows show the payments for the purchase and rental of final goods and services (expenditures), which in turn flow in the opposite direction.

Finally, the green arrows show the flows of households' saving via financial markets to firms. A financial claim in the form of a bond or a stock certificate flows in the opposite direction.

Figure 6.2 The Circular Flow Including Government and the Rest of the World

For purposes of simplicity, the circular flow illustrated in Fig. 6.1 ignored the government and foreign sectors. In this figure, these two sectors are added but only money flows are indicated (by the same color of arrows).

In addition to the flows between households and firms shown in the preceding figure, this figure illustrates other flows to and from the government and the rest of the world. Households pay taxes to government and receive transfer payments from government, with the resulting net flow of net taxes (*T*). The government also purchases goods and services from firms (*G*). Firms sell goods and services to the rest of the world (exports=*EX*) and also buy goods and services from the rest of the world (imports=*IM*), with a resulting net flow of net exports (*NX*).

This diagram illustrates the basic relationships in national income accounting. The flows from firms to factor markets illustrate the factor incomes approach, while the flows from goods markets to firms illustrate the expenditure approach.

Table 6.2 GDP: The Expenditure Approach

The expenditure approach to measuring GDP divides the economy into four expenditure sectors and then adds together the spending of these sectors. GDP is obtained as the sum of consumption expenditures (*C*), gross private domestic investment (*I*), government purchases of goods and services (*G*), and net exports (*NX*). This table illustrates the expenditure approach by reporting GDP for the U. S. in 1990. It also indicates the percent of GNP corresponding to each of the four kinds of expenditure.

Table 6.4 GDP: The Factor Incomes Approach

GDP can also be measured using an income approach. All of the payments to households for the services of factors of production they hire are added together to obtain net national income at factor cost and then some adjustments are made. This approach to measuring GDP is illustrated in this table using U.S. data for 1990.

The first five entries in the table correspond to components of factor income. To the sum of these factor incomes we must add net indirect business taxes (i.e., indirect taxes *less* subsidies) and a capital consumption (depreciation) allowance. These adjustments must be made to account for the fact that, in addition to factor payments, firms also pay indirect taxes, receive subsidies, and must replace worn out capital. The percentage contribution to GDP for each of the entries is indicated in the final column of the table.

SELF-TEST

CONCEPT REVIEW

1. The aggregate expenditure by households on consumption goods and services is called ____________ ____________.
   Total spending by firms on new plant, equipment and buildings, and additions to inventories is called ____________.
2. Payments from the government to households which are NOT payments for currently produced goods and services are called ____________ ____________.
3. Net exports is equal to ____________ minus ____________.
4. ____________ is equal to disposable income minus consumption expenditure. Disposable income equals income plus ____________ ____________ minus ____________.
5. Investment, government spending on goods and services, and exports are examples of ____________ into the circular flow of income. Taxes, saving, and imports are examples of ____________ from the circular flow of income.
6. The method of measuring GDP which adds consumption expenditure, investment, government purchases of goods and services, and net exports is called the ____________ approach. The ____________ ____________ approach measures GDP by adding together all incomes paid to households by firms.
7. The stock of raw materials, unfinished products, and finished but unsold products held by a firm is called a(n) ____________.
8. A tax which is paid by consumers when they purchase goods and services from a firm is called a(n) ____________ tax.

9. The amount by which the value of the capital stock is reduced from wear and tear and passage of time is called ____________. When we subtract this amount from gross investment we have ____________ investment. Gross domestic product is equal to net national product plus ____________.
10. The value of the output of a firm minus the value of its inputs is called ____________ ____________. We are double counting if we include expenditures on ____________ goods as well as final goods in our calculation of GDP.
11. The ____________ ____________ ____________ is a measure of the average level of prices of consumption goods and services purchased by a "typical" urban family. The ____________ ____________ measures the average level of prices of all final goods and services produced in the economy.
12. The ratio of the price of one good to the price of another is called the ____________ ____________.
13. We refer to economic activity that is legal but not reported to the government as the ____________ ____________.

TRUE OR FALSE

____1. The payment of wages to households for their labor services is an example of a real flow from firms to households.

____2. In the measurement of GDP, purchase of stocks and bonds is counted as investment.

____3. In the aggregate economy, income is equal to expenditure and to GDP.

____4. The government pays High Flyer Aircraft Company for a military jet. This is an example of a transfer payment.

____5. Net exports for the U.S. are positive if the expenditure by foreigners on goods and services produced in the U.S. is greater than the expenditure by U.S. citizens on goods and services produced in foreign countries.

____6. Disposable income is equal to consumption expenditure plus saving.

____7. Disposable income is equal to income plus transfer payments minus taxes.

____8. Imports are an example of an injection into the circular flow of income.

____9. If GDP is equal to consumption expenditure plus gross investment plus government purchases of goods and services, then exports must equal imports.

____10. Goods that are produced this year but are not sold this year do not add to this year's GDP.

____11. If there were only households and firms (i.e., no government), market price and factor cost would be equal for any good.

____12. In order to measure GDP using the factor incomes approach, we must subtract indirect taxes and add subsidies to net domestic income at factor cost.

____13. Net domestic product equals gross domestic product minus depreciation.

____14. Net investment gives the net addition to the capital stock.

____15. Gross domestic product at factor cost is a measure of the value of output produced in the U.S.

____16. If two economies have the same GDP, then the standard of living is the same in each economy.

____17. The GDP deflator is calculated as real GDP divided by nominal GDP, multiplied by 100.

____18. If you are interested in knowing whether the economy is producing a greater physical volume of output, you would want to look at real GDP rather than nominal GDP.

____19. If the price of good *A* rises much more rapidly than the prices of other goods, then good *A* is responsible for high inflation.

____20. A rise in the CPI will overstate the increase in the cost of living if relative prices also change since consumers will make substitutions.

Multiple Choice

1. Which of the following is an example of a real flow from households to firms?
   a. Goods and services
   b. Factors of production
   c. Payments for goods and services
   d. Payments for factors of production

2. Which of the following is <u>NOT</u> an example of investment in the expenditure approach to measuring GNP? General Motors
   a. buys a new auto stamping machine.
   b. adds 500 new cars to inventories.
   c. buys U.S. government bonds.
   d. builds another assembly plant.

3. Which of the following is true for the aggregate economy?
   a. Income = expenditure, but these are not generally equal to GDP.
   b. Income = GDP, but expenditure is generally less than these.
   c. Income = expenditure = GDP.
   d. Income = expenditure = GDP only if there is no government or foreign sectors.

4. Which of the following is <u>NOT</u> true?
   a. $Y = C + I + G + IM - EX$
   b. $I + G + EX = S + T + IM$
   c. $Y = C + S + T$
   d. $Y + IM = C + I + G + EX$

5. Saving can be measured as
   a. income minus taxes.
   b. income minus transfer payments.
   c. income minus taxes minus consumption expenditure.
   d. income minus net taxes minus consumption expenditure.

6. Which of the following is NOT a part of the capital stock?
   a. The house owned by the Smith family
   b. The Smith family holdings of stock in the Smith Pickle Company
   c. The pickle factory building owned by the Smith family
   d. The pickle packing machine in the pickle factory building owned by the Smith family

7. Net interest is a component of which approach to measuring GDP?
   a. Factor incomes approach
   b. Expenditure approach
   c. Injections approach
   d. Output approach

8. Which of the following is NOT a component of the factor income approach to GDP?
   a. Rental incomes
   b. Compensation of employees
   c. Corporate profits
   d. Net exports

9. To obtain the factor cost of a good from its market price, one must
   a. add indirect taxes and subtract subsidies.
   b. subtract indirect taxes and add subsidies.
   c. subtract both indirect taxes and subsidies.
   d. add both indirect taxes and subsidies.

10. Which of the following is an example of a leakage from the circular flow of income?
    a. Exports
    b. Investment
    c. Saving
    d. Subsidies

11. The value of a firm's output minus the value of inputs purchased is
    a. net exports.
    b. value added.
    c. net profit.
    d. indirect production.

12. The existence of which of the following is NOT a reason for the fact that GDP gives an underestimate of the value of total output in the economy.
    a. Household production
    b. Illegal activities
    c. The underground economy
    d. Capital consumption allowance

13. From the data in Table 6.1, compute net investment.
    a. $600 billion
    b. $630 billion
    c. $700 billion
    d. $770 billion

Table 6.1

Item	Amount (billions of $)
Consumption expenditure	3000
Gross investment	700
Depreciation	70
Gov't purchases of goods & services	1000
Imports	500
Exports	400
Transfer payments	500
Taxes	1200

14. From the data in Table 6.1, what is GDP?
    a. $4200 billion
    b. $4400 billion
    c. $4600 billion
    d. $4800 billion

15. From the data in Table 6.1, what is disposable income?
    a. $2900 billion
    b. $3400 billion
    c. $3900 billion
    d. $4100 billion

16. From the data in Table 6.1, what is saving?
    a. $ 900 billion
    b. $1000 billion
    c. $1200 billion
    d. $1400 billion

17. Table 6.2 gives price and quantity data for an economy with only two consumption goods: rubber ducks and beach towels. What is the Consumer Price Index for the current year?
    a. 100
    b. 108
    c. 110
    d. 120

Table 6.2

Item	Base year Price $	Base year Quantity	Current year Price $	Current year Quantity
Rubber ducks	5	10	5	12
Beach towels	10	5	12	4

18. Refer to the data in Table 6.2. Between the base year and the current year, the relative price of rubber ducks
    a. remained unchanged.
    b. fell.
    c. rose.
    d. Not enough information to determine what happened to the relative price of rubber ducks.

19. If 1987 is the base year for the GDP deflator, we know that
    a. nominal GDP = real GDP in 1987.
    b. nominal GDP is greater than real GDP in 1987.
    c. nominal GDP is less than real GDP in 1987.
    d. nominal GDP in 1988 will be greater than real GDP in 1988.

20. Consider the data in Table 6.3. What is the GDP deflator in 1991?
    a. 95
    b. 104
    c. 106
    d. 110

Table 6.3

Year	Nominal GDP	Real GDP	GDP deflator
1990	1000	1000	
1991	1100	1040	
1992	1190		110

21. Consider the data in Table 6.3. What is real GDP in 1992?
    a. $1040
    b. $1082
    c. $1100
    d. $1124

22. Which of the following is NOT possible?
    a. The relative prices of some goods rise during a period of high inflation.
    b. The relative prices of some goods fall during a period of high inflation.
    c. The relative prices of some goods rise during a period in which the rate of inflation is negative (i.e., the price level is falling).
    d. The relative prices of all goods rise.

SHORT ANSWER

1. In the aggregate economy, why does income equal expenditure?

2. Briefly describe how the expenditure approach measures GDP.

3. Briefly describe how the factor incomes approach measures GDP.

4. In obtaining GDP we only count expenditure on final goods. Why do we *not* count expenditure on intermediate goods?

5. How is the Consumer Price Index computed?

6. How is the GDP deflator computed?

7. Does a 5 percent increase in the CPI mean that the cost of living has increased by 5 percent? Why or why not?

8. What productive activities are not measured and thus are not counted as part of GDP?

PROBLEMS

1. Use the data for an imaginary economy given in Table 6.4 to compute the following.
   a) GDP.
   b) net investment (net *I*).
   c) net exports (*NX*).
   d) disposable income.
   e) saving.
   f) total leakages from and total injections into the circular flow of income. (Are they equal?)

Table 6.4

Item	Amount (billions of $)
Consumption expenditure (*C*)	$600
Taxes (*TX*)	400
Transfer payments (*TR*)	250
Exports (*EX*)	240
Imports (*IM*)	220
Gov't spending on goods & services (*G*)	200
Gross investment (*I*)	150
Depreciation (*Depr*)	60

2. Use the data for the same imaginary economy given in Table 6.5 to compute the following.
   a) net domestic income at factor cost.
   b) net domestic product at market prices.
   c) GDP.

Table 6.5

Item	Amount (billions of $)
Compensation of employees	$550
Indirect taxes	120
Subsidies	20
Rental income	20
Corporate profits	80
Net interest	90
Depreciation	60
Proprietor's income	70

3. Table 6.6 describes the process by which a loaf of bread is sold to a consumer as a final good. In the first stage of the production process, the farmer raises the wheat and sells enough for one loaf of bread to the miller for $.20. The miller grinds the wheat into flour and sells the flour to the baker for $.35. The baker uses the wheat to bake a loaf of bread which is sold to a grocer for $.60. Finally, the grocer sells the bread to a consumer for $.75.
   a) Complete the last column of Table 6.6 by computing the value added at each of the four stages of the production process.
   b) What is the total value added for this loaf of bread? How does it compare with the expenditure on the loaf of bread as a final good?

4. Table 6.7 gives data for an economy in which there are three consumption goods: bananas, coconuts, and grapes. Our objective will be to use these data to compute a Consumer Price Index.
   a) Complete the table by computing expenditures for the base period and the appropriate value of quantities in the current year for computing the CPI.
   b) What is the value of the basket of consumption goods in the base period? In the current period?
   c) What is the Consumer Price Index for the current period?

Table 6.6

Transaction	Price received $	Value added $
1. Farmer sells wheat to miller	0.20	
2. Miller sells flour to baker	0.35	
3. Baker sells bread to grocer	0.60	
4. Grocer sells bread to consumer	0.75	

Table 6.7

	Base period			Current period	
Goods	Quantity in basket	Price $	Expenditure $	Price $	Value of quantities $
Bananas	120	6		8	
Coconuts	60	8		10	
Grapes	40	10		9	

5. Table 6.8 gives data for an economy in which there are three final goods included in GDP: pizzas, staplers, and bombs. Our objective will be to use these data to compute a GDP deflator.
   a) Complete the table by computing expenditure on each good evaluated at base period prices.
   b) What is the value of nominal GDP in the current period?
   c) What is the value of real GDP in the current period?
   d) What is the GDP deflator in the current period?

Table 6.8

Goods	Current period: Quantity in basket	Price $	Expenditure $	Base period: Price $	Value of quantities $
Pizza	110	8	880	6	
Staplers	50	10	500	8	
Bombs	50	9	450	10	

6. Complete Table 6.9.

Table 6.9

Year	Nominal GDP	Real GDP	GDP deflator
1981	3055		94
1982		3170	100
1983	3410	3280	
1984		3500	108

ANSWERS

CONCEPT REVIEW

1. consumption expenditure; investment
2. transfer payments
3. exports; imports
4. Saving; transfer payments; taxes
5. injections; leakages
6. expenditure; factor incomes
7. inventory
8. indirect
9. depreciation; net; depreciation
10. value added; intermediate
11. Consumer Price Index; GDP deflator
12. relative price
13. underground economy

TRUE OR FALSE

1. F	5. T	9. T	13. T	17. F
2. F	6. T	10. F	14. T	18. T
3. T	7. T	11. T	15. T	19. F
4. F	8. F	12. F	16. F	20. T

MULTIPLE CHOICE

1. b	6. b	11. b	16. a	21. b
2. c	7. a	12. d	17. c	22. d
3. c	8. d	13. b	18. b	
4. a	9. b	14. c	19. a	
5. d	10. c	15. c	20. c	

SHORT ANSWER

1. When an expenditure is made, firms receive money payments. The amount received by firms in the aggregate is aggregate expenditure. All that firms receive is distributed as income to households who own the factors of production. Remember that profit is income. Since the aggregate amount firms receive is expenditure and firms pay out all they receive as income, in the aggregate economy, income equals expenditure.

2. The expenditure approach to measuring GDP adds up the total expenditure on goods and services produced in the economy made by households, firms, government, and foreigners. It is the sum of consumption expenditure, investment, government purchases of goods and services, and net exports.

3. The factor income approach measures GDP by adding up all incomes paid by firms to owners of factors of production that firms have used. This includes wages to owners of labor, interest for owners of capital, rent for land, and profits. Since proprietors' income cannot be accurately divided among these, it is included separately. Two kinds of adjustments must also be made. First, depreciation must be added to get *gross* national product since part of the expenditure on capital (investment) is just to replace capital that has worn out. Secondly, if government subsidizes firms or uses firms to collect taxes, then indirect business taxes must be added to the sum of factor incomes and subsidies must be subtracted.

4. Counting both final goods and the intermediate goods that were combined to produce it will result in "double counting." For example, counting the value of the steel that is sold to General Motors to build a car and then counting it again when the car is sold as a final good will overstate the value of final goods and services since the steel is counted twice.

5. The first step in computing the Consumer Price Index is to choose a base year. Then the value of a typical basket of consumption goods *in the base year* is computed. Next, prices of consumption goods in the current period are obtained and the value of the base year basket of goods in terms of current prices is computed. This current value of the basket is divided by the base year value and then multiplied by 100 to obtain the CPI.

6. In computing the GDP deflator, we first collect prices of goods and services in a base year. Then we evaluate the current period output at both current prices and base year prices. The value at current prices is called nominal GDP and the value at base year prices is called real GDP. The GDP deflator is the ratio of nominal GDP to real GDP, multiplied by 100.

7. A 5 percent increase in the CPI does not mean that the cost of living has increased by 5 percent if relative prices also change (and they generally will). Changes in relative prices will cause consumers to make substitutions from goods whose relative price has risen to goods whose relative price has fallen. This reduces the effect on the cost of living. The fact that some goods disappear from use and new goods appear also means that changes in the CPI do not precisely reflect changes in the cost of living.

8. Activities that produce goods and services that are not counted as part of GDP are criminal activities, production in the underground economy, and household production. The first of these is not reported because the activities themselves are illegal. The second of these refers to goods and services that are legal but are not reported to circumvent taxes or government regulations. The third includes those productive activities which households perform for themselves. Because they don't hire someone else to mow the lawn or wash the car, they are not included in GDP.

PROBLEMS

1. a) $GDP = C + I + G + (EX - IM)$ = \$970 billion
   b) Net $I = I - Depr$ = \$90 billion
   c) $NX = EX - IM$ = \$20 billion
   d) Disposable income = $GDP + TR - TX$ = \$820 billion
   e) Saving = disposable income - C = \$220 billion

f) Total leakages = $(TX - TR) + IM + S$ = $590 billion
Total injections = $I + G + X$ = $590 billion
So, total leakages = total injections.

2. a) Net domestic income at factor cost = compensation of employees + rental income + corporate profits + net interest + proprietor's income = $810 billion.
b) Net domestic product at market prices = net domestic product at factor cost + indirect taxes - subsidies = $910 billion.
c) GDP = net domestic product at market prices + depreciation = $970 billion.

3. a) Table 6.6 is completed as Table 6.6 Solution below.

Table 6.6 Solution

Transaction	Price received $	Value added $
1. Farmer sells wheat to miller	0.20	0.20
2. Miller sells flour to baker	0.35	0.15
3. Baker sells bread to grocer	0.60	0.25
4. Grocer sells bread to consumer	0.75	

b) The value added at each step is the price for which the product sold minus the cost of inputs. The total value added by the loaf of bread is the sum of the value added at each step which is $0.20 + 0.15 + 0.25 + 0.15 = $0.75. This, of course, is exactly the amount spent on the loaf of bread as a final good. Thus the loaf of bread adds $0.75 to GDP.

4. a) Table 6.7 is completed as Table 6.7 Solution below. Note that the base period quantities are evaluated at current prices to get the value of quantities in the current year.

b) The value of the basket of consumption goods in the base period is the sum of the expenditures in that period: $1600. The value of the basket of consumption goods is obtained as the sum of the values of quantities in that period: $1920.

Table 6.7 Solution

	Base period			Current period	
Goods	Quantity in Basket	Price $	Expenditure $	Price $	Value of Quantities $
Bananas	120	6	720	8	960
Coconuts	60	8	480	10	600
Grapes	40	10	400	9	360

c) The consumer price index is the ratio of the value of quantities in the current period to the base period expenditure, times 100:

$$CPI = (1920/1600) \times 100 = 120.$$

5. a) Table 6.8 is completed as Table 6.8 Solution below. Base period expenditure for each item is obtained by evaluating the current period quantity at the base year price.

Table 6.8 Solution

	Current period			Base period	
Goods	Quantity in Basket	Price $	Expenditure $	Price $	Value of Quantities $
Pizza	110	8	880	6	660
Staplers	50	10	500	8	400
Bombs	50	9	450	10	500

b) The value of nominal GDP in the current period is the sum of expenditures in the current period: $1830.
c) The value of real GDP in the current period is the sum of the current period quantities evaluated at base period prices (i.e., what the expenditures would have been at base year prices): $1560.
d) The GDP deflator for the current period is the ratio of nominal GDP to real GDP, times 100:

GDP deflator = (1830/1560) x 100 = 117.3.

6. Table 6.9 is completed as Table 6.9 Solution below. The following equation is used:

GDP deflator = (Nominal GDP/real GDP) x 100.

Table 6.9 Solution

Year	Nominal GDP	Real GDP	GDP deflator
1981	3055	3250	94
1982	3170	3170	100
1983	3410	3280	104
1984	3780	3500	108

7 AGGREGATE DEMAND AND AGGREGATE SUPPLY

CHAPTER IN PERSPECTIVE

What determines the amount of goods and services that an economy produces? What causes inflation and how can it be controlled? What are the causes of unemployment, and why does the unemployment rate fluctuate over time? The fundamental purpose of macroeconomic analysis is to address these kinds of issues; issues regarding the behavior of the national economy as a whole. These are the issues that are reflected each day in the news because they affect us all.

In this chapter we begin to build the basic tool of macroeconomic analysis: the aggregate demand and aggregate supply model. This model will prove to be very helpful as we attempt to explain the growth of real GDP and inflation as well as business cycle fluctuations in real GDP and unemployment. This chapter presents the rudiments of the model and uses them to explain recent U.S. experience with inflation and recession. In subsequent chapters we take more care in developing the underlying principles of aggregate demand and aggregate supply.

LEARNING OBJECTIVES

After studying this chapter, you will be able to:

- **Define aggregate demand and explain what determines it**
- **Explain the sources of growth and fluctuations in aggregate demand**
- **Define aggregate supply and explain what determines it**
- **Explain the sources of growth and fluctuations in aggregate supply**
- **Define macroeconomic equilibrium**
- **Predict the effect of changes in aggregate demand and aggregate supply on real GDP and on the price level**
- **Explain why real GDP grows and sometimes declines**
- **Explain why we have inflation and why its rate varies, sometimes exploding as it did in the 1970s**

Explain the OPEC recession of 1974–75, the Volcker recession of 1981–82, and the recovery of the 1980s, and the recession of 1991

HELPFUL HINTS

1. This chapter discusses the fundamental concepts of aggregate demand, aggregate supply, and macroeconomic equilibrium. The model developed here is the principal means by which we analyze macroeconomic activity. While later chapters will refine our understanding of these concepts, the basic model is introduced here. As a result, you should review this chapter until you have mastered it.

2. Although later chapters will delve more deeply into the nature of the aggregate demand and aggregate supply curves, it is important at this point to understand the basic reasons for the negative and positive slopes (respectively) of these two curves. The wise student will *carefully* study the relevant discussions in the text.

a) Three separate reasons for the negative slope of the aggregate demand curve are discussed: the real money balances effect, the intertemporal substitution effect, and the international substitution effect.

The first two of these are consequences of the fact that a change in the price level will change the level of real money. A change in real money has a direct effect on aggregate expenditure (the real money balances effect) as well as an indirect effect: a change in real money will lead to a change in interest rates which then affects aggregate expenditure (the intertemporal substitution effect). The third effect is a consequence of the fact that a change in the U.S. price level changes the *relative* price of U.S. goods and services in terms of the price of goods and services in the rest of the world. In each of these cases, an increase in the price level will cause a decrease in the aggregate quantity of goods and services demanded, thus explaining a negatively sloped *AD* curve.

b) There is a single important reason for the positive slope of the *short-run* aggregate supply curve: input prices are held constant. Given constant input prices, a change in the price level (i.e., the price of output) will affect the amount of goods and services that producers are willing to supply. For example, if the price of output rises but the price of inputs remains constant, profit-maximizing firms will increase output.

3. As in our study of microeconomics, in macroeconomics we do not define the short run and long run in terms of a length of calendar time, but rather, in terms of whether or not key variables can change. Here, in the short run, the prices of factors of production do not change, whereas, in the long run, they do change. The principal implication is that, in the short run, a change in the price level causes the price of output relative to the price of inputs to change and thus firms will change their rate of output. On the other hand, in the long run, input prices adjust and there is no long-run change in output since the initial price of output relative to input prices is restored.

4. The distinction between the short run and the long run gives rise to the differences between the factors that affect the short-run and long-run aggregate supply curves. Since input prices are held constant for the short-run aggregate supply curve but not for the long-run aggregate supply curve, a change in input prices will shift the short-run curve but not the long-run curve.

5. One of the more difficult skills to learn in macroeconomics is how to interpret different

events in terms of the models we are developing. The key is to understand whether an event will affect the aggregate demand or the aggregate supply curves. Explore the many examples in the text to help clarify this issue.

KEY FIGURES AND TABLES

Figure 7.1 The Aggregate Demand Curve and the Aggregate Demand Schedule

The aggregate demand curve illustrates the relationship between the quantity of real GDP demanded and the price level, holding other things constant. For example, if the price level is 110, the aggregate quantity of goods and services demanded is $5.5 trillion. Due to the real money balances effect, the intertemporal substitution effect, and the international substitution effect, the quantity of real GDP demanded decreases as the price level rises. Thus the aggregate demand curve is negatively sloped.

Figure 7.2 Changes in the Quantity of Real GDP Demanded

A change in the price level causes a change in the quantity of real GDP demanded which is represented as a *movement along* the aggregate demand curve. Such movements are illustrated in this figure.

The negative slope of the aggregate demand curve reflects the fact that a change in the price level causes the quantity of real GDP demanded to change in the opposite direction. The three reasons for the negative slope of the aggregate demand curve are also summarized in the figure.

Figure 7.3 Changes in Aggregate Demand

Changes in aggregate demand are represented by shifts in the aggregate demand curve. The main factors that cause changes in aggregate demand are listed here. Anything than decreases aggregate demand shifts the aggregate demand to the left and anything that increases aggregate demand shifts the curve to the right. Note that changes in the price level will *not* shift the aggregate demand curve.

Figure 7.4 The Aggregate Supply Curves and the Aggregate Supply Schedule

The two aggregate supply curves illustrate the relationship between the quantity of real GDP supplied and the price level. The short-run aggregate supply curve (*SAS*) illustrates this relationship holding everything else constant, *including input prices.* The long-run aggregate supply curve (*LAS*) illustrates the relationship holding everything *except input prices* constant.

The *SAS* curve over its full range is illustrated in part (a). Since the economy normally operates in the intermediate range, part (b) zooms in on this range. When input prices are held fixed, a rise in the price level will induce firms to increase output. Thus the *SAS* is positively sloped in this range.

Part (b) also illustrates the associated *LAS* curve which shows that, when input prices adjust to clear factor markets, aggregate supply is independent of the price level. Thus the *LAS* is vertical at the full employment level of GDP.

Figure 7.5 A Decrease in Short-Run Aggregate Supply

When input prices change, the short-run aggregate supply curve shifts. This figure illustrates a leftward (upward) shift in the *SAS* curve due to an increase the wage rates. The increase in the price of labor causes a decrease in short-run aggregate supply.

Figure 7.6 Long-Run Growth in Aggregate Supply

Any factor that increases aggregate supply in the long-run will shift both the long-run (*LAS*) and short-run aggregate supply (*SAS*) curves. This figure illustrates the effect of an increase in productive capacity. Full employment real GDP increases and both the *SAS* and *LAS* curves shift to the right.

Figure 7.7 Macroeconomic Equilibrium

Macroeconomic equilibrium occurs when the level of aggregate GDP demanded is equal to aggregate real GDP supplied. Graphically, this occurs at the intersection of the aggregate demand and short-run aggregate supply curves. This intersection gives the equilibrium value of real GDP and the price level; in this figure, the equilibrium level of real GDP is 5.5 trillion 1987 dollars and the price level is 120 (measured by the GDP deflator).

Note that when the price level is below the equilibrium price level, there is a shortage (i.e., the quantity of real GDP demanded exceeds the quantity of real GDP supplied) which causes prices (and thus the price level) to rise.

When the price level is above the equilibrium price level, there is a surplus (i.e., the quantity of real GDP supplied exceeds the quantity of real GDP demanded), which causes prices (and thus the price level) to fall. Only at the equilibrium price level will there be no tendency for change.

Figure 7.8 Three Types of Macroeconomic Equilibrium

Part (a) of this figure show an economy fluctuating over a business cycle, with the corresponding aggregate demand and supply diagrams. Macroeconomic equilibrium occurs at the intersection of the aggregate demand and *short-run* aggregate supply curves. Only if this point is also on the *long-run* aggregate supply curve will the equilibrium level of real GDP correspond to the full-employment level of real GDP. In that case, the economy is said to be at a full-employment equilibrium. Such an equilibrium is illustrated in part (c) of the figure.

If the intersection of the aggregate demand and short-run aggregate supply curves occurs at a level of real GDP *below* full-employment real GDP, then the rate of unemployment must be greater than the full-employment (natural) rate of unemployment. In that case, illustrated in part (b) of the figure, there is a recessionary gap and the economy is said to be at an unemployment equilibrium

Finally, it is quite possible that the aggregate demand and short-run aggregate supply curves will intersect at a level of real GDP which is *above* full-employment GDP. If so, there is an inflationary gap and the economy is at an above full-employment equilibrium. At such an equilibrium, illustrated in part (d), the unemployment rate will be less that the natural rate of unemployment.

Figure 7.9 The Effects of an Increase in Aggregate Demand

This figure illustrates how real GDP and the price level change when there is an increase in aggregate demand represented by a shift in the *AD* curve from AD_0 to AD_1. In the short run, input prices are fixed and so the new equilibrium occurs at the intersection of the new aggregate demand curve (AD_1) intersects the original short-run aggregate supply curve (SAS_0). As a result, real GDP and the price level both increase. Real GDP is now above its full employment level and there is an inflationary gap.

The higher price level will induce workers to demand higher wages which will shift the *SAS* curve to the left (up). The *SAS* curve will eventually shift to SAS_1 and the economy will be in equilibrium at the intersection of AD_1 and SAS_1. The price level rises even further and real GDP returns to full-employment real GDP.

Figure 7.10 The Effects of an Increase in the Price of Oil

This figure illustrates how real GDP and the price level change when there is a decrease in short-run aggregate supply due to an increase in the price of oil. In the figure, the short-run aggregate supply curve shifts to the left, from SAS_0 to SAS_1. The new equilibrium occurs at the intersection of the aggregate demand curve (AD_0) and the new short-run aggregate supply curve (SAS_1). As a result, real GDP declines and the price level rises.

This combination of recession and inflation is called stagflation.

SELF-TEST

CONCEPT REVIEW

1. The graphical representation of the relationship between the quantity of real GDP demanded and the price level is called the ____________ ____________ curve. As the price level increases, the quantity of real GDP demanded ____________.
2. There are three separate effects of the price level on the quantity of real GDP demanded. The first of these is the real money balances effect. As the price level rises, the quantity of real money ____________, which causes the quantity of real GDP demanded to ____________.
3. The second effect involves the substitution of goods now for goods later or vice versa; this is the ____________ ____________ effect. A lower price level will tend to lead to ____________ interest rates, which causes the quantity of real GDP demanded to ____________.
4. The third effect is the ____________ substitution effect. If the U.S. price level rises (holding everything else constant), the quantity of U.S.-produced goods demanded will ____________ and the quantity of foreign-produced goods demanded will ____________.
5. If the quantity of money increases (holding everything else constant) the aggregate demand curve will shift to the ____________. The aggregate demand curve will shift to the right if the government ____________ taxes.
6. With wage rates and other input prices held constant, an increase in the price level will cause the quantity of real GDP supplied to ____________. Thus the ____________-____________ aggregate supply curve is ____________ sloped. When the economy reaches its physical limit to produce, this curve becomes ____________.
7. The relationship between real GDP supplied and the price level when there is full employment is ____________-____________ aggregate supply.
8. If the quantity of real GDP demanded equals the quantity of real GDP supplied, the economy is in ____________ ____________. If this occurs when the economy is on its long-run aggregate supply curve, then the economy is said to be in ____________-____________ equilibrium. If this occurs at a level of real GDP below long-run aggregate supply, a(n) ____________ equilibrium has occurred.

9. A(n) ____________ gap is long-run real GDP minus actual real GDP when actual real GDP is below long-run real GDP. A(n) ____________ gap is actual real GDP minus long-run GDP when actual real GDP is above long-run real GDP.

10. An increase in aggregate demand (other things remaining constant, including input prices) will result in a(n) ____________ in the price level and a(n) ____________ in the level of real GDP.

11. A large increase in the price of oil (other things remaining constant) will result in a(n) ____________ in the price level and a(n) ____________ in the level of real GDP.

TRUE OR FALSE

____ 1. According to the real money balances effect, the lower the quantity of real money, the larger the quantity of real GDP demanded.

____ 2. As interest rates decline, the aggregate quantity of goods and services demanded rises.

____ 3. If the U.S. price level remains constant but the price level in the rest of the world declines, then the demand for real GDP (U.S.) declines.

____ 4. An increase in the expected rate of inflation will decrease aggregate demand.

____ 5. An increase in the foreign exchange value of the dollar will increase aggregate demand in the U.S.

____ 6. If the government decides to increase its expenditures on goods and services, the aggregate demand curve will shift to the right.

____ 7. An increase in income taxes will cause the aggregate demand curve to shift to the right.

____ 8. As the price level increases (other things remaining unchanged), the *long-run* aggregate quantity of goods and services supplied increases.

____ 9. As the price level increases (other things remaining unchanged), the *short-run* aggregate quantity of goods and services supplied increases.

____10. If the economy is on its long-run aggregate supply curve, there is full employment.

____11. If the stock of capital increases, both the long-run and short-run aggregate supply curves will shift to the right.

____12. If wages fall, both the long-run and short-run aggregate supply curves will shift to the right.

____13. An economy is initially in macroeconomic equilibrium on its long-run aggregate supply curve and then expected future profits *decrease.* If the prices of factors of production remain unchanged in the short run, the new equilibrium will be an unemployment equilibrium.

____14. An economy is initially in macroeconomic equilibrium on its long-run aggregate supply curve and then expected future profits *decrease.* The price level will rise.

____15. It is possible to have a macroeconomic equilibrium at a level of real GDP above full employment.

____16. If the economy is in an unemployment equilibrium there is an inflationary gap.

____17. If there is a significant technological advance (other things remaining unchanged), the long-run aggregate supply curve will shift to the right but the short-run aggregate supply curve will not shift.

____18. If there is significant technological advance (other things remaining unchanged), the price level will rise.

____19. The main force generating the underlying tendency of real GDP to expand over time is increases in long-run aggregate supply.

____20. The main force generating a long period of inflation is persistent increases in aggregate demand.

____21. A large increase in the price of oil, such as in 1973, resulted in an inflationary recession.

____22. Any factor that shifts the short-run aggregate supply curve to the right will also shift the long-run aggregate supply curve to the right.

____23. If an economy is producing at levels above its long-run aggregate supply, we will expect wages to rise.

MULTIPLE CHOICE

1. The aggregate demand curve (*AD*) illustrates that, as the price level falls, the quantity of
   a. real GDP demanded increases.
   b. real GDP demanded decreases.
   c. nominal GDP demanded increases.
   d. nominal GDP demanded decreases.

2. Which of the following is NOT a reason for the downward slope of the aggregate demand curve?
   a. The intertemporal substitution effect
   b. The international substitution effect
   c. The expected inflation effect
   d. The real money balances effect

3. As the price level rises, the quantity of real money
   a. increases, and thus the aggregate quantity of goods and services demanded increases.
   b. increases, and thus the aggregate quantity of goods and services demanded decreases.
   c. decreases, and thus the aggregate quantity of goods and services demanded increases.
   d. decreases, and thus the aggregate quantity of goods and services demanded decreases.

4. As the quantity of real money increases, interest rates become
   a. lower, which leads to an increase in the quantity of real GDP demanded.
   b. lower, which leads to a decrease in the quantity of real GDP demanded.
   c. higher, which leads to an increase in the quantity of real GDP demanded.
   d. higher, which leads to a decrease in the quantity of real GDP demanded.

5. Which of the following will cause the aggregate demand curve to shift to the right?
   a. An increase in interest rates (at a given price level)
   b. An increase in expected inflation
   c. An increase in taxes
   d. A decrease in the price level

6. The long-run aggregate supply curve (*LAS*) is
   a. positively sloped.
   b. negatively sloped.
   c. vertical.
   d. horizontal.

7. Long-run aggregate supply is the level of real GDP at which
   a. the aggregate demand curve intersects the short-run aggregate supply curve.
   b. there is full employment.
   c. the economy is producing its physical limit.
   d. prices are sure to rise.

8. Short-run aggregate supply is the relationship between the price level and the quantity of real GDP supplied, holding constant the
   a. prices of inputs.
   b. quantities of factors of production.
   c. level of government spending.
   d. price level.

9. The short-run aggregate supply curve (*SAS*) is positively sloped but becomes vertical at the level of real GDP at which
   a. prices begin to rise
   b. each firm is producing output at its physical limit.
   c. there is full employment.
   d. it intersects the aggregate demand curve.

10. A technological improvement will shift
    a. both the short-run aggregate supply and long-run aggregate supply curves to the right.
    b. both the short-run aggregate supply and long-run aggregate supply curves to the left.
    c. the short-run aggregate supply curve to the right but leave the long-run aggregate supply curve unchanged.
    d. the long-run aggregate supply curve to the right but leave the short-run aggregate supply curve unchanged.

11. A decrease in wages will shift
    a. both the short-run aggregate supply and long-run aggregate supply curves down.
    b. both the short-run aggregate supply and long-run aggregate supply curves up.
    c. the short-run aggregate supply curve down but leave the long-run aggregate supply curve unchanged.
    d. the long-run aggregate supply curve down but leave the short-run aggregate supply curve unchanged.

12. Macroeconomic equilibrium occurs when the
    a. economy is at full employment.
    b. economy is producing at its physical limit.
    c. aggregate demand curve intersects the short-run aggregate supply curve along its vertical portion.
    d. quantity of real GDP demanded equals the quantity of real GDP supplied.

13. Which of the graphs in Fig. 7.1 illustrates an unemployment equilibrium?
    a. (a)
    b. (b)
    c. (c)
    d. (d)

14. Which of the graphs in Fig. 7.1 illustrates a full employment equilibrium?
   a. (a)
   b. (b)
   c. (c)
   d. (d)

15. Which of the graphs in Fig. 7.1 illustrates a macroeconomic equilibrium with a recessionary gap?
   a. (a)
   b. (b)
   c. (c)
   d. (d)

16. If real GDP is greater than long-run aggregate supply, then the economy is
   a. not in macroeconomic equilibrium.
   b. in a full-employment equilibrium.
   c. in an above full-employment equilibrium.
   d. in an unemployment equilibrium.

Figure 7.1

(a)

Price Level, LAS, SAS, AD, 0, Real GDP

(b)

Price Level, LAS, SAS, AD, 0, Real GDP

(c)

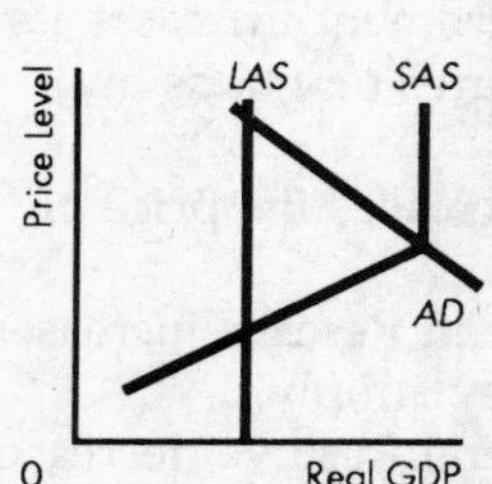

(d)

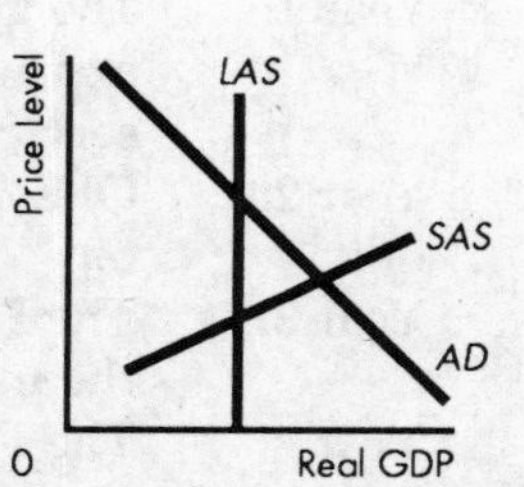

17. If input prices remain constant and firms are producing at levels less than their physical limits, an increase in aggregate demand will cause
   a. an increase in the price level and an increase in real GDP.
   b. an increase in the price level and a decrease in real GDP.
   c. a decrease in the price level and an increase in real GDP.
   d. a decrease in the price level and a decrease in real GDP.

18. We observe an increase in the price level and a decrease in real GDP. Which of the following is a possible explanation?
   a. The expectation of future profits has increased.
   b. The money supply has decreased.
   c. The price of raw materials has increased.
   d. The stock of capital has increased.

19. We observe an increase in the price level and an increase in real GDP. Which of the following is a possible explanation?
   a. The expectation of future profits has increased.
   b. The money supply has decreased.
   c. The price of raw materials has increased.
   d. The stock of capital has increased.

20. The economy cannot remain at a level of real GDP above long-run aggregate supply because input prices will
   a. fall, thus shifting the long-run aggregate supply curve to the right.
   b. fall, thus shifting the short-run aggregate supply curve down.
   c. rise, thus shifting the long-run aggregate supply curve to the left.
   d. rise, thus shifting the short-run aggregate supply curve up.

21. The fact that the short-run aggregate supply and aggregate demand curves do not shift at a fixed, steady pace explains why we observe
    a. persistent inflation.
    b. business cycles.
    c. trend growth in real GDP.
    d. large government budget deficits.

SHORT ANSWER

1. The real money balances effect implies that an increase in the price level will lead to a decrease in the aggregate quantity of goods and services demanded. Explain.

2. The intertemporal substitution effect implies that an increase in the price level will lead to a decrease in the aggregate quantity of goods and services demanded. Explain.

3. The international substitution effect implies that an increase in the price level will lead to a decrease in the aggregate quantity of goods and services demanded. Explain.

4. Why is the short-run aggregate supply curve positively sloped?

5. Why does the short-run aggregate supply curve become vertical at some high level of output?

6. Why is the long-run aggregate supply curve vertical?

7. What is meant by macroeconomic equilibrium?

8. What are the most important factors in explaining the steady and persistent increases in the price level over time in the U.S.?

PROBLEMS

1. Suppose the economy is initially in full-employment equilibrium. Assuming that input prices remain constant, graphically illustrate the effect of an increase in foreign income. What happens to the price level and the level of real GDP?

2. Suppose the economy is initially in full-employment equilibrium. Assuming that input prices remain constant, graphically illustrate the effect of an increase in the stock of human capital. What happens to the price level and the level of real GDP?

3. Suppose the economy is initially in full-employment equilibrium. Graphically illustrate the effect of an increase in wages. What happens to the price level and the level of real GDP?

4. Consider an economy that is in above full-employment equilibrium due to an increase in *AD* and given input prices. As stated in the text, the economy cannot stay at a level of real GDP above long-run aggregate supply forever. With the help of graphical representation, discuss the process by which the full-employment level of real GDP is restored.

5. Consider an economy that is initially at a full-employment equilibrium. In each of 4 successive years, an economic event occurs:

Year 1:	The government increases its expenditures on goods and services.
Year 2:	OPEC increases the price of oil.
Year 3:	The Federal Reserve increases the money supply.
Year 4:	The Federal Reserve decreases the money supply.

a) Graphically illustrate the successive consequences of these four events on the diagram in Fig. 7.2 (a). Label the initial equilibrium point *a* and label the new equilibrium points after years 1, 2, 3 and 4, *b*, *c*, *d*, and *e* respectively.
b) Suppose that each new equilibrium is achieved gradually over 1 year. In Fig. 7.2 (b), point *a* refers to the initial level of real GDP; time is measured on the horizontal axis. Plot the behavior of real GDP during the succeeding 4 years. Comment on the pattern of that behavior.

Figure 7.2

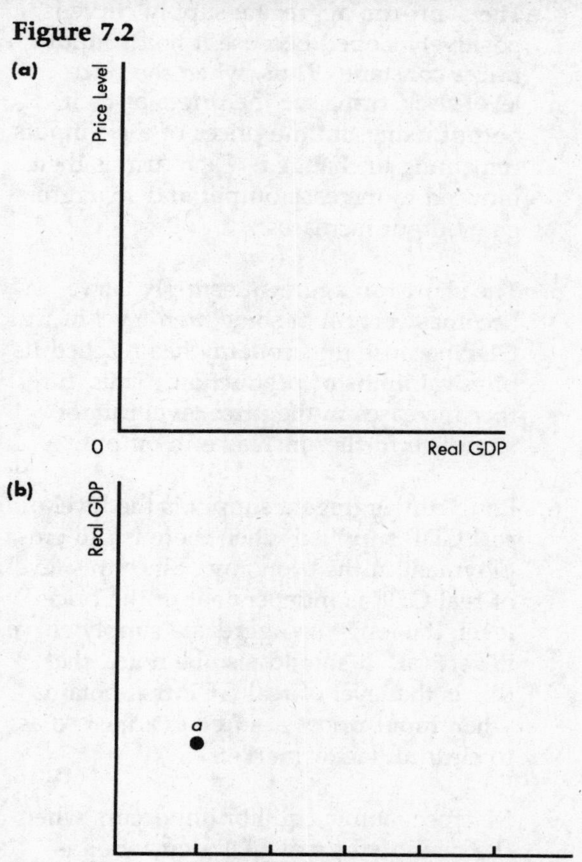

ANSWERS

Concept Review

1. aggregate demand; decreases
2. falls; decrease
3. intertemporal substitution; lower; increase
4. international; fall; rise
5. right; decreases
6. increase; short-run; positively; vertical
7. long-run
8. macroeconomic equilibrium; full-employment; unemployment
9. recessionary; inflationary
10. increase; increase
11. increase; decrease

True or False

1. F	6. T	11. T	16. F	21. T
2. T	7. F	12. F	17. F	22. F
3. T	8. F	13. T	18. F	23. T
4. F	9. T	14. F	19. T	
5. F	10. T	15. T	20. T	

Multiple Choice

1. a	6. c	11. c	16. c	21. b
2. c	7. b	12. d	17. a	
3. d	8. a	13. a	18. c	
4. a	9. b	14. b	19. a	
5. b	10. a	15. a	20. d	

SHORT ANSWER

1. The real money balances effect implies that an increase in the quantity of real money will lead to an increase in the aggregate quantity of goods and services demanded and vice versa. The quantity of *real* money is measured as the quantity of money (in dollars) divided by the price level. Thus, an increase in the price level means a decrease in the quantity of real money. The real balance effect tells us that this decline in the quantity of real money will lead to a decrease in the quantity of aggregate goods and services demanded.

2. Intertemporal substitution means the substitution of goods now for goods later or vice versa. There are two keys to understanding the intertemporal substitution effect.

   The first of these is that changes in interest rates influence households to engage in intertemporal substitution. For example, if interest rates rise, households will tend to borrow and spend less now, thus decreasing the aggregate quantity of goods and services demanded.

   The second key is that interest rates are determined by the demand for loans and the supply of loans and that these are affected by changes in the quantity of real money. In particular, a decrease in real money will make households less willing to lend. This means that the supply of loans will decrease, which will cause the interest rate to rise.

   Combining these keys, the intertemporal substitution effect is described as follows: An increase in the price level decreases the quantity of real money, which reduces the supply of loans and thus raises interest rates. The rise in interest rates will lead to a decrease in the aggregate quantity of goods and services demanded.

3. International substitution means substituting domestically produced goods for foreign produced goods or vice versa. If the price of domestic goods rises and foreign prices remain constant, domestic goods become relatively more expensive, and so households will buy fewer domestic goods and more foreign goods. This means that there will be a decrease in the quantity of real GDP demanded. Thus an increase in the price level (the prices of domestic goods) will lead to a decrease in the aggregate quantity of (domestic) goods and services demanded via the international substitution effect.

4. The short-run aggregate supply curve is positively sloped because it holds input prices constant. Thus, when the price level rises, firms see the prices of their output rising but the prices of their inputs remaining unchanged. Each firm is then induced to increase output and so aggregate output increases.

5. The short-run aggregate supply curve becomes vertical at some high level of real GDP because the economy has reached its physical limits of production. Thus, further increases in the price level cannot stimulate further increases in output.

6. Long-run aggregate supply is the level of real GDP supplied when there is full employment in the economy. Since this level of real GDP is independent of the price level, the long-run aggregate supply curve is vertical. It should also be noted that this is the level of real GDP that obtains when input prices are free to adjust so as to clear all factor markets.

7. Macroeconomic equilibrium occurs when the quantity of real GDP demanded is equal to the quantity of real GDP supplied. Graphically, macroeconomic equilibrium occurs at the intersection of the

aggregate demand and short-run aggregate supply curves.

8. The price level can rise as the result of either an increase in aggregate demand or as the result of a decrease in aggregate supply. Indeed both of these forces have contributed to periods in which the price level rose. The steady and persistent increases in the price level, however, have been due to steady and persistent increases in aggregate demand. The most important reason for this behavior of aggregate demand is persistent increases in the quantity of money.

PROBLEMS

1. The economy in Fig. 7.3 is initially at point *a* on the original *AD* curve, AD_0. An increase in foreign income will shift the *AD* curve to the right, from AD_0 to AD_1. At the new equilibrium, point *b*, the price level has risen and the level of real GDP has increased.

Figure 7.3

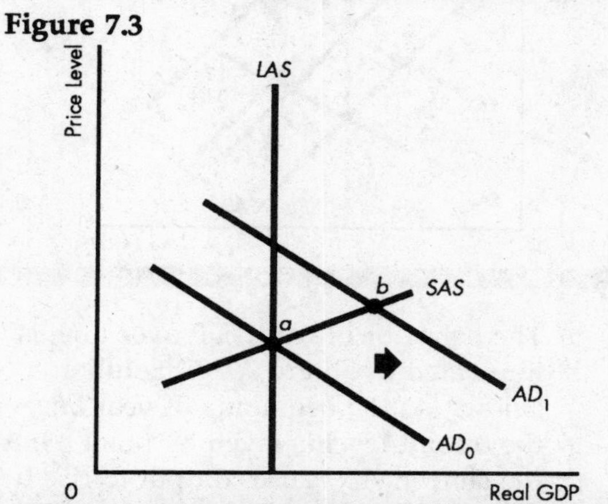

2. The economy in Fig. 7.4 is initially at point *a* on the LAS_0 and SAS_0 curves. An increase in the stock of human capital will shift both the *LAS* and *SAS* curves to the right, to LAS_1 and SAS_1 respectively. At the new equilibrium, point *b*, the price level has fallen and the level of real GDP has increased.

3. The economy in Fig. 7.5 is initially at point *a* on the SAS_0 curve. An increase in wages will shift the *SAS* curve upward, to SAS_1. At the new equilibrium, point *b*, the price level has risen and the level of real GDP has decreased.

Figure 7.4

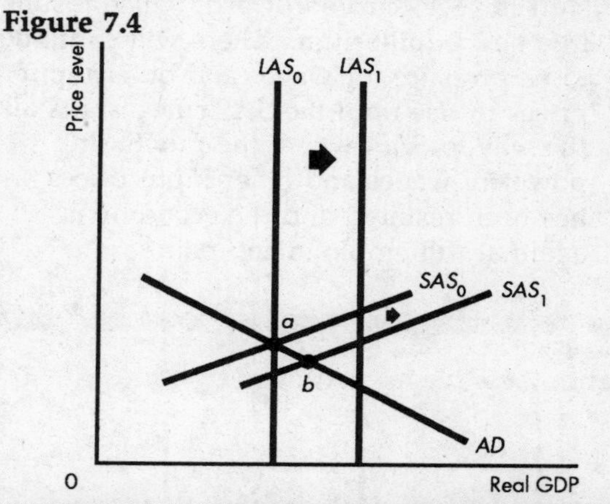

Figure 7.5

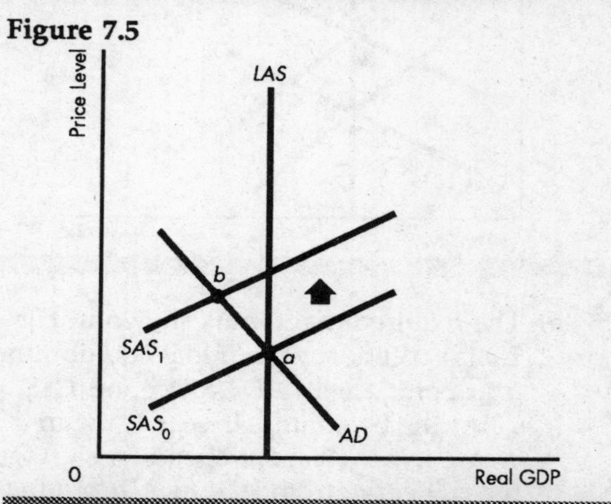

4. See Fig. 7.6. The increase in *AD* from AD_0 to AD_1 results in the above full-employment equilibrium at point *b* and causes the price level to increase. Since wages have not changed, the real cost of labor to firms has fallen and thus output is stimulated as indicated by the movement along the SAS_0 curve from point *a* to point *b*. Furthermore, the purchasing power of workers' wages has fallen. As a result, workers will demand higher wages and firms will be willing to pay them.

   In a similar way, other input prices will rise as well. This rise in input prices will shift the *SAS* curve upward, which results in a new equilibrium. There will continue to be pressure for wages and other input prices to rise until the *SAS* curve shifts all the way to SAS_1 where the purchasing power of wages and other input prices has been restored and the economy is again at full-employment, point *c*.

Figure 7.6

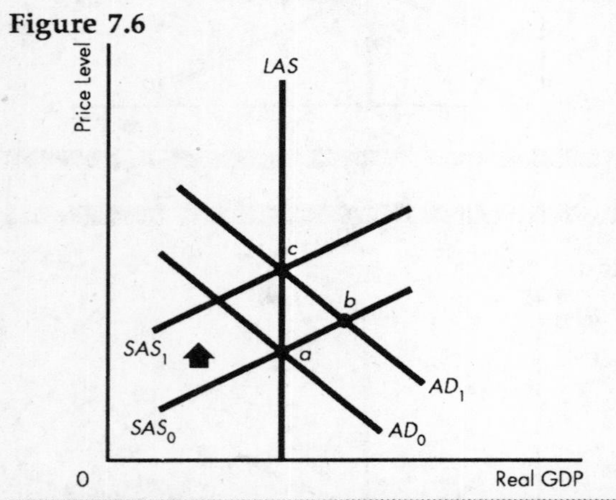

5. a) The required diagram is shown in Fig. 7.2 (a) Solution. The initial equilibrium is at point *a* with AD_0, SAS_0, and *LAS*.

   At the beginning of year 1, the increase in government spending shifts the *AD* curve from AD_0 to AD_1 producing a new equilibrium (by the end of the year) at point *b*. We note that real GDP has increased. At the beginning of year 2, OPEC increases the price of oil, which shifts the *SAS* curve from SAS_0 to SAS_2. Real GDP falls producing a new equilibrium at point *c*. At the beginning of the third year, the Fed increases the money supply (perhaps to combat the fall in output), which causes the *AD* curve to shift from AD_1 to AD_3. The new equilibrium is at point *d* and real GDP has risen. Finally, in year 4, the Fed decreases the money supply (perhaps to combat the continuing increase in the price level) and the *AD* curve shifts to the left, from AD_3 to AD_4, say. The consequence is a decline in real GDP and a new equilibrium at point *e*.

Figure 7.2 (a) Solution

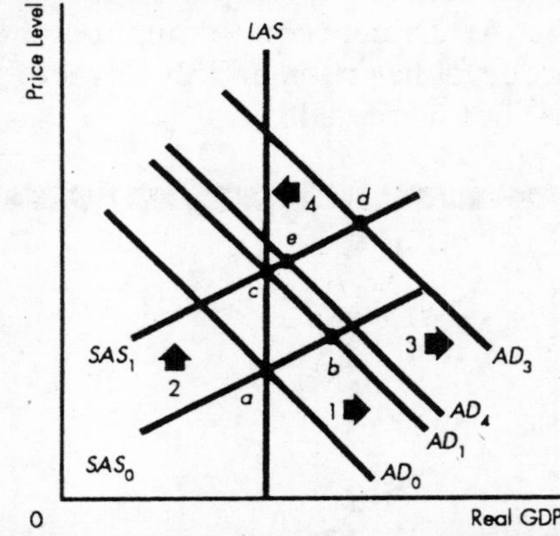

   b) The behavior of real GDP over time is illustrated in Figure 7.2 (b) Solution below. At the beginning of year one, the output level is given by point *a* but the shift in *AD* causes output to rise by the beginning of year 2 (point *b*). Similarly, as indicated in part (a) above, in years 2, 3, and 4, real GDP falls, rises, and falls again (points *c*, *d*, and *e*). These real GDP movements are characteristic of the business cycle movements in real GDP.

Figure 7.2 (b) Solution

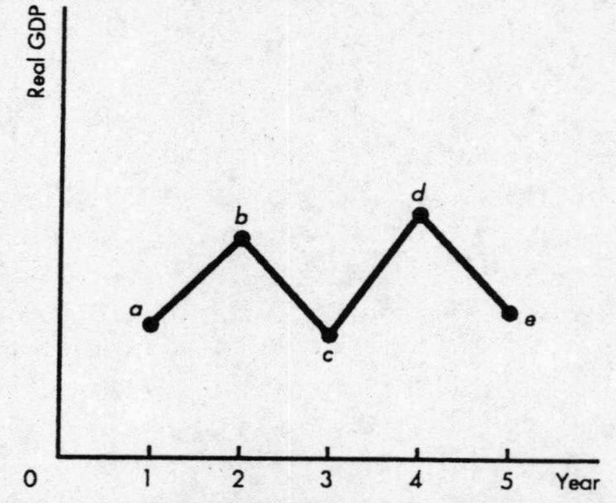

8 EXPENDITURE DECISIONS AND GDP

CHAPTER IN PERSPECTIVE

The major goal of our study of macroeconomics is to be able to explain the behavior of the aggregate economy: inflation, unemployment, business cycle fluctuations. In Chapter 7 we saw that the aggregate demand/aggregate supply model promises to be very useful in explaining these macroeconomic events. In order to effectively use the model, however, it is important to understand the factors that influence aggregate demand and aggregate supply. This chapter, as well as the following four chapters, takes a deeper look at aggregate demand.

Here we begin by carefully investigating consumption expenditure, investment, government purchases of goods and services, and net exports, the four components of aggregate expenditure. We examine the factors that affect the behavior of each of them. With our enhanced understanding, these components are brought together in this chapter and in Chapter 9 to help us explain how the levels of aggregate expenditure and GDP are determined.

LEARNING OBJECTIVES

After studying this chapter, you will be able to:

- **Describe the relative magnitudes of the components of aggregate expenditure and their relative volatility**
- **Explain how households make consumption and saving decisions**
- **Explain how firms make investment decisions**
- **Explain what determines exports, imports, and net exports**
- **Derive the aggregate expenditure schedule and aggregate expenditure curve**
- **Explain how aggregate expenditure is determined**

HELPFUL HINTS

1. Aggregate demand is the relationship between the price level and the quantity of goods and services demanded; that is, the relationship between the price level and the level of planned aggregate expenditure. The purpose of this chapter is to help us better understand the behavior of planned aggregate expenditure by separating it into its individual components and examining each of them in isolation. The behavior of consumption expenditure, investment, government purchases of goods and services, and net exports—the four components of aggregate expenditure—will be examined. As you put the discussion of this chapter in perspective, remember that the ultimate objective is a more complete understanding of aggregate demand.

2. Intuitive explanations for the behavior of consumption are at the level of the individual household: the *household* consumption function is the relationship between household consumption expenditure and household *disposable income*. Our ultimate objective, however, is to examine the behavior of *aggregate* consumption expenditure as a component of the *aggregate* demand for *real GDP*. This is why the *aggregate* consumption function is defined as the relationship between aggregate real consumption expenditure and *real GDP*.

At the level of the household, the critical behavioral concept is the marginal propensity to consume (out of disposable income). At the aggregate level, however, this must be converted to the marginal propensity to consume out of real GDP. The marginal propensity to consume out of real GDP is computed as the change in consumption divided by the associated change in real GDP. This is equal to the marginal propensity to consume (out of disposable income) times the change in disposable income divided by the change in real GDP:

$$\textit{MPC out of real GDP} = \frac{\Delta C}{\Delta Y} = \frac{\Delta C}{\Delta YD} \times \frac{\Delta YD}{\Delta Y}$$

where we note that $\Delta C/\Delta YD$ is the marginal propensity to consume (out of disposable income) and Y is real GDP. In order to find $\Delta YD/\Delta Y$ we must examine the relationship between real GDP and disposable income.

An increase in real GDP will have two effects on disposable income. The first is a direct effect: Disposable income increases by the full amount of the increase in real GDP since an increase in real GDP is an increase in income. The second effect is an indirect effect: Since net taxes increase when real GDP increases, disposable income will decrease by an amount equal to the part of the increase in real GDP that goes to net taxes. These two effects together give the net effect of an increase in real GDP on disposable income. If the proportion of an increase in real GDP that goes to net taxes is given by t, the effect of an increase in real GDP on disposable income is $(1-t)$ times the change in real GDP. For example, if 25 percent of an increase in real GDP goes to net taxes (i.e., $t = .25$), then the increase in disposable income will be 75 percent $(1-t)$ of the increase in real GDP.

This roundabout process implies that the marginal propensity to consume out of real GDP is equal to the marginal propensity to consume (out of disposable income) times $(1-t)$ where t is the proportion of an increase in real GDP which goes to net taxes.

3. The aggregate consumption function (which follows from the household consumption function) is a key relationship in our understanding of the behavior of aggregate demand and thus macroeconomic behavior. Spending the time necessary to thoroughly understand the behavior of consumption expenditure in isolation (as discussed in this chapter) will be important in the next chapter where the separate expenditure components are brought together and interaction among them is examined.

4. Investment depends on the real interest rate as well as future profit expectations. For given profit expectations, investment will increase as the real interest rate declines. The real interest rate is defined as the observed interest rate minus the expected inflation rate. Thus, changes in the observed interest rate or the expected inflation rate will affect investment through their effects on the real interest rate. An increase in the observed interest rate will (other things constant) lead to a decline in investment because the real interest rate has increased. An increase in the expected inflation rate, however, will (other things constant) lead to an increase in investment because the real rate has decreased.

5. Exports are not affected by changes in domestic real GDP, whereas imports increase as domestic real GDP increases. Since net exports are defined as exports minus imports, an increase in domestic real GDP (other things held constant) will cause net exports to decrease.

6. *Planned* expenditure is the desired level of expenditure, given the level of real GDP. However, this can differ from *actual* expenditure if firms' sales turn out to be unexpectedly high or low. If *planned* expenditure is not equal to *actual* expenditure, the economy will not be in equilibrium, firms will alter their behavior, and this will alter the level of real GDP. This process is a crucial part of the equilibrium process.

KEY FIGURES AND TABLES

Figure 8.3 The Polonius Household's Consumption Function and Saving Function

The household consumption function is the relationship between household consumption expenditure and household disposable income. Other things constant, as disposable income increases, consumption expenditure increases.

This relationship is represented graphically in part (a) of this figure. The 45° line, the line of equality, is a reference line which simply translates values measured on the horizontal axis to the vertical axis. Thus, in this figure, its height is always equal to disposable income. When the consumption function crosses the 45° line, consumption expenditure equals disposable income, which means that saving is zero. When the consumption function lies above the 45° line, saving is negative, and when the consumption function lies below the 45° line, saving is positive.

Part (b) of the figure illustrates the implied saving function: Saving is negative at low levels of disposable income but increases as disposable income increases and eventually becomes positive.

Figure 8.4 The U.S. Consumption Function

The two parts of this figure illustrate the historical relationship between consumption expenditure and two measures of income for the U.S. economy as a whole.

Part (a) plots the associated values of real disposable income and consumption in the U.S. for each year from 1970 through 1991. Note two things. First, as disposable income increases, consumption expenditure increases. Second, the points lie very close to a straight line with slope equal to 0.9. This means that the U.S. consumption function exhibits a marginal propensity to consume of 0.9.

For purposes of macroeconomic analysis, it is useful to consider consumption as a function of real GDP rather than real disposable income. This relationship for the U.S. is illustrated in part (b). It plots the associated values of real GDP and consumption expenditure in the U.S. for each year from 1970 through 1991. Note that it is positively sloped and that the marginal propensity to consume out of real GDP is about .63. This value can be reconciled with the value of the marginal propensity to consume (out of disposable income) obtained from part (a) when we recognize that about 30 percent of an increase in real GDP goes to net taxes. This means that 70 percent of the increase in real GDP will be an increase in disposable income.

Figure 8.6 Investment Demand Curves and Investment Demand Schedules

Investment demand is the relationship between investment and the real interest rate, holding other things constant. This figure illustrates that relationship in two ways: investment demand schedules and the corresponding investment demand curves. Each of these shows that, holding future profit expectations constant, investment increases as the real interest rate declines.

Furthermore, the investment demand schedules and part (b) of the figure also illustrate that, for any given real interest rate, planned investment increases as future profit expectations become more optimistic. This is represented by shifts in the investment demand curve; the curve shifts to the right as optimism increases.

Figure 8.10 Aggregate Expenditure Curve and Aggregate Expenditure Schedule

This figure illustrates the relationship between aggregate planned expenditure and real GDP in two ways: the aggregate expenditure curve and the aggregate expenditure schedule. As illustrated here, the aggregate expenditure curve is obtained as the vertical sum of each of the separate expenditure component curves. It is investment plus government purchases of goods and services plus consumption expenditure plus net exports; that is, $AE = I + G + C + EX - IM$. While only some of the expenditure components vary as real GDP varies, their sum increases as real GDP increases.

Figure 8.11 Equilibrium Expenditure and Real GDP

Equilibrium expenditure occurs when planned aggregate expenditure equals real GDP. Planned expenditure is represented graphically by the *AE* curve. The 45° line shows all points at which aggregate expenditure (measured on the vertical axis) is equal to real GDP (measured on the horizontal axis). Thus, equilibrium occurs when the *AE* curve intersects the 45° line in part (a) of the figure: at $4 trillion. This corresponds to row *d* in the table.

At levels of real GDP below $4 trillion, aggregate planned expenditure exceeds real GDP so inventories will fall. This unplanned fall in inventories is illustrated in part (b)—at point *b*. Firms will increase production to restore their inventories and real GDP rises until equilibrium is achieved.

Similarly, at levels of real GDP above $4 trillion, aggregate planned expenditure is less than real GDP so inventories will rise. Such an unplanned rise in inventories is also illustrated in part (b) – at point *f*. Firms will decrease production to reduce their inventories and real GDP falls until equilibrium is achieved.

Table 8.1 Average and Marginal Propensities to Consume and to Save

The average propensity to consume (*APC*) is defined as the ratio of consumption expenditure to disposable income. The average propensity to save (*APS*) is defined similarly: the ratio of saving to disposable income.

Part (a) of this table illustrates the computation of the *APC* and *APS* for a hypothetical relationship between disposable income and consumption expenditure. Note that, since disposable income can only be used for consumption expenditure or to add to savings, $APC + APS = 1$. Note also that, as disposable income increases, the *APC* decreases and the *APS* increases.

The marginal propensity to consume (*MPC*) is the proportion of an increase in disposable income that is spent on (consumption) goods and services and the marginal propensity to save (*MPS*) is the proportion of an increase in disposable income that is saved.

Part (b) of the table illustrates the computation of the *MPC* and *MPS*. Since an increase in disposable income must be either spent or saved, $MPC + MPS = 1$. Note that the *MPC* (and therefore the *MPS*) is constant.

SELF-TEST

CONCEPT REVIEW

1. The relationship between consumption expenditure and disposable income is called the ____________ ____________. The relationship between saving and disposable income is called the ____________ ____________. Negative saving is called ____________.
2. As disposable income increases, consumption expenditure ____________ and saving ____________.
3. The ratio of consumption expenditure to disposable income is called the ____________ ____________ ____________ ____________. The ratio of saving to disposable income is called the ____________ ____________ to save.
4. The fraction of the last dollar of disposable income that is spent on consumption goods and services is called the ____________ ____________ ____________ ____________.
5. As the real interest rate rises, planned investment expenditures ____________. The curve showing the relationship between the real interest rate and the level of planned investment (holding other things constant) is called the ____________ ____________ curve.
6. As the level of real GDP in the rest of the world increases, U.S., exports will ____________. As the level of real GDP in the U.S. increases, U.S. imports will ____________. As the foreign exchange value of the dollar rises, U.S. exports will ____________ and U.S. imports will ____________.
7. The relationship between net exports and U.S. real GDP (holding constant real GDP in the rest of the world, prices, and exchange rates) is called the ____________ ____________ ____________. As U.S. real GDP increases, net exports will ____________.
8. The graph of the relationship between the level of aggregate planned expenditure and the level of real GDP is called the ____________ ____________ curve. As real GDP increases, aggregate planned expenditure ____________.
9. ____________ expenditure occurs when planned expenditure is equal to real GDP. If planned expenditure exceeds real GDP, inventories ____________.

TRUE OR FALSE

____ 1. The largest component of aggregate expenditure in the U.S. is net exports.

____ 2. The higher a household's expected future income, the greater is its consumption expenditure today.

____ 3. As a household's disposable income increases, so does the amount it plans to save.

____ 4. If the average propensity to consume is 0.75, then the average propensity to save must be 0.25.

____ 5. If a household spends $.80 and saves $.20 out of the last dollar of disposable income, its marginal propensity to consume is 0.8.

____ 6. The sum of the marginal propensity to consume and the marginal propensity to save is equal to 1.

____ 7. The average propensity to consume is equal to the slope of the consumption function.

____ 8. While economic theory suggests that consumption expenditure increases as disposable income increases, this does not turn out to be true for the U.S.

____ 9. A change in expected future income will shift the consumption function.

____10. A change in disposable income will shift the consumption function.

____11. Net taxes increase as GDP increases.

____12. In the graph of the aggregate consumption function, the gap between the 45° line and the aggregate consumption function is equal to the sum of saving and net taxes.

____13. Investment is less volatile than consumption expenditure.

____14. The higher the real rate of interest, the greater is the amount of investment.

____15. Net investment is gross investment minus replacement investment.

____16. An increase in expected profit will shift the investment demand curve to the left.

____17. If the level of GDP in the rest of the world declines but GDP remains unchanged in the U.S., we would expect U.S. net exports to decline.

____18. If the level of GDP in the rest of the world declines but GDP remains unchanged in the U.S., we would expect the graph of the net export function to shift.

____19. Increases in the degree of specialization in the world economy imply that both imports and exports will increase.

____20. The aggregate expenditure schedule lists the level of aggregate planned expenditure that is generated at each level of real GDP.

____21. When aggregate planned expenditure exceeds real GDP, inventories will rise more than planned.

____22. Equilibrium expenditure occurs when aggregate planned expenditure equals real GDP.

MULTIPLE CHOICE

1. Which is the largest component of aggregate expenditure?
   a. Consumption expenditure
   b. Investment
   c. Government purchases of goods and services
   d. Net exports

2. Which of the following would cause a household to increase the amount it saves?
   a. A decrease in current disposable income
   b. An increase in expected future income
   c. A decrease in patience
   d. An increase in current disposable income.

3. The consumption function shows the relationship between consumption expenditure and
   a. the interest rate.
   b. the price level.
   c. disposable income.
   d. saving.

4. Consider a household with annual disposable income of $20,000. If the household makes consumption expenditures of $17,000, then its
   a. marginal propensity to consume is 0.7.
   b. marginal propensity to consume is 0.85.
   c. average propensity to consume is 0.7.
   d. average propensity to consume is 0.85.

5. The fraction of the last dollar of disposable income saved is called the
   a. marginal propensity to consume.
   b. marginal propensity to save.
   c. average propensity to save.
   d. marginal tax rate.

6. Which of the following statements is true regarding the relationship among the average propensity to consume (*APC*), the average propensity to save (*APS*), the marginal propensity to consume (*MPC*), and the marginal propensity to save (*MPS*).
   a. If the *MPC* increases, then the *MPS* must also increase.
   b. $MPC + APC = 1$.
   c. $MPC + MPS = APC + APS$.
   d. $MPC + MPS > APC + APS$.

7. The slope of the consumption function is equal to the
   a. *APC*.
   b. *APS*.
   c. *MPC*.
   d. *MPS*.

8. Which of the following would shift the consumption function upward?
   a. An increase in current disposable income
   b. An increase in expected future income
   c. A decrease in current disposable income
   d. A decrease in expected future income

9. If net taxes are one fourth (1/4) of real GDP and the marginal propensity to consume out of disposable income is .8, then the marginal propensity to consume out of real GDP is
   a. 0.2.
   b. 0.4.
   c. 0.6.
   d. 0.8.

10. Which of the following would lead to an increase in the amount of investment?
    a. A decrease in real interest rates
    b. A decrease in the utilization of capital
    c. A decrease in expected future profit
    d. A decrease in the amount of depreciation

11. If the inflation rate increases by 5 percent and the nominal interest rate increases by 3 percent, then the real interest rate
    a. decreases by 2 percent.
    b. increases by 2 percent.
    c. decreases by 8 percent.
    d. increases by 8 percent.

12. The investment demand curve shows the relationship between the level of planned investment and
    a. disposable income.
    b. real GDP.
    c. expected future profit.
    d. the real interest rate.

13. Which of the following would increase the demand for U.S. exports?
    a. A decrease in the degree of international specialization
    b. An increase in U.S. real GDP
    c. An increase in the level of GDP in the rest of the world
    d. An increase in the foreign exchange value of the dollar

14. Which of the following would increase U.S. imports from the rest of the world?
    a. A decrease in the degree of international specialization
    b. A decrease in U.S. real GDP
    c. An increase in the level of GDP in the rest of the world
    d. An increase in the foreign exchange value of the dollar

15. The net export function for the U.S. shows the relationship between net exports and
    a. the level of GDP in the rest of the world.
    b. the level of U.S. real GDP.
    c. the foreign exchange rate.
    d. disposable income.

16. Which of the following will shift the net export function upward?
    a. An increase in the foreign exchange value of the dollar
    b. An increase in the level of U.S. real GDP
    c. An increase in the level of GDP in the rest of the world
    d. An increase in interest rates

17. The aggregate expenditure curve shows the relationship between aggregate planned expenditure and
    a. disposable income.
    b. real GDP.
    c. the interest rate.
    d. consumption expenditure.

18. If unplanned inventories rise, aggregate planned expenditure is
    a. greater than real GDP, and firms will increase output.
    b. greater than real GDP, and firms will decrease output.
    c. less than real GDP, and firms will increase output.
    d. less than real GDP, and firms will decrease output.

19. If real GDP is less than aggregate planned expenditure, then
    a. aggregate planned expenditure will decrease.
    b. real GDP will increase.
    c. the price level must fall to restore equilibrium.
    d. imports must be too large.

SHORT ANSWER

1. What are the four components of aggregate expenditure?

2. What is meant by the average propensity to consume.

3. What is meant by the marginal propensity to save.

4. Explain why the marginal propensity to consume (*MPC*) and the marginal propensity to save (*MPS*) must sum to 1.

5. Explain why a lower real interest rate leads to a larger amount of investment.

6. Explain the effect on U.S. net exports of an increase in the foreign exchange value of the dollar.

7. Explain the effect of an increase in Canada's real GDP on U.S. net exports.

8. Suppose aggregate planned expenditure is greater than real GDP. Explain the process by which equilibrium expenditure is achieved.

PROBLEMS

1. Figure 8.1 illustrates the consumption function for a household. Compute the following when disposable income is $20,000:
   a) the *APC* and *APS*.
   b) *MPC* and *MPS*.
   c) level of saving.

2. From the information given by Fig. 8.1, draw a graph of the saving function for the household.

3. Consider an economy of 1 million identical households, each of which has a consumption function as illustrated in Fig. 8.1. Suppose further that net taxes are one third of real GDP.
   a) What is the marginal propensity to consume out of real GDP?
   b) Draw the graph of consumption as a function of real GDP for this economy.

Figure 8.1

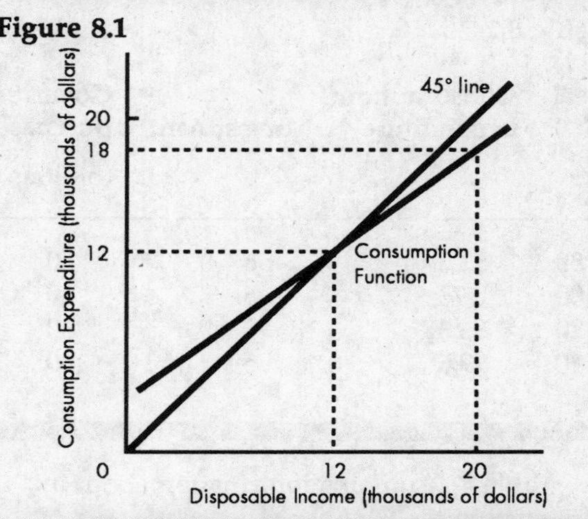

4. Table 8.1 gives the rates of return for 4 individual investment projects under consideration by a firm. Project A might be building a new factory and project B might be buying a new machine, etc. For the sake of simplicity, suppose that each project costs $1 million. What will be the amount of investment by this firm if the real interest rate is
   a) 13 percent?
   b) 10 percent?
   c) 7 percent?
   d) 3 percent?

Table 8.1 Investment Projects

Project	Real rate of return (percent)
A	4
B	12
C	8
D	6

Table 8.2

Real GDP	Consumption expenditure	Investment	Government purchase	Exports	Imports	Net exports	Aggregate expenditure
			(billions of 1987 dollars)				
80	51.2	5	30	15	11.2		
100	74	5	30	15	14		
120	86.8	5	30	15	16.8		
140	99.6	5	30	15	19.6		

5. Table 8.2 contains information about an economy.
   a) Complete the table by calculating net exports and aggregate expenditure.
   b) What is equilibrium expenditure?

ANSWERS

Concept Review

1. consumption function; saving function; dissaving
2. increases; increases
3. average propensity to consume; average propensity
4. marginal propensity to consume
5. fall; investment demand
6. increase; increase; decrease; increase
7. net export function; decrease
8. aggregate expenditure; increases
9. Equilibrium; fall

True or False

1. F	6. T	11. T	16. F	21. F
2. T	7. F	12. T	17. T	22. T
3. T	8. F	13. F	18. T	
4. T	9. T	14. F	19. T	
5. T	10. F	15. T	20. T	

Multiple Choice

1. a	5. b	9. c	13. c	17. b
2. d	6. c	10. a	14. d	18. d
3. c	7. c	11. a	15. b	19. b
4. d	8. b	12. d	16. c	

Short Answer

1. The four components of aggregate expenditure are consumption expenditure, investment, government purchases of goods and services, and net exports.

2. The average propensity to consume is the ratio of consumption expenditure to disposable income.

3. The marginal propensity to save tells us how much saving changes when disposable income changes. The marginal propensity to save is the proportion of an

increase in disposable income that is added to saving. It is computed as the change in saving divided by the change in disposable income.

4. The *MPC* gives the proportion of an increase in disposable income that is allocated to consumption spending, and the *MPS* gives the proportion that is allocated to saving. There are only two things that a household can do with any increase in disposable income: it can either spend or not spend. The portion that is spent is called consumption expenditure and the portion that is not spent (i. e., the rest) is defined as saving. Thus, the proportion of any increase in disposable income that is allocated *either* to consumption expenditure or to saving (*MPC* + *MPS*) is 1.

5. Investment projects are costly but generate a stream of revenues for the firm. A firm will undertake an investment project if it adds to profit; that is, if it adds more to revenue than it does to cost. Since the real interest rate is a part of the cost of any investment project, as the real interest rate falls, cost falls, more investment projects become profitable and thus investment increases.

6. An increase in the foreign exchange value of the dollar means that the amount of foreign currency required to buy a dollar has increased. This is the same as saying that it now requires fewer dollars to buy any given amount of foreign currency. Since U.S. goods are sold for dollars, it will now cost foreigners more to obtain the same number of dollars and so U.S. goods are now more expensive to foreigners. As a result, U.S. exports will decrease. Since foreign goods are sold for foreign currency, it will now cost U.S. citizens fewer dollars to acquire the foreign currency necessary to buy foreign goods. Thus, foreign goods have become less expensive in terms of dollars and U.S. imports will increase. The decline in exports and the increase in imports means that net exports will decline.

7. An increase in Canadian real GDP will lead to an increase in Canadian imports. Since much of Canada's imports come from the U.S., those U.S. exports are likely to rise and thus net exports will increase.

8. If aggregate planned expenditure is greater than real GDP, inventories will fall more than planned and firms will increase output to replenish those depleted inventories. As a result, real GDP increases. This procedure will continue as long as real GDP is less than aggregate planned expenditure. Thus it will stop only when equilibrium is attained; that is, when real GDP is equal to aggregate planned expenditure.

PROBLEMS

1. a) From Fig. 8.1, we see that when disposable income is $20,000, consumption expenditure is $18,000. The *APC* is the ratio of consumption expenditure to disposable income:

$$APC = (18{,}000/20{,}000) = .9$$

The *APS* is 1 - *APC*:

$$APS = 1 - .9 = .1$$

b) The *MPC* is the slope of the consumption function, 0.75. The *MPS* is 1 - *MPC*:

$$MPS = 1 - .75 = .25$$

c) Saving is equal to disposable income minus consumption expenditure:

Saving = \$20,000 - \$18,000 = \$2,000

2. The saving function is illustrated in Fig. 8.2. This function can be derived from Fig. 8.1 in several ways. We can draw the saving function by noting that saving is 0 when disposable income is \$12,000 and that the slope of the saving function, the *MPS*, is 0.25. Alternatively, we can construct the saving function by finding two points on it and drawing a line through them. One possible point has already been mentioned: the point corresponding to disposable income = \$12,000 and saving = 0 (point *a* in Fig. 8.2). From Problem 1 (c) we have a second point: disposable income = \$20,000, saving = \$2,000 (point *b* in Fig. 8.2).

Figure 8.2

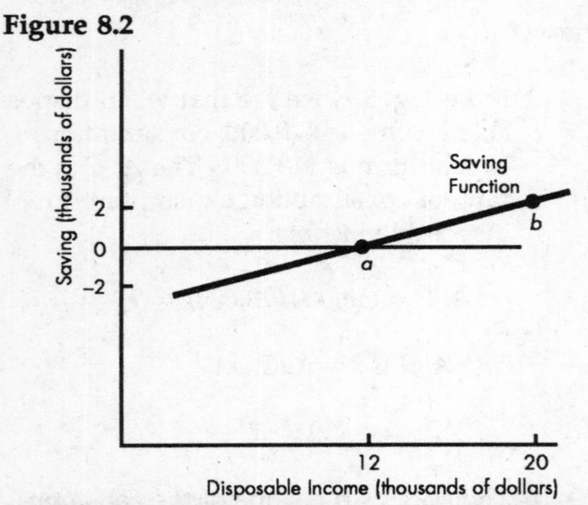

3. a) As indicated in the answer to Problem 1 (b), the marginal propensity to consume *out of disposable income* is 0.75 or 3/4. Since net taxes are 1/3 of real GDP, disposable income is 2/3 of real GDP (since disposable income = real GDP - net taxes). This implies that the marginal propensity to consume *out of real GDP* is 2/3 of 3/4 or 1/2.

b) The graph of consumption as a function of real GDP is illustrated in Fig. 8.3. This function can be derived either by finding a point on the line and using the slope of the line or by finding two points on the line. From part (a) we know that the slope of the aggregate consumption function is 1/2 (.5). We can find points on the aggregate consumption function corresponding to points on the individual household consumption functions using the following process. For example, if each of the 1 million households has a disposable income of \$20,000, each will undertake \$18,000 in consumption expenditure. Since the households are all identical, this means that when aggregate disposable income is \$20 billion, aggregate consumption expenditure is \$18 billion. Since aggregate disposable income is 2/3 of real GDP, when aggregate disposable income is \$20 billion, real GDP is \$30 billion. Thus, when real GDP is \$30 billion, aggregate consumption expenditure is \$18 billion. This gives point *a* in Fig. 8.3. Other points can be derived in similar fashion.

Figure 8.3

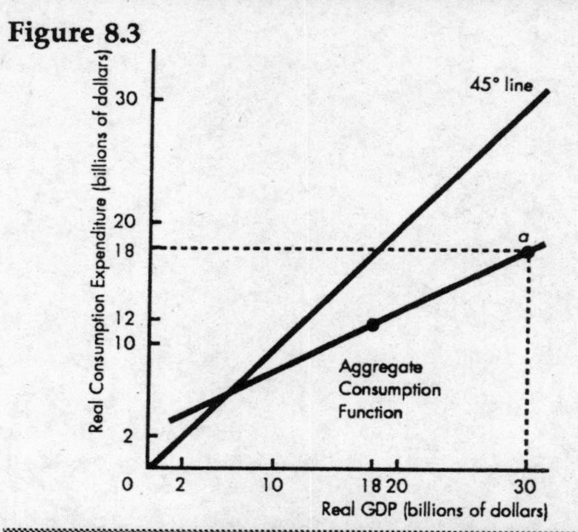

4. A project will add to the firm's profit if its real rate of return is greater than the real interest rate. Thus, the firm will undertake each project for which the real rate of return exceeds the real interest rate.

a) If the real interest rate is 13 percent, investment by the firm will be 0 since none of the projects have a real rate of return which exceeds 13 percent.
b) If the real interest rate is 10 percent, investment by the firm will be $1 million since project B is profitable.
c) If the real interest rate is 7 percent, investment by the firm will be $2 million since both projects B and C are profitable at that lower real interest rate.
d) If the real interest rate is 3 percent, investment by the firm will be $4 million since the real interest rate is now low enough that all 4 investment projects are profitable.

5. a) Table 8.2 is completed as Table 8.2 Solution below.
b) Equilibrium expenditure occurs when aggregate planned expenditure equals real GDP. As can be seen from Table 8.2 Solution, this occurs at $120 billion.

Table 8.2 Solution

Real GDP	Consumption expenditure	Investment	Government purchase	Exports	Imports	Net exports	Aggregate expenditure
			(Billions of 1987 dollars)				
80	51.2	5	30	15	11.2	3.8	90
100	74	5	30	15	14	1	110
120	86.8	5	30	15	16.8	-1.8	120
140	99.6	5	30	15	19.6	-4.6	130

9 EXPENDITURE FLUCTUATIONS AND FISCAL POLICY

CHAPTER IN PERSPECTIVE

The fundamental tool for macroeconomic analysis is the aggregate demand/aggregate supply model. This chapter further deepens our understanding of aggregate demand. In the previous chapter we examined the components of aggregate expenditure separately and then combined them and defined equilibrium expenditure. Here we examine the interactions among these expenditures in order to investigate the determination of aggregate expenditure, and thus, of aggregate demand.

Aggregate demand is defined as the relationship between the price level and aggregate expenditure. But, for any given price level, how is aggregate expenditure determined? Furthermore, a shift in the *AD* curve, represents a change in aggregate expenditure for each price level. But, by how much will aggregate expenditure change? The purpose of this chapter is to answer these questions.

LEARNING OBJECTIVES

After studying this chapter, you will be able to:

- **Explain why changes in investment and exports change consumption expenditure and have multiplier effects on aggregate expenditure**
- **Define and calculate the multiplier**
- **Explain why changes in government purchases of goods and services have multiplier effects on aggregate expenditure**
- **Explain why changes in taxes and transfer payments have multiplier effects on aggregate expenditure**
- **Explain how the government may use fiscal policy in an attempt to stabilize aggregate expenditure**
- **Explain the relationship between aggregate expenditure and aggregate demand**

HELPFUL HINTS

1. This chapter distinguishes between *autonomous* expenditure and *induced* expenditure. The difference is that autonomous expenditure is independent of changes in real GDP, while induced expenditure will vary as real GDP varies. It is important to realize, however, that even though autonomous expenditure may be independent of changes in real GDP, it will *not* be independent of changes in other variables (e.g., the price level).

2. The slope of the aggregate expenditure (*AE*) curve plays a very important role in this chapter since it determines the size of the multiplier. Thus, it is important to understand the factors that determine this slope, denoted as *g*.

The slope of the *AE* curve tells us the amount by which aggregate spending on domestic goods and services increases when there is a one-dollar increase in real GDP. Only consumption and imports have induced components. The marginal propensity to consume out of real GDP gives the increase in consumption expenditure resulting from a one-dollar increase in real GDP while the marginal propensity to import gives the increase in spending on imports resulting from a one-dollar increase in real GDP. Furthermore, any increase in imports must be subtracted from the increase in consumption expenditure since we only measure expenditure on *domestic* goods and services. Thus, we see that the slope of the AE curve is equal to the marginal propensity to consume out of real GDP minus the marginal propensity to import.

Sometimes we are not given the marginal propensity to consume out of real GDP but are given the marginal propensity to consume out of disposable income and the (constant) marginal tax rate. In such a case, we can determine the marginal propensity to consume out of real GDP by noting that an increase in real GDP will increase disposable income by (1-*t*) times the change in real GDP, where *t* is the marginal tax rate. Thus the marginal propensity to consume out of real GDP is given by the product of the marginal propensity to consume out of disposable income times (1-*t*). Problem 1 b) below is a useful exercise to check your understanding.

3. The multiplier is a very important concept. It results from the fact that the various components of aggregate expenditure interact with one another.

In particular, an initial increase in autonomous expenditure will increase real GDP directly, but that is not the end of the story. That initial increase in real GDP will generate an increase in *induced* expenditure, which further increases real GDP, and thus induces further increases in expenditure. The total effect on real GDP will be larger than the initial increase in autonomous expenditure because of the fact that there is induced expenditure, that is, because the marginal propensity to spend is greater than zero. You should become thoroughly familiar with both the intuition and the arithmetic behind the multiplier.

4. The purpose of investigating the determination of aggregate expenditure is to deepen our understanding of aggregate demand. The *AE* curve answers the question: for a given price level, how is equilibrium aggregate expenditure determined? Aggregate demand relates the resulting levels of real GDP to an array of values of the price level. Note that it is crucial to be able to distinguish between movements along the *AE* curve (resulting from changes in the price level) from shifts in the *AD* curve (resulting from changes in autonomous expenditure not related to the price level).

KEY FIGURES AND TABLES

Figure 9.1 Aggregate Expenditure

Part (a) of this figure illustrates the components of aggregate expenditure. Some of these components remain constant as real GDP increases. The sum of all such expenditure components is planned autonomous expenditure. It consists of investment, government purchases of goods and services, exports, and the autonomous component of consumption expenditure. In this figure, autonomous expenditure is $2 trillion, which does not change as real GDP changes.

Those components of aggregate expenditure which do vary as real GDP varies make up induced expenditure. Induced expenditure is the induced part of consumption minus the induced part of imports.

As illustrated in part (b) on the figure, aggregate expenditure is the sum of autonomous expenditure (represented by a blue arrow) and induced expenditure (represented by an orange arrow).

Figure 9.2 An Increase in Autonomous Expenditure

This figure illustrates the effects of an increase in autonomous expenditure. An increase in autonomous expenditure shifts the aggregate expenditure (*AE*) curve up by the amount of the increase. This leads to an increase in equilibrium expenditure that is larger than the initial increase in autonomous expenditure.

In this example, the $0.5 trillion increase in autonomous expenditure shifts the *AE* curve from AE_0 to AE_1. The new equilibrium occurs at the intersection of the new *AE* curve (AE_1) and the 45° line. Equilibrium expenditure increases by $1 trillion from $4 trillion to $5 trillion. Since an increase in autonomous expenditure of $0.5 trillion will result in a $1 trillion increase in equilibrium expenditure, the multiplier is 2.

Figure 9.3 The Multiplier and the Slope of the *AE* Curve

This figure illustrates graphically the relationship between the multiplier and the slope of the *AE* curve. Parts (a) and (b) present *AE* curves with two alternative slopes: 1/2 and 2/3 respectively. In each of the two parts of the figure, the initial increase in autonomous aggregate expenditure is the same: $1 trillion. This causes the *AE* curve in each case to shift up by $1 trillion. As is demonstrated clearly in the figure, as the slope of the *AE* curve increases from 1/2 to 2/3, the multiplier increases from 2 to 3.

Figure 9.5 The Tax Multiplier

A change in taxes will lead to a change in equilibrium expenditure in the opposite direction. The magnitude of the change in equilibrium expenditure is given by the tax multiplier. Since the change in equilibrium expenditure is in the direction opposite the change in taxes, the tax multiplier will be negative.

This figure illustrates the tax multiplier by considering the effect of a $1 trillion tax increase in an economy in which the marginal propensity to consume is 0.9 and the slope of the aggregate expenditure curve is 0.5. A tax increase of $1 trillion decreases disposable income by $1 trillion for any given level of real GDP. Since the marginal propensity to consume is 0.9, consumption will initially fall by $0.9 trillion. This is reflected by the shift in the *AE* curve from AE_0 to AE_1. The new equilibrium expenditure is $2.2 trillion, a decrease of $1.8 trillion. Thus, the tax multiplier is -1.8.

Figure 9.6 The Balanced Budget Multiplier

If an increase in government purchases of goods and services is financed by an equal increase in taxes, the effect on equilibrium expenditure is given by the balanced budget multiplier. Since this fiscal policy action combines an increase in government purchases with an equal increase in taxes, the balanced budget multiplier is the sum of the government purchases multiplier and the tax multiplier.

In the example illustrated in this figure, government purchases and taxes both increase by $1 trillion. As in Fig. 9.5, the effect of the tax increase is to shift the *AE* curve down by $0.9 trillion, from AE_0 to AE_0'. The effect of the increase in government purchases is to shift the *AE* curve up by $1 trillion, from AE_0' to AE_1. The net effect is an upward shift of the *AE* curve of $0.1 trillion. Equilibrium expenditure increases by $0.2 trillion which implies that the balanced budget multiplier in this example is 0.2.

Figure 9.8 Aggregate Expenditure and Aggregate Demand

As the price level changes, the *AE* curve shifts which results in a change in equilibrium expenditure. This is shown in part (a) of this figure. The resulting relationship between the price level and equilibrium expenditure (the quantity of real GDP demanded) is given by the aggregate demand curve as illustrated in part (b).

Part (a) shows three different *AE* curves associated with three different values of the price level. Each of these yields a different level of equilibrium expenditure. Since higher price levels are associated with lower aggregate planned expenditure and, thus, lower *AE* curves, higher price levels are associated with lower levels of real GDP demanded. This is illustrated by the negative slope of the *AD* curve in part (b).

Figure 9.9 Changes in Autonomous Expenditure and Aggregate Demand

As illustrated in this figure, a change in autonomous expenditure, *holding the price level constant,* will shift the aggregate demand curve. In the example shown here, we observe the effect of a $1 trillion increase in autonomous expenditure given a constant price level of 100.

Part (a) shows the effect on the *AE* curve: a $1 trillion upward shift from AE_0 to AE_1. This gives a new equilibrium (point *c'*) at a real GDP of $6 trillion. This means that the quantity of real GDP demanded at a price level of 100 has increased from $4 trillion to $6 trillion. As shown in part (b), this is represented by a shift in the *AD* curve to the right, from AD_0 to AD_1.

Figure 9.10 Fiscal Policy, Real GDP, and the Price Level

This figure puts the aggregate demand curve together with the short-run aggregate supply (*SAS*) curve and examines the effects of an expansionary fiscal policy (a tax cut). Part (a) keeps track of the *AE* curve and part (b) shows the effect on the *AD* curve and on equilibrium GDP and the price level.

The economy starts out at point *b* in both parts. The tax cut shifts the *AE* curve upward, from AE_0 to AE_1 and the *AD* curve to the right, from AD_0 to AD_1. At the initial price level of 100, the quantity of real GDP demanded exceeds the quantity of real GDP supplied and so the price level will rise to 125. As the price level rises, the *AE* curve shifts downward, from AE_1 to AE_2 and the economy moves to point *d* in both parts of the figure. The net effect of the tax cut is to increase both real GDP and the price level.

Table 9.1 Calculating the Multiplier

This table defines some convenient notation and then demonstrates the derivation of the formula for computing the autonomous expenditure multiplier. Using a straightforward step-by-step procedure, part (b) derives the familiar expression for the ratio of the change in equilibrium GDP to the initial change in autonomous expenditure.

SELF-TEST

CONCEPT REVIEW

1. The components of aggregate expenditure can be classified into two broad groups. The first of these, ____________ expenditure, is the sum of those components of aggregate planned expenditure that are not influenced by real GDP. The other, ____________ expenditure, is the sum of those components of aggregate planned expenditure that do vary as real GDP varies.
2. The slope of the *AE* curve is equal to the marginal propensity to consume out of ____________ ____________ minus the marginal propensity to ____________.
3. An increase in investment expenditure will shift the *AE* curve ____________.
4. The fraction of the last dollar of income paid to the government in taxes is called the ____________ ____________ rate. The higher its value, the ____________ is the slope of the *AE* curve.
5. If everyone increases saving but there is no associated increase in investment, real GDP will fall. This is called the ____________ of thrift.
6. The amount by which a change in autonomous expenditure must be multiplied to calculate the ensuing change in equilibrium real GDP is called the autonomous expenditure ____________. The larger is the value of the slope of the *AE* curve, the ____________ is its value.
7. A(n) ____________ ____________ is a mechanism that automatically decreases the fluctuations in aggregate expenditure resulting from fluctuations in its components.
8. An increase in the price level will cause the aggregate planned expenditure curve to shift ____________, which ____________ equilibrium expenditure and produces a ____________ ____________ the aggregate demand curve.
9. A(n) ____________ in government purchases will shift the *AD* curve to the right.

TRUE OR FALSE

___ 1. As real GDP increases, autonomous expenditure also increases.

___ 2. The slope of the aggregate expenditure curve is the marginal propensity to consume out of real GDP minus the marginal propensity to import.

___ 3. Anything that changes autonomous expenditure will shift the aggregate expenditure curve.

___ 4. An increase in autonomous expenditure of $1 billion will generate an increase in equilibrium expenditure of more than $1 billion.

____ 5. The higher the marginal propensity to import, the larger is the autonomous expenditure multiplier.

____ 6. The higher the marginal tax rate, the steeper is the aggregate expenditure curve.

____ 7. The multiplier is greater than 1 because an increase in autonomous expenditure leads to an induced increase in consumption expenditure.

____ 8. If a $2 billion increase in exports causes a $5 billion increase in equilibrium real GDP, the autonomous expenditure multiplier is 2.5.

____ 9. The steeper the aggregate expenditure curve, the lower is the multiplier.

____10. The tax multiplier is smaller than the autonomous expenditure multiplier.

____11. If the slope of the aggregate expenditure curve is .75, the autonomous expenditure multiplier is equal to 3.

____12. The transfer payment multiplier is larger than the government purchases multiplier.

____13. An increase in transfer payments matched by an increase in taxes will lead to an increase in real GDP equal to the size of the increase in transfer payments.

____14. Taxes and transfer payments that vary as income varies, act as automatic stabilizers in the economy.

____15. Multipliers tend to be small when the economy goes into recession and larger in recovery.

____16. An increase in the price level will shift the aggregate expenditure curve upward.

____17. An increase in the price level will shift the aggregate demand curve to the left.

____18. An increase in government expenditure will shift the aggregate expenditure curve upward and thus the aggregate demand curve to the right.

____19. An increase in taxes will shift the aggregate expenditure curve downward and thus the aggregate demand curve to the left.

____20. If the economy is at an unemployment equilibrium, an increase in aggregate demand will cause both the price level and real GDP to increase.

____21. If the economy is at an employment equilibrium, an increase in aggregate demand will cause both the price level and real GDP to increase.

MULTIPLE CHOICE

1. Autonomous expenditure is NOT influenced by
   a. the interest rate.
   b. the foreign exchange rate.
   c. real GDP.
   d. any other variable.

2. The fact that imports increase as real GDP increases implies that imports are a part of
   a. marginal expenditure.
   b. autonomous expenditure.
   c. induced expenditure.
   d. integrated expenditure.

3. The slope of the aggregate expenditure curve is equal to
   a. one minus the marginal propensity to save.
   b. one minus the marginal propensity to import.
   c. the marginal propensity to consume out of disposable income minus the marginal propensity to import.
   d. the marginal propensity to consume out of real GDP minus the marginal propensity to import.

4. An increase in autonomous expenditure will shift the *AE* curve
   a. up but leave its slope unchanged.
   b. up and make it steeper.
   c. down but leave its slope unchanged.
   d. down and make it steeper.

5. Which of the following will lead to a steeper *AE* curve?
   a. An increase in the marginal propensity to import
   b. An increase in the marginal tax rate
   c. A decrease in the marginal propensity to consume
   d. A decrease in the marginal propensity to save

6. A decrease in the marginal tax rate will
   a. make the *AE* curve flatter and increase the multiplier.
   b. make the *AE* curve flatter and decrease the multiplier.
   c. make the *AE* curve steeper and increase the multiplier.
   d. make the *AE* curve steeper and decrease the multiplier.

7. When *all* households in the economy decide to increase saving with no associated increase in investment, it turns out that real GDP decreases. This is known as the
   a. paradox of thrift.
   b. expenditure paradox.
   c. negative multiplier effect.
   d. autonomous saving effect.

8. If the slope of the *AE* curve is 0.75, what is the (autonomous expenditure) multiplier?
   a. 0.57
   b. 1.5
   c. 2.0
   d. 4.0

9. The government wants to increase aggregate expenditure by $12 billion. If the multiplier is 3, by how much should the government increase its spending on goods and services?
   a. $3 billion
   b. $4 billion
   c. $12 billion
   d. $36 billion

Fact 9.1

In the economy of Narnia, the marginal propensity to consume is 0.8, the marginal tax rate is 0.2, and the marginal propensity to import is 0.24.

10. Consider Fact 9.1. What is the slope of the aggregate expenditure curve in Narnia?
    a. 0.16
    b. 0.40
    c. 0.64
    d. 0.8

11. Consider Fact 9.1. What is the government purchases multiplier in Narnia?
    a. 5.0
    b. 2.78
    c. 1.67
    d. 1.33

12. Consider Fact 9.1. What is the transfer payment multiplier in Narnia?
    a. 5.0
    b. 2.78
    c. 1.67
    d. 1.33

13. The balanced budget multiplier is
    a. greater than the government purchases multiplier.
    b. greater than the transfer payment multiplier but less than the government purchases multiplier.
    c. greater than 1 but less than the transfer payment multiplier.
    d. less than 1.

14. Which of the following is an example of an automatic stabilizer? As real GDP increases,
    a. consumption expenditure increases.
    b. income taxes increase.
    c. spending on imports increases.
    d. investment spending in unaffected.

15. In recent years in the U.S., the multiplier has been
    a. falling due to a gradual increase in the marginal propensity to import.
    b. falling due to a gradual decrease in the marginal propensity to import.
    c. rising due to a gradual increase in the marginal propensity to import.
    d. rising due to a gradual decrease in the marginal propensity to import.

16. When an economy goes into recession, the multiplier tends to be
    a. large since the income changes are viewed to be temporary.
    b. large since the income changes are viewed to be permanent.
    c. small since the income changes are viewed to be temporary.
    d. small since the income changes are viewed to be permanent.

17. An increase in the price level will
    a. shift the *AE* curve up and increase equilibrium expenditure.
    b. shift the *AE* curve up and decrease equilibrium expenditure.
    c. shift the *AE* curve down and increase equilibrium expenditure.
    d. shift the *AE* curve down and decrease equilibrium expenditure.

18. A fall in the price level will
    a. cause autonomous expenditure to increase and thus produce a movement along the aggregate demand curve.
    b. cause autonomous expenditure to increase and thus produce a rightward shift in the aggregate demand curve.
    c. cause autonomous expenditure to increase and thus produce a leftward shift in the aggregate demand curve.
    d. have no effect on autonomous expenditure.

19. Suppose that, due to an increase in expected future profit, investment increases by $10 billion. If the multiplier is 2, the aggregate demand curve will
    a. shift to the right by the horizontal distance of $20 billion.
    b. shift to the right by a horizontal distance greater than $20 billion.
    c. shift to the right by a horizontal distance less than $20 billion.
    d. not be affected.

20. Suppose the multiplier is 2 and that the aggregate supply curve is positively sloped. Suppose further that, due to an increase in expected future profit, investment increases by $10 billion. Equilibrium real GDP will
    a. increase by $20 billion.
    b. increase by more than $20 billion.
    c. increase by less than $20 billion.
    d. be unaffected.

21. Suppose that, due to an increase in expected future profit, investment increases by $10 billion. Which of the following would reduce the effect of this increase in autonomous expenditure on equilibrium real GDP?
    a. An increase in the marginal propensity to consume
    b. A decrease in the marginal propensity to import
    c. A decrease in the marginal tax rate
    d. A steeper aggregate supply curve

SHORT ANSWER

1. What is the difference between autonomous expenditure and induced expenditure?

2. How do changes in the marginal propensity to import affect the slope of the aggregate expenditure curve?

3. How do changes in the marginal tax rate affect the slope of the aggregate expenditure curve?

4. Explain (without algebraic expressions) why the multiplier is larger if the aggregate expenditure curve is steeper.

5. Why is the tax multiplier smaller than the autonomous expenditure multiplier?

6. How does the presence of income taxes and transfer payments act as an automatic stabilizer?

7. Explain how the effects of price level changes on the *AE* curve will generate an aggregate demand curve.

PROBLEMS

1. Consider an economy with the following characteristics:
   Autonomous part of consumption expenditure = $10 billion
   Investment = $5 billion
   Government purchases of goods and services = $40 billion
   Exports = $5 billion
   Marginal propensity to consume (out of disposable income) = 0.8
   Marginal propensity to import (out of real GDP) = 0.14
   Marginal tax rate (constant) = 0.2
   a) What is autonomous expenditure in this economy?
   b) What is the slope of the *AE* curve?
   c) Draw a graph containing the *AE* curve for this economy (label it AE_0), as well as a 45° line.
   d) What is equilibrium expenditure?

2. Return to the economy of Problem 1. Now suppose that the government decides to increase its purchases of goods and services by $20 billion (from $40 billion to $60 billion).
   a) Using the graph from problem 1, draw the new *AE* curve and label it AE_1.
   b) What is the new equilibrium expenditure?
   c) What is the multiplier?
   d) What is the change in consumption, imports, and investment after the increase?

3. Return to the economy of Problem 1.
   a) What is the tax multiplier in this economy?
   b) What is the transfer payments multiplier in this economy?
   c) What is the balanced budget multiplier in this economy?

4. Now consider a new economy that is identical to the economy of Problem 1 except that the marginal propensity to import is 0.24.
   a) What is the slope of the *AE* curve in this economy?
   b) On a new graph, draw the *AE* curve for this economy, as well as a 45° line. Label it AE_2.
   c) What is equilibrium expenditure?
   d) What is the multiplier?

5. Return to the economy of Problem 1. The *AE* curve was constructed under the (implicit) assumption that the price level (*P*) was constant, at $P = 100$, say. If *P* increases to 120, suppose that autonomous expenditure decreases by $20 billion. If *P* decreases from 100 to 80, suppose that autonomous expenditure increases by $20 billion. Using this information, respond to the following.
   a) What is equilibrium expenditure when $P = 100$?
   b) What is equilibrium expenditure when $P = 120$?
   c) What is equilibrium expenditure when $P = 80$?
   d) From the answers to parts (a), (b), and (c), find three points on the aggregate demand curve and draw a line through them to represent *AD*.

ANSWERS

CONCEPT REVIEW

1. autonomous; induced
2. real GDP; import
3. upward
4. marginal tax; lower
5. paradox
6. multiplier; larger
7. automatic stabilizer
8. downward; lowers; movement along
9. increase

TRUE OR FALSE

1. F	6. F	11. F	16. F	21. F
2. T	7. T	12. F	17. F	
3. T	8. T	13. F	18. T	
4. T	9. F	14. T	19. T	
5. F	10. T	15. T	20. T	

MULTIPLE CHOICE

1. c	6. c	11. c	16. c	21. d
2. c	7. a	12. d	17. d	
3. d	8. d	13. d	18. a	
4. a	9. b	14. b	19. a	
5. d	10. b	15. a	20. c	

SHORT ANSWER

1. Autonomous expenditure does not change when real GDP changes, whereas induced expenditure does change when real GDP changes.

2. The slope of the aggregate expenditure curve is equal to the marginal propensity to consume out of real GDP *minus* the marginal propensity to import. Thus, if the marginal propensity to import increases, the slope of the *AE* curve decreases.

3. The marginal propensity to consume out of real GDP is equal to (1-*t*) times the marginal propensity to consume out of disposable income, where *t* is the (constant) marginal tax rate. This implies that the slope of the *AE* curve will decrease as the marginal tax rate increases.

4. Any initial stimulus to autonomous expenditure will generate a direct increase in real GDP. The basic idea of the multiplier is that this initial increase in real GDP will generate further increases in real GDP as increases in consumption expenditure are *induced*.

   At each round of the multiplier process, the increase in spending and thus the further increase in real GDP are determined by the slope of the *AE* curve. Since a steeper *AE* curve means a larger increase in real GDP at each round, the total increase in real GDP will also be greater. Thus, the multiplier will be larger if the *AE* curve is steeper.

5. The tax multiplier is smaller than the autonomous expenditure multiplier because a change in taxes does not have a direct effect on real GDP. Its total effect is indirect. A change in taxes will change disposable income, but, since the marginal propensity to consume is less than one, the effect on consumption expenditure (which starts the multiplier process) will be smaller than the tax change. As a result, the total effect of a tax change on real GDP will be less than the total effect of a change in autonomous expenditure of the same magnitude.

6. In the absence of income taxes and transfer payments, real GDP may fluctuate widely in response to smaller fluctuations in autonomous expenditure. This amplification of economic shocks is the autonomous expenditure multiplier at work.

   In the presence of income taxes and transfer payments that vary with real GDP, however, the effect of autonomous expenditure fluctuations is dampened. For example, an increase in autonomous expenditure implies an increase in real GDP but that increase in real GDP automatically leads to an increase in income taxes and a decrease in transfer payments. This increase in net taxes induces a fall in consumption and thus a fall in real GDP, partially offsetting the initial increase in real GDP. The net effect is a smaller increase in real GDP. In this way, income taxes and transfer payments act to automatically stabilize (reduce the movement in) real GDP.

7. The aggregate demand curve illustrates the relationship between the price level and aggregate expenditures. The aggregate expenditure diagram shows the level of equilibrium expenditure *holding the price level constant.* If the price level changes, the *AE* curve will shift and a new level of equilibrium expenditure will result. Thus, for each price level, there is a different level of equilibrium expenditure. These combinations of price level and corresponding aggregate expenditure are points on the aggregate demand curve.

   For example, if the price level rises, autonomous expenditure will decline and the *AE* curve will shift down. This will lead to a decrease in equilibrium expenditure. Since an increase in the price level is associated with a reduction in equilibrium expenditure, the *AD* curve is negatively sloped.

PROBLEMS

1. a) Autonomous expenditure is the sum of the autonomous part of consumption expenditure, investment, government purchases of goods and services, and exports. This sum is \$60 billion.
   b) The slope of the *AE* curve gives the additional amount that is spent on domestic goods and services when we increase real GDP by \$1, expressed as a fraction of the additional dollar.

   In this economy, when real GDP increases by \$1 only consumption expenditure and spending on imports increase. Since the marginal propensity to import is 0.14, 14¢ of the additional dollar of real GDP is spent on imports.

   In order to determine the amount by which consumption expenditure increases, we must first determine what happens to disposable income. Since the (constant) marginal tax rate is 0.2, 20¢ of the additional dollar is collected as tax leaving an increase in disposable income of 80¢. The marginal propensity to consume (out of disposable income) is 0.8, thus there will be an induced increase in consumption expenditure of 64¢ (0.8 times 80¢). Because we are interested only in the additional amount spent on domestic goods and services, we must subtract the 14¢ spent on imports. This gives an increase in spending on domestic goods and services of 50¢. Thus, half of the additional dollar of real GDP was so spent and the marginal propensity to spend is 0.5.
   c) See the curve labeled AE_0 in Fig. 9.1. The curve was drawn by noting that the amount of autonomous expenditure (\$60 billion) gives the vertical intercept and the slope of the *AE* curve is 0.5.

Figure 9.1

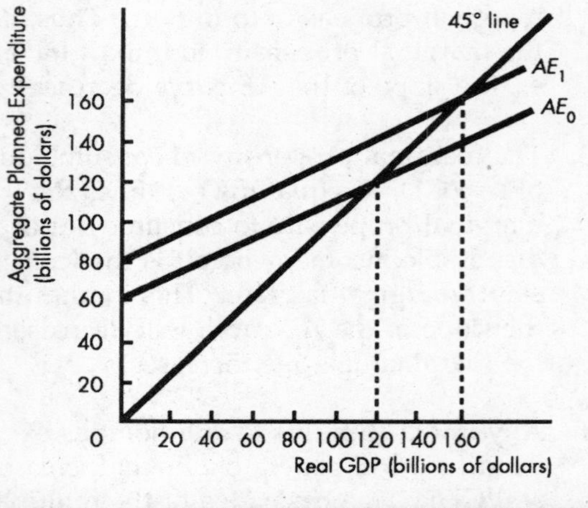

   d) Equilibrium expenditure occurs at the intersection of the AE_0 curve and the 45° line. Equilibrium expenditure is \$120 billion.

2. a) See the curve labeled AE_1 in Fig. 9.1. The new curve reflects the fact that autonomous expenditure increases by \$20 billion but the slope of the *AE* curve remains unchanged.
   b) The new equilibrium expenditure is \$160 billion. This is given by the intersection of the AE_1 curve with the 45° line.
   c) Since a \$20 billion increase in autonomous expenditure generated a \$40 billion increase in equilibrium expenditure, the multiplier is 2. This, of course, can be obtained by using the formula for the multiplier:

$$\textit{multiplier} = \frac{1}{1-g} = \frac{1}{1-0.5} = \frac{1}{0.5} = 2$$

   where *g* is the slope of the *AE* curve.

3. a) The formula for the tax multiplier is

$$\frac{-b}{1-g} = \frac{-0.8}{1-0.5} = -1.6$$

where b is the marginal propensity to consume.

b) The formula for the transfer payments multiplier is

$$\frac{b}{1-g} = \frac{0.8}{1-0.5} = 1.6$$

c) The formula for the balanced budget multiplier is

$$\frac{1-b}{1-g} = \frac{1-0.2}{1-0.5} = 0.4$$

4. a) Using the same analysis as in Problem 1 (b), we find that the slope of the *AE* curve is 0.4 in this economy.

b) See Fig. 9.2. The *AE* curve, AE_2, was constructed by noting that the amount of autonomous expenditure continued to be $60 billion but that the slope of the *AE* curve is 0.4, less than for the economy of problem 1. Therefore AE_2 is flatter than AE_0.

c) Equilibrium expenditure is $100 billion, given by the intersection of AE_2 and the 45° line.

d) The multiplier is given by the formula

$$multiplier = \frac{1}{1-g} = \frac{1}{1-0.4} = \frac{1}{0.6} = 1.67$$

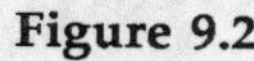

Figure 9.2

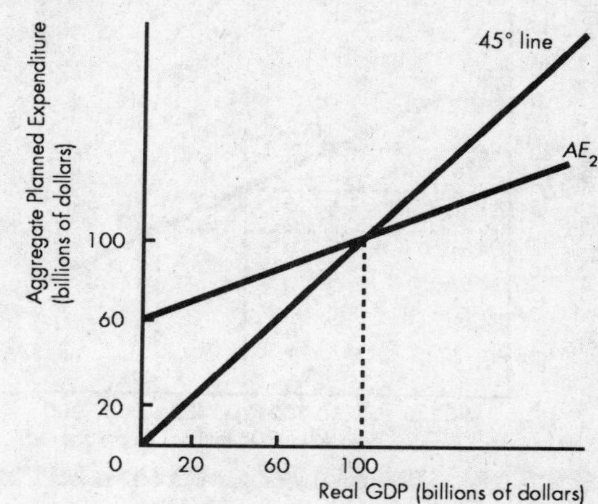

5. a) Since P = 100 was (implicitly) assumed in problem 1, equilibrium expenditure is $120 billion, as reported in the answer to Problem 1(d).

b) When P increases from 100 to 120, autonomous expenditure decreases by $20 billion. Since the multiplier is 2, equilibrium expenditure decreases by $40 billion. Thus, equilibrium expenditure is $80 billion (120 - 40).

c) When P decreases from 100 to 80, autonomous expenditure increases by $20 billion. Since the multiplier is 2, equilibrium expenditure increases by $40 billion. Thus, equilibrium expenditure is $160 billion (120 + 40).

d) See Fig. 9.3. Point *a* reflects the information in the answer to part (a) of this problem. When P = 100, equilibrium aggregate expenditure (the aggregate quantity of goods and services demanded) is $120 billion. This is a point on the aggregate demand curve. Points *b* and *c* are obtained similarly from the answers to parts (b) and (c).

Figure 9.3

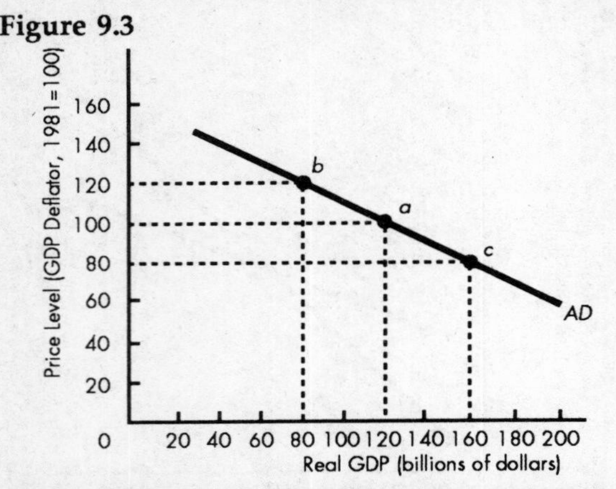
Price Level (GDP Deflator, 1981=100)
160
140
120
100
80
60
40
20
0
b
a
c
AD
20 40 60 80 100 120 140 160 180 200
Real GDP (billions of dollars)

10 MONEY, BANKING, AND PRICES

CHAPTER IN PERSPECTIVE

We have used money all our lives and yet, for most people, the source and nature of money remain largely a mystery. What exactly is money and what are its functions? How does a particular monetary system arise? What role do banks play in the creation of money? These are a few of the important issues addressed in this chapter.

Our major purpose for pursuing a deeper understanding of money and banks, however, is to help us understand the connection between money and macroeconomic activity, especially the behavior of the price level. This connection is also briefly addressed in this chapter and will be pursued further in a later chapter.

LEARNING OBJECTIVES

After studying this chapter, you will be able to:

- **Define money and state its functions**
- **Describe the different forms of money**
- **Explain how money is measured in the United States today**
- **Explain what a financial intermediary is**
- **Describe the balance sheets of the main financial intermediaries**
- **Explain the economic functions of commercial banks and other financial intermediaries**
- **Describe some of the important financial innovations of the 1980s**
- **Explain how banks create money**
- **Explain why the quantity of money is an important economic magnitude**
- **Explain the quantity theory of money**
- **Describe the historical and international evidence on the relationship between the quantity of money and the price level**

HELPFUL HINTS

1. What is money? In one basic sense, whatever meets the functions of money is money. For example, cigarettes are well documented as fulfilling the functions of money in prisoner-of-war camps and similar situations. However, you should be sure you can thoroughly answer this question on several levels. First, at the level of general definition, money is any commodity or token that is generally acceptable as a means of payment for goods and services. Second, at the level of classification, checkable deposits are money but savings deposits are not. Third, at the level of specific definitions, M1, M2, and M3 are official definitions of money.

2. If we know what money is, we must also know what money is *not* and why. Why are checks (as opposed to checkable deposits) or credit cards *not* money?

3. One of the most important concepts presented in this chapter is the money multiplier process by which banks create money. You should become thoroughly familiar with this process. Two fundamental facts allow banks to create money. First, one of the liabilities of banks is money (checkable deposits). Banks create money by creating new checkable deposits. Second, banks hold fractional reserves. This means that when a bank receives a deposit, it will only hold part of it as reserves and can loan out the rest. Note that the bank is not indulging in a scam – it is still maintaining assets (reserves plus loans) to match its liabilities (the deposits). When that loan is spent, at least part of the proceeds will likely be deposited in another bank, creating a new deposit (money).

The money multiplier process follows from this last fact: banks make loans when they receive new deposits and these loans will return to another bank creating another new deposit. The process then repeats itself, adding more money (but in progressively smaller amounts) in each round. Practice going through examples until the process becomes second nature.

4. Two important equations are introduced in this chapter.

a) The first is the equation for the simple money multiplier:

$$\textit{simple money multiplier} = \frac{1}{\textit{required reserve ratio}}$$

As discussed in the text, real world money multipliers will differ from the simple money multiplier. In the next chapter, we will derive a more sophisticated money multiplier.

b) The second is the equation of exchange:

$$MV = PY$$

where M is the quantity of money, V is the velocity of circulation, P is the price level, and Y is real GDP.

This equation simply says that the quantity of money times the average number of times each dollar is spent is equal to the dollar value of the goods and services on which it was spent. The equation is always true by definition: it is an identity.

If we further assume that the velocity of circulation and real GDP are independent of the quantity of money, the quantity theory of money is the result. These assumptions imply that when the quantity of money increases by 10 percent, the price level must increase by 10 percent in order to maintain equality between the two sides of the equation.

5. Why does the aggregate demand curve shift to the right when there is an increase in the quantity of money?

For the answer, we return to the discussion of aggregate demand in Chapter 24. There we discovered that an increase in the quantity of *real* money caused aggregate demand to increase for two reasons. The first was the real money balances effect and the second was the intertemporal substitution effect which is a result of the fact that interest rates will fall when real money increases.

At a given price level, an increase in the quantity of money is an increase in the quantity of real money. Thus, aggregate demand increases through these two effects and, since the price level is given, the aggregate demand curve shifts to the right.

KEY FIGURES AND TABLES

Figure 10.1 The Three Official Measures of Money

There are three official measures of money in the U. S.: M1, M2, and M3. As illustrated here, each consists of several components. M1 is contained in M2 and M2 is contained in M3. This figure shows the relative magnitudes of the various components of each measure of money as well as what proportion of M2 is M1 and what proportion of M3 is M2.

Figure 10.2 Aggregate Demand, Aggregate Supply, and the Quantity of Money

Using the aggregate demand-aggregate supply model, this figure illustrates the effects of an increase in the quantity of money.

In part (a), the economy is initially in an unemployment equilibrium at the intersection of AD_0 and *SAS*. The initial price level is 90 and initial real GDP is $4.4 trillion. The increase in the money supply shifts the aggregate demand curve to the right, to AD_1. The price level rises to 100 and real GDP rises to its full employment level, $4.5 trillion.

In part (b), the economy is initially in a full employment equilibrium at the intersection of the aggregate demand curve (AD_1) and the long-run aggregate supply curve, *(LAS)*. The initial price level is 100 and initial real GDP is $4.5 trillion.

Now the quantity of money increases, which shifts the aggregate demand curve to the right, from AD_1 to AD_2. Since input prices are given in the short run, the economy will move along its short-run aggregate supply curve, *(SAS)*, to the point of intersection with the new aggregate demand curve. This is a short run equilibrium at a price level of 110 and real GDP of $4.6 trillion. Thus, in the short-run, an increase in money will cause both the price level and real GDP to increase.

In the long run, however, input prices will adjust and the short-run aggregate supply curve eventually shifts to SAS_2. Thus the new long-run equilibrium will be at the intersection of the new aggregate demand curve, (AD_2), and the long-run aggregate supply curve, *(LAS)*. Thus, in the long run, the price level rises to 120 and real GDP returns to its original level of $4.5 trillion.

Figure 10.3 Money Growth and Inflation in the United States

This figure shows the historical behavior of the rate of growth of money and the rate of inflation in the United States from 1875 to 1991. Note that (1) on the average, the rate of growth of money exceeds the rate of inflation; (2) variations in the rate of inflation are correlated with variations in the rate of growth of money; (3) during World War I, the rate of inflation closely followed the rate of growth of money, but during and after World War II there was a break in the relationship; (4) before 1915 and after 1950, fluctuations in the rate of inflation have been smaller than fluctuations in the growth rate of money.

Figure 10.4 Money Growth and Inflation in the World Economy

Part (a) shows the average rate of growth of money and the average inflation rate for 60 countries. There is a clear tendency for countries with high rates of inflation to be those with high rates of growth of money. Part (b) focuses on this relationship for those countries with lower rates of inflation. While there is still a tendency for high inflation to be associated with high rates of growth of money,

money growth is not the only influence on inflation.

Table 10.2 The Three Official Measures of Money

This table simply lists the components of the three definitions of money: M1, M2, and M3. Note that M2 contains all of the components of M1 as well as additional components, and M3 contains all of the components of M2 as well as additional components.

Table 10.3 A Compact Glossary of the Components of Money

This table is a companion to Table 10.2. It gives the definitions of the components of the various official definitions of money.

Table 10.5 A Compact Glossary of Financial Intermediaries

There are five types of financial intermediaries whose deposits are part of the money supply. Each offers checkable deposits. This table lists those types and discusses their main functions, as well as indicating the approximate number of institutions and the total value of assets for each. Note that although there are more credit unions than any other type, they tend to be small; total assets are the smallest. Commercial banks are by far the most important type of financial intermediary.

SELF-TEST

CONCEPT REVIEW

1. Money is any commodity or token that is generally acceptable in exchange for goods and services. This is the first function of money: money is a(n) ____________ ____________ ____________. The alternative to using money in exchange is the direct exchange of goods for goods, called ____________.
2. The second function of money is a(n) ____________ ____________ ____________ since units of money serve as an agreed measure for stating the prices of goods and services. As a third function, money serves as a(n) ____________ ____________ ____________ since it can be held and exchanged later for goods or services. Finally, money also provides an agreed measure that allows contracts to be written for future receipts and payments. Money is thus a standard of ____________ ____________.
3. Money takes four different forms. A physical commodity that is valued in its own right and also serves as a medium of exchange is called a(n) ____________ money. A paper claim to a commodity that circulates as money is called ____________ ____________ money. An intrinsically worthless (or almost worthless) commodity that serves the functions of money is called ____________ money. Finally, a loan that the borrower promises to pay on demand which is used by the lender in exchange for goods and services is called ____________ ____________ money.
4. A firm that takes deposits from households and firms and makes loans to other

households and firms is called a(n) ____________ ____________.

5. The cash in a bank's vaults plus its deposits at Federal Reserve banks are called its ____________.
6. Assets that can be quickly converted into a medium of exchange at a reasonably certain price are known as ____________ assets. The degree to which an asset has this property is known as ____________.
7. The fraction of a bank's total deposits that are actually held in reserves is called the ____________ ____________. The ratio of reserves to deposits that banks are required, by regulation, to hold is called the ____________ ____________ ____________. Actual reserves minus required reserves equals ____________ ____________.
8. The amount by which an initial increase in bank reserves is multiplied to calculate the effect on total bank deposits is called the ____________ ____________ multiplier. This multiplier will be larger, the ____________ the required reserve ratio.
9. The proposition that an increase in money leads to an equal percentage increase in the price level is the ____________ theory of ____________. Its original basis follows from certain propositions about the equation of ____________. This equation is true by definition since one of its components is defined by it. This component, the ____________ of circulation, is the average number of times a dollar is used annually to buy the goods and services that make up GDP.

True or False

___ 1. Barter can take place only if there is a double coincidence of wants.

___ 2. Money is any commodity or token that is generally acceptable as a means of payment for goods and services.

___ 3. Unpredictable changes in the rate of inflation enhance the function of money as a standard of deferred payment.

___ 4. Only money serves as a store of value.

___ 5. Gresham's law implies that money that has not been debased (good money) will tend to drive debased money (bad money) out of circulation.

___ 6. A one dollar bill in the U.S. today is an example of convertible paper money.

___ 7. A one dollar bill in the U.S. today is an example of fiat money.

___ 8. A checkable deposit at a commercial bank is an example of private debt money.

___ 9. Some of the components of M2 are not money but have a high degree of liquidity.

____10. Other checkable deposits (like NOW accounts) are included in M2 but *not* in M1.

____11. In our modern economy, credit cards are money.

____12. Bank reserves consist of cash in the bank's vault plus its deposits at a Federal Reserve bank.

____13. Individual households are generally better at pooling risk than are financial intermediaries.

____14. A good deal of financial innovation is the result of attempts to avoid regulation.

____15. If a depositor withdraws currency from a bank, that bank's reserve ratio declines.

____16. The simple money multiplier is equal to 1 divided by the required reserve ratio.

____17. An increase in the quantity of money shifts the aggregate demand curve to the left.

____18. In the long run, an increase in the quantity of money will cause the price level to rise but will leave real GDP unchanged.

____19. The quantity theory of money implies that a 10 percent increase in the quantity of money will cause a 10 percent increase in the price level.

____20. If the quantity of money is $500 billion and nominal GDP is $2,000 billion, the velocity of circulation is one fourth.

____21. U.S. and international historical evidence shows that there is a very close correspondence between money and the price level.

____22. On average, the quantity of money has grown at a rate that exceeds the inflation rate.

Multiple Choice

1. Which of the following is NOT one of the four functions of money?
   a. Medium of exchange
   b. Measure of liquidity
   c. Standard of deferred payment
   d. Store of value

2. When a contract specifies that a certain number of dollars are to be paid in the future for services rendered, money is functioning as a
   a. medium of exchange.
   b. measure of liquidity.
   c. standard of deferred payment.
   d. store of value.

3. If prices of goods and services were stated in terms of pounds of salt, then salt is
   a. a unit of account.
   b. a standard of deferred payment.
   c. a store of value.
   d. quasi-money.

4. Which of the following is a disadvantage of a commodity money?
   a. It is valued for its own sake.
   b. Its value as money is much greater than its value as a commodity.
   c. The commodity could be used in other ways if it was not used as a medium of exchange.
   d. It has little intrinsic value.

5. The fact that debased commodity money drives money that has not been debased out of circulation is an example of
   a. liquidity.
   b. the effects of near money.
   c. convertibility.
   d. Gresham's law.

6. U.S. currency today is an example of
   a. commodity money.
   b. fiat money.
   c. convertible paper money.
   d. private debt money.

7. A checkable deposit in a financial institution is an example of
   a. commodity money.
   b. fiat money.
   c. convertible paper money.
   d. private debt money.

8. Which of the following is a component of M2 but <u>NOT</u> of M1?
   a. Traveler's checks
   b. Demand deposits
   c. Savings deposits
   d. Other checkable deposits

9. Which of the following is money?
   a. A checkable deposit
   b. A blank check
   c. A credit card
   d. A large time deposit

10. A firm that takes deposits from households and firms and makes loans to other households and firms is called a
    a. commercial bank.
    b. financial intermediary.
    c. lender of last resort.
    d. wholesale depository institution.

11. Which of the following is a liability of a commercial bank?
    a. Vault cash
    b. Loans
    c. Investment securities
    d. Demand deposits

12. Which of the following is most liquid?
    a. Demand deposits
    b. Real estate
    c. A government bond
    d. Savings deposits

13. Which of the following is <u>NOT</u> a principal service of financial intermediaries?
    a. Pooling risk
    b. Minimizing the cost of regulation
    c. Minimizing the cost of monitoring borrowers
    d. Creating liquidity

14. A bank can create money by
    a. selling some of its investment securities.
    b. increasing its reserves.
    c. lending its excess reserves.
    d. printing more checks.

15. If all banks hold 100 percent reserves, the simple money multiplier is
    a. 0.
    b. 1.
    c. 10.
    d. infinite.

16. If the required reserve ratio is 20 percent, the simple money multiplier is
    a. 1.
    b. 2.
    c. 4.
    d. 5.

17. A decrease in the quantity of money will cause
    a. both the price level and real GDP to decline in the short run; but in the long run, only the price level will fall as real GDP returns to its initial level.
    b. both the price level and real GDP to increase in the short run; but in the long run, only the price level will rise as real GDP returns to its initial level.
    c. the price level to fall in the short run; but in the long run, the price level will return to its initial level.
    d. the price level to fall and real GDP to rise in both the short run and the long run.

18. According to the quantity theory of money, an increase in the quantity of money will lead to an increase in the price level
    a. but have no effect on real GDP or the velocity of circulation.
    b. as well as increasing both real GDP and the velocity of circulation.
    c. as well as increasing real GDP but decreasing the velocity of circulation.
    d. as well as decreasing real GDP but increasing the velocity of circulation.

19. If the price level is 2, real GDP is $100 billion, and the quantity of money is $40 billion, then the velocity of circulation is
    a. 2.5.
    b. 4.
    c. 5.
    d. 10.

20. Given the historical evidence on the quantity theory of money, which of the following is NOT true?
    a. On the average, the growth rate of the quantity of money has exceeded the inflation rate in the U.S.
    b. Money supply growth is the only influence on inflation.
    c. The steadily increasing money growth rate during the 1960s and 1970s was associated with steadily rising inflation through those decades.
    d. Internationally, there is an unmistakable tendency for countries with high money growth rates to experience high rates of inflation.

SHORT ANSWER

1. What is meant by a double coincidence of wants?

2. What are the four principal functions of money?

3. What is meant when we say that money serves as a unit of account?

4. What are the main disadvantages of a commodity money?

5. Explain why credit cards are not money.

6. Explain why a savings deposit is more liquid than a 20-year corporate bond.

7. How do financial intermediaries create liquidity?

8. How do banks create money?

9. According to the quantity theory of money, what is the effect of an increase in the quantity of money?

10. Briefly summarize the historical evidence from the U.S. regarding the quantity theory of money.

PROBLEMS

1. Suppose an individual sells $1000 worth of government securities to the Federal Reserve and deposits the proceeds ($1000) in Bank 1. Note that this new deposit initially increases the quantity of money by $1000. (In the next chapter we will see how such a new deposit arises.) Assume that the required reserve ratio for all banks is 20 percent (0.2). As it stands, Table 10.1 below gives information for the first round of the simple money expansion process that will be generated by this new deposit.
   a) Follow the first six rounds of the money creation process by completing the six rows of Table 10.1.
   b) What is the total increase in the quantity of money after six rounds?
   c) What is the money multiplier?
   d) After all rounds have been completed, what will the total increase in money be?

2. Suppose the economy is in a full-employment equilibrium when there is a decrease in the quantity of money. Using an aggregate demand-aggregate supply model, show what happens to the price level and the level of real GDP in the short run and in the long run.

3. We observe an economy in which the price level is 1.5, real GDP is $240 billion, and the money supply is $60 billion.
   a) What is the velocity of circulation?
   b) According to the quantity theory of money, what will be the result of an increase in the quantity of money to $80 billion?

Table 10.1 Money Creation Process

Bank number	New deposits (dollars)	New loans (dollars)	New reserves (dollars)	Increase in money (dollars)	Cumulative increase in money (dollars)
1	1000	800	200	1000	1000
2					
3					
4					
5					
6					

ANSWERS

CONCEPT REVIEW

1. medium of exchange; barter
2. unit of account; store of value; deferred payment;
3. commodity; convertible paper; fiat; private debt
4. financial intermediary
5. reserves
6. liquid; liquidity
7. reserve ratio; required reserve ratio; excess reserves
8. simple money; smaller
9. quantity; money; exchange; velocity

TRUE OR FALSE

1. T	6. F	11. F	16. T	21. F
2. T	7. T	12. T	17. F	22. T
3. F	8. T	13. F	18. T	
4. F	9. T	14. T	19. T	
5. F	10. F	15. T	20. F	

Multiple Choice

1. b	5. d	9. a	13. b	17. a
2. c	6. b	10. b	14. c	18. a
3. a	7. d	11. d	15. b	19. c
4. c	8. c	12. a	16. d	20. b

Short Answer

1. A double coincidence of wants occurs in barter when an individual who has good A and wants to trade for good B finds an individual who has good B and wants to trade for good A.

2. Money functions as a
   - medium of exchange,
   - unit of account,
   - standard of deferred payment,
   - store of value.

3. A unit of account is an agreed measure in which prices of goods and services are stated. Money serves as a unit of account when all prices are stated in terms of units of money (e.g., dollars).

4. There are two disadvantages of commodity money discussed in the text. The first is that there is a temptation to cheat on the value of money by clipping or debasing the money. The second disadvantage is that the use of the commodity for money has a high opportunity cost. When the commodity is used as money, it cannot be used in other ways. For example, the opportunity cost of using gold as money is the forgone use of that gold for jewelry or some other function.

5. A credit card is not money but rather a mechanism for borrowing money which must later be repaid. The repayment of money takes place when the credit card bill is paid by check.

6. A savings deposit is more liquid than a 20-year corporate bond because it can more readily be converted into money (M1) at a known price. The savings deposit can be converted to money dollar for dollar by a visit to the bank. The corporate bond can be converted to money only by having a broker sell it in the bond market. Furthermore, the price of the 20-year bond fluctuates considerably and thus, the price at which the bond will be sold is uncertain.

7. Financial intermediaries create liquidity by borrowing short and lending long. They borrow funds by creating deposits which they promise to repay on short notice but loan funds for long periods of time. The deposits they create are much more liquid than the assets that result from the ultimate loan contracts. Indeed, some of the deposits created by banks are money and are thus perfectly liquid.

8. Banks create money by making new loans. When the proceeds of these loans are spent, the person receiving the money will deposit much of it in a bank deposit which is new money.

9. According to the quantity theory of money, an increase in the quantity of money will cause the price level to increase by an equal percentage amount.

10. The U.S. historical evidence suggests that, while there is definite evidence that higher rates of inflation are associated with higher rates of money growth, the relationship is not nearly so precise as the quantity theory would imply. There are other factors besides money growth that explain variations in inflation rates.

PROBLEMS

1. a) Table 10.1 is completed as Table 10.1 Solution. Note that 80 percent of each new deposit will be loaned out and 20 percent will be held as reserves. When a new loan is deposited in a bank, it becomes a new deposit and thus money.

Table 10.1 Solution Money Creation Process

Bank number	New deposits (dollars)	New loans (dollars)	New reserves (dollars)	Increase in money (dollars)	Cumulative increase in money (dollars)
1	1000	800	200	1000	1000
2	800	640	160	800	1800
3	640	512	128	640	2440
4	512	409.60	102.40	512	2952
5	409.60	327.68	81.92	409.60	3361.60
6	327.68	262.14	65.54	327.68	3689.28

b) After six rounds, the total (cumulative) increase in the quantity of money is $3689.28. This is obtained from the last column of Table 10.2 Solution.

c) The money multiplier in this case is the simple money multiplier given by

$$\textit{simple money multiplier} = \frac{1}{\textit{required reserve ratio}}$$

Since the desired reserve ratio is .2, the simple money multiplier is 5.

d) The total increase in money will be $5000 after all rounds are completed. This is obtained by multiplying the initial increase in deposits ($1000) by the simple money multiplier (5).

2. The consequences of a decrease in the quantity of money are illustrated in Fig. 10.1. The economy is initially in long run equilibrium at point *a*, the intersection of AD_0 and SAS_0 (and *LAS*). The price level is P_0 and GDP is at its full-employment level, Y^*.

A decrease in the quantity of money will shift the *AD* curve to the left, from AD_0 to AD_1. The new short-run equilibrium is at point *b*. The price level falls to P_1 and real GDP falls to Y_1. In the long run, however, input prices will also fall, which will shift the *SAS* curve down, from SAS_0 to SAS_1. A new long-run equilibrium is achieved at point *c*. Thus, in the long-run, the price level falls further to P_2, while real GDP returns to its initial level, Y^*.

Figure 10.1

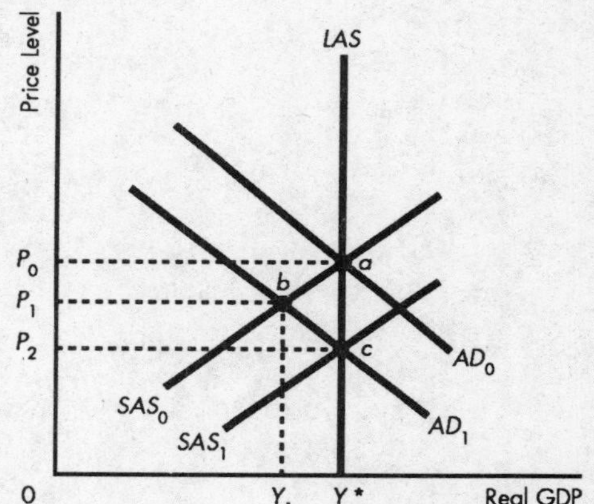

3. a) From the equation of exchange, we know that the velocity of circulation, *V*, is defined by

$$V = \frac{P \times Y}{M}$$

where *P* is the price level, *Y* is real GDP, and *M* is the quantity of money. With the values for the price level, real GDP, and the quantity of money given in this problem, we have

$$V = \frac{1.5 \times 240}{60} = \frac{360}{60} = 6$$

b) The quantity theory of money predicts that an increase in the quantity of money will cause an equal percentage increase in the price level. An increase in money from $60 billion to $80 billion is a one third (33 percent) increase. Thus, the quantity theory of money predicts that the price level will rise by a third (33 percent). Since the initial price level is 1.5, the predicted price level will be 2.0.

11 THE FEDERAL RESERVE, MONEY, AND INTEREST RATES

CHAPTER IN PERSPECTIVE

In Chapter 27 we discovered that a new bank deposit will, as it works its way through the banking system, cause a total increase in the quantity of money that is a multiple of the initial new deposit. But how might that new money-creating deposit arise? In this chapter, we find that the Federal Reserve, through its use of monetary policy tools, can create such new deposits and thus influence the quantity of money.

The reason we are so interested in the quantity of money, of course, is that, as we have seen in Chapters 24 and 27, changes in the quantity of money can have important effects on real GDP and the price level. For example, an increase in the quantity of money will increase aggregate demand, thus causing the price level to increase and the level of real GDP to increase, at least in the short run.

How does an increase in the quantity of money affect aggregate demand? We will learn that an increase in the quantity of money will cause an increase in aggregate expenditure primarily through its ability to lower interest rates. Then the question becomes: How does a change in the quantity of money cause interest rates to change? A major purpose of this chapter is to present a model that will allow us to explain the determination of interest rates.

LEARNING OBJECTIVES

After studying this chapter, you will be able to:

- **Describe the structure of the Federal Reserve System (the Fed)**
- **Describe the tools used by the Fed to influence the money supply and interest rates**
- **Explain what an open market operation is and how it works**
- **Explain how an open market operation changes the money supply**
- **Distinguish between the nominal money supply and the real money supply**
- **Explain what determines the demand for money**
- **Explain the effects of financial innovations on the demand for money in the 1980s**

- **Explain how interest rates are determined**
- **Explain how the Fed influences interest rates**

HELPFUL HINTS

1. Be sure to understand how each of the three main policy tools of the Fed works to affect the quantity of money.

a) *Required reserve ratios.* If the Fed decreases required reserve ratios, banks will suddenly find themselves with excess reserves which they will lend out, thus expanding the money supply.

Furthermore, a decrease in required reserve ratios also means that the money multiplier will have increased so that an increase in excess reserves will have a larger expansionary effect on the quantity of money. An increase in required reserve ratios will have the opposite effects.

Note that the Fed rarely changes required reserve ratios and when it does, it is generally for reasons other than to affect the quantity of money.

b) *Discount rate.* Changes in the discount rate are not very frequent either. Banks borrow from the Fed at the discount rate in order to increase their reserves. This may become necessary, for example, if a bank finds that its actual reserves are short of the amount of required reserves. Indeed, it is helpful to think of the discount rate as a penalty rate for being short of required reserves.

Thus, when the Fed raises the discount rate, it increases the penalty for having less than required reserves. This increase in the penalty will induce banks to increase their holdings of reserves, thus reducing their ability to lend and increase the money supply.

When the Fed lowers the discount rate, it encourages banks to borrow reserves which increases their ability to lend and increase the money supply.

c) *Open market operations.* This is by far the most important tool of the Fed. To help understand the effect of open market operations on the monetary base and thus the quantity of money, note that one of the liabilities of the Fed is banks' deposits at the Fed which serve as bank reserves. These deposits combined with currency in circulation (the other major liability of the Fed) constitute the monetary base. Also note that the largest class of assets on the books of the Fed is its holdings of government securities. Finally, recall that if total assets increase, due to the conventions of double entry bookkeeping, total liabilities must increase by the same amount.

An open market purchase of government securities can thus be seen as an increase in the assets of the Fed (government securities) paid for by an increase in its liabilities, principally an increase in the deposits of banks at the Fed. This increase in liabilities of the Fed is an increase in the monetary base, which will have a multiplied effect on the quantity of money.

2. Here are some further notes on open market operations.

a) To remember whether an open market purchase will lead to a decrease or an increase in money, it may be helpful to think of open market operations as an exchange of government securities for cash. For example, think of an open market purchase as the Fed acquiring government securities by giving cash to the public. Thus the money supply will increase.

b) It is important to remember that government securities are assets to the Fed just as they are to members of the public who hold them. They are liabilities of the U.S. Treasury and not the Fed.

c) There are two markets in which government securities are traded. First, there is the primary market in which the Treasury sells newly issued government securities. There is also the secondary market in which government securities previously purchased in the primary market are bought and sold. This secondary market is the *open market* in which open market operations take place.

3. Ordinary use of the term *money* does not make some important distinctions that are made in economics. In order to avoid confusion regarding the concept of the demand for money, it is important that these distinctions are clear.

For example, we often talk about our income as the amount of *money* we make over a certain period of time. When we use the term in this context, we are speaking of money as a flow — a quantity received over some period of time.

On the other hand, we may talk about how much *money* we have in our checking account or in our wallet at a certain point in time. In this context we are speaking of money as a stock — a quantity at a point in time. The distinction between these two concepts can be very important.

To avoid potential confusion, economists rarely use the term *money* when referring to a flow. Instead, they will use less ambiguous alternative terms like income or wage. In this chapter, *money* always refers to a *stock*. When we talk about the demand for *money* we are talking about the desire to hold a *stock* of *money* and not spend it. (However, it *is* being held for future spending purposes.)

4. It is crucial to distinguish between real and nominal money. Nominal money is the actual dollars you hold in the form of cash and checkable deposits. Real money is the measure of the purchasing power of that nominal money — how many goods and services you can buy with it. Clearly you only hold nominal money for this purpose, so it is the real balances that you care about.

Therefore, if the average price level rises, and all else stays the same (most especially your desired real spending), you will want the same amount of real balances as before. In order to achieve this, you will need a rise in nominal money equivalent to the rise in the average price level.

5. It is crucial to distinguish between real and nominal money. Nominal money is the actual dollars you hold in the form of cash and checkable deposits. Real money is the measure of the purchasing power of that nominal money—how many goods and services you can buy with it. Clearly you only hold nominal money for this purpose, so it is the real balances that you care about.

Therefore, if the average price level rises, and all else stays the same (most especially your desired real spending), you will want the same amount of real balances as before. In order to achieve this, you will need a rise in nominal money equivalent to the rise in the average price level.

KEY FIGURES AND TABLES

Figure 11.2 The Structure and Policy Tools of the Fed

This figure summarizes the main elements of the structure of the Federal Reserve System, as well as the three policy tools of the Fed. The central organizational unit of the Fed is the Board of Governors, which is headed by the Chairman of the Board of Governors and is supported by staff economists. There are also 12 regional Federal Reserve Banks. The Board of Governors sets required reserve ratios. The regional Federal Reserve Banks establish the discount rate with the approval of the Board of Governors. The Federal Open

Market Committee, consisting of the Board of Governors and members of the regional Federal Reserve Banks, set guidelines for open market operations, the main Fed policy tool.

Figure 11.7 The Interest Rate and the Velocity of Circulation of M1 and M2

The U.S. historical relationship between the interest rate and the velocity of circulation of M is given in part (a) of this figure. Part (b) gives the historical relationship between the interest rate and the velocity of circulation of M2. While both measures of the velocity of circulation seem to follow movements in interest rates, the relationship is much more precise for the velocity of circulation of M2. There is another notable difference between the behavior of these two velocity measures: The range over which the velocity of M has fluctuated is far greater than the range over which the velocity of M2 has fluctuated.

Figure 11.8 Money Market Equilibrium

This figure illustrates an equilibrium in the money market. The supply of real money is $3 trillion and does not vary as the interest rate varies. The real money supply curve is thus a vertical line at $3 trillion. On the other hand, the demand for real money is inversely related to the interest rate and thus the real money demand curve is negatively sloped. The equilibrium interest rate is determined by the intersection of the demand curve for real money and the supply curve of real money.

In this example, that intersection takes place at an interest rate of 5 percent. At higher interest rates, the fixed supply of real money is greater than the quantity of real money demanded; that is, households and firms are holding more money than they desire at these higher interest rates. They will therefore try to reduce the excess supply by buying financial assets. As a result of this increase in the demand for financial assets, the price of financial assets will rise and thus the interest rates earned on these assets will fall. As interest rates fall, the quantity of money demanded increases, reducing the excess supply of money. This process will continue until interest rates have fallen sufficiently that the quantity of real money demanded is equal to the quantity of real money supplied. Similarly, at interest rates below 5 percent, the same process will occur, but in the opposite direction, pushing the interest rate back to 5 percent. Note that the demand for money must do the adjusting, as the supply of money is fixed. The key point is that equilibrium must be achieved in *both* the money and financial markets; the equilibrating process must achieve joint equilibrium.

Figure 11.9 The Fed Changes the Interest Rate

This figure illustrates the ability of the Fed to influence the interest rate by conducting monetary policy which changes the supply of real money. For example, in part (a) of this figure, the Fed has purchased government securities in the open market which has led to an increase in the quantity of real money. This is represented by a rightward shift of the real money supply curve, from MS_0 to MS_1. The result is a decline in the equilibrium rate of interest by the process described in the discussion of Fig. 11.8.

In part (b), the Fed has caused the interest rate to rise by reducing the supply of real money through open market sales of government securities.

Table 11.4 Calculating the Money Multiplier

A formula for the money multiplier is derived in this table. Part 1 lists the relevant variables and defines symbols. Parts 2 and 3 give definitions of symbols for relevant variables and ratios.

Note that the monetary base is given as the sum of currency (in the hands of the nonbank public) and reserves (which includes vault cash). Money (M1) is the sum of currency (held by the nonbank public) and deposits. Part 4 uses this notation and the definition of the money multiplier to derive a convenient formula.

Note that the money multiplier depends on two key ratios: the ratio of currency to deposits (C/D) and the ratio of reserves to deposits (R/D). Increases in either of these will reduce the size of the multiplier.

Table 11.5 The Interest Rate and the Price of a Bond

The purpose of this table is to demonstrate, by use of an example, that an increase in the price of a financial asset with a fixed coupon corresponds to a decrease in the rate of return (interest) on the asset. The table demonstrates this for the simplest case, (a perpetuity), but the conclusion is quite general. The logic is straightforward since the rate of interest on an asset is the annual dollar return (coupon) as a percent of the purchase price. Thus, if the price rises, any given dollar return will be a smaller percent.

SELF-TEST

CONCEPT REVIEW

1. The central bank of the United States is called the Federal Reserve System.
2. The attempt by the Fed to control inflation and reduce business cycle fluctuations by changing the quantity of money and adjusting interest rates is called monetary policy.
3. The main policymaking body of the Fed is the Federal Open Market Committee.
4. The Fed uses three main policy tools. It can change required reserve ratios, which are the minimum reserve ratios that a bank is permitted to hold. Second it can change the discount rate which is the interest rate at which the Fed lends reserves to banks. The third tool involves the purchase and sale of government securities by the Fed. It is called open market operations.
5. The sum of Federal Reserve notes in circulation, banks' deposits at the Fed, and coinage in circulation is called the monetary base. If the Fed buys government securities on the open market, this sum will increase. The amount by which a change in this sum is multiplied to calculate the change in the quantity of money is called the money multiplier.
6. There are three main motives for holding money. The first motive, to undertake transactions and minimize the cost of transacting, is called the transactions motive. Money held as a precaution against unforeseen events and required unplanned purchases corresponds to the precautionary motive. The final motive, to avoid predicted losses from holding stocks and bonds that are expected to fall

in value, is called the speculative motive.

7. The relationship between the quantity of real money demanded and the interest rate, holding other things constant is called the demand for real money.
8. An increase in real income will shift the demand curve for real money to the right, and, if the supply of real money is constant, will cause the equilibrium interest rate to rise.
9. A bond that promises to pay a given amount of money each year is called a(n) perpetuity. If the price of this bond rises, the interest rate earned on the bond falls.
10. If the Fed buys government securities in the open market, the interest rate will likely fall.

TRUE OR FALSE

T 1. There are 12 regional Federal Reserve Banks in the United States.

F 2. An increase in required reserve ratios is intended to increase lending by banks.

F 3. If the Fed sells government securities in the open market, reserves will increase.

T 4. Federal Reserve notes are a liability of the Fed.

T 5. Federal Reserve notes are nonconvertible.

F 6. The Fed can increase the monetary base by selling government securities in the open market.

T 7. The money multiplier is given as the ratio of the change in the quantity of money to the change in the monetary base.

T 8. If there is an increase in the fraction of deposits that households and firms hold as currency, the money multiplier will decrease.

F 9. The higher the banks' required reserve ratio, the larger is the money multiplier.

T 10. If the price level increases, there will be an increase in the nominal quantity of money people will want to hold.

F 11. If the price level increases, there will be an increase in the real quantity of money people will want to hold.

T 12. The velocity of circulation is given by the ratio of real GDP to real money supply.

T 13. If interest rates rise, the velocity of circulation is likely to increase.

T 14. If interest rates rise, the quantity of money demanded is likely to decrease.

F 15. The development of highly liquid deposits and growth in the use of credit cards in recent years have caused the demand curve for real money to shift to the right.

____ 16. In the U.S., the velocity of circulation of M1 is much more stable than the velocity of circulation of M2.

____ 17. If the price of a bond rises, the interest rate earned on the bond falls.

____ 18. An increase in the demand for real money will cause the interest rate to fall.

____ 19. If households or firms find that they have more money than they want to hold, they will buy financial assets. This will cause the prices of financial assets to rise and the interest rates earned on those assets to fall.

____ 20. If the Fed wants to lower interest rates, it should sell government securities in the open market.

____ 21. If Fed monetary policy changes are foreseen by asset-holders, then interest rates will change as soon as the Fed's actions are foreseen.

MULTIPLE CHOICE

1. The U.S. central bank is the
   a. Federal Depositors Insurance Corporation.
   b. Department of the Treasury.
   c. Senate Banking Committee.
   d. Federal Reserve System.

2. The Board of Governors of the Federal Reserve System consists of
   a. 7 members, each appointed by the President for a 14-year term.
   b. 7 members, each appointed by the President for a 4-year term.
   c. 12 members, each appointed by the President for a 14-year term.
   d. 12 members, each appointed by the President for a 4-year term.

3. The main policymaking organ of the Federal Reserve System is the
   a. Board of Governors of the Federal Reserve System.
   b. Federal Monetary Policy Committee.
   c. Federal Open Market Committee.
   d. Board of Directors of the Federal Reserve Bank of New York.

4. Which of the following is NOT one of the main policy tools of the Fed?
   a. Required reserve ratios
   b. Discount rate
   c. Currency ratio
   d. Open market operations

5. The discount rate is the interest rate
   a. banks charge their very best loan customers.
   b. banks pay on certificates of deposit.
   c. the Fed pays on reserves held by banks.
   d. the Fed charges when it lends reserves to banks.

6. Which of the Fed's policy tools is most important?
   a. Reserve requirements
   b. Discount rate
   c. Currency ratio
   d. Open market operations

7. Which of the following would NOT affect the size of the monetary base?
   a. A bank exchanges government securities for a deposit at the Fed.
   b. A bank exchanges vault cash for a deposit at the Fed.
   c. The Fed buys government securities from a bank.
   d. The Fed buys government securities from someone other than a bank.

8. An open market purchase of government securities by the Fed will
   a. increase bank reserves and thus increase the monetary base.
   b. decrease bank reserves and thus decrease the monetary base.
   c. increase bank reserves and thus decrease the monetary base.
   d. decrease bank reserves and thus increase the monetary base.

9. If banks hold 10 percent of deposits as reserves and households and firms want to hold 20 percent of deposits as currency, the money multiplier is
   a. 2.8.
   b. 3.
   c. 4.
   d. 10.

10. The money multiplier will increase if either the fraction of deposits that households and firms want to hold as currency
    a. increases or the desired reserve ratio increases.
    b. increases or the desired reserve ratio decreases.
    c. decreases or the desired reserve ratio increases.
    d. decreases or the desired reserve ratio decreases.

11. Which of the following is NOT a principal motive for holding money by households and firms?
    a. Reserve motive
    b. Transactions motive
    c. Speculative motive
    d. Precautionary motive

12. The quantity of real money demanded will increase if either real income increases or
    a. the price level increases.
    b. the price level decreases.
    c. the interest rate increases.
    d. the interest rate decreases.

13. Real money is equal to nominal money
    a. divided by real GDP.
    b. minus real GDP.
    c. divided by the price level.
    d. minus the price level.

14. The higher the interest rate, the
    a. lower is the quantity of money demanded and the higher is the velocity of circulation.
    b. lower is the quantity of money demanded and the lower is the velocity of circulation.
    c. higher is the quantity of money demanded and the higher is the velocity of circulation.
    d. higher is the quantity of money demanded and the lower is the velocity of circulation.

15. Which of the following will cause the demand curve for real money to shift to the left?
    a. An increase in real GDP
    b. The expanded use of credit cards
    c. An increase in the price level
    d. An increase in the quantity of money supplied

16. If households and firms find that their holdings of real money are less than desired, they will
    a. sell financial assets which will cause interest rates to rise.
    b. sell financial assets which will cause interest rates to fall.
    c. buy financial assets which will cause interest rates to rise.
    d. buy financial assets which will cause interest rates to fall.

17. If the Fed buys government securities in the open market, the supply curve of real money will shift to the
    a. left, and the interest rate will rise.
    b. left, and the interest rate will fall.
    c. right, and the interest rate will rise.
    d. right, and the interest rate will fall.

18. If real GDP increases, the demand curve for real money will shift to the
    a. left, and the interest rate will rise.
    b. left, and the interest rate will fall.
    c. right, and the interest rate will rise.
    d. right, and the interest rate will fall.

SHORT ANSWER

1. What are the three main monetary policy tools of the Fed?

2. What are the two main liabilities of the Fed?

3. How does an open market purchase of government securities lead to an increase in the monetary base?

4. What will happen to the money multiplier if there is an increase in the fraction of deposits that households and firms want to hold as currency?

5. What are the three main motives for holding money?

6. Why do people care about the quantity of real money they hold rather than the quantity of nominal money they hold?

7. Why will the quantity of real money demanded fall when the interest rate rises?

8. The market for money is initially in equilibrium when the Fed increases the supply of money. Explain the adjustment to a new equilibrium interest rate.

9. Why will the expectation that the Fed will increase the money supply in the near future cause the interest rate to fall *now*?

PROBLEMS

1. Let D = deposits, C = currency, and R = reserves. Then let $a = C/D$, the ratio of currency to deposits, and $b = R/D$, the ratio of reserves to deposits. Table 11.1 gives alternative values for a across its top margin and alternative values for b down its left margin.

   Complete Table 11.1 by computing the money multiplier for each of the nine combinations of a and b. Note what happens to the money multiplier as the currency to deposits ratio increases. Note what happens to the money multiplier as the reserves to deposit ratio increases.

Table 11.1 Money Multipliers

	a		
b	0.1	0.2	0.3
0.05			
0.10			
0.15			

2. Calculate the money multipliers in each of the following cases.
   a) The money supply is $500 billion and the monetary base is $200 billion.
   b) Deposits = $500 billion, currency = $100 billion, and reserves = $50 billion.
   c) Reserves = $50 billion, currency = $150 billion, and the reserve to deposits ratio = 0.1.

3. Figure 11.1 illustrates the current equilibrium in the money market where *MD* is the demand curve for real money and *MS* is the supply curve for real money. Suppose the Fed wants to stimulate aggregate expenditure by lowering the interest rate to 6 percent. By how much must the Fed increase the *nominal* money supply if the price level is 2?

Figure 11.1

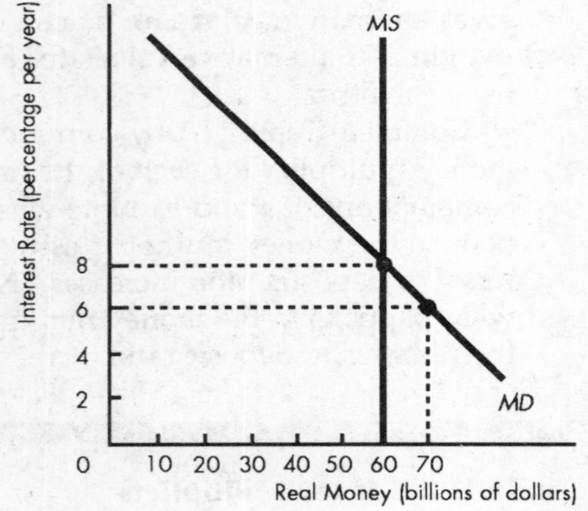

4. Having determined the amount by which the Fed must increase the nominal supply of money, we now want to determine the open market operation that will be necessary if the currency to deposits ratio is 0.2 and the required reserve ratio is 0.1. Will the Fed need to buy or sell government securities in the open market and in what amount?

5. Given the values for the currency to deposits and desired reserve ratios assumed in Problem 4, the round-by-round money multiplier process is examined here.
   a) For the open market operation in Problem 4, complete Table 11.2 by following the first six rounds of the process, then specify the effects in all other rounds, and finally give the total effects.
   b) What is the total change in money after six rounds?
   c) What is the total change in the money supply? Does this number agree with the desired change from problem 3?
   d) How much of the total change in money is a change in deposits and how much is a change in currency?

6. Consider a perpetuity with an annual coupon payment of $100. What is the interest rate on this financial asset if its price is
   a) $1000.
   b) $900.
   c) $1100.

Table 11.2 Money Multiplier Effects (billions of dollars)

Round	Excess reserves at start of round	New loans	Change in deposits	Change in currency	Excess reserves at end of round	Change in quantity of money
1						
2						
3						
4						
5						
6						
All others	—				—	
Totals	—				—	

ANSWERS

Concept Review

1. Federal Reserve
2. monetary policy
3. Federal Open Market
4. required reserve ratios, discount rate, open market operations.
5. monetary base; increase; money multiplier
6. transactions; precautionary; speculative
7. demand; real money
8. right; rise
9. perpetuity; falls
10. fall

True or False

1. T	7. T	13. T	19. T
2. F	8. T	14. T	20. F
3. F	9. F	15. F	21. T
4. T	10. T	16. F	
5. T	11. F	17. T	
6. F	12. T	18. F	

Multiple Choice

1. d	6. d	11. a	16. a
2. a	7. b	12. d	17. d
3. c	8. a	13. c	18. c
4. c	9. c	14. a	
5. d	10. d	15. b	

Short Answer

1. The three main monetary policy tools of the Fed are
   - required reserve ratios,
   - discount rate,
   - open market operations.

2. The two main liabilities of the Fed are
   - Federal Reserve notes in circulation,
   - Bank's deposits in the Fed.

3. An open market purchase of government securities by the Fed increases the monetary base by increasing one of its components: bank's deposits at the Fed. The process by which this takes place depends on whether the securities are purchased from banks or from the nonbank public.

   If the purchase is from banks, the process is direct: the Fed pays for the securities by crediting the bank's deposit at the Fed, which directly increases the monetary base.

   If the purchase is from the nonbank public, the Fed pays by writing checks on itself which the sellers of the securities deposit in their banks. The banks in turn present the checks to the Fed, which credits the banks' deposits at the Fed. Thus, in either case, the monetary base increases by the amount of the open market purchase.

4. The money multiplier will decrease if there is an increase in the fraction of deposits that households and firms want to hold as currency. This is because a currency drain reduces the proportion of each new loan that returns to the banking system as a new deposit in the money multiplier process and thus reduces the ability of the banking system to create money. At each round of the money multiplier process, part of any new loan will be held as currency and thus the amount that is deposited is less than the amount of the loan. This means that the amount of excess reserves in each successive round will be less than would be the case without the currency drain and thus the additional money created at each step will be smaller. Furthermore, the larger the ratio of currency to deposits the greater the leakage from the multiplier process.

5. The three main motives for holding money are
   - the transactions motive,
   - the precautionary motive,
   - the speculative motive.

6. Nominal money is simply the number of dollars, while real money is a measure of what money will buy. What matters to people is the quantity of goods and services that money will buy, not the number of dollars. If the price level rises by 10 percent, people will want to hold 10 percent more dollars (given real income and interest rates) in order to retain the same purchasing power.

7. Much of what constitutes money pays no interest; for example, currency and demand deposits. The interest rate is the opportunity cost of holding money since interest income on alternative financial assets that could have been held is forgone. When interest rates rise, it becomes more costly to hold money, and so people will reduce their money holdings in order to buy other financial assets and take advantage of the higher interest rates.

8. An increase in the supply of real money means that, at the current interest rate the quantity of money supplied will be greater than the quantity of money demanded. Money holders will want to reduce their money holdings and will attempt to do so by buying bonds. The increase in the demand for bonds will cause the price of bonds to rise and thus interest rates on bonds to fall. As interest rates fall, the quantity of money demanded increases, which reduces the excess supply of money. This process continues until the interest rate has fallen sufficiently that the quantity of money demanded is the same as the quantity of money supplied.

9. If economic agents expect the Fed to increase the money supply, this means that they expect the price of bonds to rise and the interest rate to fall. If this is the case, they will want to buy bonds now (i.e., increase the demand for bonds) so that they can sell them later at the higher expected price. But, this increase in the demand for bonds will cause the price of bonds to rise and the interest rate to fall now, before the Fed actually increases the money supply.

Problems

1. The completed Table 11.1 is shown here as Table 11.1 Solution. The entries are values of the money multiplier obtained from the following formula:

$$mm = \frac{1 + a}{a + b}$$

where *mm* is the money multiplier. For example, for the cell of the table corresponding to $a = 0.2$ and $b = 0.05$, we have

$$mm = \frac{1 + 0.2}{0.2 + 0.05} + \frac{1.2}{0.25} = 4.8$$

We note that for a given currency to deposits ratio (a), as the desired reserve ratio (b) increases, the money multiplier decreases. For a given desired reserve ratio (b), as the currency to deposits ratio (a) increases, the money multiplier also decreases.

Table 11.1 Solution Money Multipliers

b	a = 0.1	a = 0.2	a = 0.3
0.05	7.33	4.80	3.71
0.10	5.50	4.00	3.25
0.15	4.40	3.43	2.89

2. a) The money multiplier is the ratio of the money supply (M) to the monetary base (MB):

$$mm = M/MB = 500/200 = 2.5$$

b) Here we calculate $a = C/D$ and $b = R/D$ and use the formula derived in Table 11.6 in the text:

$$a = C/D = 100/500 = 0.2,\ b = R/D = 50/500 = 0.1$$

$$mm = \frac{1 + a}{a + b} = \frac{1 + 0.2}{0.2 + 0.1} = \frac{1.2}{0.3} = 4$$

c) Here we are given that $b = R/D = 0.1$ but we must find $a = C/D$. We know the value of C but not the value of D. We can find the value of D, however, from our knowledge of b and R: $D = R/b$. So

$$D = R/b = \$50 \text{ billion}/0.1 = \$500 \text{ billion}$$
$$a = C/D = 150/500 = 0.3$$

$$mm = \frac{1 + a}{a + b} = \frac{1 + 0.3}{0.3 + 0.1} = \frac{1.3}{0.4} = 3.25$$

3. The current equilibrium interest rate is 8 percent and the Fed would like to increase the money supply sufficiently to lower the interest rate to 6 percent. Since the quantity of real money demanded at an interest rate of 6 percent is $70 billion, the Fed will want to increase the supply of *real*

money by $10 billion: from $60 billion to $70 billion.

Real money is nominal money divided by the price level and the Fed only controls the supply of nominal money. Since the price level is 2, the supply of *nominal* money must rise by $20 billion in order to increase the supply of real money by $10 billion. Therefore, the Fed will need to increase the *nominal* money supply by $20 billion.

4. In order to increase the supply of money, the Fed will need to buy government securities in the open market since buying government securities will increase bank reserves and the monetary base. The amount of the open market purchase will depend on the money multiplier. Since $a = C/D = 0.2$ and $b = R/D = 0.1$ we can calculate the money multiplier as follows:

$$mm = \frac{1 + a}{a + b} = \frac{1 + 0.2}{0.2 + 0.1} = \frac{1.2}{0.3} = 4$$

This means that any initial increase in the monetary base will generate a total increase in money equal to 4 times its size. Thus, if we want a total increase in money of $20 billion, we need a $5 billion increase in the monetary base. This requires an open market purchase of $5 billion in government securities.

5. a) The completed table is shown as Table 11.2 Solution.

The $5 billion open market purchase will create excess reserves of $5 billion which will be loaned out; 20 percent of the loan will be held as currency, $1 billion, and the remainder will be held added to deposits, $4 billion. Of this increase in deposits, 10 percent will be held as desired reserves, $0.4 billion, and the rest will be excess reserves at the end of round 1, $3.6 billion. This then becomes the excess reserves at the beginning of round 2 and the process continues.

In subsequent rounds we compute the various entries in the table as follows:

- Excess reserves at start of round = excess reserves at end of previous round
- New loans = excess reserves at start of round
- Change in deposits = 0.8 times new loans
- Change in currency = 0.2 times new loans
- Excess reserves at end of round = 0.9 times change in deposits
- Change in quantity of money = change in deposits + change in currency

The total effects for each relevant column are obtained by using the fact that the money multiplier is 4 (from Problem 4) and the effect of all other rounds is the difference between the final total and the total after six rounds.

b) The total change in money after six rounds is $15.25 billion, the sum of the changes in the quantity of money for rounds 1 through 6.

c) The total change in the money supply is $20 billion, which can be obtained by using the money multiplier of 4. This is exactly the desired increase in the money supply from problem 3.

d) Of the $20 billion increase in money $16 billion (80 percent) is an increase in deposits and $4 billion (20 percent) is an increase in currency.

Table 11.2 Solution Money Multiplier Effects (billions of dollars)

Round	Excess reserves at start of round	New loans	Change in deposits	Change in currency	Excess reserves at end of round	Change in quantity of money
1	5	5	4	1	3.6	5
2	3.6	3.6	2.88	.72	2.59	3.6
3	2.59	2.59	2.07	.52	1.86	2.59
4	1.86	1.86	1.49	.37	1.34	1.86
5	1.34	1.34	1.07	.77	.96	1.34
6	.96	.96	.77	.19	.69	.96
All others	—	4.65	3.72	.93	—	4.65
Totals	—	20	16	4	—	20

6. The interest rate (r) on a perpetuity is obtained using the formula contained in Table 11.5 in the text:

$$r = \frac{c}{p} \times 100$$

where c = coupon and p = price of the bond.

a) $r = \frac{100}{1000} \times 100 = 10$ *percent*

b) $r = \frac{900}{900} \times 100 = 11.1$ *percent*

c) $r = \frac{100}{1100} \cdot 100 = 9.09$ *percent*

12 FISCAL AND MONETARY INFLUENCES ON AGGREGATE DEMAND

CHAPTER IN PERSPECTIVE

In a somewhat incomplete way, we have seen that fiscal policy (government actions that change taxes or government purchases) and monetary policy (Federal Reserve actions that change the money supply) can both potentially affect the economy by changing aggregate demand. In this chapter we examine in some detail the mechanisms by which such policy changes work their way through the economy to their final effects on aggregate demand and thus on the price level and real GDP. We also investigate the factors that determine whether a given monetary or fiscal policy will have a large or small effect on aggregate demand.

LEARNING OBJECTIVES

After studying this chapter, you will be able to:

- **Explain how fiscal policy (a change in government purchases or taxes) influences interest rates and aggregate demand**
- **Explain how monetary policy (a change in the money supply) influences interest rates and aggregate demand**
- **Explain what determines the relative effectiveness of fiscal and monetary policy on aggregate demand**
- **Describe the Keynesian-monetarist controversy about the influences of fiscal and monetary policy on aggregate demand and explain how the controversy was settled**
- **Explain how the mix of fiscal and monetary policy influences the composition of aggregate expenditure**
- **Explain how fiscal and monetary policy influence real GDP and the price level in both the short run and the long run**

HELPFUL HINTS

1. In Chapter 9 we examined the sector for goods and services in isolation by using the aggregate expenditure model and assuming that the interest rate is given. When the interest rate changes aggregate expenditure changes, and a new (flow) equilibrium level of real GDP results.

Similarly, in Chapter 11 we examined the money sector in isolation by using the money supply and money demand model and assuming that the level of real GDP is given. When the level of real GDP changes, the demand for real money changes and a new (stock) equilibrium rate of interest results. So the equilibrium value of real GDP is determined assuming a value for real GDP.

In this chapter we put these two sectors together and determine equilibrium real GDP and the equilibrium interest rate by examining both of the models at the same time. When the level of real GDP and the interest rate are such that both the market for goods and services and the market for money are in equilibrium at the same time, we have a simultaneous or joint equilibrium in both markets.

2. The major focus of this chapter is on the channels by which an initial change in fiscal or monetary policy is transmitted through the economy to its eventual effect on aggregate demand—the transmission channels of monetary or fiscal policy.

The graphical analysis presented in the text is of great value in studying these channels. From this analysis, we can see that the economy initially starts out in equilibrium. Next, either fiscal or monetary policy throws a market out of equilibrium. As this market changes and moves toward a new equilibrium, changes are triggered in other markets. We eventually arrive at a new, simultaneous equilibrium in all markets.

Some students may find it helpful to augment the graphical analysis with simple "arrow diagrams" which show the *sequence* of changes as the economy adjusts to an initial policy change. For example, the first and second round effects of monetary policy is represented by the following arrow diagram.

(1) First round effects:

$$\uparrow M \rightarrow \uparrow MS \overset{1}{\rightarrow} \downarrow r \overset{2}{\rightarrow} \uparrow I \rightarrow \uparrow AE \rightarrow \uparrow \textit{real GDP}.$$

Second round effects:

$$\uparrow \textit{real GDP} \rightarrow \uparrow MD \rightarrow \uparrow r \rightarrow \downarrow I \rightarrow \downarrow AE \rightarrow \downarrow \textit{real GDP}.$$

This diagram indicates that an expansionary monetary policy (e.g., an open market purchase of government securities by the Fed) will cause the quantity of money to increase ($\uparrow M$) which leads to ($\rightarrow$) an increase in the real supply of money ($\uparrow MS$). This in turn will result in a fall in the interest rate ($\downarrow r$) which will cause investment ($\uparrow I$), which is a part of aggregate expenditure, to increase ($\uparrow AE$). This will cause real GDP to begin increasing ($\uparrow$real GDP), which completes the first round. (Ignore the "*1*" and "*2*" above the first round of the arrow diagram for the moment.)

The second round effects begin with the first round increase in real GDP ($\uparrow$real GDP) which leads to an increase in the demand for real money ($\uparrow MD$). The increase in the demand for real money will cause the interest rate to rise ($\uparrow r$) and thus investment ($\downarrow I$) and aggregate expenditure will decrease ($\downarrow AE$) which will lead to a fall in real GDP ($\downarrow$real GDP). The second round effect on real GDP works in the opposite direction to the first round effect but is smaller in magnitude. This process continues until the economy eventually converges to an equilibrium in which both the goods market and the money market are simultaneously in equilibrium.

Note that an arrow diagram can be a convenient way of summarizing what we learn from the more detailed graphical analysis. Arrow diagrams can also be useful to help us see what kinds of things can weaken or strengthen the ability of policy to change aggregate demand.

3. The principle transmission channel of an increase in government purchases of goods and services (a fiscal policy) is given as follows.

(2) First round effects:

$\uparrow G \rightarrow \uparrow AE \rightarrow \uparrow real\ GDP.$

Second round effects:

$$\uparrow real\ GDP \rightarrow \uparrow MD \overset{1}{\rightarrow} \uparrow r \overset{2}{\rightarrow} \downarrow I \rightarrow \downarrow AE \rightarrow \downarrow real\ GDP.$$

The amount of government purchases on goods and services is represented by *G*. Otherwise the notation is the same as used above. The second round effects (crowding out) partially offset the first round increase in real GDP. (Once again, ignore the "*1*" and "*2*" until the next hint.)

4. The text indicates that the strength of the effect of a change in the money supply on aggregate demand depends on the responsiveness of the demand for real money to changes in the interest rate and the responsiveness of investment demand to changes in the interest rate.

The arrow diagram given in (1) can help us understand how these factors affect the strength of monetary policy by focusing on the *links* marked "*1*" and "*2*". The link between the increase in the supply of real money and the subsequent fall in the interest rate is indicated as link 1. If the demand for real money is very sensitive to interest rate changes (i.e., the *MD* curve is very flat or interest elastic), then this link is quite weak: a given increase in the supply of real money will have only a small effect on the interest rate. This in turn means a relatively small effect on investment, etc. Link 2 captures the effect of a change in the interest rate on investment. If investment is very sensitive to interest rate changes (i.e., the investment demand curve is very flat or interest elastic) then this link is quite strong: a given fall in the interest rate will have a very large effect on investment.

We can also examine the factors that determine the strength of the effect of fiscal policy on aggregate demand. Links 1 and 2 in the second round of (2) are the relevant links; indeed they are the same as links 1 and 2 for monetary policy. If the demand for real money is very sensitive to interest rate changes (i.e., the *MD* curve is very flat), then link 1 is quite weak, the amount of crowding out is small, and fiscal policy is strong. (See Problem 4b.) Similarly, if investment is very sensitive to interest rate changes (i.e., the investment demand curve is very flat), then link 2 is quite strong, the amount of crowding out is large, and fiscal policy is weak.

Thus links 1 and 2 are the critical links in the transmission process and the focus of controversy regarding the relative effectiveness of fiscal and monetary policy. It is interesting to think about the extreme Keynesian and monetarist positions in terms of these links.

The existence of a liquidity trap (horizontal *MD* curve assumed by an extreme Keynesian) makes monetary policy ineffective because it completely breaks link 1: an increase in the supply of real money will have no effect on the interest rate.

The existence of a vertical investment demand curve (assumed by an extreme Keynesian) makes monetary policy ineffective because it completely breaks link 2. Similarly, the existence of a horizontal investment demand curve or a vertical *MD* curve (assumed by an extreme monetarist) implies complete crowding out and thus ineffective fiscal policy.

Note that the same characteristics that create a strong fiscal policy create a weak monetary policy and vice versa.

KEY FIGURES AND TABLES

Figure 12.1 Equilibrium Interest Rate and Real GDP

This is the basic three-part graph used this chapter. It illustrates a simultaneous equilibrium in both money market and the market for goods and services: the combination of interest rate and real GDP which corresponds to equilibrium in the money market *and* equilibrium in the goods market.

Part (a) of the diagram illustrates the determination of the equilibrium interest rate in the money market. Once the equilibrium interest rate is determined, the level of investment is determined by the investment demand curve (*I*) in part (b). Since investment is part of aggregate planned expenditure, the level of investment (along with the other components of aggregate planned expenditure) determines the position of the *AE* curve in part (c). The position of the *AE* curve determines the level of real GDP. (*Note:* This in turn determines the amount of real money demanded and the equilibrium interest rate.)

Figure 12.2 First Round Effects of an Expansionary Fiscal Policy

Equilibrium expenditure is determined by the intersection of the aggregate expenditure, (*AE*,) curve and the 45° line. The position of the *AE curve* is determined by the level of autonomous expenditure. As the level of autonomous expenditure changes, the *AE* curve shifts which has a multiplier effect on equilibrium expenditure.

This figure illustrates these first round effects for an increase in autonomous expenditure caused by an expansionary fiscal policy. The initial level of autonomous expenditure is $1.6 trillion and is indicated by the A_0 curve. Thus, the initial aggregate expenditure curve is AE_0 and equilibrium aggregate expenditure is $4 trillion.

Starting from this equilibrium, the government increases its purchases of goods and services by $1 trillion and, thus, the autonomous expenditure curve shifts up from A_0 to A_1 and the aggregate expenditure curve shifts from AE_0 to AE_1. As a result, through a multiplier process, equilibrium expenditure and real GDP begin to rise. In the new equilibrium, equilibrium expenditure increases to $6.5 trillion.

Figure 12.3 How the Economy Adjusts to an Expansionary Fiscal Policy

Part (a) of this figure shows schematically the first round effects of an expansionary fiscal policy that was illustrated in Fig. 12.2. An increase in government purchases is an increase in autonomous expenditure which leads to an increase in aggregate expenditure and equilibrium expenditure. A multiplier process is initiated and real GDP begins to rise.

The second round effects following from rising real GDP are illustrated in part (b) of the figure. The first round increase in real GDP affects the money market by increasing the demand for real money which causes the interest rate to rise. The rising interest rate causes investment and, thus, autonomous expenditure to decline which results in a decrease in aggregate planned expenditure and equilibrium expenditure. The resulting decrease in real GDP works to offset the first round increase but the second round effect is smaller.

This figure is similar to arrow diagram (2) in Helpful Hint 3.

Figure 12.5 First Round Effects of a Decrease in the Money Supply

A change in the money supply has a direct effect on the interest rate which then effects investment expenditure. This initiates a multiplier process which causes real GDP to change. This figure illustrates these first round effects for a decrease in the money supply.

The initial situation is seen by examining all three parts of the figure. Part (a) shows that the initial real supply of money is $3 trillion MS_0, and the starting equilibrium interest rate is 5 percent. As shown in part (b), at an interest rate of 5 percent, investment spending is $1 trillion. Part (c) indicates that when investment is $1 trillion, real GDP is $4 trillion.

A $1 trillion decrease in the money supply shifts the supply curve of real money to the left, from MS_0 to MS_1. This causes the interest rate to rise to 7 percent (part (a)) which causes a decrease in investment to $0.2 trillion (part (b)). The decrease in investment shifts the investment curve in part (c) from I_0 to I_1 and the aggregate expenditure curve from AE_0 to AE_1 which causes equilibrium expenditure to fall and a multiplier process begins in which real GDP begins to fall.

Figure 12.6 How an Economy Adjusts to a Decrease in the Money Supply

Part (a) of this figure shows schematically the first round effects of a decrease in the money supply that was illustrated in Fig. 12.5. A decrease in the money supply increases the rate of interest which causes investment, a part of autonomous expenditure, to decline. As a result, aggregate planned expenditure declines which causes equilibrium expenditure to decline. A multiplier process is initiated and real GDP begins to decline.

The second round effects following from the first round fall in real GDP are illustrated in part (b) of the figure. These are the same as the second round effects following an expansionary fiscal policy shown in Fig. 12.3 but in the opposite direction. The first round decease in real GDP decreases the demand for real money which causes the interest rate to fall. The falling interest rate causes investment and, thus, autonomous expenditure to increase which results in an increase in aggregate planned expenditure and equilibrium expenditure. The resulting increase in real GDP works to offset the first round decrease but the second round effect is smaller.

This figure is similar to arrow diagram (1) in Helpful Hint 2 but here the money supply declines.

Figure 12.7 The Effectiveness of Fiscal Policy

As shown in arrow diagram (2) of Helpful Hint 3, an expansionary fiscal policy is less effective if the second round effects are strong. Thus, the larger the effect of a given change in the interest rate on investment or the larger the effect on the interest rate of a given change in the demand for real money, the larger are the second round effects and the smaller is the effect of fiscal policy on aggregate demand. This figure illustrates how these effects depend on the sensitivity of investment demand and the demand for real money to changes in the rate of interest.

Part (a) shows how the magnitude of the effect on investment (and thus aggregate demand) of an expansionary fiscal policy depends on the interest sensitivity of investment demand. An increase in government purchases increases real GDP and shifts the demand for real money curve to the right, from MD_0 to MD_1. This causes the interest rate to rise from 5 percent to 6 percent. However, the induced effect on investment depends on the interest sensitivity of investment demand. In the figure, investment demand is more sensitive to interest rate changes along ID_A than along ID_B. We see that the increase in the interest rate has a larger effect on investment when investment demand is more sensitive to interest rate changes. This means that fiscal policy is less effective when investment demand is more sensitive to interest rate changes.

Part (b) shows that the magnitude of the effect on the interest rate of an increase in the real demand for money depends on the interest sensitivity of the real demand for money. The quantity of real money demanded is less sensitive to interest rate changes along MD_A than along MD_B. An increase in government purchases increases real GDP and shifts the demand for real money curve to the right;

MD_{A0} to MD_{A1} and MD_{B0} to MD_{B1} causing the interest rate to rise. The interest rate rises by more (from 5 percent to 6 percent rather than to 5.5 percent) with MD_A, the less interest sensitive demand curve for real money. This larger increase in the interest rate means a larger decline in investment in the second round and thus less effective fiscal policy.

Figure 12.8 The Effectiveness of Monetary Policy

As shown in arrow diagram (1) of Helpful Hint 2, the larger the effect of a given change in the interest rate on investment or the larger the effect of a given change in the supply of real money on the interest rate, the larger is the effect of monetary policy on aggregate demand. This figure illustrates how these effects depend on the sensitivity of investment demand and the demand for real money to changes in the rate of interest.

Part (a) shows how the magnitude of the effect on investment (and thus aggregate demand) of an increase in the money supply depends on the interest sensitivity of investment demand. An increase in the money supply causes the interest rate to fall from 5 percent to 3 percent. However, the induced effect on investment depends on the interest sensitivity of investment demand. In the figure, investment demand is more sensitive to interest rate changes along ID_A than along ID_B. We see that the fall in the interest rate has a larger effect on investment (so monetary policy is more effective) when investment demand is more sensitive to interest rate changes.

Part (b) shows that the magnitude of the effect on the interest rate of an increase in the money supply depends on the interest sensitivity of the real demand for money. The quantity of real money demanded is less sensitive to interest rate changes along MD_A than along MD_B. An increase in the money supply shifts the money supply curve from MS_0 to MS_1 causing the interest rate to fall. The interest rate falls by more (from 5 percent to 3 percent rather than to 4 percent) with MD_A, the less interest sensitive demand curve for real money. As we can also see in part (b), for any given investment demand curve, *ID*, the larger the interest rate changes, the larger the effect on investment and, thus, the more effective is monetary policy.

Figure 12.9 Policy-Induced Changes in Real GDP and the Price Level

Fiscal or monetary policy will shift the aggregate demand curve and thus induce changes in real GDP and the price level. This figure illustrates the short-run effects of a policy-induced increase in aggregate demand.

The initial aggregate demand curve is AD_0 and the short-run aggregate supply curve is *SAS* so real GDP is $4 trillion and the price level is 130. An expansionary fiscal or monetary policy occurs which shifts the aggregate demand curve to the right, to AD_1. At the initial price level, the quantity of real GDP demanded increases to $5.5 trillion. This puts upward pressure on the price level which reduces the real money supply and causes a decrease in the quantity of real GDP demanded, represented by a movement up along the aggregate demand curve. The net effect is an increase in real GDP to $5 trillion and an increase in the price level to 140.

Figure 12.10 The Long-Run Effects of Policy-Induced Changes in Real GDP and the Price Level

As illustrated in this figure, if the economy is initially at a full employment equilibrium, a policy induced increase in aggregate demand will cause real GDP and the price level to both rise in the short run, but, in the long run, real GDP will return to its initial level and the price level will rise even further.

In the figure, the initial aggregate demand curve is AD_0 and the initial short-run aggregate supply curve is SAS_0. These curves intersect at a point on the long-run aggregate supply curve, *LAS*, so the economy begins at a full employment equilibrium with real GDP of $5 trillion and a price level of 130.

Expansionary fiscal or monetary policy will shift the aggregate demand curve to the right, to AD_1. In the short run, wage rates are fixed so the economy remains on SAS_0 and real GDP increases to $6 trillion and the price level rises to 135. Because real GDP is above its long-run level, wages will increase and the short-run aggregate supply curve will shift upward causing real GDP to begin decreasing and the price level to rise further. This will continue until the short-run aggregate supply curve has shifted to SAS_1. In the new long-run equilibrium, real GDP has returned to its full employment level of $5 trillion and the price level has risen to 145.

SELF-TEST

CONCEPT REVIEW

1. An expansionary fiscal policy will ____________ real GDP, ____________ the interest rate, and ____________ investment.
2. The tendency for an increase in government purchases to cause interest rates to rise and thus reduce investment is called ____________ ____________.
3. The tendency for an expansionary fiscal policy to decrease net exports is called ____________ ____________.
4. An increase in the money supply causes the interest rate to ____________. This will in turn cause investment to ____________, which will ____________ aggregate planned expenditure. This change in real GDP will shift the demand curve for real money to the ____________, which will cause the interest rate to ____________.
5. A change in the money supply will have a larger effect on interest rates the ____________ responsive is the demand for real money to changes in the interest rate. A change in the interest rate will have a larger effect on investment the ____________ responsive investment demand to the interest.
6. Macroeconomists whose views about the functions of the economy represent an extension of the theories of John Maynard Keynes are called ____________. Macroeconomists who believe that the economy is inherently stable and that the quantity of money is the main determinant of aggregate demand are called ____________.
7. A situation in which the demand curve for real money is horizontal at a given low interest rate is called a(n) ____________ ____________.
8. A decrease in the money supply will cause the aggregate demand curve to shift to the ____________ and, in the short run, the price level will ____________ and real GDP will ____________.

TRUE OR FALSE

____ 1. In the first round following an expansionary fiscal policy, real GDP increases.

____ 2. In the second round following an expansionary fiscal policy, real GDP increases.

____ 3. An increase in government purchases of goods and services eventually will shift the demand curve for real money to the right, increasing the interest rate.

____ 4. Crowding out will be greater if the investment demand curve is very steep.

____ 5. Crowding in is the tendency for an expansionary fiscal policy to decrease net exports.

____ 6. An increase in the supply of real money will cause the interest rate to rise.

____ 7. An increase in the demand for real money will cause the interest rate to rise.

____ 8. In general, an increase in the supply of real money will be followed by an increase in investment.

____ 9. An increase in real GDP will shift the demand curve for real money to the left.

____ 10. An increase in the rate of interest will cause the investment demand curve to shift to the left.

____ 11. A decrease in investment will decrease aggregate planned expenditure and equilibrium real GDP.

____ 12. Other things being equal, the more sensitive investment is to the interest rate, the bigger is the effect of a change in fiscal policy on aggregate demand.

____ 13. Other things being equal, the more sensitive the quantity of money demanded is to the interest rate, the bigger is the effect of a change in fiscal policy on aggregate demand.

____ 14. Other things being equal, the more sensitive investment is to the interest rate, the bigger is the effect of a change in the money supply on aggregate demand.

____ 15. Other things being equal, the more sensitive the quantity of money demanded is to the interest rate, the bigger is the effect of a change in the money supply on aggregate demand.

____ 16. An increase in the value of the dollar relative to foreign currencies will decrease net exports.

____ 17. If aggregate demand is increased by an increase in the money supply, interest rates fall and investment increases.

____ 18. If aggregate demand is increased by an increase in government purchases of goods and services, interest rates fall and investment increases.

____ 19. Keynesians consider the economy to be inherently unstable.

____ 20. Monetarists do NOT believe in the existence of a liquidity trap.

____21. With regard to the Keynesian-monetarist controversy, the statistical evidence has tended to support the extreme Keynesian position.

____22. An increase in transfer payments will increase both the price level and real GDP in the short run.

MULTIPLE CHOICE

1. Consider Fig. 12.1. Why is the situation depicted there NOT consistent with simultaneous money market equilibrium and expenditure equilibrium?
   a. The level of aggregate planned spending is inconsistent with the interest rate.
   b. The money market and the goods market are not individually in equilibrium.
   c. The expenditure equilibrium occurs at a different level of real GDP than the level of real GDP assumed when drawing the demand curve for real money.
   d. The level of investment in part (c) is inconsistent with the level of investment in part (b).

2. Suppose Fig. 12.1 depicts the actual current position of an economy. In a simultaneous money market equilibrium and expenditure equilibrium,
   a. real GDP will be less than $800 billion and the interest rate will be higher than 4 percent.
   b. real GDP will be less than $800 billion and the interest rate will be lower than 4 percent.
   c. real GDP will be more than $800 billion and the interest rate will be higher than 4 percent.
   d. real GDP will be more than $800 billion and the interest rate will be lower than 4 percent.

3. A tax cut will
   a. increase aggregate planned expenditure by causing disposable income to increase.
   b. increase aggregate planned expenditure by causing the interest rate to fall.
   c. decrease aggregate planned expenditure by causing disposable income to fall.
   d. decrease aggregate planned expenditure by causing the interest rate to rise.

4. There will be no crowding out if
   a. the demand for real money is totally unresponsive to changes in the interest rate.
   b. the supply of real money is totally unresponsive to changes in the interest rate.
   c. investment is totally unresponsive to changes in the interest rate.
   d. investment is totally unresponsive to changes in real GDP.

5. In the first round following an expansionary fiscal policy, real GDP increases. In the beginning of the second round, the demand for money
   a. increases and the interest rate declines.
   b. increases and the interest rate rises.
   c. decreases and the interest rate declines.
   d. decreases and the interest rate rises.

6. An increase in government expenditure to construct a new highway leads firms to build new factories. This is an example of
   a. crowding up.
   b. crowding down.
   c. crowding out.
   d. crowding in.

Figure 12.1

(a)

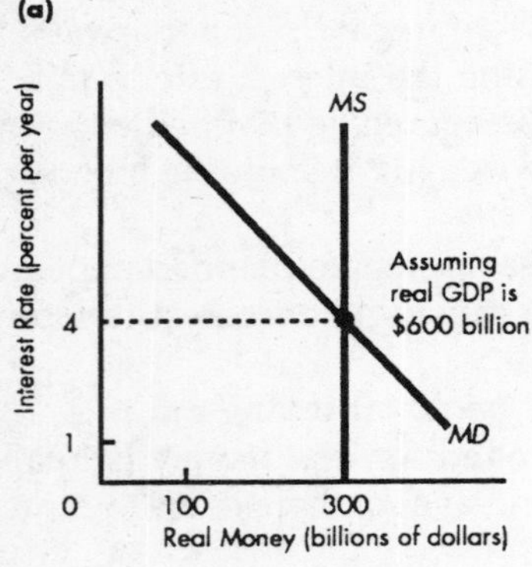

(b)

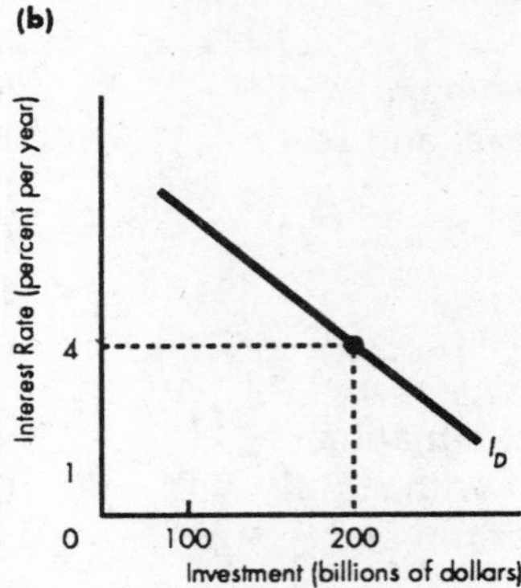

(c)

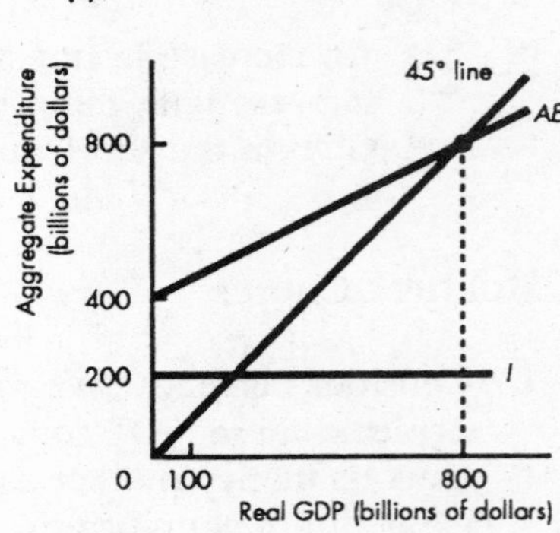

7. An increase in government purchases of goods and services will cause
   a. a decrease in the interest rate, which will lead to a decrease in the foreign exchange value of the dollar.
   b. a decrease in the interest rate, which will lead to an increase in the foreign exchange value of the dollar.
   c. an increase in the interest rate, which will lead to a decrease in the foreign exchange value of the dollar.
   d. an increase in the interest rate, which will lead to an increase in the foreign exchange value of the dollar.

8. Which of the following correctly describes the initial effects of a monetary policy? An increase in the money supply will cause
   a. investment to increase and thus aggregate planned expenditure to increase.
   b. investment to increase and thus aggregate planned expenditure to decrease.
   c. investment to decrease and thus aggregate planned expenditure to increase.
   d. investment to decrease and thus aggregate planned expenditure to decrease.

9. An increase in the money supply will, in general, eventually lead to an increase in real GDP, which will shift the demand curve for real money to the
   a. left causing the interest rate to fall.
   b. left causing the interest rate to rise.
   c. right causing the interest rate to fall.
   d. right causing the interest rate to rise.

10. Monetary policy will have the *smallest* effect on aggregate demand when the sensitivity of the demand curve for real money to the interest rate is
    a. large and the sensitivity of the investment demand curve to the interest rate is large.
    b. large and the sensitivity of the investment demand curve to the interest rate is small.
    c. small and the sensitivity of the investment demand curve to the interest rate is large.
    d. small and the sensitivity of the investment demand curve to the interest rate is small.

11. The demand for real money will be more sensitive to the interest rate,
    a. the more people care about the timing of investment.
    b. the less people care about the timing of investment.
    c. the more substitutable other financial assets are for money.
    d. the less substitutable other financial assets are for money.

12. Aggregate demand can be increased by increasing the money supply (expansionary monetary policy) or by increasing government purchases of goods and services (expansionary fiscal policy). Which of the following is a correct comparison?
    a. The interest rate will rise under the monetary policy and fall under the fiscal policy, while consumption will increase under both.
    b. The interest rate will fall under the monetary policy and rise under the fiscal policy, while consumption will increase under both.
    c. Consumption will rise under the monetary policy and fall under the fiscal policy, while the interest rate will increase under both.
    d. Consumption will rise under the monetary policy and fall under the fiscal policy, while the interest rate will decrease under both.

13. Consider an economy where the demand for real money is very sensitive to changes in the interest rate. The problem with monetary policy in this economy is that
    a. there will be a high level of crowding out.
    b. monetary policy will create changes in the exchange rate that offset the monetary policy.
    c. a change in the interest rate creates only a small change in investment demand.
    d. a change in the money supply creates only a small change in the interest rate.

14. Consider an economy where the demand for real money is very sensitive to changes in the interest rate and where the investment demand curve is also very sensitive to the interest rate. In this economy, fiscal policy
    a. is relatively ineffective while monetary policy is effective.
    b. is relatively effective while monetary policy is ineffective.
    c. and monetary policy are both effective.
    d. and monetary policy are both ineffective.

15. Which of the following sets of beliefs is characteristic of a Keynesian?
    a. The economy is inherently unstable, and fiscal policy is more important than monetary policy.
    b. The economy is inherently unstable, and monetary policy is more important than fiscal policy.
    c. The economy is inherently stable, and fiscal policy is more important than monetary policy.
    d. The economy is inherently stable, and monetary policy is more important than fiscal policy.

16. The founder of modern monetarism is
    a. Adam Smith.
    b. John Maynard Keynes.
    c. Milton Friedman.
    d. James Tobin.

17. Which of the following would characterize the extreme monetarist position?
    a. A horizontal investment demand curve and a horizontal demand curve for real money
    b. A horizontal investment demand curve and a vertical demand curve for real money
    c. A vertical investment demand curve and a horizontal demand curve for real money
    d. A vertical investment demand curve and a vertical demand curve for real money

18. If an economy is in a liquidity trap, then
    a. a change in the interest rate will have no effect on investment.
    b. a change in investment will have no effect on aggregate planned expenditure.
    c. open market operations will not shift the supply curve of real money.
    d. an increase in the supply of real money will have no effect on the interest rate.

19. Statistical evidence from a variety of historical and national experiences suggests that
    a. fiscal policy affects aggregate demand and monetary policy does not.
    b. monetary policy affects aggregate demand and fiscal policy does not.
    c. both fiscal policy and monetary policy affect aggregate demand.
    d. neither fiscal policy nor monetary policy affect aggregate demand.

20. If the economy is initially in an unemployment equilibrium, the long-run effect of an expansionary monetary policy will be
    a. an increase in both the price level and real GDP.
    b. an increase in the price level but no change in real GDP.
    c. an increase in real GDP but no change in the price level.
    d. no change in either the price level or real GDP.

21. If the economy is initially in a full employment equilibrium, the long-run effect of an expansionary monetary policy will be
    a. an increase in both the price level and real GDP.
    b. an increase in the price level but no change in real GDP.
    c. an increase in real GDP but no change in the price level.
    d. no change in either the price level or real GDP.

SHORT ANSWER

1. Trace the first and second round effects of an increase in government purchase of goods and services.

2. How does crowding out take place?

3. How does international crowding out take place?

4. Trace the first and second round effects of an increase in the supply of real money.

5. Explain how an increase in the money supply leads to an increase in aggregate planned expenditure via the exchange rate effect.

6. Why will expansionary fiscal policy have a smaller effect on real GDP if investment is very sensitive to interest rate changes?

7. Why does an increase in the supply of real money have a smaller effect on aggregate planned expenditure if the demand for real money is very sensitive to changes in the interest rate?

8. Why does an increase in the supply of real money have a larger effect on aggregate planned expenditure if investment is very sensitive to changes in the interest rate?

9. What are the principle beliefs of Keynesians and monetarists with regard to the inherent stability of the economy and the relative importance of monetary policy and fiscal policy?

10. Consider an economy initially at full employment. What are the short run and long run effects of an expansionary fiscal policy on the price level and real GDP?

PROBLEMS

1. Figure 12.2 depicts an economy. Note that MD_0 corresponds to real GDP = $400 billion, MD_1 corresponds to real GDP = $500 billion, and MD_2 corresponds to real GDP = $600 billion.
   a) What are the equilibrium values for real GDP, the interest rate, and investment?
   b) Does this correspond to a simultaneous money market equilibrium and expenditure equilibrium? Why or why not?

2. Consider again the economy depicted by Fig. 12.2. Suppose that the Fed increases the supply of real money from $300 billion to $400 billion.
   a) What is the first round effect on the interest rate?
   b) What effect will this have on investment?
   c) As a result of this change in investment, what happens to first round equilibrium GDP? Why is this first round level of GDP not the end of the story?

Figure 12.2

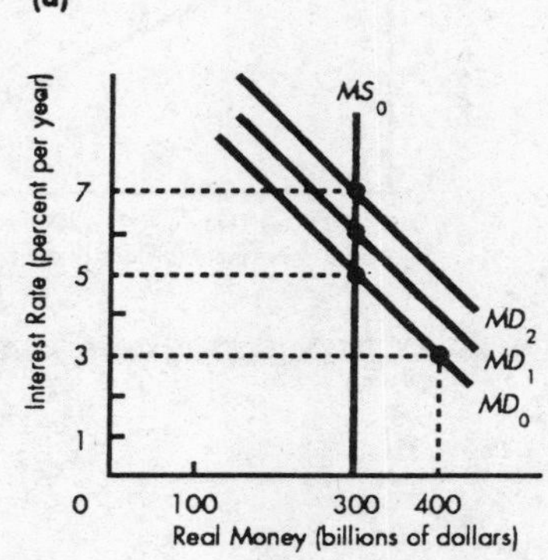

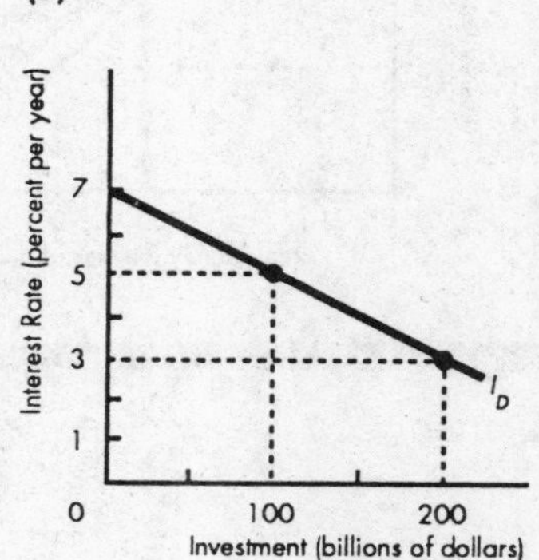

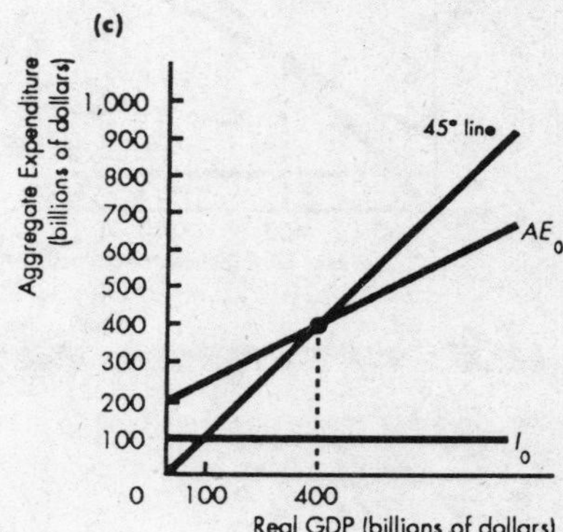

d) What are the interest rate, investment, and real GDP at the new simultaneous money market and expenditure equilibrium?

e) Using Fig. 12.2, represent graphically the new final equilibrium.

3. Figure 12.3 below depicts the same economy as in Fig. 12.2. Note that MD_0 corresponds to real GDP = \$400 billion, MD_1 corresponds to real GDP = \$500 billion, and MD_2 corresponds to real GDP = \$600 billion. Suppose that the government increases its purchase of goods and services by \$100 billion.

a) What is the initial full multiplier effect on real GDP? Why will the economy not remain at this level of real GDP?

b) As a result of this full multiplier effect on real GDP, what happens to the demand curve for real money and to the interest rate?

c) What are the interest rate, investment, and real GDP when the economy achieves simultaneous money market equilibrium and equilibrium expenditure? How much investment is crowded out? What are the differences in the effects of monetary policy and fiscal policy illustrated by Problems 2 and 3?

d) Using Fig. 12.3, represent graphically this new final equilibrium.

4. a) Graphically show that if the demand for real money is more sensitive to changes in the interest rate, monetary policy has a smaller effect on equilibrium real GDP.

b) Show also that fiscal policy has a larger effect on equilibrium real GDP.

Figure 12.3

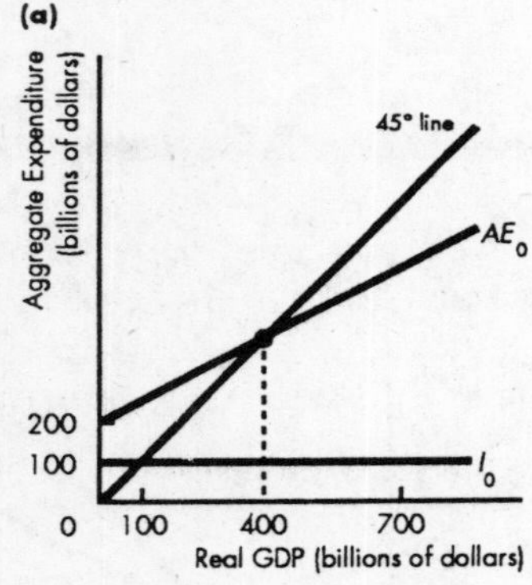

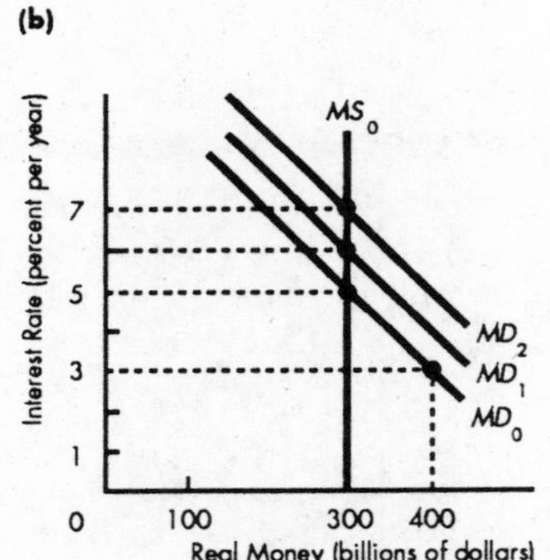

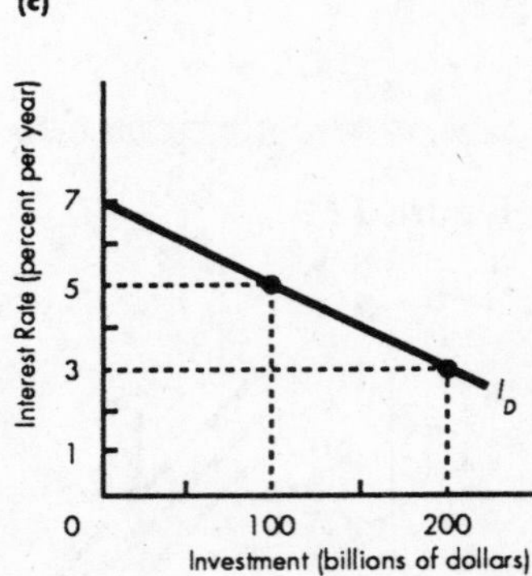

ANSWERS

CONCEPT REVIEW

1. increase; increase; decrease
2. crowding out
3. international crowding out
4. decrease; increase; increase; right; rise
5. less; more
6. Keynesians; monetarists
7. liquidity trap
8. left; decrease; decrease

TRUE OR FALSE

1. T	6. F	11. T	16. T	21. F
2. F	7. T	12. F	17. T	22. T
3. T	8. T	13. T	18. F	
4. F	9. F	14. T	19. T	
5. T	10. F	15. F	20. T	

MULTIPLE CHOICE

1. c	6. d	11. c	16. c	21. b
2. a	7. d	12. b	13. b	
3. a	8. a	13. d	18. d	
4. c	9. d	14. a	19. c	
5. b	10. b	15. a	20. a	

SHORT ANSWER

1. In the first round, an increase in government spending will increase aggregate planned expenditure and shift the AE curve upward, and the increase in aggregate planned expenditure will set off a multiplier process that starts real GDP increasing.

   In the second round, the first round increase in real GDP causes the demand curve for real money to shift to the right causing the interest rate to rise. The higher interest rate causes investment to decrease, which means that aggregate planned expenditure decreases, causing equilibrium real GDP to decline.

2. Crowding out is the tendency for expansionary fiscal policy to cause the interest rate to rise and thus investment to decline. The expansionary fiscal policy "crowds out" investment. The increase in the interest rate is a consequence of the fact that the increase in real GDP that occurs as a consequence of an increase in government expenditure on goods and services, for example, will cause the demand curve for real money to shift to the right. Thus the equilibrium interest rate will rise.

3. International crowding out is the tendency for an expansionary fiscal policy to decrease net exports. As indicated in the answer to Question 2, an expansionary fiscal policy will, in the second round, cause the interest rate to rise. As the interest rate in the U.S. rises, more U.S. dollars are demanded by people in the rest of the world which makes the dollar rise in value against other currencies. An increase in the foreign exchange value of the dollar makes U.S.-produced goods (our exports) more expensive to foreigners and makes imports less expensive. As a result, net exports decline.

4. In the first round, an increase in the supply of real money will shift the supply curve of real money to the right and lower the interest rate. The lower interest rate will cause investment to increase, which means that aggregate planned expenditure increases, setting off a multiplier process that starts real GDP increasing.

In the second round, the first round increase in real GDP causes the demand curve for real money to shift to the right causing the interest rate to rise. The higher interest rate will cause investment to decrease, which means that aggregate planned expenditure decreases, causing equilibrium real GDP to decline.

An increase in the real supply of money will shift the supply curve of real money to the right and lower the interest rate. The lower interest rate (relative to interest rates in other countries) will cause people to want to sell low-interest U.S. financial assets and buy relatively high-interest foreign financial assets. Thus the demand for dollars decreases and the demand for foreign currencies increases, which results in a lower value of the dollar relative to foreign currencies. This fall in the value of the dollar will cause net exports to increase as foreigners can now buy U.S. goods for less (in terms of their currencies) and U.S. citizens must pay more (in dollars) for foreign goods. The increase in net exports is an increase in aggregate planned expenditure, and, thus, an increase in aggregate demand.

If investment is very sensitive to changes in the interest rate, the investment demand curve will be very flat. Thus the increase in the interest rate that initiates the crowding out effect (see the answer to Question 2 above) will induce a large decrease in investment spending, which means large crowding out.

5. If the demand for real money is very sensitive to changes in the interest rate, the demand curve for real money is very flat. Thus, when the money supply increases and the supply curve for real money shifts to the right, the resulting change in the equilibrium interest rate will be small. A small interest rate change will lead to a small change in investment and a small change in aggregate planned expenditure and. thus an increase in aggregate demand.

6. If investment is very sensitive to changes in the interest rate, the investment demand curve will be very flat. Thus the increase in the interest rate that initiates the crowding out effect (see the answer to Question 2 above) will induce a large decrease in investment spending, which means large crowding out.

7. If the demand for real money is very sensitive to changes in the interest rate, the demand curve for real money is very flat. Thus, when the money supply increases and the supply curve for real money shifts to the right, the resulting change in the equilibrium interest rate will be small. A small interest rate change will lead to a small change in investment and a small change in aggregate planned expenditure.

8. If investment is very sensitive to changes in the interest rate, the investment demand curve will be very flat. Thus when the interest rate falls due to an increase in the money supply, it will induce a rather large increase in investment and thus a large increase in aggregate planned expenditure.

9. Keynesians believe that the economy is inherently unstable and that fiscal policy is much more important than monetary policy. Monetarists believe that the economy is inherently stable and that monetary policy is much more important than fiscal policy.

10. The economy is initially at full employment with real GDP at its long-run level. An expansionary fiscal policy will shift the aggregate demand curve to the right. In the short run, given the wage rate, the economy will move up the short-run ag-

gregate supply curve and both the price level and real GDP increase. Since real GDP is above its long-run level, unemployment is below its natural rate which puts upward pressure on wages. As wages increase, the short-run aggregate supply curve will shift up. In the long run, the economy will return to its long-run level of real GDP but the price level will be higher.

PROBLEMS

1. a) The equilibrium value for real GDP is at the intersection of the AE_0 curve and the 45° line: \$400 billion. The equilibrium value for the interest rate is 5 percent, since the relevant *MD* curve is MD_0 when real GDP is \$400 billion. At an interest rate of 5 percent, investment is \$100 (part b).
   b) This is a simultaneous money market and expenditure equilibrium since real GDP is \$400 billion when the interest rate is 5 percent (equilibrium expenditure) and the equilibrium interest rate is 5 percent when real GDP is \$400 billion (money market equilibrium); that is, it is simultaneous money market equilibrium and equilibrium expenditure because the values of real GDP and the interest rate that give money market equilibrium and equilibrium expenditure are the same.

2. a) The first round effect of an increase in the supply of real money from \$300 billion to \$400 billion is to lower the interest rate from 5 percent to 3 percent.
   b) The fall in the interest rate from 5 percent to 3 percent will increase investment from \$100 billion to \$200 billion.
   c) First round equilibrium GDP will increase from \$400 billion to \$600 billion. This level of GDP will not be achieved because, as real GDP begins to rise above \$400 billion, the money demand curve will start shifting to the right and causing the interest rate to rise. This will cause investment and thus the *AE* curve to shift back down somewhat.
   d) In the new simultaneous money market equilibrium and expenditure equilibrium, we must have a single real GDP and interest rate combination that (given the new money supply) leaves *both* the money market and the market for goods in equilibrium. This occurs at an interest rate of 4 percent and real GDP of \$500 billion. Investment will be \$150 billion.
   e) The new final equilibrium is illustrated in Fig. 12.2 Solution. Note that the relevant demand curve for real money is MD_1, which is drawn assuming real GDP = \$500 billion. MS_0 has shifted to MS_1, I_0 has shifted to I_1, and AE_0 has shifted to AE_1.

3. a) The full multiplier effect of an increase in government purchases of \$100 billion is to increase equilibrium GDP by \$200 billion: from \$400 billion to \$600 billion. The economy will not remain here (indeed it would likely never attain this level) because as real GDP increases, the demand curve for real money will shift to the right, raising the interest rate, which reduces investment, aggregate planned expenditure, and equilibrium real GDP.
   b) If the full multiplier effect on real GDP (from \$400 billion to \$600 billion) took place, the demand curve for real money would shift from MD_0 to MD_2, causing the interest rate to rise from 5 percent to 7 percent.

Figure 12.2 Solution

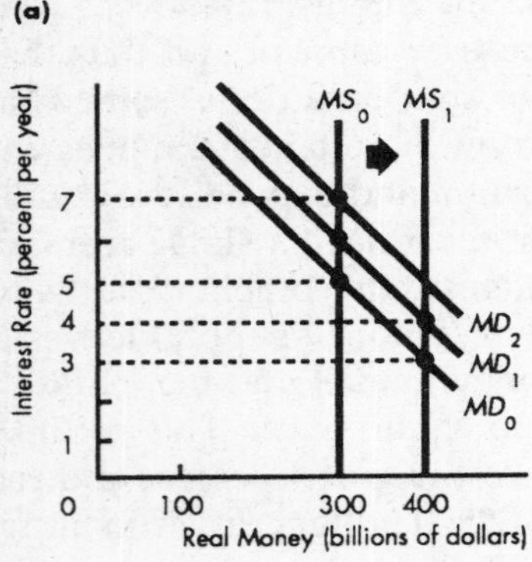

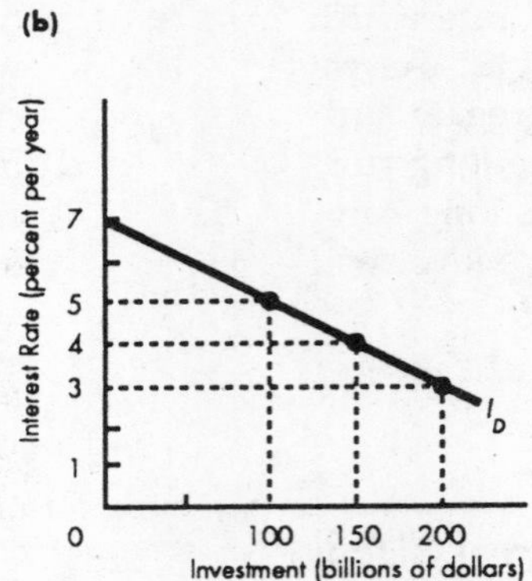

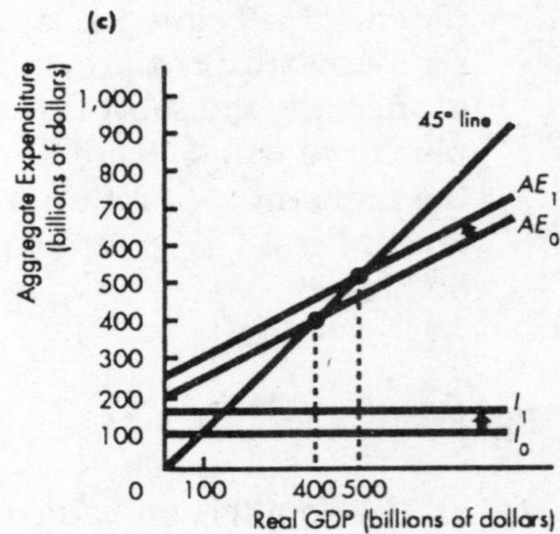

c) When the economy achieves simultaneous money market equilibrium and equilibrium expenditure, the interest rate is 6 percent and real GDP is $500 billion. Only this combination of interest rate and real GDP gives both a money market and goods market) equilibrium. Investment has fallen to $50 billion from $100 billion, so $50 billion of investment is crowded out.

Both the expansionary monetary policy of Problem 2 and the expansionary fiscal policy of Problem 3 have the *same* effect on real GDP. The monetary policy, however, *reduced* the interest rate and increased investment, while the fiscal policy *increased* the interest rate and reduced investment.

d) The new final equilibrium is shown in Fig. 12.3 Solution. Note that the relevant demand curve for real money is MD_1 which is drawn assuming real GDP = $500 billion. AE_0 has shifted up to AE_1, and I_0 has shifted down to I_1.

4. a) We know that, other things being held equal, the larger the change in the interest rate resulting from a given change in the money supply the larger the effect of monetary policy on equilibrium real GDP.

Figure 12.4 (a) shows two demand curves for real money. The steeper MD_1 curve reflects a demand for real money which is not very sensitive to interest rate changes and the flatter MD_2 curve reflects a demand for real money which is very sensitive to interest rate changes. The initial supply curve of real money is *MS*. We note that the initial equilibrium interest rate is r_0.

Observe what happens when we increase the supply of real money. *MS* shifts to *MS*″. Note that the fall in the equilibrium interest rate is large for MD_1 (the interest insensitive money demand) and small for MD_2 (the more interest sensitive money demand). Therefore we have shown that monetary policy has a smaller effect on equilibrium real GDP if the demand for real money is more sensitive to changes in the interest rate.

Figure 12.3 Solution

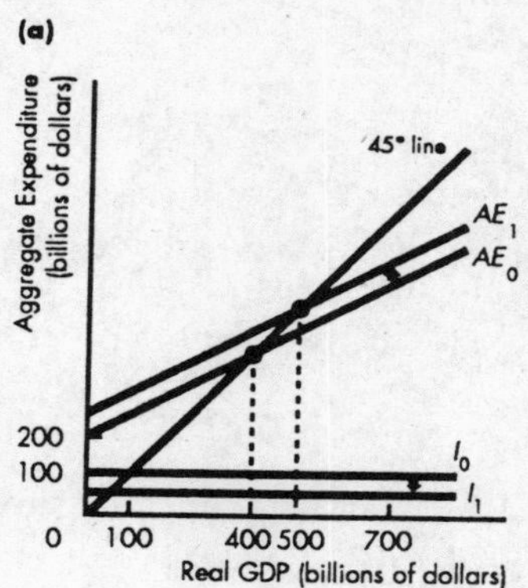

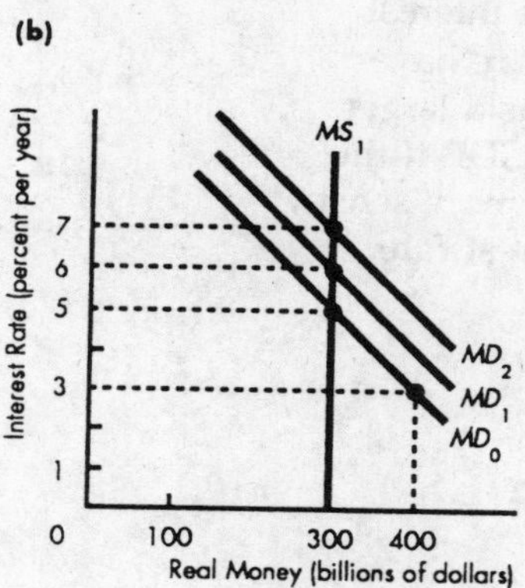

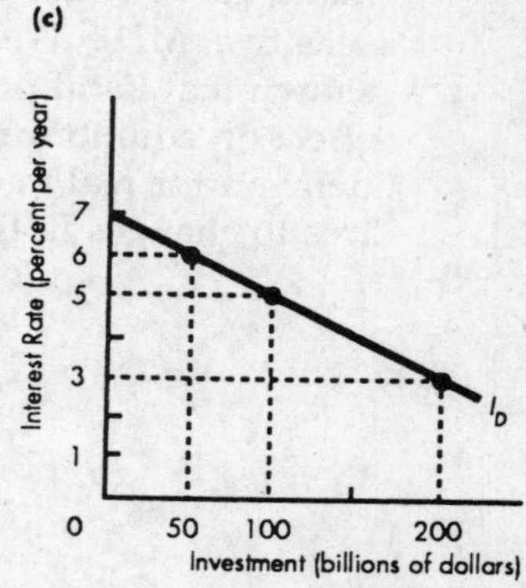

b) Fiscal policy has first and second round effects on real GDP. The second round effect is a consequence of the fact that the initial change in real GDP causes the demand curve for real money to shift, which causes the interest rate to change and leads to *crowding out* of investment. Fiscal policy has a larger effect on equilibrium GDP (is stronger) the smaller is the crowding out effect. Therefore, other things being equal, the smaller the change in the interest rate when the quantity of real money demanded changes by a given amount, the smaller is the crowding out effect and the stronger is fiscal policy.

Figure 12.4 (b) shows the same two demand curves for real money as part (a), MD_1 and MD_2. The supply curve for real money is MS and the initial equilibrium interest rate is r_0. Now we observe what happens when each of the money demand curves shifts to the right by the same amount. MD_1 shifts to $MD_1{}'$ and MD_2 shifts to $MD_2{}'$.

Figure 12.4

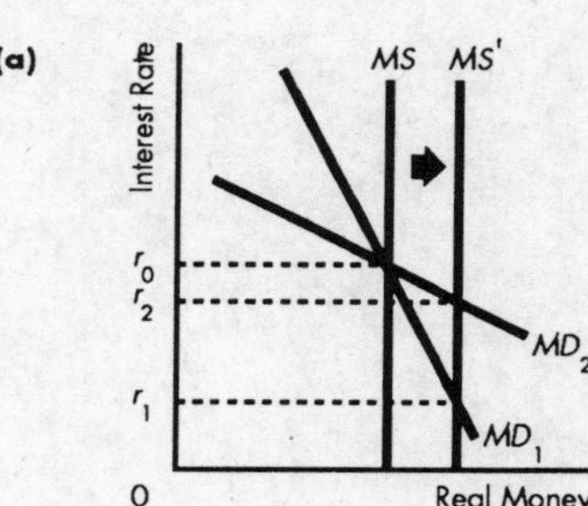

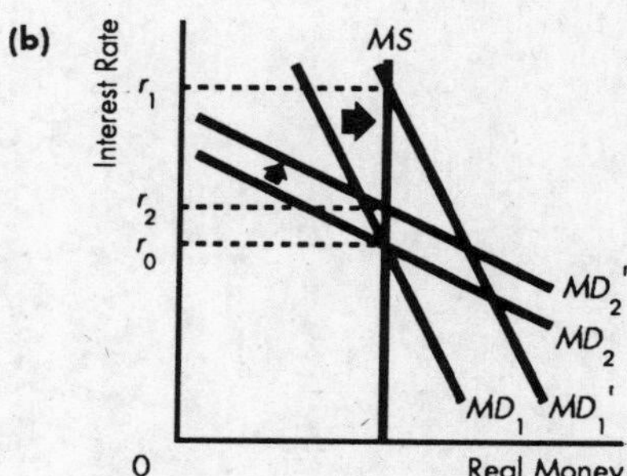

Note that the rise in the interest rate is much smaller (i.e., the crowding out effect is smaller) for the money demand curve which is more interest sensitive, MD_2. We therefore have shown that fiscal policy has a larger effect on equilibrium real GDP if the demand for real money is more sensitive to changes in the interest rate.

13 PRODUCTIVITY, WAGES, AND UNEMPLOYMENT

CHAPTER IN PERSPECTIVE

In Chapter 7 it was indicated that the behavior of the economy (inflation, unemployment, business cycle fluctuations) could be explained using the concepts of aggregate demand and aggregate supply. The basic model of macroeconomic analysis was only introduced there, however. Our objective since then has been to develop an understanding of these two fundamental concepts.

In Chapters 8 through 12 we have carefully pursued the concept of aggregate demand in order to understand how it is determined and what makes it change. In this chapter, we now turn our attention to the concept of aggregate supply.

The question of aggregate supply is: How does a change in the price level affect the quantity of real GDP supplied? Since the quantity of real GDP supplied depends in large measure on the quantity of labor employed, we find that an understanding of the labor market is critical to a complete understanding of aggregate supply. Thus we examine the labor market in order to better understand the determination of employment and real GDP. We also look at the related issue of the determination of the rate of unemployment.

LEARNING OBJECTIVES

After studying this chapter, you will be able to:

- **Explain why productivity and real GDP grow**
- **Explain how firms decide how much labor to employ**
- **Explain how households decide how much labor to supply**
- **Explain how wages, employment, and unemployment are determined if wages are flexible**
- **Explain how wages, employment, and unemployment are determined if wages are "sticky"**
- **Derive the short-run and long-run aggregate supply curves**
- **Explain what makes aggregate supply and unemployment fluctuate**

HELPFUL HINTS

1. The fundamental purpose of this chapter is to deepen our understanding of aggregate supply; that is, the relationship between the price level and the quantity of real GDP supplied. This has been broken down into constituent issues since the effect of a change in the price level on the quantity of real GDP is indirect. Our study of the aggregate production function and the labor market are part of that process.

First we ask a basic question: How is the quantity of real GDP supplied determined in general? In the short run when the capital stock and the state of technology are given, the maximum amount of real GDP that can be produced depends on the quantity of labor employed. This relationship between employment and the quantity of real GDP supplied is captured by the short-run aggregate production function.

In order to understand the determination of the quantity of real GDP supplied it is therefore necessary to pursue the second issue: How is the level of employment determined? The answer is in the labor market. The demand for labor is determined by firms and the supply of labor is determined by households. If wages are flexible and continuously adjust to clear the labor market, the level of employment will always be the equilibrium level; that is, full employment. If, on the other hand, wages are "sticky" because the money wage rate is set by a wage contract, the level of employment can deviate from its equilibrium level in the short run.

Since our interest is in aggregate supply, we want to know how the quantity of real GDP varies as the price level varies. This brings us to the third issue: How do changes in the price level affect employment and thereby real GDP? It turns out that if wages are flexible, the level of employment (and thus the quantity of real GDP supplied) is independent of the price level. Whatever the price level, the wage rate will adjust so that the unique equilibrium level of employment is achieved. This, of course, implies an aggregate supply curve which is vertical at the full-employment level of real GDP.

On the other hand, if wages are sticky, the level of employment (and thus the quantity of real GDP supplied) depends on the actual value of the price level relative to the expected value of the price level. If the price level turns out to be equal to its expected value, the equilibrium level of employment (full employment) results. If the price level is higher than expected, the level of employment turns out to be higher than the equilibrium value and thus real GDP supplied will be larger than full-employment real GDP. If the price level is lower than expected, employment will be less than equilibrium and real GDP supplied will be less than full-employment real GDP. This implies a positively sloped aggregate supply curve when wages are sticky.

2. The following arrow diagram may be helpful in understanding why the short-run aggregate supply curve is positively sloped. It shows the sequence of events that link a change in the price level with the subsequent change in the quantity of real GDP supplied. Let P = the price level, W/P = the real wage rate, L = the quantity of labor employed, and Y = the quantity of real GDP supplied. If wages are sticky we have

$$\uparrow P \rightarrow \downarrow (W/P) \rightarrow \uparrow L \rightarrow \uparrow Y.$$

If the money wage rate is fixed by contract, an (unexpected) increase in the price level ($\uparrow P$) will cause the real wage rate to fall ($\downarrow (W/P)$). At the lower real wage rate, firms will want to hire more labor ($\uparrow L$), which implies an increase in the quantity of real GDP supplied ($\uparrow Y$). Thus, the short-run aggregate supply curve is positively sloped.

If wages are flexible, an increase in the price level will have no effect on the quantity of real GDP supplied because the real wage rate will not fall.

KEY FIGURES AND TABLES

Figure 13.1 The Short-Run Aggregate Production Function

The short-run aggregate production function shows the maximum real GDP attainable at each quantity of labor input, holding constant the state of technology and the quantities of other inputs. This figure illustrates a short-run aggregate production function. Some values are given in the table and then plotted in the graph. Note two things. First, the aggregate production function is positively sloped: an increase in labor input will yield an increase in output. This is the same as saying that the marginal product of labor is positive. Second, the curve becomes flatter as labor input increases. This reflects diminishing marginal product of labor as is also shown in the graph: the additional output when we increase labor from 135 to 145 billion hours per year is larger than when we increase labor from 145 to 155 billion hours per year.

Figure 13.2 The Growth of Output

Both the natural accumulation of capital and the natural advance of technology imply that the short-run aggregate production function will shift upward over time. As illustrated here, this upward shift simply means that now more real GDP can be produced with each quantity of labor than was the case before the increase in capital or the technological advance.

Figure 13.7 Equilibrium with Flexible Wages

This figure illustrates the demand for labor curve (*LD*), the supply of labor curve (*LS*), and equilibrium in the labor market when wages are flexible. The equilibrium real wage rate is the value that equates the quantity of labor demanded with the quantity of labor supplied and is $7 an hour in this example. If the real wage rate is below the equilibrium real wage rate, the quantity of labor demanded will exceed the quantity of labor supplied, and *if real wages are flexible,* the real wage rate will be bid up until equilibrium is achieved. Similarly, if the real wage rate is above equilibrium, the quantity of labor supplied will be greater than the quantity of labor demanded and the real wage rate will fall.

Figure 13.8 Aggregate Supply with Flexible Wages

Aggregate supply is the relationship between the price level and the quantity of real GDP supplied (part c). The quantity of real GDP supplied is determined by evaluating the aggregate production at the current level of employment (part b).

In the flexible wage model, employment is determined by equilibrium in the labor market (part a). The aggregate supply curve then answers the question: What effect will a change in the price level have on the quantity of real GDP supplied? In order for a change in the price level to affect the quantity of real GDP supplied, it must cause a change in the level of employment.

In the case of flexible wages, a change in the price level will have no effect on the level of employment, since the money wage rate will change proportionately so as to leave the real wage rate and employment at their unchanged equilibrium levels. Because a change in the price level has no effect on employment in the flexible wage model, it has no effect on the quantity of real GDP supplied and thus the aggregate supply curve is vertical.

Figure 13.9 A Labor Market with Sticky Money Wages

This figure illustrates the determination of employment in a labor market in which the money wage is fixed (sticky). There is a single *real* wage rate that is consistent with equilibrium in the labor market. In the example illustrated in this figure, that real wage rate is $7. Thus, for any given price level there is a single *money* wage rate that results in labor market equilibrium. In the example here, if the price level (GDP deflator) is 100, the market clearing money wage rate is $7.

In the sticky wage model, the money wage rate is preset by a negotiated wage contract. This money wage rate is set at the level which, given the *anticipated* value of the price level, is expected to yield the single real wage rate which equates the quantity of labor demanded and the quantity of labor supplied. Since, in this example, the expected price level is 100, the money wage rate is set at $7.

If the actual price level turns out to be different from its expected value, since the money wage rate is fixed, the real wage will be different from the equilibrium real wage. The level of employment will be determined by the quantity of labor demanded at the actual real wage. For example, if the price level is 140, which is higher than the expected price level, the actual real wage rate will be $5, which is lower than the equilibrium real wage rate. Employment will be 155 billion hours per year since that is the quantity of labor demanded at a real wage rate of $5 per hour. This level of employment is greater than the equilibrium level.

Similarly, if the price level is lower than expected (e.g., 77.7), the actual real wage rate (e.g., $9) will be above equilibrium and the level of employment (145 billion hours) will be less than the equilibrium level of employment.

Figure 13.10 Aggregate Supply with Sticky Wages

The quantity of real GDP supplied depends on the quantity of labor employed. So, in order for the short-run aggregate supply curve to be positively sloped, it must be that an increase in the price level increases employment. This figure shows why the short-run aggregate supply curve is positively sloped when the labor market is characterized by sticky wages.

Since employment is determined in the labor market and, given employment, output (real GDP supplied) is determined by the short-run aggregate production function, the labor market and the short-run aggregate production function are illustrated in parts (a) and (b) of the figure. Part (c) illustrates the resulting aggregate supply curves.

Part (a) simply repeats the labor market shown in Fig. 13.9. In that figure we saw that, given the expected price level, the level of employment depends on the actual value of the price level. If the actual value of the price level is higher than expected, employment will be high. By the short-run aggregate production function, high employment means a high level of output. Thus, as the price level increases, the level of output will increase and the short-run aggregate supply curve will be positively sloped.

For example, if the expected price level is 100 and the actual price level is also 100, the real wage rate is $7, employment is 150 billion hours per year and output (real GDP) is $4.5 trillion. This corresponds to point *d* in the three parts of the figure. If the actual price level is 140 (higher than expected), the real wage rate is $5, the level of employment is 155 billion hours per year and real GDP supplied is $4.53. This corresponds to point *e* in each of the three parts of the figure. Similarly, when the price level is 77.7 (lower than expected), real GDP supplied will be $4.46 trillion (point *c*). These three points illustrate that the short-run aggregate supply curve will be positively sloped.

Figure 13.12 Unemployment with Flexible Wages

This figure examines unemployment in a labor market with flexible wages.

At a given real wage rate, the labor force consists of two groups of individuals: those who are immediately available for work at that real wage and those who are searching for the best available job. Labor supply is determined by the first group and the labor supply curve is denoted *LS* in the figure. The total labor force curve is denoted *LF*. The difference between these curves is the part of the labor force involved in search. With flexible wages, the labor market will always be in equilibrium at the intersection of the labor demand (*LD*) and labor supply (*LS*) curves. In this example, the equilibrium real wage rate is $7 and the equilibrium quantity of labor is 150 billion hours per year.

Unemployment is the difference between the labor force and actual employment. At the equilibrium real wage rate of $7, the labor force is 155 billion hours of labor while actual (equilibrium) employment is 150 billion hours per year. Thus, unemployment is 5 billion hours of labor per year. Since this is the level of unemployment when the labor market is in equilibrium, it is natural unemployment.

Figure 13.14 Unemployment with Sticky Money Wages

This figure examines unemployment in a labor market with a fixed money wage rate of $7 an hour. With the money wage rate fixed, the real wage rate depends on the price level. When money wages are sticky, employment is determined by the demand for labor given the actual real wage and may differ from the equilibrium level of employment. Unemployment is the difference between the labor force and the actual level of employment.

If the price level (GDP deflator) is 87.5, the real wage rate is $8 an hour given the fixed money wage rate of $7 an hour. This implies that employment is 147.5 billion hours of labor per year since that is the quantity of labor demanded at a real wage rate of $8. Since this is less than the quantity of labor supplied at a real wage rate of $8, actual unemployment exceeds natural unemployment.

If the price level is 116.6, the real wage is $6 an hour and employment turns out to be 152.5 billion hours per year. Since this is more than the quantity of labor supplied at a real wage rate of $6, actual unemployment is less than natural unemployment and the actual *rate* of unemployment will be below the natural *rate* of unemployment.

SELF-TEST

CONCEPT REVIEW

1. A short-run ____________ ____________ shows how maximum output varies as the quantity of labor employed varies, holding constant the stock of capital and the state of technology. The short-run ____________ ____________ ____________ shows how maximum real GDP varies as total employment of labor varies, holding constant the total stock of capital and the state of technology. It will shift ____________ over time as capital accumulates and technology advances.
2. The additional real GDP produced by one additional hour of labor input, holding other inputs and technology constant, gives the ____________ ____________ of labor. The tendency for this magnitude to decline as the quantity of labor input increases, holding everything else constant, is called the ____________ ____________ ____________ of labor.
3. The discovery of a new technique is called ____________. The act of putting the new technique into operation is called ____________.
4. The ____________ ____________ ____________ is a schedule or curve that shows the quantity of labor demanded at each level of the ____________ wage rate.

The ____________ wage rate is the wage per hour expressed in constant dollars. The ____________ wage rate is the wage per hour expressed in current dollars.

5. The ____________ ____________ ____________ is a schedule or curve that shows the quantity of labor supplied at each level of the real wage rate. According to the substitution effect, if the real wage rate rises, households will ____________ the quantity of labor they supply. According to the income effect, if the real wage rate rises, households will ____________ the quantity of labor they supply.
6. The proportion of the working age population that is either employed or unemployed (but looking for a job) is called the labor force ____________ ____________. The lowest wage at which an individual will supply any labor is called the ____________ ____________.
7. There are two leading theories about the labor market. The first of these assumes that the wage rate adjusts continually so as to keep the quantity of labor demanded equal to the quantity of labor supplied. It is called the ____________ wage theory. The second, called the ____________ wage theory, assumes that the labor market is dominated by wage contracts that set the money wage rate for a specific period of time.
8. If the wage rate adjusts continually to clear the labor market, the aggregate supply curve will be ____________. If the wage rate is set for a period of time by wage contracts, the short-run aggregate supply curve will be ____________ sloped.

TRUE OR FALSE

___ 1. The diminishing marginal product of labor implies that the demand for labor curve is negatively sloped.

___ 2. The short-run aggregate production function will shift downward when there is an increase in the stock of capital.

___ 3. A widespread drought would likely cause the short-run aggregate production function to shift upward.

___ 4. As the real wage rate rises, the quantity of labor demanded decreases, other things remaining constant.

___ 5. Suppose the money wage rate and the real wage rate are initially equal. After an increase in the price level, the money wage rate will be greater than the real wage rate.

___ 6. If the marginal product of each unit of labor increases, the demand for labor curve shifts to the right.

____ 7. If the money wage rate and the price level both rise by 10 percent, the quantity of labor demanded will increase.

____ 8. An increase in the real wage rate increases the opportunity cost of leisure.

____ 9. If the real wage rate falls, the substitution effect implies that households will increase the time spent working.

____10. If the real wage rate falls, the income effect implies that households will increase the time spent working.

____11. If the wage rate is above a person's reservation wage, that person will supply zero labor.

____12. If the real wage rate is currently high relative to what it is expected to be in the future, workers will tend to supply less labor now and more in the future.

____13. According to the flexible wage theory of the labor market, the labor market is always in equilibrium.

____14. The aggregate supply curve generated by the flexible wage theory is the same as the long-run aggregate supply curve.

____15. According to the sticky wage theory of the labor market, if the price level turns out to be higher than expected, the actual real wage will be greater than the equilibrium real wage.

____16. According to the sticky wage theory, an increase in the price level will increase employment in the short run.

____17. The sticky wage theory assumes that the quantity of labor supplied determines employment.

____18. According to the sticky wage theory, fluctuations in real GDP are due only to fluctuations in long-run aggregate supply.

____19. If there is an increase in the pace of labor turnover, the unemployment rate will rise.

____20. According to the flexible wage model, the unemployment rate is always equal to the natural rate of unemployment.

MULTIPLE CHOICE

1. The marginal product of labor curve is
   a. positively sloped and shifts when there is a change in the capital stock.
   b. positively sloped and shifts when there is a change in the quantity of labor employed.
   c. negatively sloped and shifts when there is a change in the capital stock.
   d. negatively sloped and shifts when there is a change in the quantity of labor employed.

2. Which of the following would shift the short-run aggregate production function upward?
   a. A decrease in the stock of capital.
   b. A technological advance.
   c. An increase in labor employed.
   d. An increase in the price level.

3. The demand for labor shows that, holding other things constant, as the
   a. real wage rate increases, the quantity of labor demanded decreases.
   b. real wage rate increases, the quantity of labor demanded increases.
   c. money wage rate increases, the quantity of labor demanded decreases.
   d. money wage rate increases, the quantity of labor demanded increases.

4. Why is the demand for labor curve negatively sloped?
   a. At lower wage rates, workers don't work as hard and so firms must hire more of them.
   b. The marginal product of labor declines as the quantity of labor input increases, holding other things constant.
   c. As technology advances, less labor is required to produce a given output.
   d. As the price of output rises, firms will want to hire less labor.

5. If the money wage rate is $12 per hour and the GDP deflator is 150, the real wage rate is
   a. $18 per hour.
   b. $12 per hour.
   c. $8 per hour.
   d. $6 per hour.

6. A profit maximizing firm will hire additional units of labor up to the point where
   a. workers are no longer willing to work.
   b. the marginal product of labor is zero.
   c. the marginal product of labor is a maximum.
   d. the marginal product of labor is equal to the real wage.

7. Which of the following is <u>NOT</u> a reason for a positively sloped supply of labor curve?
   a. Intertemporal substitution of labor
   b. Individuals choose to enter the labor force only if the real wage is at least as high as their reservation wage
   c. The income effect of a change in the real wage
   d. The substitution effect of a change in the real wage

8. According to the flexible wage theory of the labor market, an increase in the price level will cause the
   a. real wage rate to fall and therefore increase employment.
   b. real wage rate to fall and therefore decrease employment.
   c. money wage rate to rise by the same proportion and therefore increase employment.
   d. money wage rate to rise by the same proportion and therefore leave employment unchanged.

9. The aggregate supply curve is vertical at full-employment real GDP if
   a. the real wage rate adjusts continually so as to leave the labor market always in equilibrium.
   b. the money wage rate is fixed but the real wage rate changes due to changes in the price level.
   c. employment is determined by the quantity of labor demanded.
   d. employment is determined by the quantity of labor supplied.

10. Suppose the demand for labor and the supply of labor are both increasing over time but the demand for labor is increasing at a faster rate. Over time, therefore, we expect to see
    a. the real wage rate rising and employment falling.
    b. the real wage rate rising and employment rising.
    c. the real wage rate falling and employment rising.
    d. the real wage rate falling and employment falling.

11. According to the flexible wage theory of the labor market, an increase in real GDP implies that
    a. long-run aggregate supply has increased.
    b. aggregate demand has increased.
    c. the economy has moved up its short-run aggregate supply curve.
    d. the price level has increased.

12. According to the sticky wage theory of the labor market, a wage contract will set the money wage rate at a level
    a. equal to the real wage rate.
    b. equal to the maximum marginal product of labor.
    c. so that the money wage rate is equal to the marginal product of labor.
    d. so that, if the actual price level turns out to be what is expected, the labor market will be in equilibrium.

13. According to the sticky wage theory, employment is determined by
    a. the quantity of labor demanded at the actual real wage rate.
    b. the quantity of labor supplied at the actual real wage rate.
    c. the intersection of the demand for labor and supply of labor curves.
    d. the intersection of the aggregate demand and aggregate supply curves.

14. According to the sticky wage theory, if the actual price level turns out to be less than the expected price level, the real wage rate will be
    a. less than the equilibrium real wage rate and employment will fall.
    b. less than the equilibrium real wage rate and employment will rise.
    c. higher than the equilibrium real wage rate and employment will fall.
    d. higher than the equilibrium real wage rate and employment will rise.

15. According to the flexible wage theory, if the price level increases, then real GDP supplied will
    a. remain unchanged but, according to the sticky wage theory, real GDP supplied will increase.
    b. increase and, according to the sticky wage theory, real GDP supplied will also increase.
    c. increase but, according to the sticky wage theory, real GDP supplied will remain unchanged.
    d. decrease but, according to the sticky wage theory, real GDP supplied will increase.

16. Which of the following is <u>NOT</u> a reason for unemployment according to the flexible wage theory?
    a. When firms vary employment, they will tend to vary the number of workers rather than the number of hours per worker.
    b. Firms have imperfect information about people looking for work.
    c. Households have imperfect information about available jobs.
    d. The effects of wage contracts in labor markets.

17. The fact that labor is an economically indivisible factor of production implies that
    a. firms will tend to adjust the quantity of labor demanded by changing hours per worker rather than changing the number of workers.
    b. firms will tend to adjust the quantity of labor demanded by changing the number of workers rather than changing hours per worker.
    c. firms cannot hire fractions of workers.
    d. workers will tend to work for a single firm.

18. Which of the following would generally increase unemployment?
    a. An increase in the number of people entering retirement
    b. An increase in the number of people withdrawing from the labor force
    c. An increase in the number of people leaving school to find jobs
    d. An increase in the number of people leaving jobs to go to school

19. Figure 13.1 depicts the labor market. The price level, as measured by the GDP deflator, is 150. According to the sticky wage theory, if the price level is expected to remain constant, what money wage rate will be set by a wage contract?
    a. $8.
    b. $12.
    c. $18.
    d. $24.

Figure 13.1

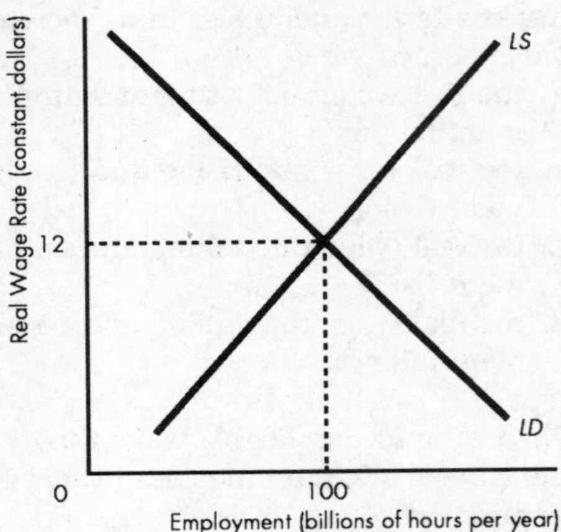

20. Refer to Fig. 13.1 and again assume that when the money wage was set, the GDP deflator was expected to remain constant at 150. If the GDP deflator actually turns out to be 200, the real wage rate will be
    a. $9 and employment will be less than 100 billion hours per year.
    b. $9 and employment will be more than 100 billion hours per year.
    c. $24 and employment will be less than 100 billion hours per year.
    d. $24 and employment will be more than 100 billion hours per year.

SHORT ANSWER

1. Why does the marginal product of labor decline as the quantity of labor employed increases?

2. Why is the demand for labor curve negatively sloped?

3. Explain why the labor force participation rate increases as the real wage rate increases. Why does this help explain why the labor supply curve is positively sloped?

4. How does the intertemporal substitution of labor help explain why the supply of labor curve is positively sloped?

5. Suppose the price level increases unexpectedly. According to the flexible wage theory of the labor market, what will happen to the money wage rate, the real wage rate, employment, and real GDP?

6. According to the sticky wage theory how is the money wage rate set ?

7. Suppose the price level increases unexpectedly. According to the sticky wage theory of the labor market, what will happen to the money wage rate, the real wage rate, employment, and real GDP?

8. How does the flexible wage theory explain observed fluctuations in unemployment?

9. How does the sticky wage theory explain observed fluctuations in unemployment?

PROBLEMS

1. Table 13.1 gives information about the short-run aggregate production function for a rather small economy; L = units of labor per day and Y = units of output per day (real GDP).
   a) Complete the last column of Table 13.1 by computing the marginal product of labor (MP_L).
   b) How much labor will be demanded if the money wage rate is $6 and the GDP deflator is 150?
   c) Draw a graph of the demand for labor and label it LD_0.

Table 13.1 Short-Run Aggregate Production Function

L	Y	MP_L
1	8	
2	15	
3	21	
4	26	
5	30	
6	33	

2. Table 13.2 gives the supply of labor schedule for the economy of problem 1.
   a) On the graph from problem 1 (c), draw the supply of labor curve and label it LS.
   b) What is the equilibrium real wage rate?
   c) What is the equilibrium level of employment?
   d) What is the level of output?

Table 13.2 Supply of Labor

Real wage rate supplied	Quantity of labor supplier
8	7
7	6
6	5
5	4
4	3
3	2

3. Suppose the economy presented in Problems 1 and 2 is characterized by flexible wages.
   a) If the GDP deflator is 100, what is the equilibrium money wage rate, the level of employment, and the level of output?
   b) If the GDP deflator is 80, what is the equilibrium money wage rate, the level of employment, and level of output?
   c) If the GDP deflator is 120, what is the equilibrium money wage rate, the level of employment, and the level of output?
   d) Draw the aggregate supply curve for this flexible wage economy.

4. Now suppose the economy of Problems 1 and 2 is characterized by sticky wages set by wage contract. Use the sticky price model to respond to the following.
   a) If the expected value of the GDP deflator over the contract period is 100, what money wage rate will be set?
   b) If during the contract period, the actual value of the GDP deflator is 100, what is the real wage rate, the level of employment, and the level of output?
   c) If during the contract period, the actual value of the GDP deflator is 83, what is the real wage rate, the level of employment, and the level of output?
   d) If during the contract period, the actual value of the GDP deflator is 125, what is the real wage rate, the level of employment, and the level of output?
   e) On the graph from Problem 3 (d), indicate three points on the short-run aggregate supply curve for this sticky wage economy. Draw part of that curve by connecting the points.

5. Now suppose that a technological advance gives a new short-run aggregate production function summarized in Table 13.3.
   a) Complete the last column of Table 13.3 by computing the marginal product of labor.

Table 13.3 New Short-Run Aggregate Production Function

L	Y	MP_L
1	10	
2	19	
3	27	
4	34	
5	40	
6	45	

   b) On the graph from Problems 1 (c) and 2 (a), draw the new demand for labor curve and label it LD_1.
   c) If wages are perfectly flexible, what will be the new equilibrium real wage rate, level of employment, and level of output. (The supply of labor curve is unchanged.)
   d) If the money wage has been set at $5 and the GDP deflator is 100, use the sticky wage model to determine the real wage rate, the level of employment, and the level of output resulting from the occurrence of a technological advance during a wage contract period.

e) In which of these two cases (flexible wages or sticky wages) does the shift in the demand curve for labor have the larger effect on employment and output?

6. Return to the original data of Problems 1 and 2. Suppose that the labor force increases as the real wage rate increases so that the labor force (*LF*) curve lies to the right of the *LS* curve by 4 units of labor. This means that 4 units of labor are used in job search.
   a) On the graph from Problems 1(c) and 2(a) draw the labor force curve and label it *LF*.
   b) What is the level of natural unemployment in this economy?
   c) What is the observed level of unemployment according to the sticky wage model if the GDP deflator is 100? 83? 125?

ANSWERS

CONCEPT REVIEW

1. production function; aggregate production function; upward
2. marginal product; diminishing marginal product
3. invention, innovation
4. demand for labor; real; real; money
5. supply of labor; increase; decrease
6. participation rate; reservation wage
7. flexible; sticky
8. vertical; positively

TRUE OR FALSE

1. T	6. T	11. F	16. T
2. F	7. F	12. F	17. F
3. F	8. T	13. T	18. F
4. T	9. F	14. T	19. T
5. T	10. T	15. F	20. T

MULTIPLE CHOICE

1. c	6. d	11. a	16. d
2. b	7. c	12. d	17. b
3. a	8. d	13. a	18. c
4. b	9. a	14. c	19. c
5. c	10. b	15. a	20. b

SHORT ANSWER

1. The marginal product is the additional real GDP produced by an additional hour of labor, *holding other inputs and technology constant.* The key to understanding the diminishing marginal product of labor is in recognizing that all other inputs (in particular, capital) are held constant. Therefore, as additional labor is employed, each unit of capital will be used by more labor. As, the use of the capital approaches its physical limits, additional units of labor will add less (but still positive amounts) to output.

2. There are two parts to the explanation of why the demand for labor curve is negatively sloped. The first part is the fact of diminishing marginal product of labor, which implies that the marginal product curve is negatively sloped. The second part is the claim that, for a profit-maximizing firm, the demand curve for labor is the same as the marginal product curve. Thus the demand curve for labor must be negatively sloped.

3. Each individual has a reservation wage below which they will not supply any labor. For example, if the wage rate is below an individual's reservation wage, the individual will not even enter the labor force. In order for an individual to be willing to enter the labor force, the real wage must be at least as great as their reservation wage. As the real wage rate rises, it will exceed the reservation wages of an increasingly larger group of people and thus the labor force increases relative to the size of the working age population; the labor force participation rate increases.

   As this rate increases, more individuals are offering to supply labor and thus the quantity of labor supplied increases. Because the original impetus was an increasing real wage rate, the real wage rate and the quantity of labor supplied are positively related.

4. Intertemporal substitution of labor involves the substitution between labor now and labor in the future. Such substitution takes place if there are differences between the current real wage rate and the real wage rate expected to exist in the future. For example, if the current real wage rate is high relative to the real wage rate expected in the future, workers will tend to increase the quantity of labor they supply now in order to take advantage of the temporary high return on labor. This means that as the real wage increases, if any part of this is expected to be temporary, the current quantity of labor supplied will increase. This implies a positive relationship between the real wage and the quantity of labor supplied.

5. According to the flexible wage theory, an increase in the price level will, at the current money wage rate, reduce the real wage rate. A fall in the real wage rate means that the labor market is now characterized by excess demand for labor; at the lower real wage rate, the quantity of labor demanded exceeds the quantity of labor supplied. Since the wage rate is flexible, the money wage rate will rise until the labor market is again in equilibrium; that is, it will rise until the real wage rate has returned to its previous level. As a result, employment returns to its previous level as does real GDP.

6. In the sticky wage theory, the money wage is set by negotiations between firms (demanders of labor) and individuals (suppliers of labor). While firms would like to pay the lowest wage rate they can and workers would like to receive the highest wage rate they can, both parties will discover that, given the necessity to agree, they are best off when the real wage rate is the equilibrium wage rate. Since the actual real wage rate will depend on the price level which will exist over the life of the wage contract, firms and individuals must determine the money wage rate based on the *expected* price level. The money wage rate will be set at the level which, if the actual price level turns out to be equal to its expected value, the labor market will be in equilibrium.

7. According to the sticky wage theory, an unexpected increase in the price level will, at the fixed money wage rate set by contract, reduce the real wage rate. Because the money wage rate cannot adjust during a contract period, this lower real wage rate will remain and, since the level of employment is determined by the demand for labor, the level of employment will increase. This, of course, implies that the quantity of real GDP supplied will increase via the aggregate production function.

8. The natural rate of unemployment is the rate that occurs when the labor market is in equilibrium. According to the flexible

wage theory, the labor market is always in equilibrium and thus the rate of unemployment is always equal to the natural rate of unemployment. Thus, any fluctuations in unemployment are the result of fluctuations in the natural rate of unemployment. As discussed in the text, changes in the natural rate of unemployment are the result of changes in the pace of labor market turnover and cannot be avoided.

9. According to the sticky wage theory, the labor market will frequently not be in equilibrium. Thus the observed rate of unemployment will deviate from the natural rate of unemployment. If the real wage rate is above equilibrium, employment will be low and the rate of unemployment will exceed the natural rate of unemployment. If the real wage rate is below equilibrium, employment will be high and the rate of unemployment will be less than the natural rate. Since, according to this view, the natural rate of unemployment is quite stable, the observed rate of unemployment varies principally because deviations of the observed rate of unemployment about the almost constant natural rate vary.

PROBLEMS

1. a) Table 13.1 is completed as Table 13.1 Solution. The marginal product of labor is the additional output produced by an additional unit of labor.
   b) The real wage rate is computed as follows.

$$\textit{real wage rate} = \frac{\textit{money wage rate}}{\textit{GDP deflator}} \cdot 100.$$

In our case, the money wage rate is \$6 per unit and the GDP deflator is 150. Therefore the real wage is \$4. Since a profit maximizing firm will hire labor until the marginal product of labor is equal to the real wage rate, we can see that the quantity of labor demanded at a real wage rate of \$4 is 5 units.

Table 13.1 Solution: Short-Run Aggregate Production Function

L	Y	MP_L
1	8	8
2	15	7
3	21	6
4	26	5
5	30	4
6	33	3

c) The graph of the demand curve for labor (labeled LD_0) is given in Fig. 13.2. The demand curve for labor is the same as the marginal product of labor curve (see Table 13.1 Solution).

Figure 13.2

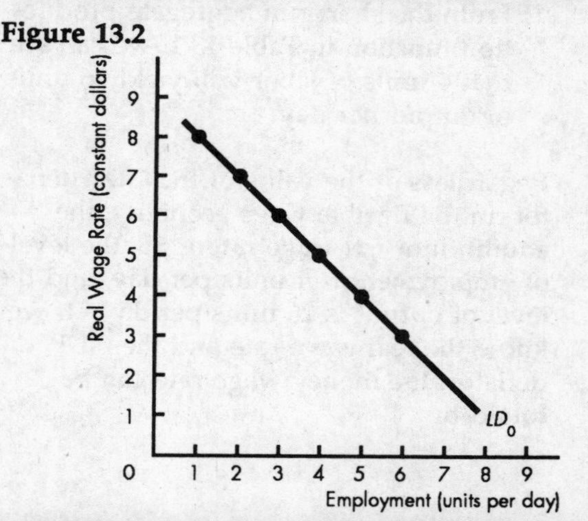

2. a) Figure 13.3 illustrates the supply curve of labor (labeled *LS*) on the same graph with the LD_0 curve from Problem 1.

Figure 13.3

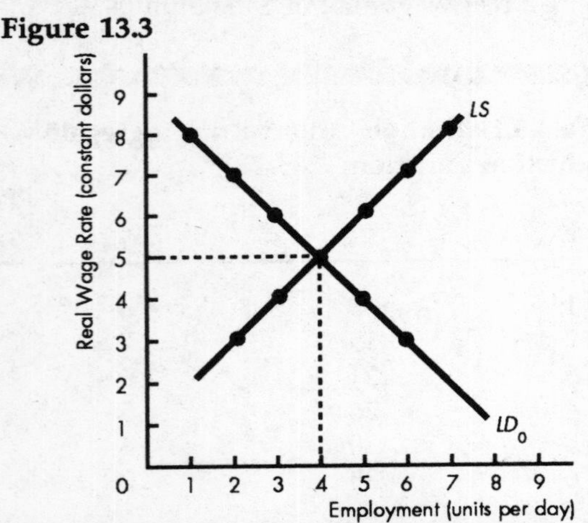

b) The equilibrium real wage rate is $5 since the quantity of labor demanded and supplied are both equal to 4 units per day. This can be seen from the graph or the tables.

c) The equilibrium level of employment is 4 units.

d) From the short-run aggregate production function in Table 13.1, we can see that 4 units of labor will yield 26 units of output per day.

3. Regardless of the value of the GDP deflator, in the flexible wage economy, the equilibrium *real* wage rate is $5, the level of employment is 4 units per day, and the level of output is 26 units per day. If we know the real wage rate and the GDP deflator, the money wage rate can be found by

$$(\textit{money wage rate} = \textit{real wage rate} \cdot \frac{\textit{GDP deflator}}{100})$$

a) If the GDP deflator is 100, a real wage rate of $5 implies a *money* wage rate of $5.

b) If the GDP deflator is 80, a real wage rate of $5 implies a *money* wage rate of $4.

c) If the GDP deflator is 120, a real wage rate of $5 implies a *money* wage rate of $6.

d) The aggregate supply curve (labeled *LAS*) for the flexible wage economy is given in Figure 13.4. Parts (a), (b), and (c) of this problem indicate that at every price level output is 26 units per day.

Figure 13.4

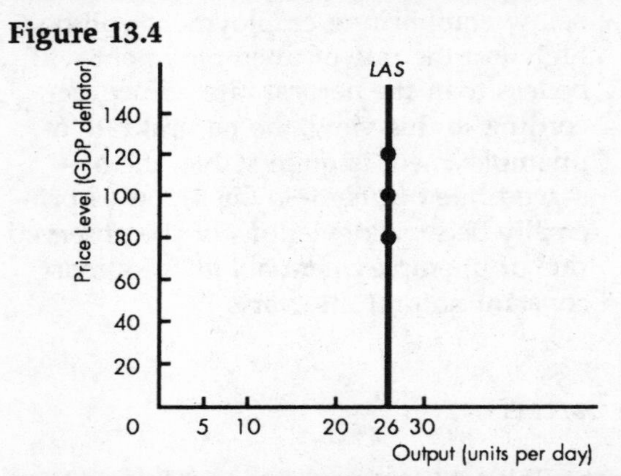

4. a) The contract money wage rate will be set so that if the actual GDP deflator turns out to be equal to the expected value of the GDP deflator (100), the real wage rate will clear the market. The real wage rate that clears the market is $5. So, since the expected GDP deflator is 100, the money wage rate will be set at $5.

b) If the actual value of the GDP deflator is 100, since the money wage rate is fixed at $5, the real wage rate is $5. This implies that employment is 4 units and output is 26 units.

c) If the actual value of the GDP deflator is 83, the real wage rate is $6 (i.e., ($5/83) × 100 = $6) since the money wage rate is fixed at $5. Employment is determined by the demand for labor which, at a real wage of $6, is 3 units per day. This implies (from Table 13.1) that output is 21 units per day.

d) If the actual value of the GDP deflator is 125, since the money wage rate is fixed at $5, the real wage rate is $4. Employment is determined by the demand for labor and is 5 units per day. From Table 13.1, this implies daily output of 30 units.

e) Figure 13.5 indicates three points on the short-run aggregate supply curve in the sticky wage economy: point *a* corresponds to output = 26, GDP deflator = 100; point *b* corresponds to output = 21, GDP deflator = 83; point *c* corresponds to output = 30, GDP deflator = 125. The points are connected to give a portion of the short-run aggregate supply curve (labeled *SAS*).

Figure 13.5

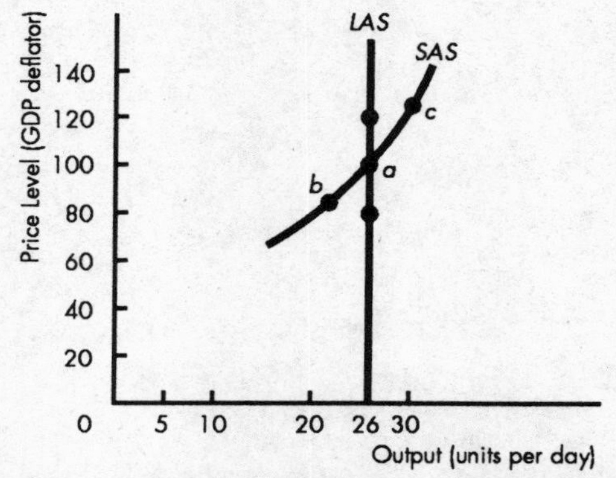

5. a) Table 13.3 is completed as Table 13.3 Solution. Note that the marginal product of each unit of labor has increased as a result of the technological advance.

b) Figure 13.6 gives the graph. Notice that the new labor demand curve, LD_1 lies to the right of LD_0.

c) It can be seen from Fig. 13.6 or Tables 13.2 and 13.3 Solution that the quantity of labor demanded equals the quantity of labor supplied at a real wage rate of $6. The level of employment is now 5 units of labor per day, which implies output of 40 units per day (from Table 13.3).

Table 13.3 Solution: New Short-Run Aggregate Production Function

L	Y	MP_L
1	10	10
2	19	9
3	27	8
4	34	7
5	40	6
6	45	5

d) In the sticky price model, the shift of the demand for labor curve will not change the contract wage rate or the supply of labor. Therefore the real wage rate remains at $5 and employment, which is determined by the new demand for labor, increases to 6 units of labor. From Table 13.3 we see that this implies output of 45 units per day.

e) Employment and output increase by more in the sticky wage model since the real wage cannot rise.

Figure 13.6

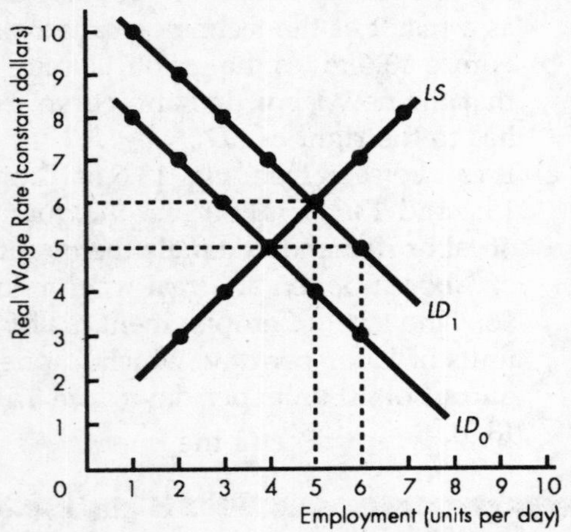

6. a) The graph with the *LF* curve along with LD_0 and *LS* is given in Fig. 13.7.

Figure 13.7

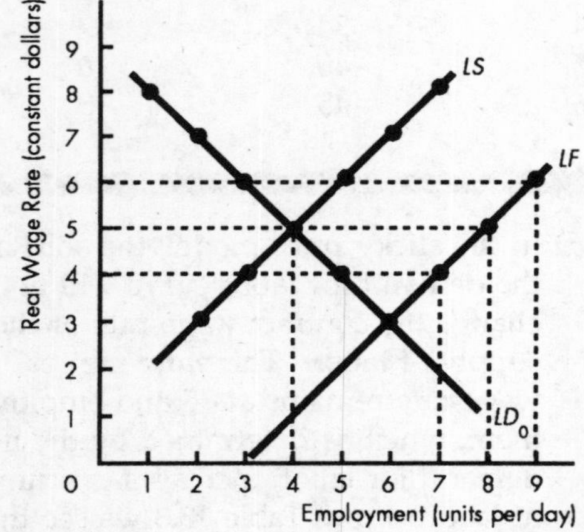

b) The level of natural unemployment is the level of unemployment (the difference between the labor force and employment) when the labor market clears (is in equilibrium). From Problem 2(c) we know that the equilibrium level of employment is 4 units at a real wage rage of $5. Since the labor force is 8 units of labor at this real wage rate, the level of natural unemployment is 4 units of labor.

c) The observed level of unemployment is the difference between the labor force and the actual level of employment at the existing real wage. When the GDP deflator is 100, the real wage rate is $5, the actual level of employment is 4 units (Problem 4b)), and the labor force is 8 units. Therefore, the level of unemployment is 4 units of labor. When the GDP deflator is 83, the real wage rate is $6, the actual level of employment is 3 units (Problem 4c)), and the labor force is 9 units. Therefore, the level of unemployment is 6 units of labor. Finally, when the GDP deflator is 125, the real wage rate is $4, the actual level of employment is 5 units (Problem 4d)), and the labor force is 7 units. Therefore, the observed level of unemployment is 2 units of labor.

14 INFLATION

CHAPTER IN PERSPECTIVE

Inflation has received secondary attention in several previous chapters but in this chapter it becomes the central focus. We learn why inflation is a problem and how the nature of the problems associated with inflation depend on whether inflation is anticipated or unanticipated. We use the aggregate demand-aggregate supply model to explain the two main causes of inflation: demand-pull and cost-push. We find that the nature of macroeconomic equilibrium depends critically on expectations about inflation. It thus becomes important to consider how expectations are formed and how expectations affect macroeconomic behavior and the *actual* rate of inflation. Finally, we discuss the relationships between inflation and interest rates and between inflation and the unemployment rate.

LEARNING OBJECTIVES

After studying this chapter, you will be able to:

- **Explain why inflation is a problem**
- **Explain how increasing aggregate demand generates a price-wage inflation spiral**
- **Explain how decreasing aggregate supply generates a cost-price inflation spiral**
- **Explain why it pays to anticipate inflation accurately**
- **Explain how inflation expectations are made**
- **Explain how inflation expectations affect *actual* inflation**
- **Explain the relationship between inflation and interest rates**
- **Explain the relationship between inflation and unemployment**

HELPFUL HINTS

1. Demand-pull inflation is initiated by an increase in aggregate demand while cost-push inflation is initiated by a decrease in aggregate supply. However, both a price-wage inflation spiral and a cost-price inflation spiral require continuing increases in aggregate demand.

2. Recall from Chapter 13 that if the expected price level turns out to be correct, employment will turn out to be at the full-employment level and thus real GDP supplied will be equal to full-employment real GDP. This is why a short-run aggregate supply curve intersects the long-run aggregate supply curve at the expected price level. If the price level is actually equal to the expected price level, the economy must be at full employment; that is, the economy must be on its long-run aggregate supply curve.

As we learn in this chapter, these same relationships hold when the *rate of inflation* is correctly anticipated. If the actual rate of inflation is equal to the expected rate of inflation, the economy will be at full employment and the economy must be on its long-run Phillips curve.

3. The rational expectation of the price level will be at the intersection of the *expected* aggregate demand curve and the *expected* short-run aggregate supply curve. Given the expected aggregate demand curve, the problem is to determine the expected short-run aggregate supply curve, the position of which is determined by the full-employment level of real GDP and the wage rate. So, it is necessary to forecast the wage rate.

In the case of sticky wages, this is straightforward since the wage rate is fixed and known. The position of the expected short-run aggregate supply curve is determined by that fixed wage.

In the case of flexible wages, however, forecasting the wage rate is complicated by the fact that the wage rate depends on the expected price level. But the reason we are trying to forecast the wage rate is to allow us to forecast the price level. As discussed in the text, this puzzle is solved by finding a forecast of the price level that gives a short-run aggregate supply curve that intersects the expected aggregate demand curve at the expected price level. This implies that when wages are flexible, the rational expectation of the price level occurs at the intersection of the expected aggregate demand curve and the expected *long-run* aggregate supply curve.

4. The rational expectation of the price level occurs at the intersection of the *expected* aggregate demand curve and the *expected* short-run aggregate supply curve (or *expected long-run* aggregate supply curve if wages are flexible). The rational expectations equilibrium, however, is at the intersection of the *actual* aggregate demand curve and the *actual short-run* aggregate supply curve.

5. Be sure you know why each of the following is true.

- If the actual price level is greater than the expected price level, real GDP is above full-employment real GDP.
- If the actual price level is less than the expected price level, real GDP is below full-employment real GDP.
- If the actual price level is equal to the expected price level, real GDP is at full-employment real GDP.

6. An important implication of the rational expectations hypothesis is that the consequences of any macroeconomic event (e.g., a monetary or fiscal policy) depend on expectations. The effect on the price level and real GDP of a given increase in the money supply will be different for different price level expectations. Its effect on the position of the aggregate demand curve does not depend on the expected price level, but the position of the short-run aggregate supply curve does depend

on the expected price level and thus so does the macroeconomic equilibrium.

For example, a given increase in the money supply can result in an increase in real GDP, no change in real GDP, or even a reduction in real GDP depending solely on the nature of the expected price level. An increase in real GDP will result if the increase in aggregate demand is not anticipated (or underanticipated); no change in real GDP will result if the increase in aggregate demand is correctly anticipated; and a reduction in real GDP will result if the increase in aggregate demand is less than anticipated (overanticipated).

7. The short-run and long-run Phillips curves are also introduced in this chapter. They can be explained by the aggregate demand-aggregate supply model. Be sure you understand why the short-run Phillips curve is negatively sloped and why it will shift when the expected rate of inflation changes.

KEY FIGURES AND TABLES

Figure 14.1 Demand-Pull Inflation

As first discussed in Chapter 7, an increase in aggregate demand increases the price level in two stages: the initial effect and the effect due to the wage response. These are illustrated in parts (a) and (b) of this figure. As the price level rises, inflation is experienced.

The economy begins in full-employment equilibrium at the intersection of AD_0 and SAS_0; the price level is 120 and real GDP is $5 trillion. Aggregate demand increases to AD_1 and, given the wage rate, the economy moves along the SAS_0 curve; the economy experiences inflation as the price level rises to 125 and real GDP rises to $5.5 trillion. This initial effect is shown in part (a).

Since employment is above full employment, wages will begin to rise and, as seen in part (b), the short-run aggregate supply curve will begin shifting upward until it reaches SAS_1. The economy experiences further inflation as the price level rises to 135 and real GDP returns to its original full employment level.

Figure 14.2 A Price-Wage Inflation Spiral

This figure is a continuation of Fig. 14.1. If aggregate demand continues to increase, the *AD* curve continues to shift to the right. This leads to a repetition of the effects that were shown in Fig. 14.1. Each time the aggregate demand curve shifts to the right, while the wage rate is fixed, the price level and real GDP will rise. Since real GDP now exceeds its full employment level, wages will rise, shifting the short-run aggregate supply curve upward. This results in a further increase in the price level. This sequence of an increase in the price level being followed by an increase in the wage rate continues as long as aggregate demand continues to increase. Thus, this perpetual demand-pull inflation gives rise to a price-wage inflation spiral.

Figure 14.3 Cost-Push Inflation

This figure illustrates the inflation effects of an upward shift in the short-run aggregate supply curve due to a large increase in the price of an important input like oil. In the figure, the economy is initially in equilibrium at the intersection of the AD_0 and SAS_0 curves. Then the increase in input cost occurs, shifting the short-run aggregate cost curve leftward to SAS_1. As a result, equilibrium occurs at the intersection of the AD_0 and SAS_1 curves: real GNP has fallen to $3 trillion and the price level has risen from 120 to 130 – an 8.3 percent rate of inflation. This simultaneous decline in real GDP and inflation is called stagflation.

Figure 14.5 A Cost-Price Inflation Spiral

This figure is a continuation of Fig. 14.3. There we saw that an increase in the price of oil will shift the short-run aggregate supply curve to the left causing a reduction of real

GDP (and employment) and cost-push inflation. If the government responds to the decline in employment by using monetary or fiscal policy to increase aggregate demand to AD_1, the price level will increase further to 135 and the original level of real GDP will be restored. If, in the face of rising prices, oil producers decide to increase the price of oil again, the short-run aggregate supply curve will shift further to the left, to SAS_2. This will result in a decline in real GDP and more inflation. As this sequence continues, the economy experiences a cost-price inflation spiral.

Figure 14.6 Rational Expectation of the Price Level

A rational expectation of the price level is given by the intersection of the expected aggregate demand curve (*EAD*) and the expected short-run aggregate supply curve (*ESAS*). Thus, forming a rational expectation requires forecasting the positions of the aggregate demand and short-run aggregate supply curves. Since the position of the short-run aggregate supply curve depends on the position of the long-run aggregate supply curve and the wage rate, one must forecast each of these. In the figure, the forecast of the long-run aggregate supply curve is denoted *ELAS*. As indicated in Helpful Hint 3, the forecast of the wage rate depends on whether wages are sticky or flexible.

Part (a) indicates the rational expectation when wages are sticky. Since the wage rate is fixed and known in this case, the position of the *ESAS* curve is readily determined. Two possibilities are illustrated here. If the wage rate is such that $ESAS_0$ is the expected short-run aggregate supply curve, then the rational expectation of the price level is 120. If, however, the expected short-run aggregate supply curve is given by $ESAS_1$, the rational expectation of the price level will be 140.

The rational expectation of the price level when wages are flexible is shown in part (b). In this case, the rational expectation of the price level is the forecast obtained by the intersection of the expected aggregate demand (*EAD*) curve and the expected *long-run* aggregate supply (*ELAD*) curve (see Helpful Hint 3). Thus, the rational expectation of the price level is 130 when wages are flexible. Since, the expected price level is at this intersection, the expected short-run aggregate supply curve also intersects these curves at the same point.

Figure 14.7 Rational Expectations Equilibrium

A rational expectations equilibrium occurs at the intersection of the actual aggregate demand curve and the actual short-run aggregate supply curve, but the position of this latter curve depends on the rational expectation of the price level. This figure illustrates, in part (a), the construction of a rational expectation of the price level and then in parts (b) and (c) illustrates a rational expectations equilibrium in two different cases.

Part (a) simply shows what is expected to happen and yields 130 as the rational expectation of the price level (see Fig. 14.6 (b)).

Given this expected price level, part (b) show a rational expectations equilibrium when aggregate demand is less than expected but the long-run aggregate and short-run supply curves turn out to be as expected. The equilibrium occurs at the intersection of the actual aggregate demand curve, (*AD*), and the actual short-run aggregate supply curve, (*SAS*) (and the same as *ESAS* in part a). Thus the price level is less than expected and real GDP is below its full-employment level.

Part (c) shows a rational expectations equilibrium when aggregate demand turns out to be as expected but long-run and short-run aggregate supply turn out to be less than expected. The equilibrium occurs at the intersection of the actual aggregate demand curve, *AD* (the same as *EAD* in part a), and the actual short-run aggregate supply curve, *SAS*. The price level is thus higher than expected and real GDP is lower but above the new full-employment real GDP.

Figure 14.8 Anticipated Inflation

As illustrated here, if inflation is fully anticipated, real GDP remains at its full-employment level and only the price level rises. In this figure the economy is initially in equilibrium at the intersection of the AD_0, SAS_0, and *LAS* curves. The price level is 120. Aggregate demand is *correctly* expected to increase to AD_1.

Since the expected long-run aggregate supply curve continues to be *LAS*, the rational expectation of the price level is 132 and the expected short-run aggregate supply curve is SAS_1. The rational expectations equilibrium is given by the intersection of the actual aggregate demand and actual short-run aggregate supply curves. Because expectations are fully correct, these actual curves are the same as their expected counterparts and the equilibrium corresponds to a price level of 132, the expected value, and real GDP of $5 trillion, which is full-employment real GDP.

As this process continues, in the next year, aggregate demand is correctly expected to rise to AD_2. The anticipated rise in the price level causes wages to rise accordingly and the short-run aggregate supply curve shifts to SAS_2. Real GDP remains at its full-employment level and the price level rises to 145, just as expected.

Figure 14.10 The Short-Run Phillips Curve

The short-run Phillips curve, denoted *SRPC*, illustrates the relationship between the rate of inflation and the rate of unemployment given the natural rate of unemployment and given the expected rate of inflation. The fact that the expected rate of inflation is held constant makes it a short run curve. For the short-run Phillips curve shown here, the natural rate of unemployment is 6 percent and and the expected rate of inflation is 10 percent.

If the actual rate of inflation is also 10 percent, the actual rate of unemployment will be the natural rate so the short-run Phillips curve passes through point *a*. If inflation is greater that anticipated, unemployment will be below its natural rate (see point *b*). If inflation is less than anticipated, unemployment will exceed the natural rate of unemployment (see point *c*).

Figure 14.11 The Short-Run and Long-Run Phillips Curves

The long-run Phillips curve, denoted *LRPC*, shows the relationship between the rate of inflation and the rate of unemployment when the actual rate of inflation equals the expected rate of inflation. It is vertical at the natural rate of unemployment, 6 percent in the figure.

Since the expected rate of inflation is held constant along any short-run Phillips curve, a change in the expected rate of inflation will shift the short-run Phillips curve vertically by the amount of the change in expected inflation. In the figure, the short-run Phillips curve shifts from $SRPC_0$ to $SRPC_1$ due to a decrease in the rate of expected inflation from 10 percent to 8 percent a year. It is important to note that the new short-run Phillips curve intersects the long-run Phillips curve at the expected rate of inflation of 8 percent (point *d*).

SELF-TEST

CONCEPT REVIEW

1. The inflation rate is the percentage rise in the ___price___ ___level___.
2. Inflation resulting from an increase in aggregate demand is called ___demand___-___pull___ inflation. Inflation resulting from a decrease in aggregate supply due to an increase in costs is called ___cost___ ___push___ inflation.

3. The short-run aggregate supply curve intersects the long-run aggregate supply curve at a price level equal to the expected price level. If the price level is higher than expected, then real GDP is greater than its full-employment level.
4. If inflation turns out to be higher than expected, borrowers gain and lenders lose.
5. A forecast that is based on all the available information, is correct on average, and minimizes the range of the forecast error is called a(n) rational expectation. The proposition that the forecasts people make are the same as the forecasts made by an economist using the relevant economic theory as well as information available is called the rational expectation hypothesis.
6. The rational expectation of the price level is given by the intersection of the expected aggregate demand curve and the expected short-run aggregate supply curve.
7. A macroeconomic equilibrium based on expectations that are the best available forecasts is called a(n) rational expectation equilibrium.
8. When aggregate demand is less than expected, actual inflation is less than expected and real GDP is less than expected.
9. An unanticipated increase in the money supply will cause the price level to increase and real GDP to increase.
10. During periods when the rate of inflation is high, nominal interest rates tend to be high. If the Fed unexpectedly increases the money supply, the immediate effect is to lower interest rates. If the Fed conducts an anticipated and continuous increase in the money supply, interest rates will rise.
11. The curve showing the relationship between inflation and unemployment for a given expected inflation rate is called the short-run phillips curve. It shows that if the actual rate of inflation is greater than the expected rate of inflation, the actual unemployment rate will be less than its natural rate.
12. The natural rate hypothesis implies that the long-run Phillips curve is vertical at the natural rate of unemployment.

TRUE OR FALSE

___ 1. If the price level at the beginning of 1990 is 120 and the price level at the beginning of 1991 is 130, the rate of inflation is 8.3 percent.

___ 2. Unanticipated inflation is a problem only at very high inflation rates.

___ 3. Unanticipated inflation produces fluctuations in real GDP, employment, and unemployment.

___ 4. An increase in the price level due to an increase in government purchases of goods and services is an example of demand-pull inflation.

___ 5. If aggregate demand is continually increasing faster than long-run aggregate supply, a price-wage inflation spiral will arise.

___ 6. A decrease in the price of oil will cause a cost-push inflation.

___ 7. If inflation exceeds expectations and workers have money wage contracts, the real wage rate has risen.

___ 8. If inflation turns out to be lower than expected, lenders gain and borrowers lose.

___ 9. A rational expectation is a forecast that is always correct.

___ 10. The rational expectations hypothesis states that people make forecasts in the same way economists do.

___ 11. In a rational expectations equilibrium the economy must exhibit full employment.

___ 12. The short-run aggregate supply curve intersects the long-run aggregate supply curve at the expected price level.

___ 13. If the expected price level falls, the short-run aggregate supply curve will shift downward by the amount of the fall.

___ 14. Only when the price level is equal to the expected price level is the economy producing at full-employment real GDP.

___ 15. In order for an increase in aggregate demand to raise the price level, the increase in aggregate demand must be anticipated.

___ 16. If an economy is in a rational expectations equilibrium and real GDP is greater than full-employment real GDP, then it must be the case that the actual price level is greater than the expected price level.

___ 17. If an increase in aggregate demand is correctly anticipated, inflation will not occur.

___ 18. Expectations of inflation are partially self-fulfilling.

___ 19. If the inflation rate rises but nominal interest rates remain unchanged, then real interest rates have fallen.

___ 20. If the inflation rate rises but real interest rates remain unchanged, then nominal interest rates have fallen.

T 21. During a period with zero expected inflation the (nominal) interest rate is 5 percent. If the expected rate of inflation rises to 6 percent, the interest rate will rise to a little more than 11 percent.

F 22. If an increase in the money supply is unanticipated, its immediate effect will be to raise interest rates.

T 23. If the Fed continues to increase the money supply at a rapid rate year after year, we would expect interest rates to be high.

T 24. The short-run Phillips curve indicates that, given the expected rate of inflation, if the actual rate of inflation increases, the rate of unemployment will decrease.

F 25. If the expected rate of inflation increases the long-run Phillips curve will shift to the right.

MULTIPLE CHOICE

1. The current year's price level is 180 and the rate of inflation over the past year has been 20 percent. What was last year's price level?
   a. 144.
   b. 150.
   c. 160.
   d. 216.

2. Which of the following would cause a perpetual demand-pull inflation?
   a. A tax cut.
   b. An increase in government purchases of goods and services.
   c. An increase in the price of oil.
   d. A positive rate of growth in the quantity of money.

3. Which of the following would cause a cost-push inflation?
   a. A tax cut.
   b. An increase in government purchases of goods and services.
   c. An increase in the price of oil.
   d. A positive rate of growth of the quantity of money.

4. If the Fed increases the money supply whenever real GDP is below its full-employment level and oil producers increase the price of oil whenever the price level increases, we are likely to observe a
   a. cost-price inflation spiral.
   b. price-wage inflation spiral.
   c. demand-pull inflation spiral.
   d. demand-push inflation spiral.

5. If the rate of inflation turns out to be lower than expected,
   a. borrowers and lenders both lose.
   b. borrowers and lenders both gain.
   c. borrowers gain and lenders lose.
   d. borrowers lose and lenders gain.

6. If the rate of inflation turns out to be lower than expected, then
   a. expectations could not be rational expectations.
   b. real GDP will be less than full-employment real GDP.
   c. the real interest rate will be lower than expected.
   d. the real wage rate will be lower than expected.

7. Which of the following is NOT true of a rational expectation forecast?
   a. It uses all available information.
   b. It makes the range of forecast errors as small as possible.
   c. It is correct.
   d. The forecast errors are zero on average.

8. Figure 14.1 illustrates an economy initially in macroeconomic equilibrium at point *a*. SAS_0 corresponds to a wage rate of $10 and SAS_1 corresponds to a wage rate of $15. If the money supply is expected to increase by 50 percent and wages are *flexible,* what is the rational expectation of the price level?
   a. 100
   b. 120
   c. 130
   d. 150

Figure 14.1

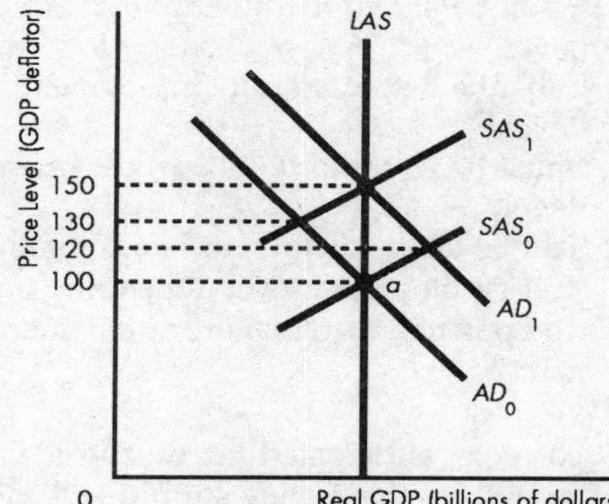

9. Figure 14.1 illustrates an economy initially in macroeconomic equilibrium at point *a*. SAS_0 corresponds to a wage rate of $10 and SAS_1 corresponds to a wage rate of $15. If the money supply is expected to increase by 50 percent and wages are *fixed at $10*, what is the rational expectation of the price level?
   a. 100.
   b. 120.
   c. 130.
   d. 150.

10. A rational expectations equilibrium is the price level and real GDP given by
   a. the intersection of the actual aggregate demand curve and the actual short-run aggregate supply curve.
   b. the intersection of the actual aggregate demand curve and the actual long-run aggregate supply curve.
   c. the intersection of the expected aggregate demand curve and the expected short-run aggregate supply curve.
   d. the intersection of the expected aggregate demand curve and the expected long-run aggregate supply curve.

11. According to the rational expectations hypothesis, a correctly anticipated increase in the money supply in an economy with a given long-run aggregate supply will result in
   a. an increase in the price level and an increase in real GDP.
   b. an increase in the price level and a decrease in real GDP.
   c. a proportional increase in the price level and no change in real GDP.
   d. no change in the price level and an increase in real GDP.

12. Suppose the money supply is expected to remain unchanged but it actually increases. According to the rational expectations hypothesis,
   a. the price level will rise and real GDP will increase.
   b. the price level will rise and real GDP will decrease.
   c. the price level will fall and real GDP will increase.
   d. the price level will fall and real GDP will decrease.

13. Figure 14.2 illustrates an economy initially in equilibrium at point *a*. If the *AD* curve is *correctly* expected to shift from AD_0 to AD_1, the new macroeconomic equilibrium will be
    a. real GDP = $380 billion and price level = 125.
    b. real GDP = $500 billion and price level = 150.
    c. real GDP = $500 billion and price level = 100.
    d. real GDP = $620 billion and price level = 125.

Figure 14.2

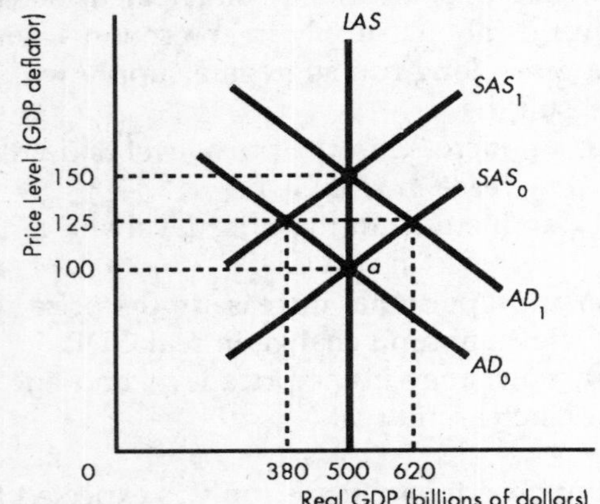

14. Figure 14.2 illustrates an economy initially in equilibrium at point *a*. If the *AD* curve is expected to shift from AD_0 to AD_1 but it actually remains at AD_0, the new macroeconomic equilibrium will be
    a. real GDP = $380 billion and price level = 125.
    b. real GDP = $500 billion and price level = 150.
    c. real GDP = $500 billion and price level = 100.
    d. real GDP = $620 billion and price level = 125.

15. Figure 14.2 illustrates an economy initially in equilibrium at point *a*. If the *AD* curve is expected to remain at AD_0 but, in fact, shifts to AD_1, the new macroeconomic equilibrium will be
    a. real GDP = $380 billion and price level = 125.
    b. real GDP = $500 billion and price level = 150.
    c. real GDP = $500 billion and price level = 100.
    d. real GDP = $620 billion and price level = 125.

16. If the actual price level is higher than the expected price level, then real GDP
    a. must be above its full-employment level.
    b. must be below its full-employment level.
    c. must be equal to its full-employment level.
    d. can be above, below, or equal to its full-employment level depending on the position of the aggregate demand curve.

17. A correctly anticipated increase in the rate of growth of the money supply will cause nominal interest rates to
    a. fall and real interest rates to fall.
    b. fall and leave real interest rates unchanged.
    c. rise and real interest rates to rise.
    d. rise and leave real interest rates unchanged.

18. Suppose that initially the nominal rate of interest is 8 percent and the expected rate of inflation is 5 percent. If the expected rate of inflation increases to 8 percent, what will the new nominal rate of interest be?
    a. 3 percent.
    b. 8 percent.
    c. 11 percent.
    d. 16 percent.

19. Which of the following will shift the short-run Phillips curve to the right?
    a. Either an increase in the expected rate of inflation or a decrease in the natural rate of unemployment.
    b. Either an increase in the expected rate of inflation or an increase in the natural rate of unemployment.
    c. Either a decrease in the expected rate of inflation or a decrease in the natural rate of unemployment.
    d. Either a decrease in the expected rate of inflation or an increase in the natural rate of unemployment.

20. Given the expected rate of inflation, an increase in the actual rate of inflation will cause a
    a. movement along the short-run Phillips curve and a decrease in the unemployment rate.
    b. movement along the short-run Phillips curve and an increase in the unemployment rate.
    c. shift of the short-run Phillips curve and a decrease in the unemployment rate.
    d. shift of the short-run Phillips curve and an increase in the unemployment rate.

Short Answer

1. Explain how a price-wage inflation spiral arises.

2. Explain how a cost-price inflation spiral arises.

3. What is a rational expectation?

4. How is a rational expectation of the price level calculated
    a. if wages are sticky?
    b. if wages are flexible?

5. What will happen to the price level and real GDP if the government increases its purchases of goods and services and that increase is not anticipated (i.e., the price level is not expected to change)?

6. What will happen to the price level and real GDP if the government increases its purchases of goods and services and that increase *is* anticipated?

7. What will happen to the price level and real GDP if aggregate demand is expected to increase but it does not?

8. What is the relationship between the expected rate of inflation and interest rates?

9. How can an increase in the anticipated growth rate of the money supply increase interest rates while an increase in the quantity of money will lower interest rates?

10. Why is the short-run Phillips curve negatively sloped?

Problems

1. Table 14.1 gives the initial aggregate demand and short-run aggregate supply schedules for an economy in which the expected price level is 80.
    a) What is full-employment real GDP?
    b) What is actual real GDP and the actual price level?

Table 14.1

Price level	Real GDP demanded	Real GDP supplied
60	600	400
80	500	500
100	400	600
120	300	700
140	200	800

Table 14.2

Price level	Real GDP demanded	Real GDP supplied
60	800	
80	700	
100	600	
120	500	
140	400	

2. In year 1 the economy is in the macroeconomic equilibrium characterized in Problem 1. It is *expected* that in year 2, aggregate demand will be as given in Table 14.2.
   a) What is the *vertical* amount of the expected shift in the aggregate demand curve when real GDP is $500 billion?
   b) What is the rational expectation of the price level for year 2 if
      i) wages are sticky?
      ii) wages are flexible?
   c) Assuming that wages are flexible, the expected shift in aggregate demand will cause the short-run aggregate supply (*SAS*) curve to shift. What will the new *SAS* curve be? For each price level, give the new values of real GDP supplied in the last column of Table 14.2.
   d) Suppose that, in fact, aggregate demand does NOT change but remains as given in Table 14.1. Still assuming that wages are flexible, what will real GDP and the price level be in year 2?
   e) Compare the actual change in the price level with the expected change.

3. In year 1 the economy is in the macroeconomic equilibrium characterized by Problem 1. It is *expected* that in year 2 aggregate demand will NOT change but remain as given in Table 14.1. But, in fact, in year 2 aggregate demand *does* change to the aggregate demand given in Table 14.2.
   a) What is the rational expectation of the price level for year 2 if wages are sticky? Flexible?
   b) Assuming that wages are flexible, what is the relevant *SAS* curve, the one given in Table 14.1 or the one you have given by completing Table 14.2?
   c) What will real GDP and the price level turn out to be in year 2?
   d) Compare the actual change in the price level with the expected change.

4. In year 1 the economy is in the macroeconomic equilibrium characterized by Problem 1. It is *expected* that in year 2, aggregate demand will be as given in Table 14.2. It turns out that expectations are correct: the actual aggregate demand in year 2 is as given in Table 14.2.
   a) Assuming wages to be flexible, what is the rational expectation of the price level for year 2?
   b) Assuming wages to be flexible, what will real GDP and the price level turn out to be in year 2?
   c) Compare the actual change in the price level with the expected change.

5. Assuming that wages are flexible, graphically illustrate the rational expectations equilibrium in an economy for which aggregate demand is higher than expected. Compare the actual equilibrium with the expected equilibrium.

6. Assuming that wages are flexible, graphically illustrate the rational expectations equilibrium in an economy for which aggregate demand is higher than expected *and* long-run aggregate supply is lower than expected. Compare the actual equilibrium with the expected equilibrium.

ANSWERS

CONCEPT REVIEW

1. price level
2. demand-pull; cost-push
3. expected price level; greater
4. gain; lose
5. rational; rational expectations
6. short-run aggregate supply
7. rational expectations
8. less; less
9. increase; increase
10. high; lower; rise
11. short-run Phillips; less
12. natural rate

TRUE OR FALSE

1. T	6. F	11. F	16. T	21. T
2. F	7. F	12. T	17. F	22. F
3. T	8. T	13. T	18. T	23. T
4. T	9. F	14. T	19. T	24. T
5. T	10. F	15. F	20. F	25. F

MULTIPLE CHOICE

1. b	5. d	9. b	13. b	17. d
2. d	6. b	10. a	14. a	18. c
3. c	7. c	11. c	15. d	19. b
4. a	8. d	12. a	16. a	20. a

SHORT ANSWER

1. An increase in aggregate demand will initially increase both the price level and real GDP as the aggregate demand curve shifts along the prevailing short-run aggregate supply curve. Since the economy is now above full-employment real GDP, wages will increase shifting the short-run aggregate supply curve leftward so that the price level will rise further and real GDP will return to its full-employment level. This is the process of demand-pull inflation. If aggregate demand does not increase further, there will be no further increase in the price level.

   If, however, aggregate demand continues to increase, the process just described will continually repeat itself. The price level will rise followed by a wage increase on and on. The economy is experiencing a price-wage inflation spiral.

2. An increase in costs (consider an increase in the price of oil) will shift the short-run aggregate supply curve leftward which will result in an increase in the price level and a decline in real GDP—stagflation. This is cost-push inflation. If, in the face of the decline in real GDP, the govern-

ment initiates an expansionary monetary or fiscal policy, aggregate demand will increase causing a further increase in the price level and an increase in real GDP (perhaps to its full-employment level). Given the increase in the price level, oil producers may decide to further increase the price of oil which will shift the short-run aggregate supply curve again and the process just discussed will repeat itself. As long as the process continues, we observe continual cost increases followed by price level increases—a cost-price inflation spiral.

3. A rational expectation is a forecast that is based on all available information, is correct on average, and makes the range of the forecast error as small as possible.

4. A rational expectation of the price level is obtained by using the aggregate demand and aggregate supply model to predict the price level. The actual price level will be given by the intersection of the aggregate demand curve and the short-run aggregate supply curve. Therefore we want to determine where we expect these curves to be and then see where they intersect. The problem is that the short-run aggregate supply curve depends on the wage rate so we must also forecast the wage rate.
   a. In the case of sticky wages, the wage rate is fixed so the forecasting problem is easy. The position of the expected short-run aggregate supply curve is determined by the fixed wage rate.
   b. In the case of flexible wages, however, forecasting the wage rate is complicated by the fact that the wage rate depends on the expected price level. But the reason we need a forecast of the wage rate is to find the expected price level. We resolve this problem by recognizing that if the price level turns out to be equal to the expected price level, the short-run aggregate supply curve intersects the aggregate demand curve at the point where the latter curve intersects the long-run aggregate supply curve. Since the long-run aggregate supply curve does not depend on the expected price level, the rational expectation of the price level is obtained at the intersection of the aggregate demand curve and the *long-run* aggregate supply curve.

5. An increase in government purchases of goods and services will shift the aggregate demand curve to the right. If the price level is not expected to change, the short-run aggregate supply curve remains unchanged and the increase in aggregate demand will cause the price level to rise and real GDP to increase.

6. If the shift in the aggregate demand curve is anticipated, the expected price level will rise by the amount of the vertical shift in the aggregate demand and thus the short-run aggregate supply will shift up by that amount. So, when an increase in aggregate demand is fully anticipated, the aggregate demand curve and the short-run aggregate supply curve will shift upward by the same amount. As a result, the price level will rise and real GDP will remain unchanged.

7. If the expected price level increases due to an expected increase in aggregate demand but there is no change in actual aggregate demand, only the short-run aggregate supply curve shifts up. Thus, the intersection between the new short-run aggregate supply and the original aggregate demand curve will be at a higher price level and a lower level of real GDP.

8. When the rate of inflation is expected to rise, the interest will also rise to compensate for the increased rate at which the

purchasing power of money is eroding. The essential point is that lenders and borrowers are interested in the quantity of goods and services that a unit of money will buy. Lenders will insist on the higher interest rate (to compensate for the loss of purchasing power of money) and borrowers will be willing to pay it because they realize that the dollars they pay back will buy fewer goods and services.

9. If the Fed increases the money supply *unexpectedly*, the immediate effect will be to lower the interest rate as equilibrium is restored in the money market. If, on the other hand, the Fed continues to increase the money supply year after year people are likely to expect it to continue. Thus inflation occurs and there is an increase in expected inflation. This will cause (nominal) interest rates to rise.

10. The short-run Phillips curve shows the relationship between the rate of inflation and the rate of unemployment given the expected rate of inflation and the natural rate of unemployment. Explaining its negative slope requires us to explain why an increase in the rate of inflation will be associated with a decrease in employment (and vice versa). We know that if the actual rate of inflation is equal to the expected rate of inflation, the economy will be at full employment so the rate of unemployment is equal to its natural rate. If the actual rate of inflation increases to a level above the expected rate of inflation then aggregate demand must be increasing more rapidly than expected so real GDP exceeds its full-employment level which implies that unemployment is now less than the natural rate of unemployment. Since an increase in the rate of inflation has caused a decrease in the rate of unemployment, the short-run Phillips curve is negatively sloped. The same logic implies that a decrease in the actual rate of inflation below its expected level will be associated with an increase in the rate of unemployment.

Problems

1. a) Full-employment real GDP is the quantity of real GDP supplied when the expected price level is equal to the actual price level. The last column of Table 14.1 gives the quantity of real GDP supplied at various price levels assuming that the *expected* price level is constant at 80. Since when the *actual* price level is also 80, the quantity of real GDP supplied is $500 billion, that is the value of full-employment real GDP.
   b) Actual real GDP and the actual price level are determined by the intersection of the aggregate demand curve and the short-run aggregate supply curve. Real GDP is $500 billion and the price level is 80, since at a price level of 80, the quantity of real GDP demanded equals the quantity of real GDP supplied ($500 billion).

2. a) The price level associated with $500 billion of real GDP demanded for the original aggregate demand curve (Table 14.1) is 80. The price level associated with $500 billion of real GDP demanded for the new expected aggregate demand curve (Table 14.2) is 120. Therefore the aggregate demand curve is expected to shift upward by 40.
   b) i) If wages are sticky and not expected to change, the relevant expected short-run aggregate supply curve is the original one associated with Table 14.1. The rational expectation of the price level is 100 since that is the price level that equates the expected quantity of real GDP demanded (from Table 14.2) with the

expected quantity of real GDP supplied (from Table 14.1). That is the price level predicted by the aggregate demand-aggregate supply model.

ii) If wages are flexible, the rational expectation of the price level is given by the intersection of the expected aggregate demand curve (Table 14.2) and the expected long-run aggregate supply curve. Long-run aggregate supply is equal to $500 billion and is not expected to change. Since the price level associated with $500 billion of real GDP demanded is 120, the rational expectation of the price level.

c) The quantities of real GDP supplied for the new *SAS* curve are given in the last column of Table 14.2 Solution. The original expected price level is 80. From part (b) we know that, when wages are flexible, the new expected price level is 120, which implies that the *SAS* curve shifts up by 40. Thus, at each quantity of real GDP supplied, the price level on the new *SAS* curve is 40 points higher than on the original *SAS* curve (Table 14.1). For example, real GDP supplied of $500 billion now requires a price level of 120 rather than 80. Similarly, real GDP supplied of $400 billion now requires a price level of 100 rather than 60. (*Note:* The values in parentheses in the table are inferred by extrapolation rather than calculated from Table 14.1.)

d) The new macroeconomic equilibrium in year 2 will occur at the intersection of the actual *AD* curve and the relevant *SAS* curve. Since the *AD* curve was expected to shift and wages are flexible, the relevant *SAS* curve is the one associated with the expected price level of 120 (the *SAS* curve in Table 14.2 Solution). But the *AD* curve did not actually shift, so the *AD* curve is given in Table 14.1. The intersection of these curves is at real GDP equals $400 billion and price level equals 100. When the price level is 100, the quantity of real GDP demanded is equal to the quantity of real GDP supplied at $400 billion.

e) The price level was expected to rise from 80 to 120 but, in fact, only rises from 80 to 100.

Table 14.2 Solution: Aggregate Demand and Supply

Price level	Real GDP demanded	Real GDP supplied
60	800	(200)
80	700	(300)
100	600	400
120	500	500
140	400	600

3. a) Since neither aggregate demand nor long-run aggregate supply are expected to change, the rational expectation of the price level remains at 80 whether wages are sticky or flexible.

b) The answer to part (a) implies that the relevant *SAS* curve is the one given in Table 14.1.

c) The rational expectations equilibrium will occur at the intersection of the actual *AD* curve and the relevant *SAS* curve. The actual *AD* curve is given in Table 14.2 while the relevant *SAS* curve is given in Table 14.1. Thus real GDP will be $600 billion and the price level will be 100.

d) The price level was expected to remain unchanged at 80 but, in fact, the price level rises from 80 to 100.

4. a) Since aggregate demand is expected to increase and wages are flexible, the rational expectation of the price level for year 2 is the same as in Problem 2: 120.
   b) The rational expectations equilibrium will occur at the intersection of the actual *AD* curve and the relevant *SAS* curve. Since the expected price level is 120, the relevant *SAS* curve is the one given in Table 14.2 Solution. The actual *AD* curve is also given in Table 14.2. Thus real GDP will be $500 billion and the price level will be 120.
   c) The price level was expected to rise from 80 to 120, which is exactly what happens.

5. Figure 14.3 illustrates the rational expectations equilibrium. The expected aggregate demand curve is given by *EAD* which intersects the expected long-run aggregate supply curve, (*ELAS*), at point *a*. Thus the rational expectation of the price level is P_0, which implies that the relevant short-run aggregate supply curve is *ESAS*. The actual aggregate demand curve, *AD*, is higher than expected and the *actual* short-run aggregate supply curve is the same as *ESAS*. The rational expectations equilibrium occurs at point *b*, the intersection of *AD* and *ESAS*. The equilibrium price level, P_1, is higher than expected and thus real GDP is above capacity (i.e., above Y_0).

Figure 14.3

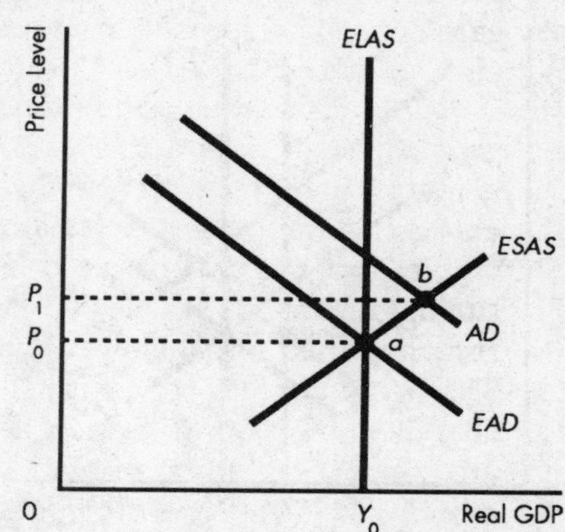

6. Figure 14.4 illustrates the rational expectations equilibrium in this case. The expected aggregate demand curve, (*EAD*), intersects the expected long-run aggregate supply curve, (*ELAS*), at point *a*. Thus the rational expectation of the price level is P_0, which implies that the expected short-run aggregate supply curve is *ESAS*. The actual aggregate demand curve, *AD*, is higher than expected. Also, the actual long-run aggregate supply curve, *LAS*, is lower than expected, which means that the actual short-run aggregate supply curve corresponding to an expected price level of P_0 is given by *SAS*.

   The rational expectations equilibrium occurs at point *b*, the intersection of *AD* and *SAS*. The equilibrium price level is P_2, which is much higher than expected. Real GDP can be above, below, or at the expected full-employment real GDP, Y_0, depending on the relative magnitudes of the unanticipated shifts, but real GDP will be above the new actual full-employment real GDP, Y_1.

Figure 14.4

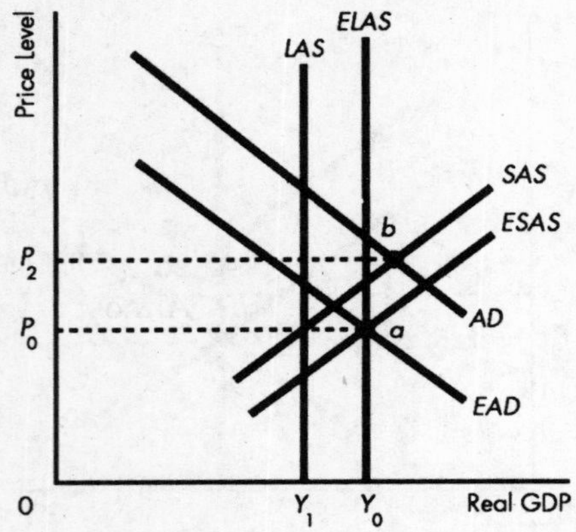

15 RECESSIONS AND DEPRESSIONS

CHAPTER IN PERSPECTIVE

The most recent recession occurred in 1990-1991. Why did real GDP fall and the unemployment rate rise while the rate of inflation fell only slightly? The recession of 1981 and 1982 was the deepest since the Great Depression. What caused real GDP to fall steeply and the unemployment rate to rise to above 10 percent? Why did the rate of inflation fall? Almost a decade earlier, the U.S. experienced another recession. Why did real GDP fall and unemployment rise during 1974 and 1975? Why did the rate of inflation *increase* during that recession?

In this chapter we use the aggregate demand and aggregate supply model that has been developed over the last several chapters to interpret the events mentioned in the previous paragraph. We also use these tools to examine the largest recession of all—the Great Depression. We find that all of the effort spent mastering recent chapters has a big payoff here. The model we have developed turns out to be very informative as we use it to analyze real world macroeconomic events.

LEARNING OBJECTIVES

After studying this chapter, you will be able to:

- **Describe the origins of the 1991 recession and the other recessions of the 1970s and 1980s**
- **Describe the course of money, interest rates, and expenditure as the economy contracts**
- **Describe the labor market in recession**
- **Compare and contrast the flexible and sticky wage theories of the labor market in recession**
- **Describe the onset of the Great Depression in 1929**
- **Describe the economy in the depths of the Great Depression between 1929 and 1933**
- **Compare the economy of the 1930s with that of today and assess the likelihood of another Great Depression**

HELPFUL HINTS

1. This chapter should be very rewarding to those who have spent the effort needed to understand the previous eight chapters. First of all it introduces no new analytical structure. Instead, the power of the fully developed aggregate demand and aggregate supply model is demonstrated by analyzing some interesting macroeconomic episodes, including the Great Depression. You should be pleased that you have mastered this powerful analytical tool.

2. As you examine various macroeconomic episodes, there are several key factors that you should focus on. First, are changes in aggregate demand and/or aggregate supply expected or unexpected? Second, as you follow the various changes, be sure you can understand what is going on in the labor and money markets that underlie the goods and services market. It is these markets that will tell you what is happening to the key variables: employment, unemployment, and interest rates.

3. Throughout this chapter we use our two competing theories (flexible wages and sticky wages in the labor market) to explain real world events. It is important to note that there is no dispute over the facts such as the level of prices or real GDP. The dispute centers around what changes in the economy created the facts, and therefore, also touches on what government policies might affect the economy.

It is *very* important to note that these are theories, not statements of facts, and that their explanations of the facts could be incorrect. Only proper empirical investigation over time will cast light on the validity of the theories.

KEY FIGURES AND TABLES

Figure 15.1 The OPEC Recession

This figure illustrates the effects of a large negative aggregate supply shock using the OPEC oil price shock as an example. In 1973 the economy was at the intersection of the AD_{73} and the SAS_{73} curves; real GDP was $3.3 trillion and the price level was 41. When OPEC dramatically increased the price of crude oil in 1973, the short-run aggregate supply curve shifted leftward by a large amount, to SAS_{75}. The aggregate demand curve shifted to the right (to AD_{75}) but by a much smaller amount. Thus the new equilibrium was at the intersection of the AD_{75} and SAS_{75} curves; real GDP had fallen to $3.2 trillion and the price level had risen to 49.

Figure 15.2 The Volcker Recession

This figure illustrates a recession following a shift in the aggregate demand curve which is less than expected using the Volcker recession as an example. In 1980 the economy was in equilibrium at the intersection of the AD_{80} and SAS_{80} curves; real GDP was $3.8 trillion and the price level was 74. At this time the price level had been rising at a rate of about 10 percent per year and that rate of inflation was expected to continue. Thus, the short-run aggregate supply curve for 1982 shifted all the way to SAS_{82}. The Fed under its chairman, Paul Volcker, however, significantly reduced the rate of growth of the money supply below what had occurred in the recent past and had been expected to continue. As a result the aggregate demand curve actually shifted up by only a small amount to AD_{82}. The new equilibrium, at the intersection of the AD_{82} and SAS_{82} curves, was at a lower level of real GDP ($3.75 trillion) and a higher price level (84). But the new price level was lower than the expected price level.

Figure 15.3 The 1990-1991 Recession

In 1990, the economy was in equilibrium at the intersection of the AD_{75} and SAS_{75} curves; real GDP was $4.9 trillion and the price level was 113. The Gulf crisis of that year affected both aggregate demand and aggregate supply. The increased uncertainty arising from that crisis and the ensuing Gulf War caused aggregate demand to fall in spite of an increase in government purchases associated with the war. Thus the aggregate demand curve shifted to the left, to AD_{91}. At the same time, the price of oil rose substantially which shifted the short-run aggregate supply curve to the left as well (to SAS_{91}). As a result, real GDP fell to $4.8 trillion in 1991 and the price level rose to 117.

Figure 15.5 The Labor Market in Recession: Sticky Wage Theory

Here the behavior of the labor market during the OPEC recession is examined assuming that the sticky wage theory is correct. Part (a) of the figure illustrates the downward shift of the short-run aggregate production function which resulted from the dramatic increase in the price of crude oil. This also caused the marginal product of labor to fall, which shifted the labor demand curve in part (b) downward from LD_{73} to LD_{75}. The labor market began in 1973 in equilibrium at the intersection of the LD_{73} and LS_{73} curves. The rate of unemployment was equal to the natural rate. Due to past increases in the population and thus increases in the current labor force, the labor supply curve shifted to the right, from LS_{73} to LS_{75}. We have already discussed the shift in the labor demand curve resulting from the decline in the marginal product of labor. As the price level rose (due to the aggregate supply shock) the real wage rate fell from $12.07 per hour to $11.97 per hour. Note that the labor supply curves are fairly steep. Thus the fall in the real wage rate was not enough to clear the labor market and employment, which is determined by labor demand, was only 161 billion hours per year. At the real wage rate of $11.97 per hour the quantity of labor supplied was 163 billion hours per year. Thus there was an increase in unemployment above natural unemployment.

Figure 15.6 The Labor Market in Recession: Flexible Wage Theory

This figure is the counterpart to Fig. 15.5 assuming that the flexible wage theory is correct. The only differences between the figures are that part (a) of Fig. 15.5 is omitted here since it is exactly the same and the labor supply curves are much flatter (more sensitive to changes in the real wage rate) here. The labor demand curves are the same as those in the previous figure and the magnitudes of the shifts are the same. Since the labor supply curve is flatter here, the fall in the real wage rate from $12.07 to $11.97 per hour is enough to clear the labor market at the employment level of 161 billion hours per year. The fall in employment is a fall in natural employment. Thus the flexible wage theory, by assuming a flat labor supply curve, can explain the behavior of the labor market during the OPEC recession.

SELF-TEST

CONCEPT REVIEW

1. The principal cause of the OPEC recession was a severe shock to aggregate ________. The principal cause of the Volcker recession was a severe shock to aggregate ________. The ________-________ recession resulted from shocks to both.
2. A situation in which real GDP stops growing or even declines but inflation speeds

up is called ___stagflation___. This situation was experienced during the ___Opec___ recession.

3. At the onset of a recession, interest rates may rise, fall, or remain steady. But once the recession is underway, interest rates will ___fall___ due to a(n) ___decline___ in the demand for real money.
4. The main component of aggregate expenditure that falls during a recession is ___investment___.
5. The OPEC recession shifted the short-run aggregate production function ___downward___. This shift ___lowered___ the marginal product of labor, which implies that the demand for labor curve shifted to the ___left___.
6. Proponents of the sticky wage theory believe that the quantity of labor supplied is ___less___ responsive to changes in real wages than is believed by proponents of the flexible wage theory.
7. The principal initial cause of what became the Great Depression was a shift in aggregate ___demand___. During the first few years of the Great Depression the money supply ___fell___ by 20 percent. During this period, real interest rates were ___high___.

TRUE OR FALSE

___F___ 1. The OPEC oil price increase in 1973-1974 caused the short-run aggregate supply curve to shift rightward.

___T___ 2. The primary cause of the Volcker recession was a dramatic slowdown in the growth of the money supply.

___F___ 3. The reduction in the growth rate of the money supply conducted by Volcker was generally anticipated by households and firms.

___F___ 4. The 1990-1991 recession was the result of a decrease in aggregate supply and an increase in aggregate demand.

___F___ 5. During the early stages of a recession, interest rates may rise or fall but later they typically rise.

___T___ 6. During a recession, the demand for real money grows less rapidly and may even decline.

___F___ 7. During a recession, the main component of aggregate expenditure that falls is consumption.

___T___ 8. The demand for labor fell as a result of the OPEC oil price increase.

___F___ 9. In order for the flexible wage theory to explain the behavior of the labor market (real wages and employment), it must be assumed that the supply of labor curve is not very sensitive to changes in the real wage.

___T___ 10. During the OPEC recession, the real wage rate fell.

____11. According to the sticky wage model of the labor market, the increase in unemployment during the OPEC recession was due to an increase in natural unemployment due to job market turnover.

____12. By now, the evidence implies that the sticky wage theory is false.

____13. The stock market crash of 1929 was the cause of the Great Depression.

____14. The major initial factor leading to the Great Depression was uncertainty about the future, which led to a reduction in investment and consumer expenditure.

____15. Real GDP fell during the Great Depression in spite of the fact that the nominal money supply increased.

____16. The stock market crash of 1987 caused the recession of 1988.

____17. The existence of the Federal Depositors Insurance Corporation reduces the likelihood that something like the Great Depression could happen again.

____18. A recession today is likely to be much less severe than during the 1920s or 1930s due to the fact that the government sector is much larger today.

Multiple Choice

1. During the OPEC recession, which was caused by an aggregate
   a. supply shock, the rate of inflation increased.
   b. supply shock, the rate of inflation decreased.
   c. demand shock, the rate of inflation increased.
   d. demand shock, the rate of inflation decreased.

2. During the Volcker recession, which was caused by an aggregate
   a. supply shock, the rate of inflation increased.
   b. supply shock, the rate of inflation decreased.
   c. demand shock, the rate of inflation increased.
   d. demand shock, the rate of inflation decreased.

3. Stagflation means that real GDP stops growing or even declines *and*
   a. the rate of inflation declines.
   b. the rate of inflation increases.
   c. the rate of inflation remains stable.
   d. the economy experiences deflation.

4. Once a recession is underway, interest rates will
   a. decrease due to a decrease in the demand for real money.
   b. decrease due to an increase in the demand for real money.
   c. increase due to a decrease in the demand for real money.
   d. increase due to an increase in the demand for real money.

5. The OPEC oil price increase shifted the short-run aggregate production function
   a. upward and lowered the marginal product of labor.
   b. upward and raised the marginal product of labor.
   c. downward and lowered the marginal product of labor.
   d. downward and raised the marginal product of labor.

6. The sticky wage theory suggests that the quantity of labor supplied is
   a. not very sensitive to changes in the real wage rate and that the rate of unemployment is equal to the natural rate of unemployment during a recession.
   b. not very sensitive to changes in the real wage rate and the rate of unemployment is greater than the natural rate of unemployment during a recession.
   c. very sensitive to changes in the real wage rate and that the rate of unemployment is less than the natural rate of unemployment during a recession.
   d. very sensitive to changes in the real wage rate and that the rate of unemployment is less than the natural rate of unemployment during a recession.

7. According to the flexible wage theory, the increase in the unemployment rate during the OPEC recession was an increase in the
   a. deviation of the rate of unemployment from the natural rate of unemployment resulting from a real wage rate that is too high to clear the labor market.
   b. deviation of the rate of unemployment from the natural rate of unemployment resulting from an increase in job market turnover.
   c. natural rate of unemployment resulting from a real wage that is too high to clear the labor market.
   d. natural rate of unemployment resulting from an increase in job market turnover.

8. During the OPEC recession, the real wage rate
   a. fell and employment fell.
   b. fell and employment rose.
   c. rose and employment fell
   d. rose and employment rose.

9. During the Great Depression (1930-1933), the money wage rate
   a. rose and the real wage rate remained about the same.
   b. rose and the real wage rate rose.
   c. fell and the real wage rate remained about the same.
   d. fell and the real wage rate rose.

10. During the Great Depression, the money supply
    a. increased and the real interest rate was low.
    b. increased and the real interest rate was high.
    c. decreased and the real interest rate was low.
    d. decreased and the real interest rate was high.

11. During the Great Depression, aggregate demand was expected to
    a. fall but it didn't fall as rapidly as expected.
    b. fall but it fell faster than expected.
    c. rise but it actually fell.
    d. rise, which it did due to an increase in the money supply.

12. The major cause of the Great Depression was
    a. a dramatic increase in the prices of raw materials during 1929.
    b. a fall in the money supply during 1929.
    c. a fall in investment and consumer spending due to uncertainty about the future.
    d. the stock market crash of 1929.

13. During the Great Depression the real rate of interest was
    a. high because the rate of inflation was negative.
    b. high because the rate of inflation was positive.
    c. low because the rate of inflation was negative.
    d. low because the rate of inflation was positive.

14. Which of the following is NOT a reason why a recession as deep as the Great Depression is quite unlikely in the U.S.?
    a. The Federal Depositors Insurance Corporation.
    b. The value of the dollar is defined in terms of gold.
    c. The Fed is prepared to lend reserves to banks.
    d. Multi-income families.

15. The Federal Depositors Insurance Corporation (FDIC)
    a. keeps reserve requirements high so that banks can meet large withdrawals.
    b. loans reserves to banks.
    c. insures deposits thereby reducing the incentive for depositors to make large withdrawals.
    d. insures banks against large withdrawals.

16. Multi-income families reduce the probability of another Great Depression by
    a. reducing the probability of everyone in the family being simultaneously unemployed.
    b. investing more in the economy.
    c. paying more taxes.
    d. increasing fluctuations in consumption.

Short Answer

1. What is meant by stagflation?

2. What caused the OPEC recession? What happened to rate of inflation?

3. What caused the Volcker recession? What happened to the rate of inflation?

4. What caused the 1990-1991 recession?

5. What was the major cause of the Great Depression? What happened to the rate of inflation?

6. What is the basic controversy among economists about the behavior of the labor market during recession? Why is the controversy important for designing an appropriate antirecessionary economic policy?

7. List the four important features of the U.S. economy that make severe depression less likely today.

8. How do government transfer payments in the U.S. help to reduce the severity of a recession caused by an unexpected decrease in aggregate demand?

Problems

1. Show graphically and discuss what would have happened to the rate of inflation and real GDP if the Volcker reduction in the rate of growth of money had been anticipated. Would there have been a Volcker recession? How does this compare with what did happen?

2. Show graphically and discuss what would have happened to the rate of inflation and real GDP during the OPEC recession if the Fed had increased the rate of growth of

the money supply. How does this compare with what did happen?

3. Table 15.1 gives data for a hypothetical economy in years 1 and 2. What is likely to have caused this recession?

Table 15.1

	Year 1	Year 2
Real GDP (billions of dollars)	500	450
Price level (GDP deflator)	100	105
Expected price level	100	110

4. Table 15.2 gives data for a hypothetical economy in years 1 and 2. What is likely to have caused this recession?

Table 15.2

	Year 1	Year 2
Real GDP (billions of dollars)	500	450
Price level (GDP deflator)	100	105
Expected price level	100	100

5. Table 15.3 gives some money market data for a hypothetical economy that underwent a negative aggregate supply shock (like the OPEC oil price increases) at the beginning of year 2. Using a graph of the money market, offer an explanation of the increase in the interest rate in year 2 and the decrease in year 3.

Table 15.3

	Year 1	Year 2	Year 3
Real money supply (billions of dollars)	120	110	100
Interest rate	8	10	6

6. Table 15.4 gives some labor market data for a hypothetical economy that experienced a negative aggregate supply shock (like the OPEC oil price increases) between years 1 and 2. Assume that, due to past population growth, the labor supply is increasing over time
   a) Using a graph of the labor market, explain this change in the real wage rate and employment, assuming that the flexible wage theory is true.
   b) Using a separate graph of the labor market, explain this change in the real wage rate and employment, assuming that the sticky wage theory is true.

Table 15.4

	Year 1	Year 2
Real wage rate (constant dollars)	500	450
Employment (billions of hours)	100	105

ANSWERS

Concept Review

1. supply; demand; 1990-1991
2. stagflation; OPEC
3. fall; decline
4. investment
5. downward; lowered; left
6. less
7. demand; fell; high

True or False

1. F	5. F	9. F	13. F	17. T
2. T	6. T	10. T	14. T	18. T
3. F	7. F	11. F	15. F	
4. F	8. T	12. F	16. F	

Multiple Choice

1. a	5. c	9. c	13. a
2. d	6. b	10. d	14. b
3. b	7. d	11. b	15. c
4. a	8. a	12. c	16. a

Short Answer

1. Stagflation is a situation in which there is stagnation in the rate of growth of real GDP (either no growth or even a decline) and an increasing rate of inflation.

2. The major cause of the OPEC recession was a large negative aggregate supply shock in the form of a fourfold increase in the price of crude oil by OPEC during late 1973 and early 1974. The upward shift in the short-run aggregate supply curve resulted in stagflation. Not only did real GDP fall but the rate of inflation increased.

3. The major cause of the Volcker recession was an unanticipated reduction in the rate of growth of aggregate demand. This was the result of the Federal Reserve decision (under Paul Volcker's leadership) to reduce the rate of growth of the money supply. Thus the aggregate demand curve did not shift up by as much as expected. This caused real GDP to fall and the rate of inflation to fall below the level expected (which was the level that had been occurring in the recent past).

4. The Gulf Crisis in 1990 caused reductions in both aggregate demand and aggregate supply. The increase in government purchases to carry out the Gulf War increased aggregate demand but that was more than offset by a decrease in aggregate demand due to the increased uncertainty associated with the crisis. The net effect was a decrease in aggregate demand. The Gulf Crisis also resulted in a large increase in the price of oil which shifted the short-run aggregate supply curve to the left. The combined effect was a decrease in real GDP and an increase in the price level but only a slightly lower rate of inflation than had existed before the recession.

5. The major cause of the Great Depression was an unanticipated fall in aggregate demand, which was the consequence of reduced investment and reduced consumer expenditure (especially on durable goods) due to uncertainty and pessimism. For several years (1930-1933) aggregate demand fell by more than expected. This caused real GDP to fall and the rate of inflation to fall. In fact the rate of inflation was negative during that period; that is, the economy experienced deflation.

6. Economists disagree about two aspects of the labor market: (1) the sensitivity of the supply of labor curve to changes in the real wage rate and (2) the speed with which the real wage rate adjusts to clear the labor market.

Some economists believe that the labor supply curve is not very sensitive to changes in the real wage rate and that wages themselves are sticky and adjust only slowly. As a consequence, when a recession occurs, the real wage does not fall by enough to clear the labor market in the short-run and thus there is an excess supply of labor (unemployment).

Other economists believe that the labor supply curve is very sensitive to changes in the real wage rate and that wages are flexible. When a recession occurs, the real wage can fall sufficiently to clear the labor market. Any increase in unemployment is thus interpreted to be an increase in natural unemployment.

These issues have significant implications for the design of an appropriate policy as a response to recession. If the sticky wage theory is correct, then it may be useful to consider expansionary monetary or fiscal policies to counteract recession. Whereas, if the flexible wage theory is correct, since the (short-run) aggregate supply is vertical in that theory, expansionary monetary or fiscal policy will simply increase the rate of inflation and have no effect on real GDP.

7. The four important features of the U.S. economy that make severe depression less likely today are:
• Bank deposits are insured
• The Fed is prepared to be the "lender of last resort"
• Taxes and government spending play a stabilizing role
• Multi-income families are more economically secure.

8. When a recession arises, unemployment increases and disposable income declines. This decline in disposable income will lead to a reduction in consumption expenditure, which will have a multiplied negative effect on real GDP. Transfer payments, however, reduce these secondary effects of a recession by reducing the amount by which disposable income falls. As incomes fall and unemployment increases, government transfer payments increase in the form of higher unemployment benefits or other welfare payments. As a result, the fall in disposable income is reduced and the decline in consumption is less.

PROBLEMS

1. Figure 15.1 (based on Fig. 15.2 in the text) illustrates the effect of the Volcker reduction in the money supply growth rate if it had been anticipated. The economy starts at the intersection of the AD_{80} and SAS_{80} curves with real GDP of $3.8 trillion and price level equal to 74. This, of course, corresponds to the facts. The Federal Reserve increases the money supply by only a small amount shifting the aggregate demand curve to AD_{82}. Since this shift is anticipated, the short-run aggregate supply curve will shift up to SAS^*_{82} and the equilibrium in 1982 will be at the intersection of the AD_{82} and SAS^*_{82} curves. Real GDP has *increased* from $3.8 trillion to approximately $3.84 trillion (the increase in natural real GDP) and the price level has increased from 74 to 78 (approximately). Thus if the Volcker monetary policy had been anticipated, the rate of inflation would have fallen (and done so even faster) without a recession. Recall that, in fact, the policy was not anticipated. Aggregate demand was expected to shift by much more than it did. As a result, real GDP fell to $3.75 trillion and

the price level rose to 84 (less than expected but more than 78).

Figure 15.1

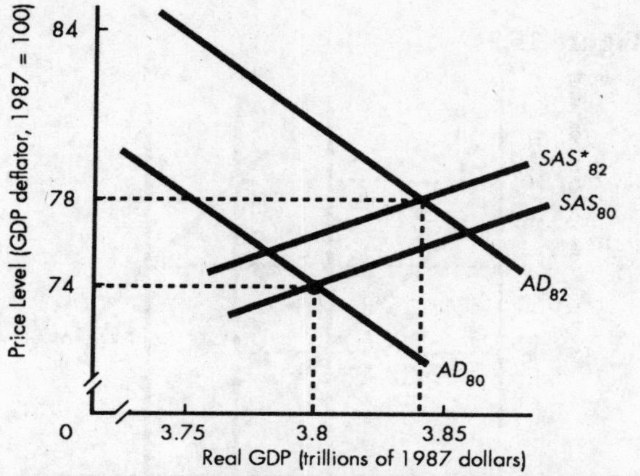

Figure 15.2

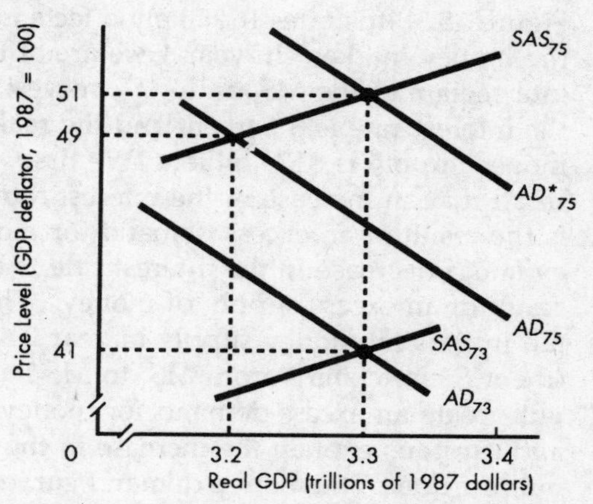

2. The economic situation in 1973, before the effect of the oil price increase, is depicted in Figure 15.2, which is based on Figure 15.1 in the text. The economy is at the intersection of the AD_{73} and SAS_{73} curves. Real GDP is $3.3 trillion and the price level is 41. Recall, from the discussion of the text that the increase in the price of oil caused a large upward shift in the short-run aggregate supply curve, to SAS_{75} in the figure here. The upward shift in aggregate demand was much smaller, to AD_{75}, and thus the intersection of SAS_{75} and AD_{75} (the new equilibrium) occurred at a lower level of real GDP ($3.2 trillion) and a higher price level (49). If the Fed had increased the money supply further, the aggregate demand curve would have been higher and the fall in real GDP reduced, although at the cost of a higher price level. For example, suppose the Fed increases the money supply sufficiently to give the aggregate demand curve denoted AD^*_{75}. This results in a new equilibrium with real GDP remaining at $3.3 trillion and the price level rising to 51.

3. We note that the price level has increased and real GDP has fallen. This would be the result when the upward shift in the short-run aggregate supply curve is greater than the upward shift in the aggregate demand curve. But that would be the case for either a negative aggregate supply shock or an increase in aggregate demand that is less than anticipated. To see which of these has occurred, we look at the price level that was expected in year 2 and compare it to the actual price level. Since the actual price level is lower than the expected price level, it must be the case that the fall in real GDP is due to an increase in aggregate demand that was less than expected. Actual real GDP must be less than natural real GDP.

4. Once again we note that the price level has increased and real GDP has fallen. In this case, however, the actual price level in year 2 is greater than the price level that was expected. Thus, the fall in real GDP must be due to a negative aggregate supply shock. Actual GDP is greater than natural GDP but natural real GDP has

fallen because of the negative aggregate supply shock.

5. Figure 15.3 illustrates the likely effects in the money market. In year 1 we are at the intersection of the MS_1 and MD_1 curves; the interest rate is 8 percent and the real money supply is \$120 billion. We first recall that an increase in the interest rate is the result of an excess demand for money and a decrease in the interest rate is the result of an excess supply of money. The fall in the real money supply in year 2 (the MS curve shifts from MS_1 to MS_2) will create an excess demand for money and can thus explain the increase in the interest rate. The money demand curve may also have increased or decreased (depending on what has happened to real GDP in year 2) but any decrease must have been small. For simplicity, in the figure we assume that the MD curve did not shift (i.e., $MD_2 = MD_1$). We see that in year 3, the money supply fell further (MS_2 to MS_3) and that the interest rate fell. Therefore there must have been an excess supply of money. The only way this could occur is if the MD curve shifted to the left by an amount greater than the shift in the MS curve; for example, to MD_3. This is likely to happen because the recession will have caused real GDP to fall which will reduce the demand for money.

6. a) Figure 15.4 illustrates a flexible wage model. The initial year 1 equilibrium is at the intersection of the LD_1 and LS_1 curves (real wage rate = \$10 per hour and employment = 80 billion hours per year). Note that the LS_1 curve is rather flat (flat enough to lie above the year 2 equilibrium point). As the population increases between year 1 and year 2, the labor supply curve shifts to the right to LS_2. The negative aggregate supply shock has reduced the marginal product of labor and thus the labor demand curve shifts down to LD_2. The new equilibrium corresponds to the real wage rate of \$9 and employment of 78 billion hours per year.

Figure 15.3

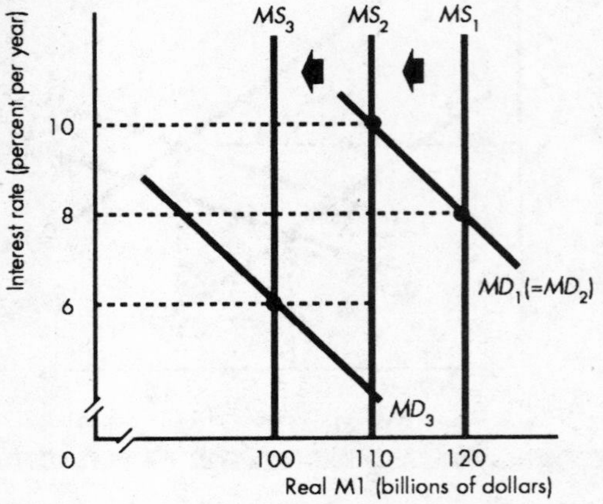

Figure 15.4

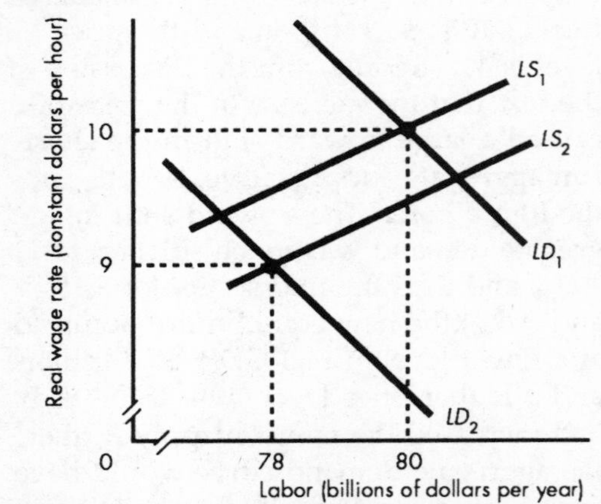

b) Figure 15.5 illustrates the sticky wage model. The initial year 1 equilibrium is at the intersection of the LD_1 and LS_1 curves. Note that the LS_1 curve here is much steeper than in the flexible wage model of part (a). The LD_1 curve is the same as above as is the LD_2 curve, which is the labor demand curve after the reduction in the marginal product of labor due to the supply shock. Due to population growth, the *LS* curve shifts out to LS_2 (the same horizontal shift as in Fig. 15.4). The real wage falls to $9 per hour due to an increase in the price level following the aggregate supply shock. This is not low enough to clear the labor market, so employment, which is determined by labor demand, is 78 billion hours per year.

Figure 15.5

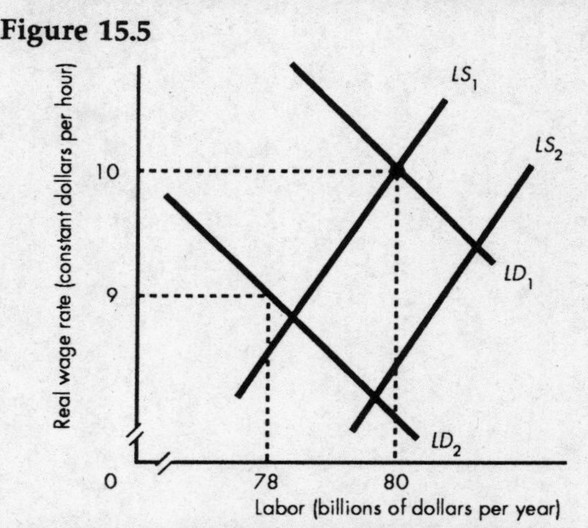

16 STABILIZING THE ECONOMY

CHAPTER IN PERSPECTIVE

Early in our study of macroeconomics we learned that business cycle fluctuations have been characteristic of the behavior of the U.S. economy. Severe recessions have occurred frequently and at times we have experienced periods of considerable inflation. There is a strong consensus that we would be better off if these fluctuations could be reduced. In our development of the complete aggregate demand and aggregate supply model, we saw that monetary policy and fiscal policy can be used to shift the aggregate demand curve and therefore potentially affect these fluctuations.

In this chapter we discuss the use of policy to reduce the magnitude of business cycle fluctuations. It appears, for example, that if the economy enters a recession, expansionary monetary or fiscal policy could be used to increase aggregate demand and eliminate the recession. Similarly, contractionary policies could be used to reduce inflationary pressures. Here we examine the potential and the problems associated with the use of policy to stabilize the economy.

LEARNING OBJECTIVES

After studying this chapter, you will be able to:

- **Describe the goals of macroeconomic stabilization policy**
- **Explain how the economy influences government popularity**
- **Describe the main features of fiscal policy since 1960**
- **Describe the main features of monetary policy since 1960**
- **Distinguish between fixed-rule and feedback-rule stabilization policies**
- **Explain how the economy responds to aggregate demand and aggregate supply shocks under fixed-rule and feedback-rule policies**
- **Explain why lowering inflation usually brings recession**

HELPFUL HINTS

1. Like the previous chapter, this chapter introduces some new concepts but no new analytical tools. The model that is used here to analyze the effects of policy is the model whose development was completed in Chapter 14. Thus, like Chapter 15, this chapter represents a payoff for all the effort required in mastering that model.

2. This chapter is intended to give us a more realistic perspective regarding the use of policy in the real world. In previous chapters we have abstracted from numerous complications that arise in the real-world use of the aggregate demand and aggregate supply model in making policy decisions.

This simplified our task and maximized our learning. In this chapter we learn of the problems that confront a policymaker. Among the most important problems is the inability to predict the *magnitude* or the *timing* of factors which affect aggregate demand or aggregate supply.

a) Our macroeconomic model is a good guide to the *qualitative* effects of changes in factors that affect aggregate demand and aggregate supply. For example, we know that an increase in the money supply will shift the aggregate demand curve to the right. When conducting policy, however, qualitative knowledge is not enough. We must also have *quantitative* knowledge. We must know *how much* a given increase in the money supply will increase aggregate demand.

While we may have an understanding of the direction of the effect, knowledge of the magnitude of effect is much more difficult to obtain and much more limited. This reduces the potential for policy to be used to "fine tune" the economy.

b) In addition to direction and magnitude, we must also know *when*. The full effect on aggregate demand of policy changes made today will not be immediate. Much if not most of that effect will occur only with considerable time lag. Thus, it is important that policymakers be able to predict these time lags in order to be confident that the future effect of a policy change made today will be appropriate when the effect actually occurs.

Unfortunately, that is extremely difficult. Not only are these lags often long but, to make matters more difficult, they are variable in length. This makes them unpredictable. As a result, policymakers may initiate a policy today which, when it has its effect sometime in the future, turns out to shift aggregate demand in the "wrong" direction because circumstances have changed. In such a case, policy will actually turn out to be destabilizing and thus worse than doing nothing at all.

The following analogy may be helpful. Consider the goal of driving a car from your house to the house of a friend living a distance away. The policy goal is to get the car from here to there. To make this simple, consider a single policy tool: the steering wheel. If you want the car to turn right, you turn the steering wheel clockwise. If you want the car to turn left, you turn the steering wheel counterclockwise. Note that not only is the direction in which the steering wheel is turned important, but the magnitude is also important in order to turn the car without accident.

Most of us can steer a car rather well because there is essentially no lag between the time we turn the steering wheel and the turning of the front wheels of the car. Consider how the task would be complicated if there is a time lag of one minute. Much better predictions of where the car will be one minute hence will be required. Consider how the task would be complicated further if there is not only a time lag but the length of that time lag is variable and thus unpredictable. You might choose to stay home (a fixed policy).

3. Many students (and policymakers!) fall into the trap of thinking that it is obvious that feedback rules must be better than fixed rules, since theoretically feedback rules seem to be able to do everything fixed rules can, plus more. Do not fall into this trap! There are many problems with the actual implementation of feedback rules in the real world: They require very good knowledge of the economy; they introduce unpredictability into the economy; they can generate *bigger* fluctuations in aggregate demand, due to the lags mentioned previously; they do not work for aggregate supply shocks.

These reasons make it far from obvious that feedback rules are better than fixed rules.

KEY FIGURES AND TABLES

Figure 16.1 Macroeconomic Performance: Real GDP and Inflation

The two main macroeconomic stabilization policy targets are real GDP growth and inflation. This figure shows the performance of real GDP growth and inflation since 1960. The difference between the nominal GDP growth rate and the real GDP growth rate is the rate of inflation, as indicated by the green shaded area. It is readily apparent that both real GDP growth and inflation have experienced considerable variability over this period.

Figure 16.3 The Fiscal Policy Record: A Summary

This figure summarizes the behavior of fiscal policy since 1960 by showing the performance of government spending, taxes, and the deficit. Each of these is expressed as a percentage of GDP. Note that government spending has clearly tended to increase over this period while taxes have demonstrated only a slight upward trend. This widening gap between government spending and taxes is reflected in the generally worsening deficit.

Also note that movements in government spending and taxes, and, thus, movements in the deficit, follow a cycle that has generally made fiscal policy expansionary in the year before an election and contractionary in the year following an election.

Figure 16.4 The Monetary Policy Record: A Summary

This figure complements Fig. 16.3. It summarizes the behavior of monetary policy since 1960 by showing the rate of growth of M2. There have been wide fluctuations in the M2 growth rate with a tendency for that growth rate to decrease immediately following an election and to increase as the next election approaches.

Figure 16.6 Two Stabilization Policies: Aggregate Demand Shock

Suppose the economy is in recession because of a temporary decline in aggregate demand. This figure compares the effects of two alternative monetary policy responses to this state of affairs: a fixed rule and a feedback rule.

In part (a) of the figure, the Fed is assumed to follow a fixed policy rule which specifies holding the money supply constant. Thus the aggregate demand curve remains at AD_1 and, since the short-run aggregate supply curve remains at *SAS*, the economy continues in recession with the price level at 90 and real GDP at $4 trillion. As the aggregate demand curve gradually shifts back to AD_0, the price level gradually increases to 100 and the level of real GDP gradually returns to its full-employment level at $5 trillion.

In part (b), the Fed is assumed to follow a feedback rule specifying that the Fed should increase the money supply whenever aggregate demand falls and decrease the money supply whenever aggregate demand rises. Thus, the Fed would respond to the temporary fall in aggregate demand that caused the recession by increasing the money supply and thus the aggregate demand curve would shift from AD_1 to AD_0. The feedback policy rule would thus immediately eliminate the recession.

Figure 16.7 Stabilization Policy and Aggregate Supply: A Factor Price Increase

This figure illustrates the alternative effects of a fixed policy rule versus a feedback policy rule when there is a shift in the short-run aggregate supply curve due to a large increase in the price of inputs created by a powerful input supplier. For example, a large union may be able to increase the wages of its members or a monopoly supplier of raw materials may be able to increase the price of raw materials.

In the figure, the economy is initially in equilibrium at the intersection of the AD_0 and SAS_0 curves. Then there is an increase in input costs, shifting the short-run aggregate cost curve leftward to SAS_1. As a result, equilibrium occurs at the intersection of the AD_0 and SAS_1 curves: Real GDP has fallen to $4 trillion and the price level has risen to 120. Under a fixed rule, policy will not be used to shift the aggregate demand curve and nothing changes. The economy remains in recession until input prices fall to their original level and the initial equilibrium is restored.

Under a feedback policy, however, the Fed and/or Congress will initiate expansionary monetary and/or fiscal policies in order to bring the economy out of recession and the aggregate demand curve will shift from AD_0 to AD_1. Thus, real GDP will return to $5 trillion and the price level will rise further to 130. The feedback rule leads policymakers to "accommodate" the cost increase and increases the likelihood that it will happen again.

Figure 16.8 Stabilization Policy and Aggregate Supply: A Decrease in Productivity

This figure assumes that real business cycle theories are correct and thus the only relevant aggregate supply curve is the long-run aggregate supply curve. In that context, it illustrates the alternative effects of a fixed policy rule and a feedback policy rule when there is a decrease in productivity.

The economy is initially in equilibrium at the intersection of the AD_0 and LAS_0 curves. When productivity declines, long-run real GDP falls from $5 trillion to $4 trillion, equilibrium real GDP falls to $4 trillion and the price level rises from 100 to 120.

Under a fixed policy rule, this is where the economy remains. Under a feedback rule, however, there is a futile attempt to increase real GDP by increasing the money supply and thus shifting the aggregate demand curve to AD_1. The new equilibrium level of GDP will remain at $4 trillion, its new long-run level, and the price level will rise even further to 140.

Figure 16.9 Lowering Inflation

The economy represented here is initially experiencing an ongoing 10 percent rate of inflation that is fully anticipated. The effects of a reduction in the rate of growth of aggregate demand are illustrated in this figure using two equivalent approaches. Part (a) illustrates the effects using the aggregate demand-aggregate supply model and part (b) uses the Phillips curve.

The economy begins at the intersection of the AD_0 and SAS_0 curves in part (a); the price level is 100 and real GDP is $5 trillion. Since the expected rate of inflation is equal to the actual rate of inflation of 10 percent, the economy is on the $SRPC_0$ curve at the point corresponding to a 10 percent rate of inflation and a 6 percent rate of unemployment (the natural rate).

If the inflation rate is expected to continue at 10 percent, the aggregate demand curve is expected to shift to AD_1 next year so wages rise accordingly and the short-run aggregate supply curve shifts to SAS_1. In part (a), next year's equilibrium depends on the position of the actual aggregate demand curve. Policymakers have decided to reduce the growth of aggregate demand to 4 percent so the aggregate demand curve shifts to AD_2 which is less than expected. The equilibrium occurs at the intersection of AD_2 and SAS_1, the price level is 108 and real GDP is $4 trillion. Thus, while the expected rate of inflation is 10 percent, the actual rate of inflation is 8 percent and, as seen in part (b), the economy moves along $SRPC_0$ to a rate of unemployment of 9 percent.

If the slowdown in aggregate demand is announced and believed, the expected aggregate demand curve is AD_2 and the short-run aggregate supply curve is SAS_2, as seen in part (a). Thus, real GDP remains at $5 trillion and the price level rises to only 104. The decline in the expected rate of inflation to 4 percent shifts the short-run Phillips curve to $SRPC_1$ in part (b). The rate of inflation is 4 percent, as expected, and the rate of unemployment remains at its natural rate of 6 percent.

SELF-TEST

CONCEPT REVIEW

1. Delivering a macroeconomic performance that is as smooth and predictable as possible is the ____________ problem.
2. The ____________ ____________ is a statement of the federal government financial plan, itemizing programs and their costs as well as tax revenues. The difference between the amount the government spends on its programs and the taxes it receives is called the government ____________.
3. Ray Fair has studied the effects of economic performance on voter behavior. He has found that for each ____________ percentage point ____________ in the real GDP growth rate, the incumbent political party gets a 1 percentage point increase in voter share; for each ____________ percentage point ____________ in the inflation rate, the incumbent party gets a 1 percentage point decrease in voter share.
4. A(n) ____________ ____________ ____________ is a business cycle whose origins are fluctuations in aggregate demand brought about by policies designed to improve the change of a government being re-elected. This is illustrated by the fact that there is a tendency for the money supply growth rate to ____________ immediately following an election and to ____________ as the next election approaches.
5. Macroeconomic policies can be classified into two broad categories. A(n) ____________ policy rule specifies an action to be pursued regardless of the state of the economy. A(n) ____________ policy rule specifies how actions will change when the state of the economy changes.
6. Inflation that has its origins in cost increases is called ____________-____________ inflation.
7. A theory that is based on flexible wages and ascribes aggregate fluctuations to

random shocks to the economy's long-run aggregate supply is called a(n) ____________ ____________ ____________ theory.

8. Attempting to keep the growth rate of nominal GDP steady is called ____________ ____________ ____________.

TRUE OR FALSE

____ 1. Fluctuations in real GDP growth contribute to fluctuations in the national trade balance.

____ 2. Keeping inflation steady will cause wide fluctuations in the value of the dollar abroad.

____ 3. In the U.S., fiscal policy is implemented by the House of Representatives and the Senate.

____ 4. The Federal reserve conducts monetary policy.

____ 5. The President has the power to formulate and implement monetary policy.

____ 6. According to Ray Fair's study of the effect of economic performance on voter behavior, a one percentage point decrease in the inflation rate brings in as many additional votes as a one percentage point increase in real GDP growth.

____ 7. A business cycle whose origins are changes in aggregate demand designed to improve the chance of a government being re-elected is called a political business cycle.

____ 8. There has been a tendency for the federal deficit to increase in the year immediately following an election and then decrease as the next election approaches.

____ 9. "Allow the money supply to grow at the constant rate of 3 percent per year" is an example of a feedback policy rule.

____10. It is obvious that a feedback policy rule is superior to a fixed rule.

____11. The less is known about the current state of the economy, the stronger the case for a fixed policy rule.

____12. The use of feedback rules can increase the degree of unpredictability in the economy.

____13. The inflation resulting from expansionary monetary policy is an example of cost-push inflation.

____14. The use of a feedback rule rather than a fixed rule increases the likelihood of cost-push inflation.

____15. According to real business cycle theory, the short-run and long-run aggregate supply curves are the same.

____16. According to real business cycle theory, an increase in aggregate demand will increase real GDP in the short run.

____17. The rate of growth of nominal GDP is equal to the rate of growth of real GDP minus the inflation rate.

____18. The Fed could lower the rate of inflation without creating a recession if its inflation reduction policy is fully expected.

____19. When the Fed conducts an inflation reduction policy a recession usually occurs.

MULTIPLE CHOICE

1. The two main macroeconomic stabilization policy targets are
   a. the foreign exchange rate and the federal deficit.
   b. inflation and the federal deficit.
   c. real GDP growth and the foreign exchange rate.
   d. real GDP growth and inflation.

2. Monetary policy actions are formulated and monitored by
   a. Congress.
   b. the President.
   c. the Federal Open Market Committee.
   d. the U.S. Treasury Department.

3. The policy role of the administration, including the President of the U.S., is to
   a. advise and persuade Congress and the Federal Reserve.
   b. determine how much the government will be able to spend.
   c. send directives to the Federal Reserve regarding the conduct of monetary policy.
   d. set tax policy.

4. The Council of Economic Advisors (CEA) advises the
   a. President.
   b. Federal Reserve.
   c. House of Representatives.
   d. Senate.

5. According to Ray Fair's study of the effect of economic performance on voter behavior, the incumbent political party gets a 1 percentage point increase in voter share for each
   a. 3 percentage point increase in the real GDP growth rate or for each 1 percentage point decrease in the inflation rate.
   b. 1 percentage point increase in the real GDP growth rate or for each 3 percentage point decrease in the inflation rate.
   c. 2 percentage point increase in the real GDP growth rate or for each 1 percentage point decrease in the inflation rate.
   d. 1 percentage point increase in the real GDP growth rate or for each 2 percentage point decrease in the inflation rate.

6. According to the political business cycle theory, we would expect the money supply growth rate to
   a. increase immediately following an election and to decrease as the next election approaches.
   b. decrease immediately following an election and to increase as the next election approaches.
   c. increase immediately following an election and continue to increase as the next election approaches.
   d. decrease immediately following an election and continue decreasing as the next election approaches.

7. Which of the following is true?
   a. The behavior of fiscal policy has generally been consistent with the political business cycle theory while the behavior of monetary policy has generally been inconsistent.
   b. The behavior of fiscal policy has generally been inconsistent with the political business cycle theory while the behavior of monetary policy has generally been consistent.
   c. The behavior of both fiscal policy and monetary policy has generally been inconsistent with the political business cycle theory.
   d. The behavior of both fiscal policy and monetary policy has generally been consistent with the political business cycle theory.

8. Which of the following is an example of a fixed "policy" rule?
   a. Wear your boots if it snows.
   b. Leave your boots home if it does not snow.
   c. Wear your boots every day.
   d. Take your boots off in the house if they are wet.

9. Under a fixed policy rule, a decrease in aggregate demand will cause the price level to
   a. decrease and real GDP to decrease.
   b. decrease and real GDP to remain unchanged.
   c. remain unchanged and real GDP to decrease.
   d. remain unchanged and real GDP to remain unchanged.

10. Suppose that, starting from a full-employment equilibrium, there is a temporary unexpected decline in aggregate demand. Our feedback rule is increase the money supply whenever there is a fall in aggregate demand and decrease the money supply whenever there is a rise in aggregate demand. In this case, our rule would result in
    a. an increase in real GDP to above its full-employment level and a rise in the price level above its original value.
    b. real GDP jumping back to its full-employment level and the price level jumping back to its original value.
    c. an increase in real GDP but not back to full-employment level and no effect on the price level.
    d. a slow increase in real GDP back to its full-employment level and a slow rise in the price level.

11. Which of the following is <u>NOT</u> an argument *against* a feedback rule?
    a. Feedback rules require greater knowledge of the economy than we have.
    b. Feedback rules introduce unpredictability.
    c. Aggregate supply shocks cause most economic fluctuations.
    d. Aggregate demand shocks cause most economic fluctuations.

12. Which of the following is the basic reason for the claim that feedback rules generate bigger fluctuations in aggregate demand? Policymakers
    a. use the wrong feedback rules to achieve their goals.
    b. must take actions today which will not have their effects until well into the future.
    c. do not really want to stabilize the economy.
    d. try to make their policies unpredictable.

13. Under a feedback policy rule that increases the money supply growth rate when real GDP is below its long-run level, an increase in the price of oil will cause the price level to rise by
    a. less than under a fixed policy and real GDP to return to its long-run level.
    b. less than under a fixed policy and real GDP to remain below its long-run level.
    c. more than under a fixed policy and real GDP to return to its long-run level.
    d. more than under a fixed policy and real GDP to remain below its long-run level.

14. A fixed rule for monetary policy
    a. requires considerable knowledge of how changes in the money supply affects the economy.
    b. would be impossible for the Fed to achieve.
    c. minimizes the threat of cost-push inflation.
    d. would result in constant real GDP.

15. According to real business cycle theories,
    a. any decline in real GDP is a decline in productivity.
    b. wages are flexible but labor market equilibrium does not necessarily imply full employment.
    c. fluctuations in aggregate demand change full-employment real GDP.
    d. fluctuations in aggregate demand cannot affect the price level.

16. According to real business cycle theories, if the Fed increases the money supply when real GDP declines,
    a. real GDP will increase but only temporarily.
    b. real GDP will increase permanently.
    c. real GDP and the price level will both be unaffected.
    d. real GDP will be unaffected but the price level will rise.

17. Under a fixed policy rule, if productivity growth slows down, the real GDP growth rate will
    a. fall and the price level will fall.
    b. fall and the price level will rise.
    c. rise and the price level will fall.
    d. rise and the price level will rise.

18. If the Fed reduces the rate of growth of the money supply unexpectedly, in the short run the rate of inflation will
    a. decrease and the rate of unemployment will increase.
    b. decrease and the rate of unemployment will decrease.
    c. actually increase and the rate of unemployment will increase.
    d. actually increase and the rate of unemployment will decrease.

SHORT ANSWER

1. What are the two main macroeconomic policy targets?

2. Who implements fiscal policy?

3. Why is macroeconomic policy usually expansionary in the year before an election?

4. Distinguish between a fixed rule and a feedback rule.

5. How does incomplete knowledge of full-employment real GDP affect the argument for feedback rules?

6. The purpose of policy is to stabilize. How can feedback rules result in even greater variability in aggregate demand?

7. Why is a feedback rule undesirable if real business cycle theories are correct?

8. If the Fed announced its intention to reduce the rate of inflation by reducing the rate of growth of the money supply, expected inflation would decline accordingly and thus a reduction in the actual rate of inflation could be achieved without a recession. Why does this not seem to be the case?

PROBLEMS

1. Assume that the Fed knows exactly how much and when the aggregate demand curve will shift, both in the absence of monetary policy and when the Fed changes the money supply.

   In this environment, compare the effects on real GDP and the price level of a temporary decline in aggregate demand which returns gradually to its previous level over several periods under fixed and feedback policy rules. Assume the economy is initially at full-employment real GDP and that full-employment real GDP is constant. Illustrate graphically on a separate graph for each of the following rules:
   a) First, assume that the Fed follows the fixed rule: Hold the money supply constant.
   b) Now assume that the Fed follows the feedback rule: Increase the money supply whenever aggregate demand falls and decrease the money supply whenever aggregate demand rises.

2. Consider an economy which experiences a temporary increase in aggregate demand. The Fed follows a feedback rule similar to the one given in Problem 1(b) but now we assume that the Fed does NOT have perfect knowledge of how much and when aggregate demand will shift.

   In Year 1 the economy is in macroeconomic equilibrium at full-employment real GDP, but, as the year ends, there is a burst of optimism about the future, which initiates a (temporary) rise in aggregate demand.

   As a result, in Year 2, real GDP increases and the rate of unemployment falls below its natural rate. Given its feedback rule, the Fed reduces the money supply "to keep the economy from overheating." The effect on aggregate demand, however, takes place only after a time lag of one year.

   In Year 3, this burst of optimism returns to its previous level and thus, so does aggregate demand. In addition, the monetary policy implemented in Year 2 finally has its effect on aggregate demand in Year 3.

   Analyze the behavior of real GDP and the price level using three graphs, one each for Years 1, 2, and 3. Assume that all changes in aggregate demand are unanticipated and that full-employment real GDP is constant. Did a feedback monetary policy rule stabilize aggregate demand?

3. Assume that real business cycle theories are correct. There is a fall in full-employment real GDP. First illustrate graphically the effect on real GDP and the price level if the Fed follows the fixed rule: Hold the money supply constant. Then, on the same graph, illustrate the effect on real GDP and the price level if the Fed follows the feedback rule: Increase the money supply whenever real GDP falls and decrease the money supply whenever real GDP rises.

4. Suppose the Fed decides to start an anti-inflationary policy. Figure 16.1 shows the initial state of the economy (point *a*) and the expected state next period (point *b*). The Fed decides to carry out a gradual policy of inflation reduction. In year 1, it will reduce the growth in *AD* to 5 percent, and in year 2 it will reduce the growth in

AD to 2.5 percent. If the policy is initially unexpected, show on the graph what will occur over the next two years.

Figure 16.1

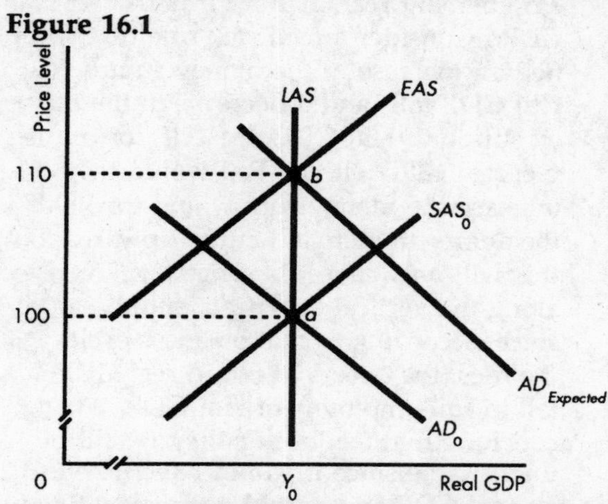

ANSWERS

Concept Review

1. stabilization
2. federal budget; deficit
3. 1; increase; 3; increase
4. political business cycle; decrease; increase
5. fixed; feedback
6. cost-push
7. real business cycle
8. nominal GDP targeting

True or False

1. T	5. F	9. F	13. F	17. F
2. F	6. F	10. F	14. T	18. T
3. T	7. T	11. T	15. T	19. T
4. T	8. F	12. T	16. F	

Multiple Choice

1. d	5. b	9. a	13. c	17. b
2. c	6. b	10. b	14. c	18. a
3. a	7. d	11. d	15. a	
4. a	8. c	12. b	16. d	

Short Answer

1. The two main macroeconomic policy targets are real GDP growth and inflation.

2. Fiscal policy involves changes in government expenditure and taxes, both of which are under the control of Congress, including the House of Representatives and the Senate. The President or other members of the administration may advise or persuade but the decisions are made by Congress.

3. Research by Ray Fair indicates that a one percentage point increase in real GDP growth brings in as many additional votes as a three percentage point decrease in the inflation rate. As a result, since the incumbent political party wants to be reelected, there is a tendency to favor policies that increase real GDP over those that decrease inflation. Expansionary policies in the year before an election will be of political benefit to the incumbent party since their short-run effect will be to increase real GDP growth with a small increase in the inflation rate. In the long run (i.e., after the election), the net effect will be no increase in real GDP growth but a much higher rate of inflation.

4. The difference between a fixed rule and a feedback rule is whether or not the specified action depends on the state of the economy or not. A fixed rule specifies an action that will be pursued regardless of the state of the economy whereas a feedback rule specifies actions that may change depending on the state of the economy.

5. In general, the goal of a feedback policy is to stabilize real GDP at its full-employment level. If real GDP falls below its full-employment level, policy would be used to stimulate aggregate demand and if real GDP rises above it full-employment level, policy would be used to reduce the rate of growth of aggregate demand. If, however, policymakers do not know the level of full-employment real GDP, they will not always know whether the economy is above or below full employment and so they will not know whether the appropriate feedback policy is to increase or decrease the rate of growth of aggregate demand.

6. Policy actions (e.g., an open market operation) will affect aggregate demand only after a time lag. This means that a policy action that is taken today will have its intended effect only sometime in the future. Thus, it is necessary for policy makers to forecast the state of the economy for a year or two into the future in order to be confident that the future effect of the policy action taken today will be appropriate when the effect occurs. This is very difficult to do since the lags are long (one to two years) and unpredictable. As a result, policymakers face a very good chance that the policy action taken today will turn out to have an effect in the future, which is the opposite of what would be appropriate at the time; that is, policy could destabilize aggregate demand rather than stabilize aggregate demand.

7. Real business cycle theories claim that real GDP is always at its full-employment level, that the economy is always on its long-run aggregate supply curve. Thus, since a policy action will not affect full-employment real GDP it cannot affect real GDP. Consider a feedback rule that specified an increase in the money supply if real GDP falls and a decrease in the money supply if real GDP rises. If, for example, real GDP fell, the Fed would then increase the money supply and thus shift the aggregate demand curve upward. But this will only cause the price level to rise along the vertical aggregate supply curve since, according to real business cycle theories, the observed fall in real GDP is a fall in full-employment real GDP. We conclude that feedback policy would be undesirable since it would have no effect on real GDP and would only cause fluctuations in the price level.

8. The problem is that expected inflation may not in fact decline as a result of the announcement by the Fed. The Fed may have a credibility problem since expectations will be much more strongly affected by the record of actions by the Fed than by its announcement. If people don't believe the Fed, they will not adjust expectations. Then, if the Fed carries out the policy, a recession will result in spite of the fact that an announcement was made.

PROBLEMS

1. a) The behavior of real GDP and the price level under the fixed rule is illustrated in Fig. 16.2 (a). The economy is initially at point *a* on the aggregate demand curve AD_0: The price level is P_0, and real GDP is at its full-employment level, denoted Y_0. The temporary decline in aggregate demand shifts the

aggregate demand curve downward to AD_1.

Since the money supply is held constant under the fixed rule, the new equilibrium is at point *b*: The price level has fallen to P_1 and real GDP has fallen to Y_1. The economy is in recession. As the aggregate demand curve gradually returns to AD_0, the price level gradually rises to P_0 and real GDP gradually returns to full-employment GDP, Y_0.

b) The behavior of real GDP and the price level under the feedback rule is illustrated in Fig. 16.2 (b). Once again the economy is initially at point *a* on the aggregate demand curve AD_0. The temporary decline in aggregate demand temporarily shifts the aggregate demand curve to AD_1. Given the Fed's feedback rule, it will increase the money supply sufficiently to shift the AD_1 curve back to AD_0. Thus the Fed offsets the decline in aggregate demand and equilibrium remains at point *a*: the price level remains at P_0 and real GDP remains at its full-employment level, Y_0.

As the temporary causes of the decline in aggregate demand dissipate, the aggregate demand curve will begin gradually shifting upward. The Fed will then decrease the money supply just enough to offset these shifts. As a result, the aggregate demand curve will remain at AD_0 and equilibrium will remain at point *a*.

Figure 16.2

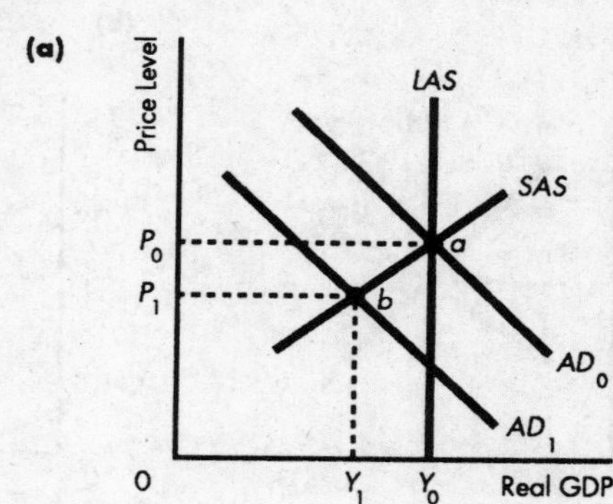

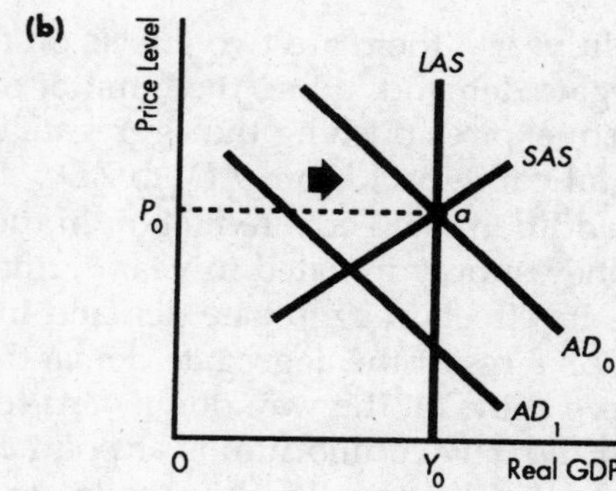

2. The state of the economy in years 1, 2, and 3 is illustrated in Fig. 16.3, parts (a), (b), and (c), respectively. The initial equilibrium (point *a*) in year 1 is illustrated in part (a). The economy is producing at full-employment real GDP (Y_1) and the price level is P_1.

   In year 2, the aggregate demand curve shifts to AD_2 in part (b) due to the burst of optimism. The Fed also reduces the money supply but there is no immediate effect on aggregate demand. Thus the equilibrium in year 2 occurs at the intersection of the AD_2 and *SAS* curves; at point *b* in part (b). Real GDP has risen to Y_2, which is above full-employment and the price level has risen to P_2.

Figure 16.3

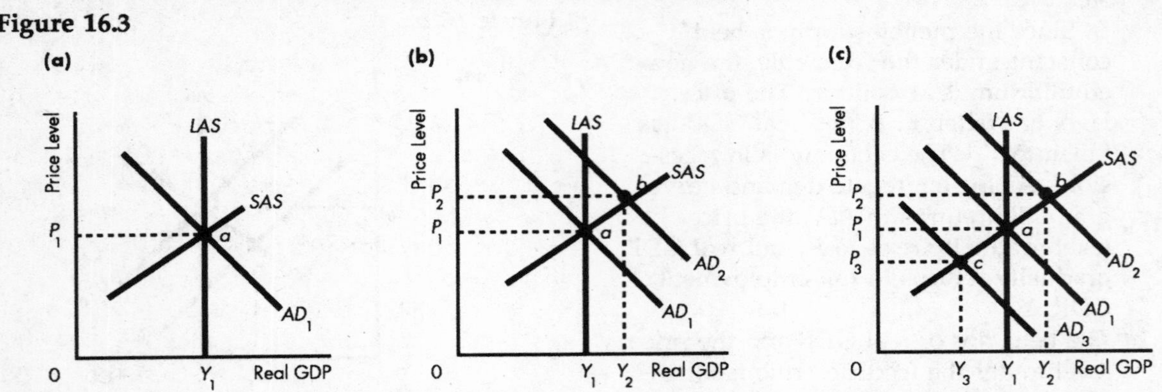

In year 3 there are two effects on aggregate demand. First, the burst of optimism expires pushing the aggregate demand curve back from AD_2 to AD_1. But, in addition, the Fed's reduction in the money supply initiated in year 2, finally has its effect on aggregate demand in year 3. As a result the aggregate demand curve shifts all the way downward to AD_3 and the new equilibrium is at point *c* in part (c). The price level has fallen to P_3 and real GDP has fallen to Y_3 which is below its full-employment level. The Fed's feedback policy in year 2 has caused a recession in year 3 even though it looked like the right policy when it was implemented.

Note that if the Fed had been following a fixed rule it would not have changed the money supply in year 2 and as a result, in year 3, the equilibrium would have been at point *a* and real GDP would have been at its full-employment level. Because of imperfect knowledge on the part of the Fed and the delayed effect of policy changes, the feedback rule has resulted in destabilizing aggregate demand; that is, policy has *increased* the variability of aggregate demand.

3. The effects on real GDP and the price level are illustrated in Fig. 16.4. Since we are assuming that real business cycle theories are correct, the only aggregate supply curve is the long-run aggregate supply curve. The economy is initially in equilibrium at the intersection of the AD_O and LAS_O curves, point *a*. Real GDP is Y_O and the price level is P_O. Then full-employment real GDP falls and the aggregate supply curve shifts to the left, from LAS_O to LAS_1.

   If the Fed follows the fixed policy rule, it will hold the money supply constant and the aggregate demand curve will remain at AD_O. Thus the new equilibrium is at point *b*: Real GDP will fall to Y_1 (the new full-employment level) and the price level will have risen to P_1.

   If, on the other hand, the Fed follows the feedback rule, the fall in real GDP will lead the Fed to increase the money supply, which will shift the aggregate demand curve to the right, from AD_O to AD_1. Note that monetary policy will have no effect on full-employment real GDP and thus no effect on the (long-run) aggregate supply curve. Therefore, under the feedback policy rule, the new equilibrium is at point *c*: Real GDP has remained at Y_1 but the price level has risen to P_2. The consequence of a feedback rule is a larger increase in the price level (i.e., higher inflation) with no effect on real GDP.

Figure 16.4

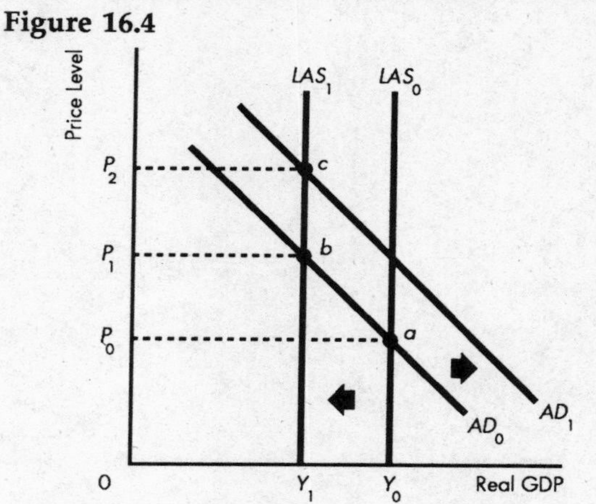

4. The anti-inflationary policy is illustrated in Fig. 16.1 Solution. It will reduce the growth of aggregate demand to a (vertical) distance of 5 percent. However, the actual *SAS* will be based on the expected inflation rate of 10 percent, and therefore SAS_1 is the relevant curve, yielding an equilibrium in year 1 at the point *c*, with a fall in real GDP, and a rise in inflation of, say, 7.5 percent, less than expected.

In year 2, the Fed allows aggregate demand to rise a further 2.5 percent, or a vertical rise to 107.625 (105 x 102.5), crossing the long-run aggregate supply curve at the point *d*, where AD_2 and *LAS* cross.

The actual impact on the economy depends on how much adjustment of expectations occurs. If the policy is now credible, and if wages can adjust sufficiently, there will be a shift in the short-run aggregate supply curve to SAS_2, and the equilibrium will be at the point *d*, with a very small inflation, and with real GDP back to the natural rate.

Figure 16.1 Solution

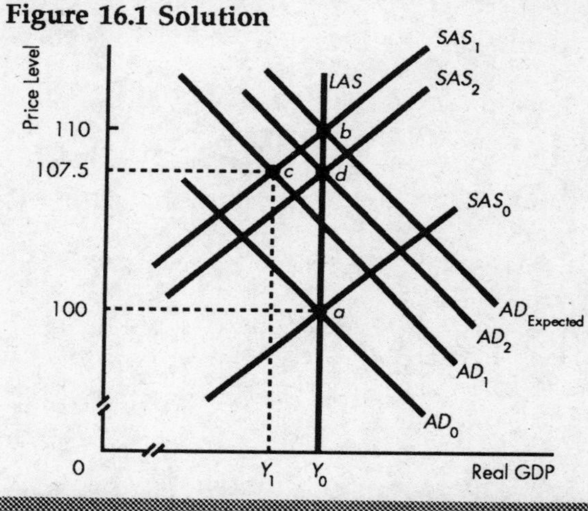

17 THE DEFICIT

CHAPTER IN PERSPECTIVE

The subject of this chapter is one of the most prominent economic and political topics we face. The government budget deficit is widely discussed and widely misunderstood. Why has the deficit gotten to be so large? How concerned should we be about recent large and persistent deficits? What kind of burdens do large deficits place on current and future generations? Do deficits cause inflation? How can the deficit be eliminated? These are the important issues that are addressed in this chapter.

LEARNING OBJECTIVES

After studying this chapter, you will be able to:

- **Explain why, during the past decade, the federal government spent more each year than it raised in taxes**
- **Distinguish between debt and the deficit**
- **Distinguish between the *nominal* deficit and the *real* deficit**
- **Explain why the deficit appears to be larger than it really is**
- **Describe the different means available for financing the deficit**
- **Explain why the deficit makes the Fed's job harder**
- **Explain why a deficit can cause inflation**
- **Explain why a deficit can be a burden on future generations**
- **Describe the measures that are being taken to eliminate the deficit**

HELPFUL HINTS

1. To understand why money financing of a deficit is inflationary, it is useful to recall our discussion in Chapter 28 of the conduct of monetary policy by the Federal Reserve. Money financing is financing a deficit by selling bonds to the Federal Reserve System. The effect on the money supply is just like an open market purchase of government securities. The only difference is that the initial deposit created at the Fed when the Fed buys these government bonds is owned by the government (the Treasury) rather than the public. As these deposits are spent, bank reserves increase and the money multiplier process begins.

2. Note that since tax revenue depends (positively) on real GDP and government transfer payments depend (negatively) on real GDP, the size of the deficit fluctuates with business cycle fluctuations in real GDP. During business cycle recessions, the deficit will increase, and during booms, the deficit will decrease.

We have also noted in discussions of fiscal policy in previous chapters that changes in the deficit are expected to have an effect on real GDP. For example, an expansionary fiscal policy which will increase the deficit will increase real GDP. Thus, in addition to the affect of a change in real GDP on the deficit, a change in the deficit through fiscal policy will effect real GDP. The deficit both affects and is affected by real GDP.

For many purposes we are interested in isolating the effect of the deficit on real GDP. In those cases we adjust the deficit for the effect of the business cycle and use the cyclically adjusted deficit.

3. The measurements that reflect the nominal and real deficits are sometimes confusing to students. The nominal deficit measures the addition to federal debt from the current fiscal year, measured in terms of the amount of extra *dollars* that are owed. The real deficit measures the addition to federal debt from the current fiscal year, measured in terms of the amount of extra *goods and services* owed by the federal government. Clearly, the latter more correctly measures the government's obligations. In times of positive inflation, the nominal deficit overestimates the real obligations of the government.

4. The previous discussion of real and nominal deficits implies that arguments about the federal deficit and its impact on the economy overestimate the problem. The theory of Ricardian equivalence also implies that worries about the deficit are too strong— indeed, the strong version of the theory implies that the size of the deficit is completely irrelevant!

Ricardian equivalence argues that any current federal deficit suggests that future taxpayers will have to raise taxes in order to pay off the accumulated debt. Rational individuals will take this into account, and realize that they, as taxpayers, have some outstanding debt, and will carefully save up to pay it off when it comes due or will leave a bequest to their children large enough to pay off the debt.

As a result, the strong version of the theory argues that the rise in savings by individuals will match the rise in borrowing from the federal government, leaving interest rates unchanged, and therefore leaving the economy unaffected by the deficit.

Of course, the crucial (as yet unanswered) question is whether the arguments of the theory are true or not. However, it would seem likely that at the very least, partial Ricardian equivalence is true. As a result, we should discount the problem of the deficit to some degree.

KEY FIGURES AND TABLES

Figure 17.1 The Deficit

This figure shows the historical pattern of government expenditure, revenue, and the deficit as a percent of GDP from 1975 through 1991 in the U.S. The deficit is the difference between expenditure and revenue. Over this period there has always been a deficit though it has become larger and more persistent since 1982.

Figure 17.4 The Business Cycle and the Deficit

A recession leads to a fall in taxes and an increase in government transfer payments. Thus we expect the deficit to rise during recessions. Similarly, a business cycle boom leads to an increase in tax revenue and a fall in government transfer payments. Thus we expect the deficit to decrease during booms.

This figure illustrates the historical relationship between the business cycle (measured as percentage deviations of real GDP from trend) and the deficit. We see that, in general, our expectations are confirmed: deficits tend to be largest during recessions (e.g., the OPEC recession and the Volcker recession) and smallest during booms.

Figure 17.5 The Real Deficit and the Nominal Deficit

The nominal deficit is the measured deficit. The real deficit removes the distortion of inflation from the nominal deficit and is a superior measure, especially during periods of inflation. This figure shows the historical values of both the real and nominal deficits.

Note three things. First, the real and nominal deficits move up and down together. Second, during periods of inflation the real deficit is smaller than the nominal deficit. Third, the real deficit has only become large and persistent during the 1980s. It is this latter fact that has given rise to the recent increased concern about the deficit.

Figure 17.9 The Laffer Curve

This figure illustrates a hypothetical Laffer curve which shows the relationship between tax rates and tax revenue. It may be helpful to think of the curve given here as applying to an income tax. The Laffer curve simply reflects the fact that as the tax rate on income rises, income producing activities will be reduced.

If the percentage decrease in income is greater than the percentage increase in the tax rate, tax revenue declines. Note that if the tax rate is zero, tax revenue will be zero. If the tax rate on income is 100 percent, tax revenue will also be zero since no one will undertake the effort to produce income if they can keep none of it. In between these extremes, there is likely to be positive tax revenue.

As the tax rate increases from zero, tax revenue increases since the percentage decrease in income will be less than the percentage increase in the tax rate. Eventually, however, the tax rate is sufficiently high and thus the disincentive to earn additional income sufficiently large that this relationship is reversed and tax revenue falls. Between these ranges is a tax rate at which tax revenue is a maximum. In the figure, that tax rate is 40 percent.

SELF-TEST

CONCEPT REVIEW

1. The federal government's budget ______________ is equal to its total tax revenue minus its total expenditure in a given time period. If revenue exceeds expenditure, the federal government has a budget ______________. If revenue is less than expenditure, the federal government

has a budget ____________. If revenue equals expenditure, the federal government has a ____________ budget.

2. A measure of the deficit that would occur if the economy were at full employment is called the ____________ ____________ deficit.
3. The change in the real value of outstanding government debt is the ____________ deficit. Because of inflation, this measure of the deficit is ____________ than the nominal deficit.
4. Financing the government deficit by selling bonds to the Federal Reserve System is called ____________ financing. Financing the government deficit by selling bonds to any holder other than the Federal Reserve System is called ____________ financing.
5. The view that debt financing and paying for government spending with taxes are equivalent is called Ricardian __________.
6. The power to eliminate by veto any specific item in a budget is called a(n) ____________-____________ veto.
7. The percentage of tax levied on a particular activity, like income earning, is called a(n) ____________ ____________. The activity on which the tax is levied is called the ____________ ____________. The product of these is ____________ ____________.
8. The curve that shows the amount of tax revenue that will be collected at each tax rate is called the ____________ curve.

TRUE OR FALSE

____ 1. The federal deficit is the total amount of borrowing the federal government has undertaken.

____ 2. It is only government purchases of goods and services, not transfer payments, that are crucial in analyzing the federal deficit.

____ 3. An increase in tax revenues will decrease the budget deficit.

____ 4. The last year in which the U.S. federal government had a budget surplus was 1982.

____ 5. The major reason for the increase in the deficit as a percent of GDP is the fact that tax revenue as a percent of GDP has fallen, while government expenditure as a percent of GDP has remained fairly stable.

____ 6. The budget deficit generally decreases during recessions.

____ 7. If the total dollar value of government debt has remained constant between year 1 and year 2, but inflation has been experienced between those years, there will be a real surplus.

____ 8. The real deficit will always be less than the nominal deficit.

____ 9. The real deficit has been persistently large only since the early 1980s.

____10. To finance a deficit, the government must sell bonds.

____11. If the government finances a deficit by selling bonds to households, the money supply must increase.

____12. Financing a deficit by selling bonds to the Federal Reserve System is likely to be inflationary.

____13. Deficits are inevitably inflationary.

____14. For a given level of government expenditure, a deficit causes crowding out of investment only if real interest rates rise.

____15. If Ricardian equivalence holds, the real interest rate will not change when the government increases the amount it spends.

____16. Ricardian equivalence has been proven to be false.

____17. A federal government deficit that is currently bond-financed, will not be inflationary as long as the eventual monetary finance of the deficit is far enough in the future.

____18. The Omnibus Budget Reconciliation Act of 1990 is intended to reduce the budget deficit.

____19. An increase in the tax rate will always result in an increase in tax revenue.

____20. The Laffer curve shows the relationship between the size of the deficit and the real interest rate.

MULTIPLE CHOICE

1. Suppose the government starts with a debt of $0. Then, in year 1, there is a deficit of $100 billion; in year 2, there is a deficit of $60 billion; in year 3, there is a surplus of $40 billion; and in year 4, there is a deficit of $20 billion. What is government debt at the end of year 4?
   a. $20 billion.
   b. $140 billion.
   c. $180 billion.
   d. $220 billion.

2. Which of the following would <u>NOT</u> increase the budget deficit?
   a. An increase in interest on the government debt.
   b. An increase in government purchases of goods and services.
   c. An increase in government transfer payments.
   d. An increase in indirect business taxes.

3. Which of the following is the correct explanation for the increasing size of the deficit relative to GDP in the 1980s?
   a. Government spending relative to GDP has increased, while tax revenue relative to GDP has remained fairly stable.
   b. Government spending relative to GDP has remained fairly stable, while tax revenue relative to GDP has fallen.
   c. Government spending relative to GDP has fallen, while tax revenue relative to GDP has risen.
   d. Government spending and tax revenue relative to GDP have both increased substantially, but tax revenue relative to GDP has increased less rapidly.

4. During a recession, tax revenue
   a. declines and government expenditure declines.
   b. declines and government expenditure increases.
   c. increases and government expenditure declines.
   d. increases and government expenditure increases.

5. A large deficit is of greater concern if it occurs during a period of
   a. recession.
   b. increasing inflation.
   c. low inflation and sustained economic growth.
   d. high unemployment.

6. What are the main elements of government spending that have increased (relative to GDP) since 1970?
   a. Transfer payments and debt interest.
   b. Government purchases of goods and services and defense spending.
   c. Government purchases of goods and services and debt interest.
   d. Government purchases of goods and services and transfer payments.

7. Consider the information in Table 17.1. What is the real deficit in year 2?
   a. $0.
   b. $180 billion.
   c. $198 billion.
   d. $360 billion.

Table 17.1

	Year 1	Year 2
Government debt	$180 billion	$198 billion
Price level	1.0	1.1

8. If, in a given year, government debt increases by 6 percent and the rate of inflation is 10 percent,
   a. the real deficit has increased by 4 percent.
   b. the real deficit has increased by 6 percent.
   c. the real deficit has increased by 10 percent.
   d. there is a real surplus.

9. When the deficit is financed by selling bonds to the Federal Reserve, it is called
   a. credit financing.
   b. debt financing.
   c. money financing.
   d. reserves financing.

10. Money financing of a deficit may be preferred by government because
    a. the Fed is willing to pay a higher price for bonds than households and firms.
    b. debt financing leaves the government with an ongoing obligation to pay interest.
    c. it reduces the prospect of inflation.
    d. it disciplines the government to reduce its level of spending.

11. An increase in the deficit will leave future generations with a smaller capital stock if it causes
    a. the supply of loans to increase more than the demand for loans.
    b. the demand for loans to increase more than the supply of loans.
    c. the demand for loans to increase by the same amount as the supply of loans.
    d. the supply of loans to increase and the demand for loans to decrease.

12. Ricardian equivalence implies that, for a given level of government spending, as the deficit increases
a. the real rate of interest falls.
b. the real rate of interest rises.
c. saving increases.
d. consumption expenditure increases.

13. Which of the following is NOT a proposal for reducing the U.S. deficit?
a. Line-item veto.
b. Balanced budget amendment.
c. Increase tax rates.
d. Money financing of the deficit.

14. A decrease in tax rates
a. can increase tax revenue if the percent increase in the tax base it causes is greater than the percent fall in the tax rate.
b. can increase tax revenue if the percent increase in the tax base it causes is less than the percent fall in the tax rate.
c. cannot increase tax revenue since each activity being taxed will be taxed at a lower rate.
d. cannot increase tax revenue since the tax base will decline as well.

15. The curve that relates the tax rate and tax revenue is called the
a. tax curve.
b. revenue curve.
c. Laffer curve.
d. Buchanan curve.

16. Consider Table 17.2. What is the equilibrium interest rate in the private market?
a. 4 percent.
b. 6 percent.
c. 8 percent.
d. 10 percent.

Table 17.2 The Market for Loanable Funds

Private quantity demanded (billions of $)	Quantity supplied (billions of $)	Real interest rate (percent)
400	1,600	12
600	1,400	10
800	1,200	8
1,000	1,000	6
1,200	800	4
1,400	600	2

17. Consider Table 17.2. The government enters the loanable funds market to borrow $400 billion to finance the deficit. If the Ricardian equivalence does not hold, what will be the new equilibrium interest rate?
a. 4 percent.
b. 6 percent.
c. 8 percent.
d. 10 percent.

18. Consider Table 17.2. The government enters the loanable funds market to borrow $400 billion to finance the deficit. If Ricardian equivalence does not hold, what will be the amount loaned to private investors in billions of dollars once this market has reached a new equilibrium?
a. $400.
b. $600.
c. $800.
d. $1,000.

19. Consider Table 17.2. The government enters the loanable funds market to borrow $400 billion to finance the current deficit. If Ricardian equivalence does hold, what will be the new equilibrium interest rate?
    a. 4 percent.
    b. 6 percent.
    c. 8 percent.
    d. 10 percent.

SHORT ANSWER

1. What changes in the government budget (spending and taxes) since 1970 are the principal cause of continuing large government deficits?

2. What is the cyclically adjusted deficit?

3. Why does debt financing of a permanent deficit lead to an ever-increasing deficit?

4. Why will a permanent debt-financed deficit lead to inflation?

5. How might a deficit be a burden on future generations of Americans?

6. According to Ricardian equivalence, why will there be no increase in the real interest rate when the government debt finances its spending?

7. What is the argument for a line-item veto for the president as a deficit reduction device?

8. Why will an increase in the tax rate NOT always lead to an increase in tax revenue?

PROBLEMS

1. Table 17.3 gives information about the price level and the government budget in an economy. Based on the information given, complete the table by computing the following for each year: the surplus or deficit (and noting which by negative sign for deficit, or positive sign for surplus), the government debt, real government debt, and the real surplus or deficit (and noting which by negative sign for deficit, or positive sign for surplus).

Table 17.3

Year	Price level	Taxes	Gov't spending	Surplus or deficit	Gov't debt	Real gov't debt	Real surplus or deficit
1	1.00	100	120	-20	20	20	-20
2	1.11	110	140				
3	1.20	120	130				
4	1.30	130	135				
5	1.52	140	145				

Table 17.4

Year	Real GDP	Taxes	Gov't spending	Deficit	Cyclically adjusted deficit
1	500	100	120		
2	450				
3	400				

2. Table 17.4 gives the path of real GDP in an economy over time. In this economy, capacity real GDP is constant at $500 billion. Furthermore, a $10 billion increase in real GDP will cause taxes to increase by $2 billion and government spending to decrease by $2 billion. The effects are

symmetric if real GDP decreases. Complete the table by first computing the values for taxes and government spending in each year. Then compute the actual deficit and the cyclically adjusted deficit.

3. The government decides to permanently increase its spending by $100 billion, which it will cover by a permanent debt-financed deficit. Before this decision, government debt is zero. Assume that the interest rate remains constant at 10 percent. Complete Table 17.5 by computing the deficit, government debt, and interest payment (to be paid at the beginning of the next year) for the first four years. What is the size of government debt in four years?

Table 17.5

Year	Deficit (billions of $)	Government debt (billions of $)	Interest payment (billions of $)
1	100.0		
2			
3			
4			

4. Using a graph of the demand and supply of loans and a graph of investment demand, show the effect on investment of a decision to finance government spending by way of debt financing if the Ricardian equivalence proposition
   a) is true.
   b) is false and households do not increase saving.

ANSWERS

Concept Review

1. balance; surplus; deficit; balanced
2. cyclically adjusted
3. real; smaller
4. money; debt
5. equivalence
6. line-item
7. tax rate; tax base; tax revenue
8. Laffer

True or False

1. F	5. F	9. T	13. F	17. F
2. F	6. F	10. T	14. T	18. T
3. T	7. T	11. F	15. F	19. F
4. F	8. F	12. T	16. F	20. F

Multiple Choice

1. b	5. c	9. c	13. d	17. c
2. d	6. a	10. b	14. a	18. c
3. a	7. a	11. b	15. c	19. b
4. b	8. d	12. c	16. b	

Short Answer

1. In general, the deficit has risen because the level of government spending as a percentage of GDP has risen, while tax revenue as a percent of GDP has remained rather stable. The components of spending that have shown the most consistent growth are transfer payments and interest payments on government debt. Defense spending decreased during much of this period but increased in the 1980s.

2. The size of the deficit rises during recessions and falls during booms because tax revenue goes up as income rises and government transfer payments rise as income falls. The cyclically adjusted deficit adjusts for these effects of the business cycle on the size of the deficit. It is the deficit that would occur if the economy were at full employment.

3. The government pays interest on all of the government debt. Whenever the government has a budget deficit, government debt increases and thus interest payments will increase. This increase in interest payments means that the size of the deficit will be larger next year and thus the debt and interest payments will increase still further. Through this process, the interest payment increases each year and thus adds more to the deficit each succeeding year.

4. A permanent debt-financed deficit will lead to inflation, since the deficit will be ever-increasing as a result of ever-increasing interest payments on government debt (see Short Answer Question 3). There will be a point beyond which the government cannot or will not continue debt financing the deficit and will turn to money financing. This, of course will cause inflation.

   Since people who buy bonds know this they will expect higher inflation in the future and the nominal rate of interest will be driven up. This will cause people to reduce their demand for money. The reduction in the demand for money will lead to an increase in the demand for goods and will thus cause inflation now.

5. A deficit will be a burden on future generations of Americans to the extent that government debt is owned by foreigners. Future generations of Americans will have to pay the higher interest payments on the increased government debt, but to the extent that they also receive those interest payments there is no net burden. However, if part of the debt is owned by foreigners, American taxpayers will make all the interest payments but only receive part. The part that is received by foreigners will be a net burden.

   An additional burden to future generations would occur if the deficit causes real interest rates to rise and thus crowds out investment. In this case, the capital stock inherited by future generations will be less than it would otherwise have been.

6. According to Ricardian equivalence, when the government decides to debt finance its spending, people recognize that taxes must rise in the future in order to cover the additional spending and higher interest payments. In order to be able to pay these higher taxes, they will cut back consumption and increase saving by enough to meet those future tax liabilities. The increase in saving necessary will be equal to the increase in government spending. An increase in saving is an increase in the supply of loans and an increase in the deficit (government spending) is an increase in the demand for loans. Since the demand and supply of loans both increase by the same amount, the real interest rate is unchanged.

7. A line-item veto would allow the President to veto specific spending items in a bill without vetoing the entire spending bill. Under the current veto power, in order to veto some special-interest spending item, the President must veto the entire bill, including those parts all agree are appropriate. As a result, the President is reluctant to use the all-or-nothing veto power to control spending. The president, it is argued, would be less reluctant to use the line-item veto which implies greater ability to reduce government spending

and enhances the President's ability to control spending.

8. It is important to recognize that tax revenue is the product of the tax rate and the tax base and that an increase in the tax rate may well cause the tax base to decrease. For example, an increase in the tax rate on gasoline will cause people to consume less gasoline. If the tax base falls by enough to offset the effect of the tax rate increase, tax revenue can actually fall.

PROBLEMS

1. Table 17.3 is completed below as Table 17.3 Solution. The surplus or deficit is computed as the difference between taxes and government spending. A deficit is a negative value for this difference. Government debt is the sum of all the deficits up to that point in time minus the sum of all the surpluses up to that point in time. Real government debt is actual (nominal) government debt divided by the price level. The real surplus or deficit is real government debt in the current year minus real government debt in the previous year. Once again, a negative difference indicates a real deficit.

Table 17.3 Solution

Year	Price level	Taxes	Gov't spending	Surplus or deficit	Gov't debt	Real gov't debt	Real surplus or deficit
1	1.00	100	120	-20	20	20	-20
2	1.11	110	140	-30	50	45	-25
3	1.20	120	130	-10	60	50	-5
4	1.30	130	135	-5	65	50	0
5	1.52	140	145	-5	70	46	+4

2. Table 17.4 is completed in Table 17.4 Solution. The change in taxes in each year is 20 percent of the change in real GDP. So, for example, when real GDP falls by $50 billion in year 2, taxes fall by $10 billion. The change in government spending in each year is also 20 percent of the change in real GDP but moves in the opposite direction. Thus, when real GDP falls by $50 billion in year 2, government spending increases by $10 billion. The (actual) deficit, of course, is the difference between taxes and government spending. We ignore the negative sign in the table because there is never a surplus. The cyclically adjusted deficit is the deficit that would have existed if the economy had been at full employment. Note that in year 1 real GDP is at its full employment ($500 billion). Thus the cyclically adjusted deficit is equal to the actual deficit that year ($20 billion). In subsequent years we find the cyclically adjusted deficit by asking what would happen to the deficit if sufficient real GDP were added or subtracted so as to be at capacity. In year 2, for example, real GDP is $450 billion which is $50 billion below its full-employment level. The actual deficit is $40 billion. What would happen to that deficit if we were to (hypothetically) add $50 billion to real GDP? Taxes would rise by $10 billion and government spending would decline by $10 billion implying that the deficit would fall by $20 billion, leaving a cyclically adjusted deficit of $20 billion. In spite of the fact that the actual deficit fluctuates, the cyclically adjusted deficit is constant here because the actual deficit changes only in response to business cycle changes.

Table 17.4 Solution

Year	Real GDP	Taxes	Gov't spending	Deficit	Cyclically adjusted deficit
1	500	100	120	20	20
2	450	90	130	40	20
3	400	80	140	60	20

3. Table 17.5 is completed in Table 17.5 Solution. Because the government debt is initially zero, the year 1 deficit becomes year 1 debt. The interest rate of 10 percent must be paid on the government debt which means that the interest payment (due at the beginning of year 2) is $10 billion which becomes part of the deficit in year 2. It is similar for subsequent years.

Table 17.5 Solution

Year	Deficit (billions of $)	Government debt (billions of $)	Interest payment (billions of $)
1	100.0	100.0	10.00
2	110.0	210.0	21.00
3	121.0	331.0	33.10
4	133.1	464.1	46.41

4. a) The effect is shown in Fig. 17.1. Before the decision, the market for loans is in equilibrium at the intersection of the D_0 and S_0 curves. This yields a real interest rate of r_0, which implies that investment is I_0. Once the government decides on debt financing, the demand for loans curve increases from D_0 to D_1. If the Ricardian equivalence proposition is true, the supply of loans curve increases (horizontally) by the same amount: S_0 shifts to S_1. Since the shifts are the same amount, the real interest rate remains at r_0 and thus, investment spending remains at I_0. There is no crowding out.

   b) If, however, households do not increase their saving in response to the increase in the deficit, the demand curve for loans will shift from D_0 to D_1 but the supply of loans curve will remain at S_0. This means that the equilibrium real interest rate will rise to r_1 and that investment will fall from I_0 to I_1. Thus, investment is crowded out.

Figure 17.1

(a)

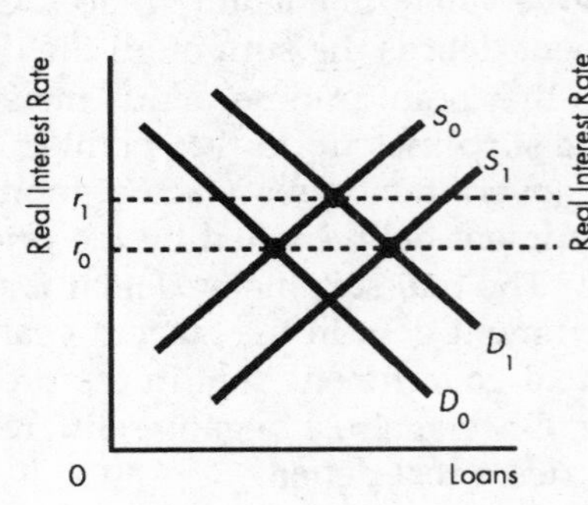

(b)

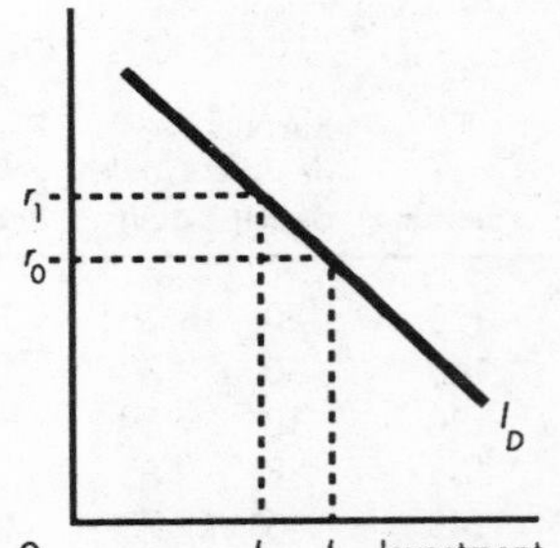

18 TRADING WITH THE WORLD

CHAPTER IN PERSPECTIVE

Over the past two decades in the U.S., the volume of imports and exports as a percent of GDP has doubled. As the U.S. has become more dependent on international trade, issues associated with international trade have become more prominent in public discussion. Today, much is said and some is even done about our relationships with key trading partners and there seems to be much support among some political leaders for protectionist policies.

We first address the basic issue of why nations trade. What is the nature of the gains that make trade worthwhile? What determines which goods a country will import and which it will export? We then turn to more difficult issues such as: If there are significant gains to free trade, why do countries frequently restrict imports? What are the effects of a tariff or a quota or some other trade restriction?

These are timely issues which are not widely understood and which will likely become increasingly important.

LEARNING OBJECTIVES

After studying this chapter, you will be able to:

- **Describe the patterns and trends in international trade**
- **Explain comparative advantage**
- **Explain why all countries can gain from international trade**
- **Explain how prices adjust to bring about balanced trade**
- **Explain how economies of scale and diversity of taste lead to gains from international trade**
- **Explain why trade restrictions lower the volume of imports and exports and lower our consumption possibilities**
- **Explain why we have trade restrictions even though they lower our consumption possibilities**

HELPFUL HINTS

1. It is useful to recall the discussion of opportunity cost, comparative advantage, and gains from trade in Chapter 3. The current chapter applies the fundamental concepts of opportunity cost and comparative advantage to the problem of trade between nations. The basic principles are the same whether we are talking about trade between individuals in the same country or between individuals in different countries.

Many students (and others involved in debates about trade) seem confused by the concept of comparative advantage, partially because they implicitly conceive of *absolute advantage* as the sole reason for trade. A country has an absolute advantage if it can produce all goods using less inputs than another country. However, such a country can still gain from trade.

To see this, consider comparing California to North Dakota. California has better weather and in combination with widespread irrigation has an absolute advantage in the production of all agricultural products—indeed, California frequently has more than one harvest a year! This would seem to imply that California has no need to trade with North Dakota. However, North Dakota has a *comparative advantage* in the production of wheat. Therefore, California will specialize in fruits and trade them for wheat. California could easily grow its own wheat, but to do so would have too high an opportunity cost—the lost fruit crops. By specializing and trading, both California and North Dakota can gain.

2. In addition to the gains from trade, this chapter also discusses the economic effects of trade restrictions. One of the important things we learn is that the economic effects of a tariff and a quota are the same. We note that a voluntary export restraint (VER) is also a quota but a quota imposed by the exporting country rather than the importing country.

All these trade restrictions raise the domestic price of the imported good, reduce the volume of and value of imports. They will also reduce the value of exports by the same amount as the reduction in the value of imports. The increase in price that results from each of these trade restrictions produces a gap between the domestic price of the imported good and the foreign supply price of the good.

The difference between the alternative trade restrictions lies in which party captures this excess. In the case of a tariff, the government receives the tariff revenue. In the case of a quota imposed by the importing country, domestic importers who have been awarded a license to import capture this excess through increased profit. When a VER is imposed, the excess is captured by foreign exporters who have been awarded licenses to export by their government.

3. The major point of this chapter is that gains from free trade can be considerable. Why then do countries have such a strong tendency to impose trade restrictions? The key is that while free trade creates overall benefits to the economy as a whole, there are both winners and losers. The winners gain more in total than the losers lose, but the latter tend to be concentrated in a few industries.

It is therefore not surprising that free trade will be resisted by some acting on the basis of rational self-interest. Even though only a small minority benefit from any given trade restriction, while the overwhelming majority will be hurt, it is not surprising to see trade restrictions implemented. The reason is that the cost of a given trade restriction to each of the many is individually quite small, while the benefit to each of the few will be individually large. Thus, the few will have a significant incentive to see that restriction takes place, while the many will have little incentive to expend time and energy in resisting trade restriction.

KEY FIGURES

Figure 18.2 Opportunity Cost in Pioneerland

This figure shows the production possibility frontier for the imaginary country of Pioneerland. Currently it is producing and consuming 15 billion bushels of grain and 8 million cars a year at point *a* on the production possibility frontier. Opportunity cost is measured as the slope of the production possibility frontier at this point. At point *a*, 1 car costs 9,000 bushels of grain, or 9,000 bushels cost 1 car.

Figure 18.3 Opportunity Cost in Magic Empire

This figure shows the production possibility frontier for the imaginary country of Magic Empire. Currently it is producing and consuming 18 billion bushels of grain and 4 million cars a year at point *a* on the production possibility frontier. Opportunity cost is measured as the slope of the production possibility frontier at this point. At point *a*, 1 car costs 1,000 bushels of grain, or 1,000 bushels cost 1 car.

Figure 18.4 International Trade in Cars

The price at which a good trades internationally and the quantity traded are determined by the international market for the good. This figure illustrates a hypothetical international market for cars using the example of Pioneerland and Magic Empire.

Magic Empire has a comparative advantage in the production of cars and so supplies cars to the world market. At higher prices, Magic Empire is willing to supply more cars although it must receive at least 1 thousand bushels of grain (its opportunity cost of a car) to be willing to produce.

The supply curve in the figure gives Magic Empire's export supply of cars. Similarly, the demand curve in the figure gives Pioneerland's import demand for cars. It shows that as the price of a car falls, the quantity of cars that Pioneerland wants to import increases although it will not buy any cars at a price above 9 thousand bushels of grain (its opportunity cost of a car). The equilibrium price when trade takes place is at the intersection of these two curves. The price of a car (under free trade) is 3 thousand bushels of grain and 4 million cars per year are imported by Pioneerland from Magic Empire.

Figure 18.5 Expanding Consumption Possibilities

This figure clearly illustrates the gains from trade experienced by Pioneerland and Magic Empire. Without trade, each country consumes what it produces. Its consumption is constrained by the production possibility frontier. The gain from trade for each country is that, with trade, while production is constrained by the production possibility frontier, consumption can exceed that frontier. Consumption is only constrained by the consumption possibility curve which (except for a single point) lies beyond the production possibility curve.

Part (a) of the figure shows the situation for Pioneerland. Without trade, Pioneerland produces and consumes at point *a*: 8 million cars and 15 billion bushels of grain. With trade (at 1 car trading for 3 thousand bushels of grain), Pioneerland produces at point *b*: 5 million cars and 30 bushels of grain.

But, because of trade, consumption can be different. Indeed, with trade, Pioneerland consumes at point *c*: 9 million cars and 18 billion bushels of grain. This is 1 million more cars and 3 billion more bushels of grain than were consumed without trade (at point *a*). This additional consumption is the gain from trade for Pioneerland. A similar analysis in part (b) illustrates that Magic Empire also gains from trade.

Figure 18.7 The Effects of a Tariff

The effects of a tariff on the price of a good and the quantity traded are shown in this figure by using the Pioneerland and Magic Empire example of trade in cars. Pioneerland imposes a tariff of $4,000 per car on cars imported from Magic Empire. This shifts the export supply curve upward by $4,000 since Magic Empire must also be able to cover the tariff. Thus the price of a car in Pioneerland increases from $3,000 to $6,000 and the quantity of cars traded falls to 2 million per year. The total revenue from the tariff (which is received by the government of Pioneerland) is $8 billion: $4,000 per car times 2 million cars. Although this figure does not show it directly, Pioneerland's grain exports will also decrease because Magic Empire's income from export of cars has fallen.

Figure 18.8 The Effects of a Quota

This figure illustrates the effects of a quota on domestic price and quantity traded again using the Pioneerland and Magic Empire example. Pioneerland imposes a quota of 2 million cars per year. This restriction is indicated in the graph by a vertical line at 2 million cars. This becomes the effective supply curve for the purpose of determining the price, which turns out to be $6,000. The quantity traded, of course, is 2 million cars per year, the quota limit. At 2 million cars, Magic Empire is willing to supply cars for $2,000 each. This $4,000 per car difference between the selling price and the price received by the exporter is captured by the importer.

SELF-TEST

CONCEPT REVIEW

1. The goods and services purchased from people in foreign countries are called ____________. The goods and services sold to people in foreign countries are called ____________. The value of exports minus the value of imports is called the ____________ of ____________.

2. A country is said to have a(n) ____________ ____________ in the production of a good if it can produce that good at a lower opportunity cost than any other country. A country is said to have a(n) ____________ ____________ if for all goods its output per unit of inputs is higher than any other country.

3. The restriction of international trade is called ____________. A tax imposed by the importing country on an imported good is called a(n) ____________. The result of imposing such a tax is to ____________ the price that consumers in the importing country pay and ____________ the quantity traded. When such a tax is imposed the tax revenue is received by the ____________.

4. The international agreement negotiated after World War II and designed to limit government restriction of international trade is called the ____________ ____________ on ____________ and ____________.

5. A restriction that specifies a limit on the quantity of a particular good that can be imported is called a(n) ____________. The result of such a limit is to ____________ the price that consumers in the importing country pay. The extra revenue from such a limit is received by the ____________.

6. An agreement between two governments in which the government of the exporting country agrees to restrict the quantity of its exports to the importing country is called a(n) ________ ________ ________. Such an agreement will ________ the price that consumers in the importing country pay for the good.
7. When a good is sold in a foreign market at a lower price than in a domestic market or for a price that is lower than the cost of production it is called ________.
8. A tariff that enables domestic producers to compete with subsidized foreign producers is called a ________ ________.

TRUE OR FALSE

____ 1. The United States imports more manufactured goods than it exports.

____ 2. The United States is a net exporter of agricultural products.

____ 3. When a U.S. citizen stays in a hotel in France, the U.S. is exporting a service.

____ 4. In the U.S., international trade has become less important as a percent of GDP since 1950.

____ 5. If there are two countries, A and B, and two goods, X and Y, and country A has a comparative advantage in the production of X, then country B must have a comparative advantage in the production of Y.

____ 6. If country A must give up 3 units of Y to produce 1 unit of X and B must give up 4 units of Y to produce 1 unit of X, then A has a comparative advantage in the production of X.

____ 7. If countries specialize in goods for which they have a comparative advantage, then some countries will gain and others will lose but the gains will be larger than the losses.

____ 8. Trading according to comparative advantage allows all trading countries to consume outside their production possibility frontier.

____ 9. If a country has an absolute advantage, it will not benefit from trade.

____10. Countries may exchange similar goods for each other due to economies of scale in the face of diversified tastes.

____11. When governments impose tariffs, they are increasing their country's gain from trade.

____12. Tariffs in the U.S. are much higher than they were before World War II.

____13. The General Agreement on Tariffs and Trade (GATT) has successfully reduced trade restrictions in the world.

____14. A tariff on a good will raise its price and reduce the quantity traded.

____15. A tariff not only reduces the total value of imports but it reduces the total value of exports as well.

____16. A quota will cause the price of the imported good to fall.

____17. The government will raise no revenue from a quota.

____18. The "excess revenue" created by a voluntary export restraint is captured by the exporter.

____19. Japan is dumping steel if it sells it in Japan at a lower price than it sells it in the U.S.

____20. Elected governments are likely to be slow to reduce trade restrictions even though the gains would be much larger than the losses because there would be many fewer losers than gainers.

MULTIPLE CHOICE

1. The U.S. is a
   a. net exporter of manufactured goods and net importer of agricultural products.
   b. net exporter of manufactured goods and net exporter of agricultural products.
   c. net importer of manufactured goods and net importer of agricultural products.
   d. net importer of manufactured goods and net exporter of agricultural products.

2. Which of the following is a U.S. export of a service?
   a. A U.S. citizen buys a restaurant meal while traveling in Switzerland.
   b. A Swiss citizen buys a restaurant meal while traveling in the U.S.
   c. A U.S. citizen buys a clock made in Switzerland.
   d. A Swiss citizen buys a computer made in the U.S.

3. The country with which the U.S. has the largest international trade deficit is
   a. Canada.
   b. Japan.
   c. Mexico.
   d. the European Economic Community.

4. Suppose there are two countries, A and B, producing two goods, *X* and *Y*. Country A has a comparative advantage in the production of good *X* if less
   a. of good *Y* must be given up to produce one unit of *X* than in country B.
   b. labor is required to produce one unit of *X* than in country B.
   c. capital is required to produce one unit of *X* than in country B.
   d. labor and capital are required to produce one unit of *X* than in country B.

5. Suppose there are two countries, A and B, producing two goods, *X* and *Y* and that country A has a comparative advantage in the production of *X*. If the countries trade, the price of *X* in terms of *Y* will be
   a. greater than the opportunity cost of *X* in country A and less than the opportunity cost of *X* in country B.
   b. less than the opportunity cost of *X* in country A and greater than the opportunity cost of *X* in country B.
   c. greater than the opportunity cost of *X* in both countries.
   d. less than the opportunity cost of *X* in both countries.

6. Compared to a no-trade situation, international trade according to comparative advantage allows each country to consume
   a. more of the goods it exports but less of the goods it imports.
   b. more of the goods it imports but less of the goods it exports.
   c. more of both goods it exports and goods it imports.
   d. less of both goods it exports and goods it imports.

7. In country A, it requires one unit of capital and one unit of labor to produce a unit of *X* and it requires two units of capital and two units of labor to produce a unit of *Y*. What is the opportunity cost of good *X*?
   a. The price of a unit of capital plus the price of a unit of labor.
   b. One unit of capital and one unit of labor.
   c. Two units of capital and two units of labor.
   d. One half unit of *Y*.

8. If country A has an absolute advantage in the production of everything,
   a. no trade will take place because country A will have a comparative advantage in everything.
   b. no trade will take place because no country will have a comparative advantage in anything.
   c. trade will probably take place and all countries will gain.
   d. trade will probably take place but country A will not gain.

9. The imposition of a tariff on imported goods will increase the price consumers pay for imported goods and
   a. reduce the volume of imports and the volume of exports.
   b. reduce the volume of imports and increase the volume of exports.
   c. reduce the volume of imports and leave the volume of exports unchanged.
   d. will not affect either the volume of imports or the volume of exports.

10. Who benefits from a tariff on good *X*?
    a. Domestic consumers of good *X*.
    b. Domestic producers of good *X*.
    c. Foreign consumers of good *X*.
    d. Foreign producers of good *X*.

11. Which of the following is responsible for significant reduction in trade restrictions since World War II?
    a. The Smoot-Hawley Act.
    b. The voluntary exports restraint agreement between the U.S. and Japan.
    c. The United Nations.
    d. The General Agreement on Tariffs and Trade.

12. A tariff on good *X* which is imported by country A will cause
    a. the demand curve for *X* in country A to shift upward.
    b. the demand curve for *X* in country A to shift downward.
    c. the supply curve of *X* in country A to shift upward.
    d. the supply curve of *X* in country A to shift downward.

13. Country A and country B are currently engaging in free trade. Country A imports good X from country B and exports Y to B. If country A imposes a *tariff* on X, country A's X producing industry will
    a. expand and its Y producing industry will contract.
    b. expand and its Y producing industry will expand.
    c. contract and its Y producing industry will contract.
    d. contract and its Y producing industry will expand.

14. Country A and country B are currently engaging in free trade. Country A imports good X from country B and exports Y to B. If country A imposes a *quota* on X, country A's X producing industry will
    a. expand and its Y producing industry will contract.
    b. expand and its Y producing industry will expand.
    c. contract and its Y producing industry will contract.
    d. contract and its Y producing industry will expand.

15. When a *tariff* is imposed, the gap between the domestic price and the export price is captured by
    a. consumers in the importing country.
    b. the person with the right to import the good.
    c. the government of the importing country.
    d. foreign exporters.

16. When a *quota* is imposed, the gap between the domestic price and the export price is captured by
    a. consumers in the importing country.
    b. the person with the right to import the good.
    c. the government of the importing country.
    d. foreign exporters.

17. When a voluntary export restraint agreement is reached, the gap between the domestic price and the export price is captured by
    a. consumers in the importing country.
    b. the person with the right to import the good.
    c. the government of the importing country.
    d. foreign exporters.

18. Country A imports good X from country B and exports Y to B. Which of the following is a reason why country A might prefer arranging a voluntary export restraint rather than a quota on X?
    a. So as NOT to reduce the volume of its own exports of Y.
    b. To prevent country B from retaliating by restricting country A's exports.
    c. To keep the domestic price of X low.
    d. To increase government revenue.

SHORT ANSWER

1. What is meant by comparative advantage?

2. How is it that *both* parties involved in trade can gain?

3. Why do countries exchange similar manufactured goods with each other?

4. How does a tariff on a particular imported good affect the domestic price of the good, the export price, the quantity imported, and the quantity of the good produced domestically?

5. How does a tariff on imports affect the exports of the country?

6. How does a quota on a particular imported good affect the domestic price of the good, the export price, the quantity im-

ported, and the quantity of the good produced domestically?

7. How does a voluntary export restraint (by the foreign exporting country) on a particular imported good affect the domestic price of the good, the export price, the quantity imported, and the quantity of the good produced domestically?

8. Why might a government prefer a quota to a tariff?

9. Why might an importing country prefer to arrange a voluntary export restraint than to impose a quota or a tariff?

10. Who benefits and who loses if the U.S. obtains a "voluntary" export restraint on Japanese cars? Why might the United Auto Workers (a union) lobby strongly for such a trade restriction?

PROBLEMS

1. Consider a simple world in which there are two countries, Atlantis and Beltran, each producing two goods, food and cloth. The production possibility frontier for each country is given in Table 18.1 below.
   a) Assuming a constant opportunity cost in each country, complete the table.
   b) What is the opportunity cost of food in Atlantis? Of cloth?
   c) What is the opportunity cost of food in Beltran? Of cloth?
   d) Draw the production possibility frontiers on separate graphs.

Table 18.1

Atlantis		Beltran	
Food (units)	Cloth (units)	Food (units)	Cloth (units)
0	500	0	800
200	400	100	600
400		200	
600		300	
800		400	
1,000		--	--

2. Suppose that Atlantis and Beltran engage in trade.
   a) In which good will each country specialize?
   b) If 1 unit of food trades for 1 unit of cloth, what will happen to the production of each good in each country?
   c) If 1 unit of food trades for 1 unit of cloth, draw the consumption possibility frontiers for each country on the corresponding graph from Problem 1 (a).
   d) Before trade, if Atlantis consumed 600 units of food, the most cloth it could consume was 200 units. After trade, how many units of cloth can be consumed if 600 units of food are consumed?

3. Continue the analysis of Atlantis and Beltran trading at the rate of 1 unit of food for 1 unit of cloth.
   a) If Atlantis consumes 600 units of food and 400 units of cloth how much food and cloth will be consumed by Beltran?
   b) Given the consumption quantities and the production quantities from problem 2 (b), how much food and cloth will Atlantis and Beltran import and export?

4. Figure 18.1 gives the import demand curve for shirts for country A, labeled *D*, and the export supply curve of shifts for country B, labeled *S*.
   a) What is the price of a shirt under free trade?
   b) How many shirts will be imported by country A?

Figure 18.1

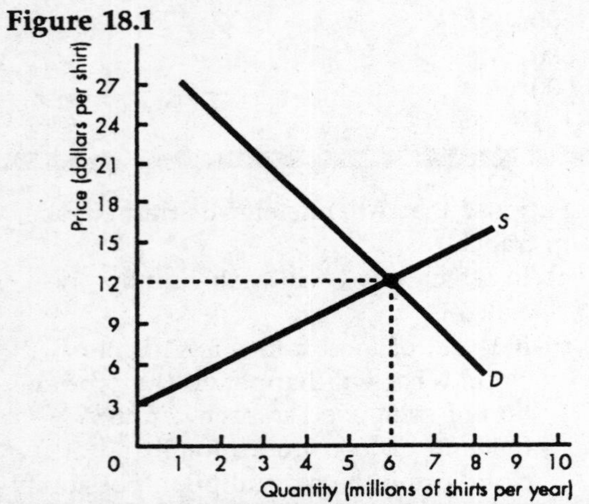

5. Suppose the shirtmakers in country A of Problem 4 are concerned about foreign competition and so the government of country A imposes a tariff of $9 per shirt. Using Fig. 18.1, answer the following questions.
   a) What will happen to the price of a shirt in country A?
   b) What is the price the exporter will actually receive?
   c) How many shirts will be imported by country A?
   d) What is the revenue from the tariff? Who captures it?

6. Suppose that instead of a tariff, country A imposes a quota of 4 million shirts per year. Again, use Fig. 18.1 to answer the following questions.
   a) What will be the price of a shirt in country A?
   b) What price will the exporter actually receive?
   c) How many shirts will be imported by country A?
   d) What is the difference between the total amount paid by consumers and the total amount received by exporters—the "excess profit?" Who captures it?

7. Finally, suppose that instead of a tariff or a quota, country A induces country B to impose a voluntary export restraint (VER) of 4 million shirts per year.
   a) What will be the price of a shirt in country A?
   b) How many shirts will be imported by country A?
   c) Is there any "excess" profit here? If so, how much is it and who captures it?

ANSWERS

CONCEPT REVIEW

1. imports; exports; balance; trade
2. comparative advantage; absolute advantage
3. protectionism; tariff; increase; decrease; government
4. General Agreement; Tariffs; Trade
5. quota; raise; importer
6. voluntary export restraint; raise
7. dumping
8. countervailing duty

TRUE OR FALSE

1. T	6. T	11. F	16. F
2. T	7. F	12. F	17. T
3. F	8. T	13. T	18. T
4. F	9. F	14. T	19. F
5. T	10. T	15. T	20. T

MULTIPLE CHOICE

1. d	6. c	11. d	16. b
2. b	7. d	12. c	17. d
3. b	8. c	13. a	18. b
4. a	9. a	14. a	
5. a	10. b	15. c	

SHORT ANSWER

1. Comparative advantage simply means lowest opportunity cost. A country is said to have a comparative advantage in the production of some good if it can produce that good at a lower opportunity cost than any other country.

2. In order for two potential trading partners to be willing to trade, they must have different comparative advantages; that is, different opportunity costs. If they do, then they will trade and both parties will gain. If the parties do not trade, they will each face their own opportunity costs. A price at which trade takes place must be somewhere between the opportunity costs of the two traders. This means that the party with the lower opportunity cost of the good in question will gain because it will receive a price above its opportunity cost. Similarly, the party with the higher opportunity cost will gain because it will pay a price below its opportunity cost.

3. The exchange of similar manufactured goods is the result of economies of scale in the face of diversified tastes. With international trade, each manufacturer faces the entire world market. Thus they can specialize very narrowly to satisfy a particular taste and still take advantage of economies of scale.

4. A tariff on an imported good will *raise its price to domestic consumers* as the export supply curve shifts upward. The export price is determined by the original export supply curve. As the domestic price of the good rises, the quantity of the good demanded falls and thus the relevant point on the original export supply curve is at a lower quantity and a *lower export price*. This lower quantity means that the *quantity imported falls*. The rise in the domestic price will also lead to an *increase in the quantity of the good supplied domestically*.

5. When country A imposes a tariff on its imports of good *X*, not only does the volume of imports shrink but the volume of exports of *Y* to country B will shrink by the same amount. Thus a balance of trade is maintained. As indicated in the answer to Short Answer Question 4, the export price of good *X* falls when a tariff is imposed. This fall in the price received by the exporter means that the price of imports in the foreign country has risen; i.e., if the amount of *Y* that country B gets for an *X* has fallen, the quantity of *X* that must be given up to obtain a *Y* has increased. This implies that the quantity of *Y* (A's export) demanded by country B will fall and thus A's exports decline.

6. The effect of a quota on the domestic price of the good, the export price, the quantity imported, and the quantity of the good produced domestically are exactly the same as the effects of a tariff discussed in the answer to Short Answer 4. The only difference is that the increase in the domestic price is here not the result of a

vertical shift in the export supply curve but the result of the fact that the quota forces a vertical effective export supply curve at the quota amount.

7. The effect of a voluntary export restraint (VER) is exactly the same as that of a quota. Indeed a VER is a quota. The only difference is that the government of the exporting country is able to distribute the excess revenue from the quota rather than the government of the importing country.

8. Tariffs and quotas have the same effects on prices and quantities (see the answers to Questions 4 and 6 above). The difference is that the excess revenue raised by a tariff is captured by the government whereas the excess revenue raised by a quota is captured by those persons who have been given the right to import by the government. In either case the government is in a position to benefit. It may prefer to use quotas in order to reward political supporters by giving them rights to import and thus allowing them to capture large profits. Second, quotas give the government more precise control over the quantity of imports. Also, it is politically easier to impose a quota than a tariff.

9. The only difference between a quota and a voluntary export restraint (VER) is which government has the ability to reward its political supporters. As discussed in the answer to Short Answer 8, under a quota, the importing country's government can take advantage of the quota to reward its political supporters. Under a VER, it is the exporting country's government that has this ability. An importing country may prefer a VER in order to avoid a tariff or quota war with the exporting country.

10. If the U.S. arranges a voluntary export restraint (VER) on Japanese cars, U.S. producers of cars and their input suppliers benefit because the price of cars is higher. U.S. car buyers (a much larger group), however, lose because they must pay higher prices for cars. In addition, U.S. industries that would have exported to Japan (e.g., agricultural products, timber, and services) will lose because the demand for their products will fall (see the answer to Short Answer 5, which is applicable here). Since the United Auto Workers represent an important input in the U.S. car industry, they would lobby strongly for trade restrictions in order to at least temporarily retain jobs in the industry.

PROBLEMS

1. a) Completed Table 18.1 is shown here as Table 18.1 Solution. The values in the table are calculated using the opportunity cost of each good in each country. See parts (b) and (c) below.

Table 18.1 Solution

Atlantis Food (units)	Atlantis Cloth (units)	Beltran Food (units)	Beltran Cloth (units)
0	500	0	800
200	400	100	600
400	300	200	400
600	200	300	200
800	100	400	0
1,000	0	--	--

b) In order to increase the output (consumption) of food by 200 units, cloth production (consumption) falls by 100 units in Atlantis. Thus the opportunity cost of a unit of food is 1/2 unit of cloth. This opportunity cost is constant as are all others in this problem, for simplicity. Similarly, the opportunity cost of clothing in Atlantis is 2 units of food.

c) In Beltran a 100 unit increase in the production (consumption) of food requires a reduction in the output (consumption) of cloth of 200 units. Thus the opportunity cost of food is 2 units of cloth. Similarly the opportunity cost of cloth in Beltran is 1/2 units of food.

d) Figure 18.2 parts (a) and (b) illustrate the production possibility frontiers for Atlantis and Beltran, respectively labeled PPF_A and PPF_B. The rest of the diagram is discussed in the solution to Problems 2 and 3.

2. a) We see from the solutions to Problems 1 (b) and (c) that Atlantis has lower opportunity cost (1/2 unit of cloth) in the production of food, Atlantis will specialize in the production of food. Beltran, with the lower opportunity cost for cloth (1/2 unit of food) will specialize in cloth.

b) Each country will want to produce every unit of the good in which they specialize as long as the amount they receive in trade exceeds their opportunity cost. For Atlantis, the opportunity cost of a unit of food is 1/2 unit of cloth but it can obtain 1 unit of cloth in trade. Since the opportunity cost is constant (in this simple example), Atlantis will totally specialize by producing all of the food it can: 1000 units per year (point *b* in Fig. 18.2(a). Similarly, in Beltran, the opportunity cost of a unit of cloth is 1/2 unit of food but a unit of cloth will trade for 1 unit of food. Since the opportunity cost is constant, Beltran

Figure 18.2

(a)

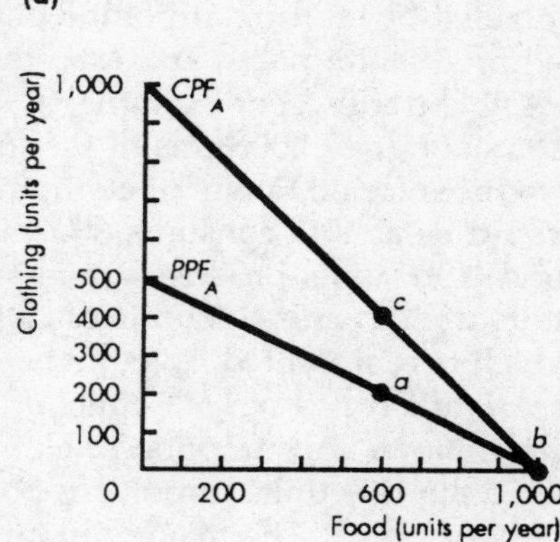

(b)

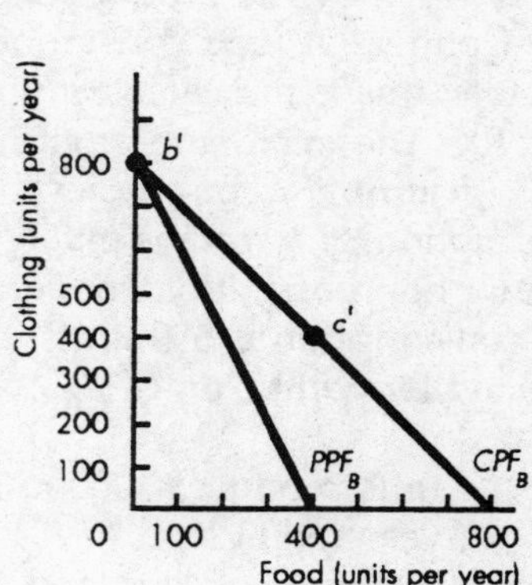

will totally specialize in the production of cloth and will produce 800 units per year (point *b′* in Fig. 18.2(b)).

c) The consumption possibility frontiers for Atlantis and Beltran (labeled CPF_A and CPF_B) are illustrated in Fig. 18.2, parts (a) and (b), respectively. These frontiers are straight lines that indicate all the combinations of food and cloth that can be consumed with trade. The position and slope of the consumption possibility frontier for an economy depend on the terms of trade between the goods and the production point of the economy.

The consumption possibility frontier for Atlantis (CPF_A), for example, is obtained by starting at point *b* on PPF_A, the production point, and examining possible trades. For example, if Atlantis traded 400 units of the food it produces for 400 units of cloth, it would be able to consume 600 units of food (1000 units produced minus 400 units traded) and 400 units of cloth, which is represented by point *c*.

d) If Atlantis consumes 600 units of food, trade allows consumption of cloth to be 400 units, 200 units more than possible without trade. The maximum amount of cloth that can be consumed *without trade* is given by the production possibility frontier. If food consumption is 600 units, this is indicated by point *a* on PPF_A. The maximum amount of cloth consumption for any level of food consumption *with trade* is given by the consumption possibility frontier. If food consumption is 600 units, this is indicated by point *c* on CPF_A.

3. a) Since Atlantis produces 1000 units of food per year (point *b* on PPF_A), to consume 600 units of food and 400 units of cloth (point *c* on CPF_A) it must trade 400 units of food for 400 units of cloth. This means that Beltran has traded 400 units of cloth for 400 units of food. Since Beltran produces 800 units of cloth, this implies that Beltran must consume 400 units of food and 400 units of cloth (point *c′* on CPF_B).

   b) Atlantis exports 400 units of food per year and imports 400 units of cloth. Beltran exports 400 units of cloth per year and imports 400 units of food.

4. a) The price of a shirt under free trade will occur at the intersection of country A's import demand curve for shirts and country B's export supply curve of shirts. This occurs at a price of $12 per shirt.

   b) Country A will import 6 million shirts per year.

5. a) The effect of the $9 per shirt tariff is to shift the export supply curve (*S*) upward by $9. This is shown as a shift from *S* to *S′* in Fig. 18.1 Solution. The price is now determined by the intersection of the *D* curve (which is unaffected by the tariff) and the *S′* curve. The new price of a shirt is $18.

   b) Of this $18, $9 is the tariff, so the exporter only receives the remaining $9.

   c) Country A will now import only 4 million shirts per year.

   d) The tariff revenue is $9 (the tariff per shirt) times 4 million (the number of shirts imported), which is $36 million. This money is received by the government of country A.

Figure 18.1 Solution

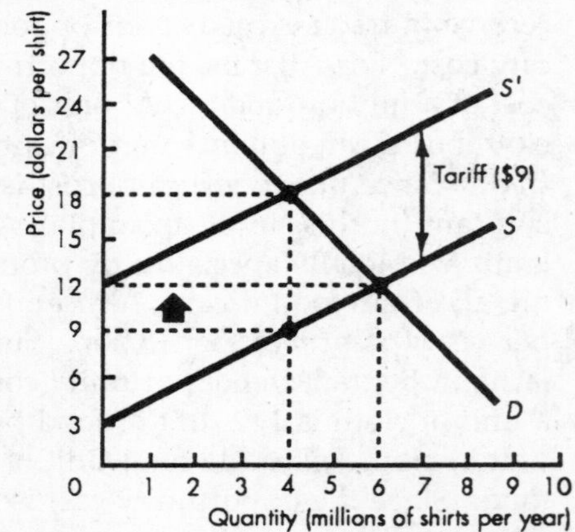

6. a) The quota restricts the quantity that can be imported to 4 million shirts per

year regardless of the price and is represented by a vertical line in Fig. 18.3 (which corresponds to Fig. 18.1). The market for shirts will thus clear at a price of $18 per shirt.

b) This $18 price is received by the people who are given the right to import shirts under the quota. The amount received by the exporter is $9, given by the height of the *S* curve at a quantity of 4 million shirts per year.

c) Country A will import 4 million shirts per year, the quota limit.

d) The "excess profit" is $9 per shirt (the $18 received by the importer minus the $9 received by the exporter) times 4 million shirts, which is $36 million. This is captured by the importers who have been rewarded by the government of country A since they have been given the right to import under the quota. This is essentially a right to make an "excess profit."

7. a) The effect of a VER of 4 million shirts per year will be the same as a quota of 4 million shirts per year. Indeed, a VER *is* a quota but one which is imposed by the government of the exporting country rather than the government of the importing country. Thus the situation under a VER is illustrated by Fig. 18.3. The price of a shirt will be $18.

b) Country A will import 4 million shirts per year, the VER limit.

c) The "excess profit" is the same as under a quota (Problem 6 (d)), $36 million. The only difference is that it is captured by those persons in the exporting country which have been given the right to export (at the higher price) under the VER.

Figure 18.3

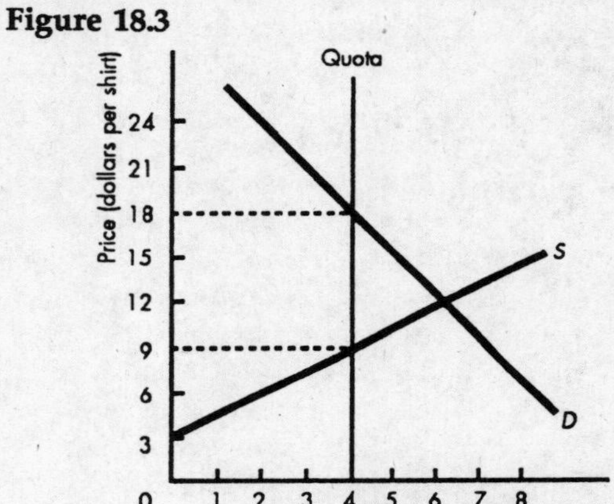

19 THE BALANCE OF PAYMENTS AND THE DOLLAR

CHAPTER IN PERSPECTIVE

With the increase in the importance of international trade for the U.S. there has also been an increase in concerns about our economic relationships with other countries. Daily new stories indicate that there are many who are greatly concerned by the continuing large U.S. trade deficit. Similarly, many are greatly concerned by the fact that the U.S. dollar has fallen in value relative to the currencies of many of our major trading partners, especially Japan. There are others who argue that the foreign exchange value of the dollar has not fallen enough.

What has caused the large and apparently chronic U.S. trade deficits and how are they financed? Is there a link between large government budget deficits and large trade deficits? Why should we be concerned about continuing large trade deficits? What makes the foreign exchange value of the dollar fluctuate and why has its value fallen against other major currencies, especially the Japanese yen? These are some of the basic questions addressed in this chapter. Understanding how to think about them will help us better understand important international economic relationships that affect us all.

LEARNING OBJECTIVES

After studying this chapter, you will be able to:

- **Explain how international trade is financed**
- **Describe a country's balance of payments accounts**
- **Explain what determines the amount of international borrowing and lending**
- **Explain why the United States changed from being a lender to a borrower in the mid-1980s**
- **Explain how the foreign exchange value of the dollar is determined**
- **Explain why the foreign exchange value of the dollar fluctuated in the 1980s**
- **Explain the effects of changes in the exchange rate**

- **Explain what determines interest rates and why they vary so much from one country to another**

HELPFUL HINTS

1. The previous chapter demonstrated the gains from trade between countries. Indeed, as noted in Chapter 3, these are the same gains that result from trade *within* countries as well. However, there is an important difference between trade within a single country and trade between countries.

When individuals in the same country engage in trade, they use the same currency and so trade is straightforward. On the other hand, international trade is complicated by the fact that individuals in different countries use different currencies. If the person selling the good is from Japan he will want payment to be in Japanese yen, but if the person buying the good is from the U.S., she will likely be holding only U.S. dollars. This problem complicates trade between individuals in different countries.

This chapter addresses this complication by looking at the balance of payments of a country as well as the foreign exchange market.

2. Note that the balance of payments must balance. Individual accounts in the balance of payment, can be in deficit or surplus but that will be offset by a surplus or deficit in another account. It may be useful to reconsider the example of Joanne given in the text.

3. It is important to understand foreign exchange rates as prices determined by supply and demand. They are prices of currency determined in markets for currency. The demand for U.S. dollars in the foreign exchange market, for example, is the demand for dollar (denominated) assets, including U.S. money. That demand will arise from the desire on the part of foreigners to purchase U.S. goods and services (which requires dollars) and the desire on the part of foreigners to purchase U.S. financial or real assets. The supply of dollar assets is determined by the government and the Fed and depends on the exchange rate regime.

4. The law of one price is not relevant only in the context of international trade. Anytime there is a discrepancy in the price of the same good in two markets, natural economic forces (unless restricted) will eliminate that discrepancy and thus establish a single price. Suppose that the price in market 1 rises relative to the price in market 2. Individuals will now buy in the market with the lower price and not in the market with the higher price. This increase in the demand in market 2 and decrease in demand in market 1 will cause the two prices to come together. This same principal is true in international markets as well: natural market forces will result in a single price for the *same* good.

5. Purchasing power parity is the manifestation of the law of one price in international trade. Purchasing power parity implies that, as long as exchange rates can adjust, they will adjust so that money (of whatever country) will have the same purchasing power in all countries. This means that if one country experiences inflation while others do not, exchange rates will adjust so that the purchasing power of money will be the same in all countries.

For example, suppose that in year 1 the price of good *A* (the only traded good) is $5 in the U.S. and 600 yen in Japan. Since the exchange rate is 120 yen per dollar, there is purchasing power parity; that is, at this exchange rate the dollar price of good *A* is the same in both countries ($5) and the yen price of *A* is the same in both countries (600 yen).

Now suppose that the U.S. experiences inflation and that, as a consequence, in year 2 the price of *A* in the U.S. is $6. There has been no inflation in Japan and the price of *A* there continues at 600 yen. Note what would happen if the exchange rate remained at 120 yen per dollar. The dollar price in the U.S. is now $6 but the dollar price in Japan is still $5. Furthermore, the yen price in Japan is still 600 yen but the yen price in the U.S. is now 720 yen. Thus there is no longer purchasing power parity.

The yen per dollar exchange rate must fall in order to restore purchasing power parity (i.e., to restore one price). Natural market forces will cause this to occur. The inflation in the U.S. will cause the demand for dollar assets to decline, which will result in a fall in the yen per dollar exchange rate. This will continue as long as there is a discrepancy between the dollar (or yen) prices in the two countries. Thus the exchange rate will fall to 100 yen per dollar at which point purchasing power parity will be restored. The dollar price of good *A* will be $6 in both countries and the yen price will be 600 yen in both countries.

6. Note that it is *not* the edict of a government which fixes the exchange rate of its currency but rather the willingness of its central bank to supply all of the domestic currency denominated assets that are demanded at the fixed exchange rate.

KEY FIGURES AND TABLES

Figure 19.1 The Balance of Payments

The historical record of the three balance of payments accounts for the U.S. over the period 1975-1990 is given here. Note that the sum of the balances from each account for any year must be zero since the total balance of payments must be in balance.

There are three important features to notice. First, the behavior of the current account balance and the capital account balance has been fundamentally different in the 1980s. From 1975 until the early 1980s, the current account balance was generally in surplus although the average surplus was small. However, since 1982 the current account balance has exhibited a very large deficit though the size of the deficit began decreasing in the late 1980s.

The second feature to notice is that the capital account is essentially a mirror image of the current account indicating that the current account deficit has been financed almost exclusively by borrowing from the rest of the world.

The third important feature is that fluctuations in holdings of official reserves have been much smaller than in the other two accounts.

Figure 19.2 The Twin Deficits

This figure shows the historical behavior of the current account deficit and the government budget deficit over the period 1975-1990. Notice that there is a tendency for these two deficits to rise and fall together. Consequently, they are referred to as the twin deficits. Notice also that the size of both deficits increased during the 1980s.

Figure 19.4 Exchange Rates

This figure shows the behavior of the exchange rate of the U. S. dollar over the period 1975—1991. The exchange rate is the price at which foreign currencies and the dollar are traded. The red line shows the exchange rate in terms of yen per dollar while the blue line shows a trade-weighted index of the value of the dollar.

The decline in the yen value of a dollar means that the dollar has depreciated against the yen. On the other hand, the dollar appreciated against all other currencies during the first half of the 1980s and depreciated against all other currencies during the second half of the 1980s.

Figure 19.6 Three Exchange Rate Regimes

This figure illustrates the effects of an increase in the demand for dollar assets under the three exchange rate regimes. Part (a) shows the effects under a fixed exchange rate regime, part (b) shows the effects under a flexible exchange rate regime, and part (c) examines the consequences under a managed exchange rate regime. The difference in the effects arises from the difference in the supply curve of dollar assets under each of the three regimes.

Under a fixed exchange rate regime, part (a), the Fed is prepared to supply as many dollar assets as are demanded at the fixed exchange rate. This implies that the supply curve will be horizontal at that pegged exchange rate and thus an increase in the demand for dollar assets will call forth an equal increase in the quantity supplied and the exchange rate will remain unchanged.

Under a flexible exchange rate, part (b), the supply curve of dollar assets is vertical because the Fed does not respond at all to changes in the demand for dollar assets. Thus, an increase in the demand for dollar assets will cause the yen per dollar exchange rate to increase with no increase in the quantity of dollar assets.

The behavior of a managed exchange rate, part (c), is between these two extremes. Under a managed exchange rate the Fed will respond partially to changes in the exchange rate and thus the supply curve of dollar assets is positively sloped. In this case the increase in the demand for dollar assets will cause an increase in both the yen per dollar exchange rate and the quantity of dollar assets supplied.

Table 19.2 The Current Account Balance, Net Foreign Borrowing, and the Financing of Investment

Key equations from our study of the national income accounts in Chapter 6 imply that there is an important relationship between the balance of trade deficit, the government budget deficit, and the private sector deficit. This figure demonstrates this relationship using those equations.

Part (a) of the figure defines some symbols to be used and gives some corresponding numerical values for the U.S. in 1990. Part (b) lists the two key equations from national income accounting, (1) and (2), and then takes the difference between them to obtain equation (3). It is equation (3) which describes the important relationship.

In part (c), equation (3) is solved for the balance of trade surplus (*EX* - *IM*) and given as equation (4). This equation states that the balance of trade surplus/deficit (*EX* - *IM*) is equal to the sum of the government budget surplus/deficit (*T* - *G*) and the private sector surplus/deficit (*S* - *I*). Part (d) shows how investment is financed by solving equation (3) for investment to obtain equation (7).

Table 19.4 The Demand for Dollar Assets

The demand for dollar assets is characterized in this table. The first part indicates that, just like any other case, the demand for dollar assets obeys the law of demand: the quantity of dollar assets demanded is negatively related to the price of a dollar in terms of foreign currency. For example, if the yen price of the dollar rises, the quantity of dollar assets demanded declines. The second part of the figure lists several factors that will cause the demand curve for dollar assets to shift.

Table 19.5 The Supply of Dollar Assets

This table is a counterpart to Table 19.4. It characterizes the other half of the foreign exchange market, the supply of dollar assets. As discussed in the text and illustrated in Fig. 19.6, the slope of the supply curve for dollar assets depends on the type of exchange rate regime.

Under a fixed exchange rate regime, the supply curve of dollar assets is horizontal at the fixed exchange rate. Under a flexible exchange rate regime, the supply curve of dollar assets is vertical, and under a managed exchange rate regime, it is positively sloped.

The bottom section of the table indicates that the supply curve of dollar assets will shift if the Fed changes the monetary base or there is a government budget surplus or deficit.

SELF-TEST

CONCEPT REVIEW

1. The international trading, borrowing, and lending activities of a country are recorded in its ____________ of ____________ ____________. It consists of three accounts. The expenditures on imported goods and services and the receipts from the sale of exported goods and services are recorded in the ____________ account. The ____________ account records lending to and borrowing from the rest of the world. The change in a country's holdings of foreign currency is shown in the ____________ ____________ account.
2. A country that is borrowing more from the rest of the world than it is lending is called a(n) ____________ ____________. A country that is lending more to the rest of the world than it is borrowing is called a(n) ____________ ____________.
3. A country that during its entire history has borrowed more from the rest of the world than it has loaned is called a(n) ____________ nation.
4. The balance of trade deficit is ____________ ____________ the sum of the government budget deficit and the private sector deficit.
5. The market in which the currencies of different countries are exchanged for each other is called the ____________ ____________ market. The price at which one currency exchanges for another is called the ____________ ____________ ____________.
6. There are three foreign exchange regimes. In the first of these the value of the exchange rate is pegged by a central bank. This is a(n) ____________ exchange rate. A(n) ____________ exchange rate is a regime in which the exchange rate is determined by market forces without government intervention. A(n) ____________ exchange rate is a regime in which the government does not peg the exchange rate but does intervene in the foreign exchange market in order to influence the price of its currency.
7. The international organization that monitors balance of payments and exchange rate activities of all countries is called the ____________ ____________ ____________.
8. The fall in the price of a currency in terms of another currency is called currency ____________.

9. The supply curve of dollar assets is horizontal under a(n) ____________ exchange rate regime, it is vertical under a(n) ____________ exchange rate regime, and it is positively sloped under a(n) ____________ exchange rate regime.

10. Buying low and selling high when there is a difference in price in two places is called ____________. This activity implies the law of ____________ ____________, which states that any given commodity will be available for a single price.

11. The equality of the value of money across all countries once differences in risk are taken into account is called ____________ ____________ ____________.

12. When interest rates are equal across countries we have ____________ ____________ ____________.

TRUE OR FALSE

____ 1. The sale of U.S. manufactured computers to a firm in Canada will be recorded in the current account of the balance of payments accounts.

____ 2. If there is a current account deficit then there must also be a deficit in either the capital account or the official settlements account.

____ 3. If the U.S. borrows more from the rest of the world than it loans to the rest of the world, the U.S. has a capital account surplus.

____ 4. If a nation is a net borrower from the rest of the world, it must be a debtor nation.

____ 5. If a country has a large government budget deficit and the private sector deficit is small, the balance of trade deficit will be large.

____ 6. If investment is greater than saving, the private sector has a deficit.

____ 7. At any given time, the exchange rate between the U.S. dollar and the Japanese yen is almost identical, no matter where in the world the transaction is taking place.

____ 8. The U.S. is currently maintaining a fixed exchange rate.

____ 9. If the exchange rate between the U.S. dollar and the Japanese yen changes from 130 yen per dollar to 140 yen per dollar, the U.S. dollar has appreciated.

____10. Foreign exchange rates are set by the International Monetary Fund.

____11. If the interest rate on U.S. dollar denominated assets rises, the demand for dollar denominated assets decreases.

____12. If the foreign exchange value of the dollar is expected to rise, the demand for dollar denominated assets increases.

____13. Under a fixed exchange rate regime in the U.S., the supply curve of dollar assets is horizontal at the pegged exchange rate.

____14. Under a flexible exchange rate regime in the U.S., an increase in the monetary base by the Federal Reserve would cause the foreign exchange price of the dollar to rise.

____15. Under a flexible exchange rate regime in the U.S., an increase in the government budget deficit will cause the foreign exchange price of the dollar to rise.

____16. Arbitrage will tend to result in a single price for any given commodity.

____17. If the yen price of the dollar is 100 yen per dollar and the price of a traded good is $10 in the U.S., purchasing power parity implies that the price in Japan will be 1000 yen.

____18. The purchasing power parity theory can be tested by comparing the price of nontraded goods in different countries.

____19. Interest rate parity is the result of arbitrage in the markets for assets.

____20. Countries with currencies that are expected to appreciate will have higher interest rates than countries with currencies that are expected to depreciate.

Multiple Choice

1. Which of the following is NOT one of the balance of payments accounts?
   a. Current account.
   b. Nontraded goods account.
   c. Official settlements account.
   d. Capital account.

2. Suppose the U.S. initially has all balance of payments accounts in balance (no surplus or deficit). Then U.S. firms increase the amount they import from Japan, financing that increase in imports by borrowing from Japan. There will now be a current account
   a. surplus and a capital account surplus.
   b. surplus and a capital account deficit.
   c. deficit and a capital account surplus.
   d. deficit and a capital account deficit.

3. The country Plato came into existence at the beginning of year 1. Given the information in Table 19.1, in year 4 Plato is a net
   a. lender and a creditor nation.
   b. lender and a debtor nation.
   c. borrower and a creditor nation.
   d. borrower and a debtor nation.

Table 19.1

Year	Borrowed from rest of world (billions of dollars)	Loaned to rest of world (billions of dollars)
1	60	20
2	60	40
3	60	60
4	60	80

4. Assuming that Plato is on a floating exchange rate, in which year or years in Table 19.1 did Plato have a current account surplus?
   a. Year 1.
   b. Year 2.
   c. Years 1 and 2.
   d. Year 4 only.

5. A nation is currently a net lender and a debtor nation. Which of the following statements applies to that nation?
   a. It has loaned more than it borrowed abroad this year, but borrowed more than it loaned during its history.
   b. It has borrowed more abroad than it loaned this year and also borrowed more than it loaned during its history.
   c. It has loaned more than it borrowed abroad this year and also loaned more than it borrowed during its history.
   d. Its debts must be currently growing.

6. Suppose that in a country, government purchases of goods and services is $400 billion, taxes (net of transfer payments) is $300 billion, saving is $300 billion, and investment is $250 billion. The current account
   a. surplus is $150 billion.
   b. surplus is $50 billion.
   c. deficit is $150 billion.
   d. deficit is $50 billion.

7. The country of Question 6 has a government budget
   a. surplus and a private sector surplus.
   b. surplus and a private sector deficit.
   c. deficit and a private sector surplus.
   d. deficit and a private sector deficit.

8. Suppose the exchange rate between the U.S. dollar and the British pound is 2 pounds per dollar. If a radio sells for 38 pounds in Britain, what is the dollar price of the radio?
   a. $19.
   b. $26.
   c. $38.
   d. $76.

9. The market in which the currency of one country is exchanged for the currency of another is called the
   a. money market.
   b. capital market.
   c. foreign exchange market.
   d. forward exchange market.

10. Under a flexible exchange rate regime, if the foreign exchange value of a country's currency starts to rise, that country's central bank will
    a. increase the supply of assets denominated in its own currency.
    b. decrease the supply of assets denominated in its own currency.
    c. decrease the demand for assets denominated in its own currency.
    d. do nothing.

11. Suppose that the dollar-yen foreign exchange rate changes from 140 yen per dollar to 130 yen per dollar. Then the yen has
    a. depreciated against the dollar and the dollar has appreciated against the yen.
    b. depreciated against the dollar and the dollar has depreciated against the yen.
    c. appreciated against the dollar and the dollar has appreciated against the yen.
    d. appreciated against the dollar and the dollar has depreciated against the yen.

12. Which of the following will shift the demand curve for dollar assets to the right?
    a. An increase in the demand for foreign goods by U.S. citizens.
    b. A decrease in the demand for U.S. goods by foreigners.
    c. The dollar is expected to appreciate.
    d. The government has a budget deficit.

13. Which of the following will shift the supply curve of dollar assets to the right under flexible exchange rates?
    a. An increase in the demand for foreign goods by U.S. citizens.
    b. A decrease in the demand for U.S. goods by foreigners.
    c. The dollar is expected to appreciate.
    d. The government has a budget deficit.

14. Under a flexible exchange rate regime, the supply curve of dollar assets is
    a. vertical.
    b. horizontal.
    c. positively sloped.
    d. negatively sloped.

15. Under a flexible exchange rate regime, a U.S. government budget deficit will cause the foreign exchange price of the dollar to
    a. fall and the quantity of dollar assets held to fall.
    b. fall and the quantity of dollar assets held to rise.
    c. rise and the quantity of dollar assets held to fall.
    d. rise and the quantity of dollar assets held to rise.

16. Under a flexible exchange rate regime, an increase in interest rates in the U.S. relative to those in Japan would cause
    a. the dollar to appreciate against the yen.
    b. the dollar to depreciate against the yen.
    c. an increase in the supply of dollar assets.
    d. a decrease in the supply of dollar assets.

17. Under a managed exchange rate regime, a decrease in interest rates on dollar assets will cause the foreign exchange price of the dollar to
    a. fall and the quantity of dollar assets to fall.
    b. fall and the quantity of dollar assets to rise.
    c. rise and the quantity of dollar assets to fall.
    d. rise and the quantity of dollar assets to rise.

18. Suppose the exchange rate between the U.S. dollar and the Japanese yen is initially 120 yen per dollar. According to purchasing power parity, if prices remain unchanged in Japan and there is a 10 percent increase in the U.S. in the prices of
    a. nontraded goods, the exchange rate will become about 108 yen per dollar.
    b. nontraded goods, the exchange rate will become about 132 yen per dollar.
    c. traded goods rise, the exchange rate will become about 108 yen per dollar.
    d. traded goods rise, the exchange rate will become about 132 yen per dollar.

19. If the interest rate in the U.S. is greater than the interest rate in Japan, interest rate parity implies that
    a. the inflation rate is higher in Japan.
    b. Japanese financial assets are poor investments.
    c. the yen is expected to depreciate against the dollar.
    d. the yen is expected to appreciate against the dollar.

20. Which of the following would cause the dollar to depreciate against the yen?
    a. An increase in the U.S. monetary base.
    b. An increase in interest rates in the U.S.
    c. A decrease in interest rates in Japan.
    d. An increase in U.S. exports purchased by Japan.

SHORT ANSWER

1. What are the three balance of payments accounts and what do they each record?

2. What is the relationship between a country's trade deficit, its government budget deficit, and its private sector deficit?

3. What are the likely effects of a government budget deficit on the trade deficit?

4. What is meant by the foreign exchange rate between the U.S. dollar and the Japanese yen?

5. If the U.S. maintained a fixed exchange rate regime, how would the Fed keep the exchange rate at its pegged level?

6. Why is the supply curve of dollar assets horizontal under a fixed exchange rate regime?

7. Why did the dollar appreciate significantly against the yen during 1981 and 1982?

8. The existence of arbitrage implies the law of one price. Explain.

9. What is purchasing power parity?

10. What is interest rate parity?

PROBLEMS

1. The international transactions of a country for a given year are reported in Table 19.2.

Table 19.2

Transaction	Amount (billions of dollars)
Exports of goods and services	$100
Imports of goods and services	130
Transfers to the rest of the world	20
Loans to the rest of the world	60
Loans from the rest of the world	
Increase in official reserves	10

a) What is the amount of loans from the rest of the world?
b) What is the current account balance?
c) What is the capital account balance?
d) Does this country have a flexible exchange rate?

2. The information in Table 19.3 is for a country during a given year.

Table 19.3

Variable	Amount (billions of dollars)
GDP	$800
Taxes (net of transfer payments)	200
Government budget deficit	50
Consumption	500
Investment	150
Imports	150

a) What is the level of government expenditure on goods and services?
b) What is the private sector surplus or deficit?
c) What is the value of exports?

d) What is the current account surplus or deficit?

3. Suppose that the exchange rate between the U.S. dollar and the German mark is 2 marks per dollar.
   a) What is the exchange rate in terms of dollars per mark?
   b) What is the price in dollars of a camera selling for 250 marks?
   c) What is the price in marks of a computer selling for 1000 dollars?

4. Suppose the interest rate is Japan in 4 percent per year and that the interest rate in the U.S. is 9 percent per year. Furthermore, the exchange rate today is 100 yen per dollar but you expect the exchange rate in one year to be 95 yen per dollar; that is, you expect the dollar to depreciate against the yen. You have $100 to lend today and want to know whether the expected return would be higher on a one year loan in Japan or in the U.S.
   a) If you loan the $100 in the U.S., how much will you receive in dollars at the end of one year?
   b) If you convert the $100 to yen and loan it in Japan, how much will you receive in yen at the end of one year? How much do you expect that to be worth in terms of dollars?
   c) In which country is your expected return higher?

ANSWERS

CONCEPT REVIEW

1. balance; payments accounts; current; capital; official settlements
2. net borrower; net lender
3. debtor
4. equal to
5. foreign exchange; foreign exchange rate
6. fixed; flexible; managed
7. International Monetary Fund
8. depreciation
9. fixed; flexible; managed
10. arbitrage; one price
11. purchasing power parity
12. interest rate parity

TRUE OR FALSE

1. T	6. T	11. F	16. T
2. F	7. T	12. T	17. T
3. T	8. F	13. T	18. F
4. F	9. T	14. F	19. T
5. T	10. F	15. F	20. F

MULTIPLE CHOICE

1. b	6. d	11. a	16. a
2. c	7. c	12. c	17. b
3. b	8. a	13. d	18. c
4. d	9. c	14. a	19. d
5. a	10. d	15. b	20. a

SHORT ANSWER

1. The three balance of payments accounts are
   - The current account, which records the value of exports and the value of imports as well as transfers between countries and interest received from and paid to other countries.
   - The capital account, which records the amount that a country borrows from the rest of the world and the amount that it lends to the rest of the world.

- The official settlements account, which records the changes in a country's holdings of official reserves.

2. The national income accounting identities allow us to show that a country's balance of trade deficit is equal to the sum of its government budget deficit and its private sector deficit.

3. A government budget deficit will likely cause the trade deficit to increase because it will increase imports and decrease exports. A government deficit will increase aggregate planned expenditure which will increase aggregate demand. Part of the increase in expenditure will be on goods and services produced in foreign countries (i.e., imports). In addition, if the economy is producing at full-employment, part of domestic production which has been going to exports will be diverted to satisfy the increase in domestic demand and thus exports decrease.

4. The foreign exchange rate between the U.S. dollar and the Japanese yen is the number of yen required to purchase one dollar in the foreign exchange market.

5. If the U.S. is operating under a fixed exchange rate regime, any change in the demand for dollar assets must be met with an equal change in the supply of dollar assets by the Fed in order to leave the exchange rate unchanged at its pegged level. This means that the Fed must be prepared to supply whatever quantity of dollar assets are demanded at the official exchange rate. For example, if the exchange rate is initially at its pegged level and the demand for dollar assets increases, the Fed must increase the supply of dollar assets by the same amount to keep the foreign exchange value of the dollar from rising. The Fed would increase the supply of dollar assets by buying foreign currency (foreign bank deposits) with dollar assets in the form of U.S. bank deposits. Thus official reserves will increase when the Fed increases the supply of dollar assets.

6. As indicated in the previous answer, under a fixed exchange rate regime, the Fed must stand ready to supply whatever quantity of dollars are demanded at the official exchange rate. Since the quantity of dollar assets supplied adjusts to maintain the exchange rate at its pegged level, the supply curve of dollar assets is horizontal.

7. The period of 1981 and 1982 was a period of deep recession in the U.S. caused by a significant reduction in the rate of growth of the monetary base. The restrictive monetary policy by the Fed caused the supply of dollar assets to fall (relative to demand). This put upward pressure on the yen price of the dollar. Furthermore, the increase in U.S. interest rates associated with the restrictive monetary policy caused the demand for dollars to increase, which put additional upward pressure on the yen price of the dollar.

8. The law of one price says that any given commodity will be available for a single price. Arbitrage involves the attempt to make a profit by exploiting different prices for the same commodity.

   If, for example, good *A* is selling for a high price in one market and a low price in another, a profit could be made by buying *A* in the market with the low price and selling it in the market with the high price. As more of *A* is purchased in the market with the low price, the price will rise, and as more of *A* is sold in the market with the high price the price, will fall. Thus, arbitrage will move the prices toward each other. The tendency to buy low and sell high will continue to exist until the price of the commodity is the same in both markets. Thus arbitrage implies a single price for the commodity.

9. Purchasing power parity follows from arbitrage and the law of one price. It means that the value of money is the same in all countries once the differences in risk are taken into account. For example, if the exchange rate between the dollar and the yen is 120 yen per dollar, purchasing power parity says that a good that sells for 120 yen in Japan will sell for 1 dollar in the U.S. Thus, the exchange rate is such that money (dollars or yen) has the same purchasing power in both countries.

10. Interest rate parity also is an implication of arbitrage. It occurs when interest rates are equal across countries after accounting for the fact that loans in different countries are denominated in different currencies. In order to calculate the true interest rate, it is necessary to account for the fact that different currencies will appreciate or depreciate at different rates. A country whose currency is expected to depreciate will have higher interest rates to compensate for the expected depreciation.

PROBLEMS

1. a) The amount of loans from the rest of the world is $100 billion. This is obtained by recognizing that the overall balance of payments must balance; the sum of the positive entries (exports, loans from the rest of the world, and increase in official reserves) must equal the sum of the negative entries (imports, transfers to the rest of the world, and loans to the rest of the world).
   b) The current account balance is a $50 billion deficit: exports minus imports minus transfers to the rest of the world.
   c) The capital account balance is a surplus of $40 billion: loans from the rest of the world minus loans to the rest of the world.
   d) This country does NOT have a flexible exchange rate because official reserves increased. Official reserves would have remained unchanged under flexible exchange rates.

2. a) Since we know that the government budget deficit is $50 billion and the taxes (net of transfer payments) is $200 billion, we can infer that government expenditure on goods and services is $250 billion.
   b) The private sector surplus or deficit is given by saving minus investment. Investment is given as $150 billion but we must compute saving. Saving is equal to GDP minus taxes minus consumption: $100 billion. Thus there is a private sector deficit of $50 billion.
   c) We know that GDP is consumption plus investment plus government expenditure on goods and services plus net exports (exports minus imports). Since we know all these values except exports, we can obtain that value by solving for exports. The value of exports equals GDP plus imports minus consumption minus investment minus government expenditure on goods and services; the value of exports equals $50 billion.
   d) There is a current account deficit of $100 billion. This can be obtained in two ways. First we can recognize that the balance of trade surplus of deficit is given by the value of exports ($50 billion) minus the value of imports ($150 billion). The alternative method is to recognize that the balance of trade deficit is equal to the sum of the government budget deficit ($50 billion) and the private sector deficit ($50 billion).

3. a) If one dollar can be purchased for 2 marks, then the price of a mark is half a dollar per mark.
   b) At an exchange rate of 2 marks per dollar, it takes 125 dollars to obtain the 250 marks needed to buy the camera.
   c) At an exchange rate of 2 marks per dollar, it takes 2000 marks to obtain the 1000 dollars needed to buy the computer.

4. a) Loaning $100 at an interest rate of 9 percent means that you will receive $109 at the end of one year.
   b) At the current exchange rate (100 yen per dollar) you can obtain 10,000 yen for your $100, which you can loan in Japan at an interest rate of 4 percent. This means that at the end of one year you will receive 10,400 yen. Since you expect the dollar to depreciate so that the exchange rate in a year is 95 yen per dollar, you expect to be able to buy $109.47 with the 10,400 yen.
   c) The expected return is slightly higher in Japan than in the U.S.

20 GROWTH AND DEVELOPMENT

CHAPTER IN PERSPECTIVE

What makes countries rich or poor? Is it the quantity of natural resources? Why is it that a country like Japan with few natural resources has been able to increase its per capita income from about 17 percent of that in the U.S. at the end of World War II to a per capita income that is about the same as in the U.S. today? Similarly, how has a country like Singapore, with almost no natural resources, been able to experience such rapid economic growth? In this chapter we address these and related questions as we look at the problems and prospects for economic growth and development.

LEARNING OBJECTIVES

After studying this chapter, you will be able to:

- **Describe the international distribution of income**
- **Explain the importance of economic growth**
- **Explain how the accumulation of capital and technological progress brings higher per capita incomes**
- **Describe the obstacles to economic growth in poor countries**
- **Explain the possible effects of population control, foreign aid, free trade, and demand stimulation on economic growth and development**
- **Evaluate policies designed to stimulate economic growth and development**

HELPFUL HINTS

1. There are two main points made in this chapter:
   a) Countries become rich by achieving high rates of growth in per capita income and maintaining them over a long period of time.
   b) The higher the rate of capital accumulation and the faster the pace of technological improvement, the higher the rate of growth in per capita income.

2. It is probably equally important to note the things that are apparently *not* important determinants of economic growth.
   a) *An abundance of natural resources.* Most of the recent success stories of economic development (e.g., Hong Kong and Singapore) have occurred in the absence of natural resources. Natural resources can be helpful (e.g., the oil-rich countries) but they are not necessary. This is hopeful because a country can do very little about its lack of natural resources.
   b) *Aggregate demand stimulus.* Our development of the aggregate demand and aggregate supply model informs us that aggregate demand stimulus may affect real GDP in the short run but will only be inflationary in the long run. The evidence confirms this. There is no relationship between inflation and economic growth.
   c) *Restriction of international trade.* Indeed, this chapter points out that unrestricted international trade has been a part of the most dramatic success stories of economic growth. From the discussion of the gains from international trade in Chapter 18, it should be no surprise that protection from international competition will decrease the rate of economic growth.

KEY FIGURES AND TABLES

Figure 20.1 The World Lorenz Curve, 1985

The Lorenz curve graphically illustrates the degree of inequality in the distribution of income. On the horizontal axis is measured the cumulative percentage of the population and on the vertical axis is measured the cumulative percentage of income. The population is ordered from low income to high income. The Lorenz curve for an equal distribution of income would be shown by a 45° line indicating that 20 percent of the population had 20 percent of the income, and so on.

The Lorenz curve for the United States illustrated here reflects the distribution of income across families. Since it is bowed out, it shows that there is inequality in the distribution of income: 20 percent of the population has much less than 20 percent of the income. The world Lorenz curve illustrated here reflects the distribution of average per capita income across countries of the world. It shows even more inequality.

Figure 20.4 Technological Change

This figure illustrates the consequences of technological change as well as increases in the capital stock on economic growth. The U.S. and Ethiopia are assumed to have been using the same technology and thus were on the same per capita production function in 1790 (PF_{1790}). The U.S., however, had more capital per capita and so the U.S. produced farther up the PF_{1790} curve. Output per capita in the U.S. exceeded per capita output in Ethiopia in 1790 even though each country used the same technology.

From 1790 to 1990 two things happened in the U.S. Technological improvement shifted the per capita production function upward and the per capita stock of capital increased. Both of these increased output per capita and thus were responsible for economic growth.

In Ethiopia, however, there was no technological improvement and no accumulation of capital per worker. Thus, output per capita has not increased and Ethiopia has not experienced economic growth.

Figure 20.5 Investment Trends

Part (a) of the figure compares the behavior of average investment rates (investment as a percentage of income) from 1960 to 1990 for industrial countries and developing countries. The first thing to notice is that investment rates are reasonably high for both groups of countries: investment is generally 20 percent or more of income. In addition, it is interesting to note that the investment rate in the developing countries increased throughout the 1960s and into the 1970s. Since 1975, that rate has fallen off somewhat but has remained higher than the average investment rate for industrial countries. On the other hand, the investment rate in industrial countries was rather stable at about 24 percent from 1960 to 1974. Thereafter, the investment rate in industrial countries dropped.

Part (b) of the figure compares the investment rates of two countries that have had very different growth experiences since 1960: Singapore and Ethiopia. Note that in 1960 the investment rate in both countries was the same, slightly more than 10 percent. Since then, however, the investment rate in Singapore has risen dramatically to 40 percent or more. Ethiopia, however, has maintained about the same low investment rate. It is no accident that Singapore has experienced phenomenal economic growth over this period, while growth in Ethiopia has been extremely slow.

Figure 20.6 Population Growth and Number of Dependents

Countries that have high population growth rates also tend to have a high percentage of their population under the age of 15 and therefore dependent. This is illustrated in this figure. Each point in the graph corresponds to the population growth rate and percentage of population under the age of 15 for a single country. There seems to be a clear positive relationship between them. This means that countries with high population growth rates face an obstacle to economic development, since a much larger part of the population is dependent, requiring the use of resources for consumption but not yet contributing to production.

SELF-TEST

CONCEPT REVIEW

1. A country in which there is little industrialization, very little capital equipment, and low per capita incomes is called a(n) ____________ country. A country that is poor but is accumulating capital and developing an industrial base is called a(n) ____________ country.
2. Countries in which there is a rapidly developing broad industrial base and per capita income is growing quickly are called ____________ ____________ countries. A country with a large amount of capital equipment and in which people are highly specialized, enabling them to earn high per capita incomes is called a(n) ____________ country.
3. A country in which productive capital and firms are almost exclusively state owned, in which there is limited reliance on market processes for allocation of resources, and in which the production and distribution of most goods and services is through government agencies is called a(n)

____________ country.

4. The distribution of income among countries is ____________ unequal than the distribution of income among families in the U.S.
5. If poor countries have a slow growth rate of real per capita GDP and rich countries have a faster growth rate, the gap between the rich and poor ____________.
6. The relationship between inputs and outputs is called the ____________ function. There are three classes of inputs. The first, ____________, includes nonproduced natural resources. The second, ____________, increases as the number of workers increases. The third, ____________, includes machines and factories as well as human skills and knowledge.
7. The relationship between per capita output and the per capita stock of capital in a given state of technology is called the ____________ ____________ ____________ function. It will shift ____________ if there is a technological advance.
8. Other things equal, the larger is saving, the ____________ will be the rate of capital accumulation. Other things equal, the larger the government budget deficit, the ____________ will be the rate of capital accumulation.
9. The situation in which a country is locked into a low income condition that reinforces itself is called a(n) ____________ ____________.

TRUE OR FALSE

___ 1. The poorest countries in the world are underdeveloped countries.

___ 2. The distribution of income among families in the U.S. is more unequal than the distribution of income among countries.

___ 3. In order for a poor country to close the real per capita income gap between itself and rich countries, it must attain and maintain a high rate of economic growth.

___ 4. The per capita production function illustrates the relationship between per capita output and per capita labor inputs.

___ 5. An economy will move along its per capita production function to a higher level of per capita output if it increases the amount of per capita capital.

___ 6. When a country adopts a better technology, its per capita production function will shift upward.

___ 7. Faster growing countries typically have lower rates of capital accumulation.

___ 8. Countries with higher population growth rates generally have a smaller percentage of the population under age 15.

____ 9. Other things equal, a larger current account deficit will accommodate more investment.

____ 10. A country that borrows heavily from the rest of the world will not become overburdened by that debt if it purchases productive capital with its borrowings and the growth rate of income provided by the investment exceeds the interest rate.

____ 11. Foreign aid has almost always made a decisive difference in the economic growth of countries receiving it.

____ 12. Stimulation of aggregate demand by rich countries will not help poor countries in the long run.

____ 13. Stimulation of aggregate demand by poor countries, however, will help poor countries in the long run.

____ 14. The most dramatic economic growth success stories have almost always involved rapid expansion of international trade.

____ 15. Countries with higher rates of inflation tend to have higher growth rates of per capita income.

MULTIPLE CHOICE

1. Which of the following is <u>NOT</u> an attribute of a developing country?
   a. Poverty.
   b. A stable stock of capital.
   c. A developing industrial base.
   d. A developing commercial base.

2. Which of the following relies LEAST on the market as a mechanism for allocating resources?
   a. Industrial countries.
   b. Newly industrialized countries.
   c. Communist countries.
   d. Oil rich countries.

3. The Lorenz curve depicting the distribution of average per capita income across countries lies
   a. on the 45° line.
   b. to the left of the 45° line.
   c. to the right of the 45° line but not as far out as the Lorenz curve depicting the distribution of income of families within the U.S.
   d. to the right of the 45° line and farther out than the Lorenz curve depicting the distribution of income of families within the U.S.

4. Which of the following is <u>NOT</u> a characteristic of a per capita production function?
   a. As the stock of capital increases, the per capita production function shifts upward.
   b. The state of technology is held constant for a given per capita production function.
   c. The law of diminishing returns applies to the per capita production function.
   d. Per capita output increases as the per capita stock of capital increases.

5. Suppose rich country *A* enjoys a per capita income of $100,000 per year and poorer country *B* has a per capita income of only $1,000. With constant populations, what happens to the income gap between the two countries (initially $99,000) if per capita income in the poor country grows at a rate of 100 percent, while growth in the rich country is only 2 percent?
   a. The income gap between the two must narrow because the poor country grows faster.
   b. The income gap stays the same.
   c. The income gap widens despite the faster growth in the poor country.
   d. The income gap initially widens, then narrows.

6. Human capital is
   a. the skill and knowledge of workers.
   b. labor.
   c. the machines made by humans.
   d. the machines used by humans.

7. Which of the following would be the best way to increase the rate of economic growth?
   a. Discover new supplies of natural resources.
   b. Develop new technologies.
   c. Increase the population growth rate.
   d. Decrease the population growth rate.

8. As capital is accumulated and capital per unit of labor increases,
   a. this leads to less output because workers tend to become less hard working when they work with large machines.
   b. this increases the productivity of labor and economic growth.
   c. the marginal productivity of capital increases.
   d. this leads to a reduced rate of economic growth as workers lose their jobs to the machines.

9. Which of the following is NOT a principal obstacle to economic growth for poor countries?
   a. Multinational corporations.
   b. Population growth.
   c. Low saving rates.
   d. International debt.

10. Population growth can reduce economic growth if
    a. per capita productivity increases as well.
    b. the population increase consists of able-bodied workers.
    c. the population increase consists of children or other dependents not yet in the work force.
    d. too many workers push up wages.

11. For a given level of saving, investment will be higher the
    a. higher is the government budget deficit and the higher is the current account deficit.
    b. higher is the government budget deficit and the lower is the current account deficit.
    c. lower is the government budget deficit and the higher is the current account deficit.
    d. lower is the government budget deficit and the lower is the current account deficit.

12. When a country is locked into a self-reinforcing low-income situation, it is said to be in
    a. an underdevelopment trap.
    b. a liquidity trap.
    c. a deindustrialization trap.
    d. an undercapitalized trap.

13. Stimulating aggregate demand in the rich countries will
    a. raise the growth rate in these countries, but not in the developing nations.
    b. have no impact on long-run growth rates in the rich countries, but will help the poor countries.
    c. stimulate saving in the poor countries.
    d. have no impact on the income levels of the poor countries.

14. Which of the following has been a key ingredient in the most dramatic success stories of economic development?
    a. Population control.
    b. Foreign aid.
    c. Natural resources.
    d. Relatively unrestricted international trade.

15. Which of the following will NOT increase the long-run economic growth rate of a poor country?
    a. An increase in the saving rate.
    b. An increase in the growth of technology.
    c. An increase in the rate of growth of aggregate demand.
    d. An increase in the rate at which capital is accumulated.

16. Which of the following best characterizes the current general feeling among economists about the role of foreign aid in stimulating economic growth?
    a. Foreign aid has generally had a distinct positive effect on economic growth.
    b. Foreign aid has generally had a distinct negative effect on economic growth.
    c. Foreign aid is most helpful if it is used to increase per capita consumption.
    d. There is some controversy about the direction of the effect on economic growth but agreement that the sale of foreign aid is too small to make a decisive difference.

SHORT ANSWER

1. How does the inequality of the distribution of average per capita income across countries compare to the inequality of the distribution of income across families in the U.S.?

2. Use the concept of a per capita production function to explain why an increase in the rate of capital accumulation will lead to faster economic growth.

3. What effect does a technological improvement have on the per capita production function?

4. Explain the relationship among investment, saving, the current account deficit, and the government budget deficit.

5. Why is international debt an obstacle to the economic growth of a poor country?

6. How can an underdevelopment status be self-reinforcing?

7. Which approach to overcoming the obstacles to economic growth has been most successful? Why has it been successful?

8. Why will aggregate demand stimulation fail to help a poor country become rich?

PROBLEMS

1. Consider two countries, High and Low. High currently has a real per capita income of $10,000 while Low currently has real per capita income of only $5,000. The rate of growth of real per capita income in High is 1 percent per year.
    a) Suppose the rate of growth of real per capita income in Low is 10 percent per year. What will the gap in real per

capita income between High and Low be after 1 year? After 4 years?

b) Suppose the rate of growth of real per capita income in Low is 20 percent per year. What will the gap in real per capita income between High and Low be after 4 years? How many years will it take for Low to surpass High?

2. This problem illustrates the effect of capital accumulation and technological growth on economic growth. Figure 20.1 shows two per capita production functions for an economy. Suppose we begin on the curve labeled PF_1.

a) What is the effect on output per capita of an increase in capital per capita from 1 machine per worker to 3 machines per worker? From 3 machines per worker to 5 machines per worker? From 1 machine per worker to 5 machines per worker directly?

b) Now suppose that there is a technological improvement that shifts the per capita production function from PF_1 to PF_2. What is the effect on output per capita of this technological improvement if there is 1 machine per worker? If there are 5 machines per worker?

c) Now suppose that the technological improvement that shifts the *PF* curve occurs at the same time as the capital per capita increases from 1 machine per worker to 5 machines per worker. What is the effect on output per capita?

3. Suppose a country is saving $10 billion per year. What is investment in this country if

a) the current account and government budget are both in balance (no deficit or surplus)?

b) the government budget is in balance but there is a current account deficit of $10 billion?

c) the government budget is in balance but there is a current account surplus of $10 billion?

d) the current account is in balance but there is a government budget deficit of $10 billion?

e) the current account is in balance but there is a government budget surplus of $10 billion?

Figure 20.1

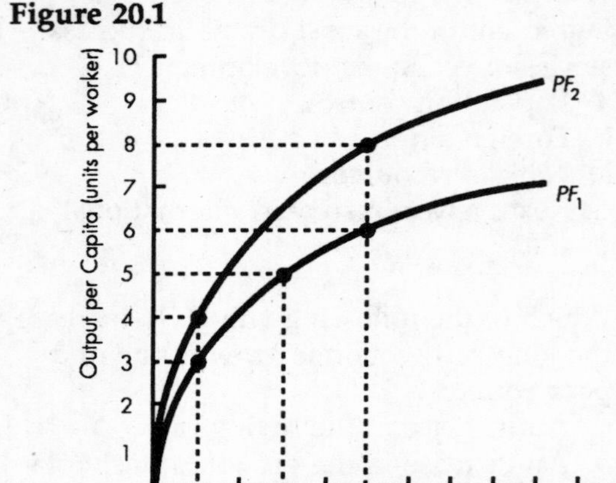

4. Graveland is a poor country with no natural resources except gravel. Initially, income is $500 per year, taxes and government spending are each $100 per year, all disposable income is consumed, there are no exports or imports, and there is no technological change (all figures are per capita).

a) In this economy, what is the level of saving and of investment? Is there economic growth?

b) Suddenly, there is a worldwide gravel shortage and Graveland is able to export gravel at a huge profit. Exports soar from zero to $700, income rises to $1,900, and consumption rises to $1,100 per year. There are still no imports and initially government spending and taxes are constant. What happens to the current account? What is investment now? Is the growth rate now positive?

c) Suppose that Graveland starts to import capital goods at a rate of $500 per year. What happens to the current account? Saving? Investment? Future growth?

ANSWERS

CONCEPT REVIEW

1. underdeveloped; developing
2. newly industrialized; industrial
3. communist
4. more
5. widens
6. production; land; labor; capital
7. per capita production; upward
8. larger; smaller
9. underdevelopment trap

TRUE OR FALSE

1. T	4. F	7. F	10. T	13. F
2. F	5. T	8. F	11. F	14. T
3. T	6. T	9. T	12. T	15. F

MULTIPLE CHOICE

1. b	5. d	9. a	13. d
2. c	6. a	10. c	14. d
3. d	7. b	11. c	15. c
4. a	8. b	12. a	16. d

SHORT ANSWER

1. The distribution of average per capita income across countries is much more unequal than the distribution of income across families in the U.S.

2. The per capita production function illustrates how per capita output increases as the per capita stock of capital increases, given the state of technology. If the rate of capital accumulation increases, then the per capita stock of capital is increasing more rapidly, which means that per capita output is increasing more rapidly; that is, there is faster economic growth. This is illustrated graphically by more rapid movements up along the graph of the per capita production function.

3. The per capita production function gives the relationship between per capita output and the per capita stock of capital *given the state of technology.* If the state of technology improves, each unit of capital is now more productive and so the per capita production function shifts upward.

4. The national accounting equations discussed in Chapter 6 can be used to show that investment is equal to saving plus the current account deficit minus the government budget deficit.

5. If a poor country has a large international debt, it needs a current account surplus in order to make interest payments and pay back the debt. From the equation given in the answer to the previous question we see that this means some of the country's saving will have to be used to make these payments. This will leave less of saving to finance investment.

6. The problem with many poor countries is that they have a low per capita stock of capital. In order to increase it, they must

increase the saving rate, but the saving rate will not increase because a low per capita stock of capital results in low per capita output which implies low saving. Thus the existence of a low per capita capital stock leads to conditions that generate a low per capita capital stock.

7. Of the several approaches suggested for overcoming the obstacles to economic growth, the one that has proven most successful is the expansion of relatively unrestricted international trade. By producing goods for which they have a comparative advantage, countries like Hong Kong and Singapore have substantially increased per capita income by reaping the gains from trade.

8. A poor country will become rich only if it is able to increase the rate of growth of real GDP for a long period of time. If a poor country stimulates aggregate demand, there is likely to be an increase in real GDP but only in the short run while input prices are fixed. As we have learned in previous chapters, once input prices adjust, real GDP will return to capacity real GDP and the only remaining effect will be a permanent increase in the price level. Only increases in long-run aggregate supply (full-employment real GDP) will have a permanent effect on real GDP.

PROBLEMS

1. a) Since the rate of growth is 1 percent per year in High, real per capita income will increase from $10,000 to $10,100 after 1 year. Since the rate of growth is 10 percent per year in Low, real per capita income will increase from $5000 to $5500. Thus the real per capita income gap between High and Low has fallen from $5000 to $4600. In High, real per capita income next year will be 1.01 times real per capita income this year. In Low, real per capita income next year will be 1.10 times real per capita income this year. If we carry this out for 4 years, we find that after 4 years, real per capita income will be $10,406 in High and $7320 in Low. Thus, after 4 years, the real per capita income gap will have fallen to $3086.
   b) If the growth rate in Low is 20 percent, after 4 years real per capita income will be $10,368, while real per capita income in High will be $10,406 (since the growth rate in High is still 1 percent per year). Thus, after 4 years, the real per capita income gap between High and Low will have fallen from $5000 to $38. Real per capita income in Low will surpass real per capita income in High early in year 5.

2. a) From PF_1 in Fig. 20.1 we see that as the capital per capita increases from 1 machine per worker to 3 machines per worker, output per worker increases from 3 units to 5 units. As the machines per worker increase from 3 to 5, output per worker increases from 5 to 6 units. Thus the law of diminishing returns holds. We note that if we increase the machines per worker from 1 directly to 5, output per worker increases from 3 directly to 6 units.
   b) If there is 1 machine per worker, the upward shift from PF_1 to PF_2 implies that output per worker increases from 3 units to 4 units. If, however, there are 5 machines per worker, the upward shift from PF_1 to PF_2 implies that output per worker increases from 6 units to 8 units.
   c) If we increase the machines per worker from 1 to 5 at the same time as the shift from PF_1 to PF_2 occurs, output per

worker will increase from 3 units to 8 units.

3. Using key national income equations (discussed in Chapter 6), the text shows that *Investment = Saving + Current account deficit - Government budget deficit*. This is the equation that is used to determine the level of investment in each of the situations given.
   a) If the current account deficit and the government budget deficit are both zero; investment is equal to saving, which is $10 billion.
   b) If the current account deficit is $10 billion (the government budget deficit is still zero) it can be added to saving to finance investment of $20 billion.
   c) If there is a current account surplus of $10 billion, this must be subtracted from saving: investment will be zero. All of saving is loaned to foreigners to finance the excess of exports over imports.
   d) If there is a government budget deficit of $10 billion (the current account is in balance) it must be subtracted from saving: investment will be zero. All of saving is loaned to the government to finance its budget deficit.
   e) If there is a government budget surplus of $10 billion, we add that amount to saving and thus $20 billion is available for investment.

4. a) For the equation *Investment = Saving + Current account deficit - Government deficit*, since there are initially no deficits, clearly investment equals saving. However, consumption equals disposable income. Therefore saving is zero, as is investment. Since there is no investment, there is no capital accumulation and no economic growth.
   b) If exports are $700 and imports are still zero, then net exports (the current account in this case) are $700. From our equation, we can see that investment equals saving of $700 (since *Saving = Income - Taxes - Consumption* or $700 = $1,900 - $100 - $1,100) plus a current account deficit of -$700 minus a government deficit of zero so investment equals zero. Since investment equals zero, and there is no technological change, growth stays constant at zero after Graveland reaches the new level of income.
   c) Net exports now equal $700 - $500 or $200. Saving and income are initially unchanged, as is the government deficit, so that investment equals $700 + (-$200) - 0 = $500. Clearly, this investment will raise the capital stock, and will create future growth.

21 ECONOMIC SYSTEMS IN TRANSITION

CHAPTER IN PERSPECTIVE

Through each of the previous chapters of the text we have looked to capitalist economies in general and the U.S. economy in particular both as the object of description and as a source of examples. However, capitalism is not the only system that has been used to solve the fundamental problem of scarcity. Much of the world's population lives in countries with economic systems that have not been capitalist. The first major objective of this chapter is to briefly examine these alternative economic systems. A main focus is on the Soviet-style system of central planning.

Many formerly socialist countries are currently undergoing transitions from centrally planned economies to market economies. This chapter looks at these transitions in progress in the former Soviet Union, in several of the countries of Eastern Europe, and in China. The chapter also briefly discusses alternative strategies for making such a transition.

LEARNING OBJECTIVES

After studying this chapter, you will be able to:

- **Describe the fundamental economic problem that confronts all nations**
- **Describe the alternative systems that have bee used to solve the economic problem**
- **Describe the Soviet style system of central planning**
- **Describe the economic problems confronting the former Soviet Union**
- **Describe the economic problems of other Eastern European countries**
- **Describe the process of economic change in China**
- **Describe and evaluate the alternative strategies for making the transition from a centrally planned economy to a market economy**

HELPFUL HINTS

1. It is appropriate that the textbook ends where it began, emphasizing the universal problems that face any economy regardless of the kind of economic system that organizes its economic activity. Foremost among these is the fundamental and universal problem of scarcity, which makes choice necessary. No economic system can eliminate scarcity. Each simply confronts the problem in a different way and thus induces a different incentive structure.

An additional underlying notion that is relevant under any economic system is the postulate of the rationality of economic agents that has been maintained throughout the text. In particular, we have assumed that individuals will pursue their own best interest as they understand it. This is a postulate about basic human attributes and is independent of economic environment. It is the case, however, that the specific way in which that pursuit of self-interest will be manifest will be different under different economic systems since alternative systems provide different incentive structures. Socialism does not change the desire to pursue one's interest as indicated by the fact that managers of socialist enterprises receive bonuses if they achieve certain targets.

2. The topic of this chapter is of great current practical interest and likely will continue to be for some time. Much of the socialist world is in a process of reform. In addition to the ongoing economic reforms in China rapid and fundamental changes are also taking place in the republics of the former Soviet Union as well as in other formerly socialist countries of Eastern Europe. It will be interesting for you to examine these changes as they progress using the principles taught here.

KEY FIGURES AND TABLES

Figure 21.1 The Fundamental Economic Problem

The fundamental economic problem is scarcity—households want to consume more goods and services than the available resources allow. Households have preferences about the goods and services they consume and the use of factors of production they control. Factors of production are combined using a technology to produce goods and services. Any economic system must decide *what* goods and services to produce, *how* to produce them (i.e., what technologies to use), and *for whom* to produce them (i.e., how the goods and services will be distributed among households).

Figure 21.2 Alternative Economic Systems

Alternative economic systems differ along two dimensions: (1) the nature of ownership of capital and land, and (2) the type of incentive structure. This figure creates a diagram in these two dimensions in order to easily compare the economic systems of different countries.

On the horizontal scale, the range of capital and land ownership patterns is given with all capital and land owned by individuals at the left and all capital and land owned by the state at the right. On the vertical scale, the range of incentive structures is given with an incentive system bases solely on market prices at the top and an incentive system based on administered prices or sanctions at the bottom. Using these two scales we can place a country in the figure according to its actual system.

The upper-left corner of the space corresponds to capitalism since all capital and land are owned by individuals and the incentive system is based on market prices. Similarly, the lower-right corner corresponds to socialism, the lower-left corner corresponds to welfare state capitalism, and the upper-right corner corresponds to market socialism. It is useful to note that no country is located exactly at a corner. This reflects the fact that all countries have elements of both capitalism and socialism but differ in degree.

Figure 21.3 Capitalism's Solution to the Economic Problem

Under capitalism, factors of production are privately owned by and under the control of households. The allocation of these factors of production, as well as goods and services produced by firms using them, takes place in response to market incentives without any central planning. Under capitalism, household preferences paramount.

Households plan to sell factors of production in order to buy goods and services; that is., households supply factors of production and demand goods and services. Firms, on the other hand, plan to buy factors of production in order to produce goods and services by some technology chosen by the firm. Firms plan to sell these goods and services to households. Thus, firms demand factors of production and supply goods and services. The plans of households and firms are brought into balance through the operation of factor markets and goods markets. In each of these markets, market prices are determined which equate quantity demanded with quantity supplied.

Changes in market prices have important incentive effects for both households and firms. For example, if the price of labor rises, households have an incentive to increase the quantity of labor they supply and firms have an incentive to reduces the quantity they demand. Under capitalism, the choices of *what, how,* and *for whom* are made by the interaction of households and firms in markets.

Figure 21.4 Socialism's Solution to the Economic Problem

Under socialism, as under capitalism, households have preferences about goods and services they consume and about the use of their labor, the only factor of production over which they have any control. However, unlike capitalism, under socialism, capital and land are controlled by central planners who determine *what* goods and services will be produced by state enterprises, *how* they will be produced, and *for whom.* As a result, planners preferences play the predominant role in determining what goods will be available even though households can decide, on the basis of their own preferences, whether or not to buy the goods produced.

Prices are also set by the planners, but not at levels that equate quantity demanded and quantity supplied. As a result, socialist economies experience chronic shortages and surpluses. Rather than price incentives, firms respond to rewards and penalties imposed by superiors.

Table 21.1 A Compact Summary of Key Periods in the Economic History of the Soviet Union

In order to understand the nature and consequences of Soviet socialism, it is important to have a knowledge of the economic history of the Soviet Union since the Bolshevik revolution. The key aspects of that history are summarized here. As a consequence of the Bolshevik revolution under Lenin, the Soviet economic system began to change but the fundamental changes took place under Stalin during the 1930s. The Soviet-style system of planning described in this chapter was largely put in place by Stalin. This compact summary ends with the breakup of the Soviet Union in 1991 and the creation of the Commonwealth of Independent States in 1992.

Table 21.3 A Compact Summary of Key Periods in the Economic History of the People's Republic of China

The People's Republic of China was established in 1949. Since then, the Chinese economic system has undergone several changes. Although at first Mao Zedong followed the Soviet model of socialism, in 1958, he initiated the Great Leap Forward, which was a significant economic reform. It was an economic failure. During the cultural revolution, real GDP actually fell. Since the reforms of 1978 initiated by Deng Xiaoping, however, China has experienced a very rapid rate of growth. These reforms introduced many elements of capitalism into the Chinese economy.

SELF-TEST

CONCEPT REVIEW

1. The universal fundamental economic problem of ______________ cannot be abolished by any economic system.
2. A set of arrangements that induce people to take certain actions is a(n) ______________ ______________.
3. ______________ is a system based on private ownership of capital and land and on an incentive system based on market prices. ______________ is a system based on state ownership of capital and land and on an incentive system based on administered prices arising from a central economic plan.
4. ______________ ______________ is an economic system that combines state ownership of capital and land with incentives based on a mixture of market and administered prices. ______________ ______________ ______________ is a system that combines the private ownership of capital and land with state intervention in markets that change the price signals people respond to.
5. The ______________ ______________ ______________, initiated by Mao Zedong in China, was an economic plan based on small-scale, labor-intensive production.
6. An industry owned and operated by a publicly owned authority directly responsible to the government is called a(n) ______________ industry. The process of selling state-owned enterprises is called ______________.

TRUE OR FALSE

____ 1. Scarcity is a greater problem for capitalist economies than for socialist economies.

____ 2. Under capitalism all capital is owned by the state.

____ 3. Capitalism has an incentive system based on market prices.

____ 4. Under socialism resources are allocated by freely functioning markets.

____ 5. Under market socialism there is decentralized planning.

____ 6. Under capitalism, household preferences carry the most weight.

____ 7. Great Britain is an example of a pure capitalist economy.

____ 8. The architect of the economic management system that was used by the Soviet Union beginning in the 1930s was Vladimir Lenin.

____ 9. A key element of Soviet-style central planning is the iterative nature of the planning process.

____10. During the 1980s, private plots constituted about 25 percent of the agricultural land of the Soviet Union but produced less than 3 percent of total agricultural output.

____11. Money played a very important role in transactions between state enterprise in the Soviet Union.

____12. The central planning system of the Soviet Union could not cope with the transition from an investment to a consumption economy.

____13. Of all the formerly planned economies of Eastern Europe, the transition to a market has been the most dramatic and complete in East Germany.

____14. The Great Leap Forward initiated by Mao Zedong in China in 1958 was one of the significant economic successes in modern China.

____15. Economic growth rates in China have increased considerably since the market-oriented economic reforms initiated by Deng Xiaoping in 1978.

____16. The most rapidly growing sector of the Chinese economy during the 1980s was non-state industrial firms.

____17. The scale of government is larger in Japan than in most other capitalist countries.

____18. In Japan, government economic intervention through the Ministry of Trade and Industry has been probusiness.

____19. In recent years, European welfare states have increasingly been selling state-owned enterprises to private groups.

____20. The fact that the socialist economy is a complete organism supports the case for gradual transition to a market economy.

MULTIPLE CHOICE

1. Which economic system is characterized by private ownership of capital and considerable state intervention in markets?
   a. Capitalism.
   b. Socialism.
   c. Market socialism.
   d. Welfare state capitalism.

2. Which economic system is characterized by private ownership of capital and reliance on market prices to allocate resources?
   a. Capitalism.
   b. Socialism.
   c. Market socialism.
   d. Welfare state capitalism.

3. Which economic system is characterized by state ownership of capital and reliance on market prices to allocate resources?
   a. Capitalism.
   b. Socialism.
   c. Market socialism.
   d. Welfare state capitalism.

4. Which economic system is characterized by state ownership of capital and central planning?
   a. Capitalism.
   b. Socialism.
   c. Market socialism.
   d. Welfare state capitalism.

5. In a socialist economy, prices are set to
   a. achieve equality between demand and supply.
   b. achieve social objectives.
   c. achieve household preferences.
   d. avoid shortages.

6. Which of the following has had a predominantly socialist economic system?
   a. China.
   b. Great Britain.
   c. Japan.
   d. Sweden.

7. The Soviet Union was founded in 1917 following the Bolshevik revolution led by
   a. Boris Yeltsin.
   b. Mikhail Gorbachev.
   c. Joseph Stalin.
   d. Vladimir Ilyich Lenin.

8. The Soviet Union collapsed in 1991 and was replaced by
   a. the Commonwealth of Independent States.
   b. Belorussia.
   c. GOSPLAN.
   d. the Supreme Soviet.

9. Which of the following did NOT exist in the former Soviet Union?
   a. Money.
   b. State enterprises.
   c. Resource markets.
   d. A central planning committee.

10. Which of the following is NOT a key element of Soviet style economic planning and control?
    a. Iterative planning process.
    b. Exchange of money between state enterprises.
    c. Administrative hierarchy.
    d. Taut and inflexible plans.

11. An important reason for the much slower growth rates experienced by the Soviet Union during the 1980s is
    a. the transition from an investment to a consumption economy.
    b. rising oil prices.
    c. high income tax rates.
    d. flexible prices.

12. Which of the following is NOT a major problem confronting the republics of the former Soviet Union as they make the transition to the capitalist economic system?
    a. Collapse of traditional trade flows.
    b. Value and legal systems alien to capitalism.
    c. Fiscal crisis.
    d. Deflation.

13. Which of the formerly planned Eastern European economies has made the transition to a market economy most readily?
    a. Poland.
    b. Czechoslovakia.
    c. East Germany.
    d. Hungary.

14. The People's Republic of China dates from
    a. 1917.
    b. 1927.
    c. 1936.
    d. 1949.

15. During the Great Leap Forward in China under Mao Zedong,
   a. there was a dramatic increase in agricultural production but not industrial production.
   b. the application of new technologies resulted in a significant general increase in production.
   c. China experienced very slow economic growth.
   d. China became a major exporter of grains and cotton.

16. The economic reforms of 1978 under Deng Xiaoping
   a. moved China off the "capitalist road" it had been on under Mao Zedong.
   b. abolished collectivized agriculture.
   c. have resulted in slower economic growth in China.
   d. have made China more dependent on food imports.

17. Which of the following is <u>NOT</u> a feature of China's economic reforms that have resulted in a high rate of economic growth?
   a. Elimination of inflation.
   b. An efficient taxation system.
   c. Gradual price deregulation.
   d. Massive entry of new non-state firms.

18. Which of the following is <u>NOT</u> a feature of the Japanese economy that appears to be responsible for its dramatic economic success?
   a. Reliance on free-market, capitalist methods.
   b. An abundance of natural resources.
   c. Small scale of government.
   d. Pro-business government intervention by the Ministry of Trade and Industry.

19. Which of the following countries has an economic system closest to market socialism?
   a. Japan.
   b. The former Soviet Union.
   c. Yugoslavia.
   d. Great Britain.

20. Which of the following countries has an economic system closest to welfare state capitalism?
   a. Japan.
   b. The former Soviet Union.
   c. Yugoslavia.
   d. Great Britain.

SHORT ANSWER

1. Distinguish between a capitalist economic system and a welfare state capitalist system.

2. Distinguish between a socialist economic system and a market socialist system.

3. Why did the economic growth rate in the Soviet Union decline significantly during the 1970s and 1980s?

4. Why did the Soviet Union experience a high rate of inflation in 1991?

5. Briefly describe the economic reforms proclaimed by Deng Xiaoping in China in 1978. What has been their effect?

6. What choices must be made in the transition from socialism to a market economy?

7. How has the fact that the Japanese government is the smallest (relative to income) in the capitalist world contributed to its rapid growth?

8. What is meant by privatization?

PROBLEMS

1. New Commonwealth (N.C.) is a capitalist country in which markets operate freely and consumers and producers respond to price incentives. Table 21.1 gives the demand and supply schedules for shoes in terms of collars, the currency of N.C.

Table 21.1

Price per pair of shoes (collars)	Quantity of shoes demanded (millions of pairs)	Quantity of shoes supplied (millions of pairs)
2	4	2
4	3	3
6	2	4
8	1	5

   a) Illustrate the market for shoes in N.C. graphically.
   b) What is the price of a pair of shoes? How many pairs of shoes are produced in N.C.? How many pairs will consumers buy?

2. Now, suppose that the demand for shoes in N.C. increases. Quantity demanded increases by 2 million pairs at each price.
   a) Illustrate the change in the shoe market on the same graph you constructed for Problem 1.
   b) What happens to the price of shoes? How does this affect the quantity supplied? The quantity demanded?

3. Bulmania is a socialist country in which the Central Planning Committee (CPC) sets prices and output targets for all goods. Table 21.2 gives the demand schedule for shoes in terms of cubles, the currency of Bulmania. The CPC sets the price at 4 cubles per pair of shoes and the output target at 3 million pairs of shoes.

Table 21.2

Price per pair of shoes (cubles)	Quantity of shoes demanded (millions of pairs)
2	4
4	3
6	2
8	1

   a) Illustrate the market for shoes in Bulmania graphically if the target output of shoes is achieved. How many pairs of shoes are produced and how many do consumers want to buy?
   b) Using the same graph, illustrate the market for shoes if the target level of output is not achieved: Only 2 million pairs of shoes are produced. Why are the quantity supplied and the quantity demanded not brought into equality?

4. Now, suppose that the demand for shoes in Bulmania increases: Quantity demanded increases by 2 million pairs at each price. On a new graph, illustrate the new shoe market in Bulmania if the target output of shoes is achieved. How many pairs of shoes are produced and how many do consumers want to buy? Why are these not brought into equality?

ANSWERS

CONCEPT REVIEW

1. scarcity
2. incentive structure
3. Capitalism; Socialism
4. Market socialism; Welfare state capitalism
5. Great Leap Forward
6. nationalized; privatization

TRUE OR FALSE

1. F	5. T	9. T	13. T	17. F
2. F	6. T	10. F	14. F	18. T
3. T	7. F	11. F	15. T	19. T
4. F	8. F	12. T	16. T	20. F

MULTIPLE CHOICE

1. d	5. b	9. c	13. c	17. a
2. a	6. a	10. b	14. d	18. b
3. c	7. d	11. a	15. c	19. c
4. b	8. a	12. d	16. b	20. d

SHORT ANSWER

1. Both capitalism and welfare state capitalism are characterized by private ownership of capital and land. They differ with regard to incentive structure. Capitalism has an incentive system based on market prices while welfare state capitalism is characterized by considerable state intervention in markets.

2. Both socialism and market socialism are characterized by state ownership of capital and labor. They differ with regard to incentive structure. Under socialism, incentives are based on administered prices or sanctions arising from a central economic plan. Under market socialism, incentives are based on a mixture of market and administered prices.

3. The three major factors contributing to the slow growth of the Soviet economy are: transition from an investment to a consumption economy, external shocks, and taut and inflexible plans.

   It is much easier for a centrally planned economy to accommodate expansion of the capital stock than to handle the complexities of producing a large variety of types, sizes, colors, designs, and styles of consumer goods. As the orientation of the Soviet economy changed in the 1960s to a consumption economy, central planning hindered growth.

   Much of the previous economic growth in the Soviet Union was a result of the rising price of oil and trade with its Eastern European allies. During the 1980s, however, the price of oil fell and the Soviet Union's traditional trading partners initiated economic reforms and began to look west for trading opportunities.

   The inflexibility of central planning did not allow the Soviet Union to adjust to its changing circumstances.

4. During the heyday of central planning, the Soviet government was able to acquire the revenue it needed to finance its expenditures from the profits of state enterprises. With the collapse of central planning, however, this source of revenue was greatly diminished. With no change in spending, the government was forced to run large deficits which it financed by printing money. The result was rapid inflation.

5. In 1978 Deng Xiaoping abolished collective agriculture (state-owned and state-operated farms) and raised prices paid to farmers for many crops. Agricultural land

was leased to farmers for the payment of a fixed tax and a commitment to sell part of its output to the state. The main thing is that individual farmers were free to decide what to plant and how to produce.

Since farmers now were able to profit from their productivity, there were new incentives for efficiency. The effects have been striking. The production of agricultural products increased dramatically with the output of some products (those for which the set price was increased the most) increasing by many times their previous level. China went from being the world's largest importer of agricultural products to being an exporter of these products. The overall growth rate in the economy increased to 7 percent per year.

6. When a country decides to abandon socialism and move toward a market economy it must make three important choices. First, it must decide the style of market economy to adopt. Should it choose U.S. style capitalism, Japanese style capitalism, or some style of welfare state capitalism? Second, it must choose the sequencing of reforms. For example, should prices be deregulated before or after a system of private ownership of capital and land is established? Third, it must decide the speed of reform. Should the transition be undertaken gradually or in a "big bang?"

7. The small scale of the Japanese government, less than one fifth of the economy, means not only that the level of government spending is low but, more important, taxes are low. Thus it is likely that taxes provide less of a disincentive for work and productivity. Lower taxes also usually mean higher saving and therefore more rapid capital accumulation.

8. Privatization is the process of selling state-owned enterprises to private groups. In recent years, privatization of previously nationalized industries has been increasingly pursued by the Western European welfare state capitalist governments as well as by formerly centrally planned economies of Eastern Europe.

PROBLEMS

1. a) The market for shoes in N.C. is illustrated in Fig. 21.1. The demand curve is given by D_0 and the supply curve by S.

Figure 21.1

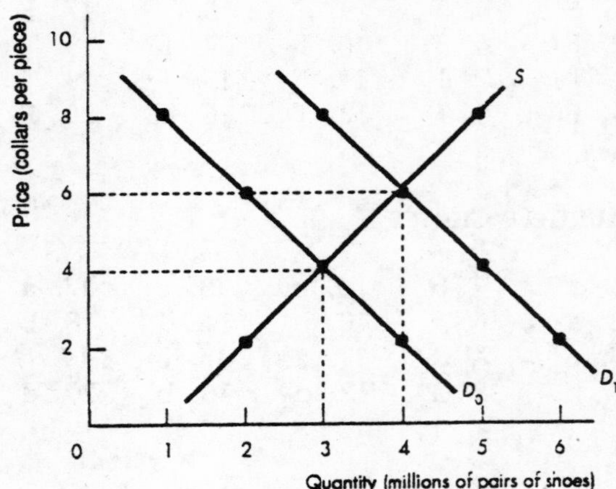

b) From Table 21.1 and Fig. 21.1 we see that the equilibrium market price of a pair of shoes is 4 collars. At this price, the quantity of shoes produced and the quantity desired by consumers are equal at 3 million pairs. In a free market, of course, the price always adjusts so that these quantities are equal.

2. a) The new demand curve is D_1 in Fig. 21.1. It lies to the right of D_0 by 2 million pairs of shoes.

b) The increase in demand creates excess demand (a shortage) at the original price. This puts upward pressure on the price and the excess demand is eliminated by the resulting increase in quantity supplied and decrease in quantity demanded. The new market price for a pair of shoes is 6 collars. The rise in the price of shoes induces producers to increase quantity supplied from 3 million to 4 million pairs of shoes. It also induces consumers to reduce quantity demand from 5 million to 4 million pairs of shoes.

3. a) The demand and supply curves in the Bulmania shoe market are illustrated in Fig. 21.2. The demand curve is given by D_0. Because producers do not respond to prices, the supply curve will be vertical at the existing level of output. Since the target level of output is achieved, the supply curve is vertical at 3 million pairs of shoes and is denoted S_0.

There are 3 million pairs of shoes produced. This is independent of the price. At the set price of 4 cubles per pair, consumers want to buy 3 million pairs.

b) If only 2 million pairs of shoes are produced, the supply curve is vertical at 2 million as represented by S_1 in Fig. 21.2. Quantity supplied has fallen to 2 million pairs of shoes but, at the set price of 4 cubles per pair, quantity demanded remains at 3 million pairs. Thus, there is a shortage of 1 million pairs of shoes. Since the price is set by the CPC it will not adjust to equate quantity supplied and quantity demanded.

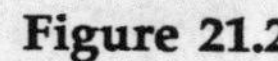
Figure 21.2

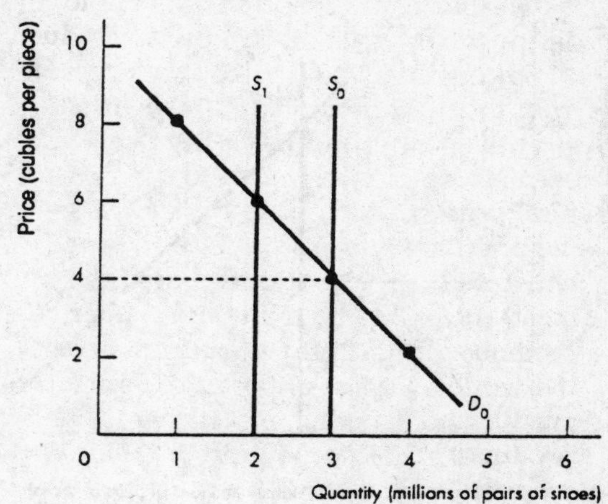

4. The shoe market in Bulmania after the increase in demand is given in Fig. 21.3. The new demand curve is D_1 and the supply curve, S_0, is vertical at 3 million pairs of shoes, the target output. While 3 million pairs of shoes are produced, at the CPC administered price of 4 cubles per pair, consumers want to buy 5 million pairs. Thus, there is a shortage of 2 million pairs of shoes. As in Problem 3.b), the price cannot adjust to bring quantity supplied and quantity demanded into equality and eliminate the shortage.

Figure 21.3

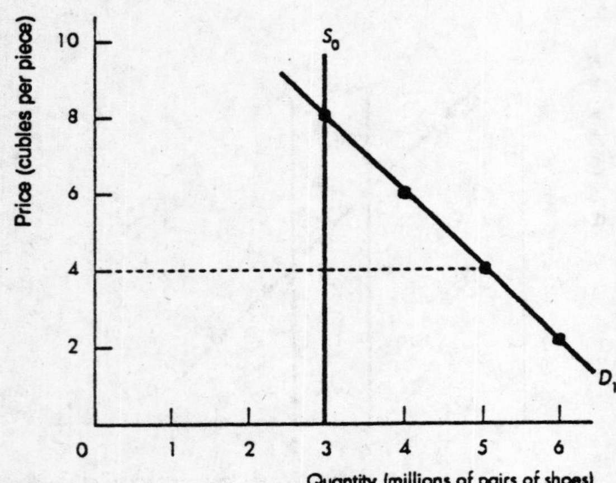
Price (cubles per piece)
10
8
6
4
2
0
1
2
3
4
5
6
S_0
D_1
Quantity (millions of pairs of shoes)